Multinationals and the Constitutionalization of the World Power System

This collection offers a powerful and coherent study of the transformation of the multinational enterprise as both an object and subject of law within and beyond States. The study develops an analysis of the large firm as being a system of organization exercising vast powers through various instruments of private law, such as property rights, contracts and corporations.

The volume focuses on the firm as the operational unit of governance within emerging systems of globalization, whilst exploring in-depth the forms within which the firm might be regulated as against the inhibiting parameters of national law. It connects, through the ordering concept of the firm in globalization, the distinct regimes of constitutionalization, national and international law.

The study will be of interest to students and academics in globalization and the regulation of multinational corporations, as well as law, economics and politics on a global scale. It will also interest government leaders and NGOs working in the areas of MNE regulations.

Jean-Philippe Robé is a French and New York qualified partner in the Paris office of Gibson, Dunn & Crutcher and a specialist in International Business Law. He teaches Globalization and Legal Pluralism at Sciences Po, Paris. He has published widely and has given numerous lectures on enterprise law and corporate governance. In 2016 he was awarded the prestigious *Prix du Cercle Montesquieu* for his book '*Le temps du monde de l'entreprise – Globalisation et mutation du système juridique*'.

Antoine Lyon-Caen is Professor of Law at the University of Paris West – Nanterre La Défense. He recently rejoined the Board of Lyon-Caen & Thiriez, solicitors to the State Council and Court of Cassation, France. He is the author of many legal publications.

Stéphane Vernac lectures in Law at the University of Picardie Jules Verne, France. He is the author of publications on the relationship between labour law and company law and on the regulation of private organizations.

Globalization: Law and Policy

Globalization: Law and Policy builds an integrated body of scholarship that critically addresses key issues and theoretical debates in comparative and transnational law and the principles governance and policy on which they are developed. Volumes in the series focus on the consequential effects of globalization, including emerging frameworks and processes for the internationalization, legal harmonization, juridification, and democratization of law among increasingly connected political, economic, religious, cultural, ethnic, and other functionally differentiated governance communities. Legal systems, their harmonization and incorporation in other governance orders, and their relationship to globalization are taking on new importance within a coordinated network of domestic legal orders, the legal orders of groups of states, and the governance frameworks of non-state actors. These legal orders engage a number of important actors, sources, principles, and tribunals-including multinational corporations as governance entities, contract and surveillance as forms of governance that substitute for traditional law, sovereign wealth funds and other new forms of state activity, hybrid supra national entities like the World Bank and the International Monetary Fund, and international tribunals with autonomous jurisdiction, including the International Criminal Court, the World Trade Organization, and regional human rights courts. The effects have been profound, especially with respect to the role of states, and especially of developed states as their long time position in global affairs undergoes significant transformation. Comparative and transnational law serve as natural nexus points for vigorous and sometimes interdisciplinary approaches to the study of state and non-state law systems, along with their linkages and interactions. The series is intended as a resource for scholars, students, policy makers, and civil society actors, and includes a balance of theoretical and policy studies in single-authored volumes and collections of original essays.

Larry Catá Backer is the W. Richard and Mary Eshelman Faculty Scholar, Professor of Law and International Affairs at the Pennsylvania State University. Previously he served as Executive Director of the Comparative and International Law Center at the University of Tulsa. He has published widely on comparative and transnational law.

Multinationals and the Constitutionalization of the World Power System

Edited by
Jean-Philippe Robé, Antoine Lyon-Caen & Stéphane Vernac

Routledge
Taylor & Francis Group
LONDON AND NEW YORK

First published 2016
by Routledge
2 Park Square, Milton Park, Abingdon, Oxon OX14 4RN

and by Routledge
711 Third Avenue, New York, NY 10017

First issued in paperback 2018

Routledge is an imprint of the Taylor & Francis Group, an informa business

British Library Cataloguing in Publication Data
A catalogue record for this book is available from the British Library

Library of Congress Cataloging-in-Publication Data
A catalog record for this book has been requested

ISBN 13: 978-1-138-60655-5 (pbk)
ISBN 13: 978-1-4724-8292-1 (hbk)

Typeset in Times New Roman
by Apex CoVantage, LLC

Contents

Tables

Contributors

Larry Catá Backer is the W. Richard and Mary Eshelman Faculty Scholar and Professor of Law and International Affairs at the Pennsylvania State University (BA Brandeis University, MPP Harvard University Kennedy School of Government, JD Columbia University). He is a member of the American Law Institute (ALI), the European Corporate Governance Institute and the European China Law Studies Association. His research focuses on governance-related issues of globalization and related constitutional theories of public and private governance, with a focus on institutional frameworks where public and private law systems converge: the multinational corporation, the production chain, the state investor in private markets, the social responsibility of states and enterprises, emerging problems of polycentricity where multiple systems might be simultaneously applied to a single issue or event, and problems of translation between Western and Marxist Leninist (especially Chinese) constitutional systems. He teaches courses in corporate law, transnational law and international organizations. His publications include *Lawyers Making Meaning: The Semiotics of Law in Legal Education* (Springer: 2013), and *Signs in Law, A Source Book* (Springer: 2014), both with Jan Broekman; casebooks; *Comparative Corporate Law* (Carolina Academic Press: 2002) and *Law and Religion: Cases, Materials, and Readings,* with Frank S. Ravitch (West: 2015); an edited collection of essays, *Harmonizing Law in an Era of Globalization* (Carolina Academic Press: 2007); and a number of articles and contributions to published collections of essays. Shorter essays on various aspects of globalization and governance appear on his essay site, "Law at the End of the Day" (http://lcbackerblog.blogspot.com). His publications and other work are available on his personal website (www.backerinlaw.com/Site/) or through the Social Science Research Network (http://ssrn.com/author=259226).

Véronique Champeil-Desplats is Professor of Public Law at the University of Paris Ouest Nanterre la Défense. Her three fields of expertise in the legal academic world are theory of law, constitutional law and fundamental rights. Her work on the theory of law relates mostly to the epistemology and the methodology of legal sciences. Developing an analytical approach to law, she concentrates on the work of some key authors (A. Ross, N. Bobbio, and R. Guastini) and concepts (sources of law, hierarchy of norms, norms, effectiveness, power and constraint in the interpretation of the legal texts). Concerning constitutional law, she concentrates more particularly on constitutional review: study of case law of constitutional courts and analysis of the power of constitutional judges. Finally, on fundamental rights, she mainly studies the notions used in this field in France, the relations between positivism and human rights, the relations between human rights and economic liberties, the function of fundamental rights in the interaction between legal systems.

Christian Chavagneux holds a PhD in Economics from the University Paris Ouest and a Master's degree in International Political Economy from the London School of Economics. He is a columnist for the monthly publication *Alternatives Économiques* and the digital daily *AlterEco Plus*. His publications include *A Brief History of Financial Crises* (La Découverte: 2013).

Charley Hannoun is a Law Professor at the University of Cergy-Pontoise, Director of the Center for Research in Economic Law (LEJEP) and of the Master II in Company Law. He is also Founder of a law firm at the Paris Bar. Besides writing numerous articles, he has dedicated recent years to the general theory on company law and corporate governance as well as the multinational corporations' duty of care to prevent the health and environmental risks and the possible violations of human rights; he notably published *The Law and the Groups of Companies* (LGDJ: 1991) and two collective books entitled *The Companies' Control: Evolution and Perspectives* (L'Harmattan: 2007) and *The Dematerialization of the Company. Essays on the Immaterial Dimensions of the Company* (L'Harmattan, 2010). He also participated in a research seminar entitled "The Company, Collective Ownership, the Common World," organized by the Collège des Bernadins.

Paddy Ireland is Professor of Law at the University of Bristol. He is also Dean of the Faculty of Social Sciences and Law. He has written extensively about the history and theory of corporate law, and is also interested in the ways in which financial property forms were legally constituted. He is currently researching the property aspects of the Household Responsibility System in China.

Sheldon Leader is Founder and Director of the Essex Business and Human Rights Project, and Professor of Law, University of Essex. His interest is in the relationship between economic non-State actors and human rights, drawing on political philosophy, labor law, company law and economic law. His most recent relevant publications include "Corporate Accountability", in M. Bovens, R.E. Goodin and T. Schillemans (eds.), *The Oxford Handbook on Public Accountability*, (Oxford University Press: 2014); "Labor Rights in the World Economy", in *Business and Human Rights*, L. Blecher et al. eds. (American Bar Association: 2014); "Project Finance and Human Rights" in Bohoslavsky et al. (eds.), *Making Sovereign Financing and Human Rights Work* (Hart: 2014); "Statehood, Power, and the New Face of Consent" in *Indiana Journal of Global Legal Studies* (forthcoming).

Antoine Lyon-Caen specializes in labor law, international and European law, and social sciences, and is Professor at Paris Ouest Nanterre University.

Jean De Munck is a philosopher and sociologist. He specializes in the sociology of the norm. With Marie Verhoeven, he directed the book *Les mutations du rapport à la norme* (De Boeck: 1997). He connects research in the field of sociology and research in the fields of epistemology and political philosophy. In his book *L'institution sociale de l'esprit* (Presses Universitaires de France: 1999) he developed an approach to rationality in social sciences in discussion with the works of Putnam, Habermas, and Gadamer, and contemporary approaches of the mind. As a sociologist, he specializes in legal sociology, with an interest in the development of alternative dispute resolution mechanisms. He writes on the capability approach of Amartya Sen and on social and civil dialogue in Europe. He is professor at the Catholic University of Louvain (Belgium), and he has taught in Paris and Bogotá.

Ronen Palan is Professor of International Political Economy, City University London. He published many books and articles on the theme of the offshore economy and tax havens.

Elsa Peskine is Lecturer at the Paris Ouest Nanterre La Défense University. She codirects the Institute of Legal Research on the Company and Industrial Relations (IRERP). Her fields of research concern labor law and more specifically labor law affecting groups or networks of companies.

Jean-Philippe Robé holds a PhD in legal science from the European University Institute in Florence and an LLM degree from the University of Michigan Law School in Ann Arbor. A member of the Paris and New York bars, he is a partner in one of the most prestigious US law firms. The author of numerous articles on legal science and on the impact of the business firm on the legal, economic and political systems, he teaches law at the Sciences Po Law School in Paris. His latest book, *Le temps du monde de l'entreprise – globalisation et mutation du système juridique* has been published by Éditions Dalloz. It is a collection of his main articles, published in French and in English, with an introduction putting his work in context.

John Gerard Ruggie is the Berthold Beitz Professor in Human Rights and International Affairs at Harvard's Kennedy School of Government and Affiliated Professor in International Legal Studies at the Harvard Law School. From 1997 to 2001, he served as United Nations (UN) Assistant Secretary-General for Strategic Planning, and from 2005 to 2011 as the UN Special Representative for Business and Human Rights. He is a Fellow of the American Academy of Arts and Sciences. His most recent book, *Just Business: Multinational Corporations and Human Rights* (W. W. Norton: 2013), has been translated into Chinese, Japanese, Korean, Portuguese, and Spanish. In June 2014 he received the Harry LeRoy Jones Award of the Washington Foreign Law Society, annually honoring "an individual who has made an outstanding contribution to the development and application of international law".

Tatiana Sachs is Lecturer at the University Paris Ouest Nanterre La Défense and member of the Institute of Legal Research on the Company and Industrial Relations (IRERP). Her research focuses on labor law and on the different economic analysis of labor law. She has written a book titled *The Economic Reason in Labor Law. A Contribution on Law and Economics* (LGDJ: 2013) and a few articles about the impact of economics on the recent evolution of French and European labor law.

Gunther Teubner is the former Otto Kahn Freund Professor at the London School of Economics. At present he is Principal Investigator at the Excellence Cluster "Normative Orders" at the Goethe University Frankfurt. His research areas are social theory of law, private law theory, contract law and comparative Law. Recent publications include *Transnational Societal Constitutionalism* (Indiana University: 2013), *Constitutional Fragments: Societal Constitutionalism in the Globalization* (Oxford University Press: 2012), *Networks as Connected Contracts* (Hart: 2011) and *Contractual Networks* (Hart: 2008).

Stéphane Vernac is Lecturer at the University of Picardie Jules Verne – Amiens (Center of Private Law and Criminal Science of Amiens, or CEPRISCA) and Associate Researcher at the Center for Scientific Management (CGS, MINES ParisTech). He has written about the power of the firm and he is interested in the way in which labor law and commercial law create conditions for the emergence of organizational power. He has published books (*The Firm, Blind Spot of Knowledge*, with B. Segrestin and B. Roger, Edition Sciences Humaines: 2014; *The Extensive Purpose Corporation, a New Statute for the Firm*, with B. Segrestin, K. Levillain, and A. Hatchuel, Presses des Mines: 2015), and many articles on the theme of liabilities of firms.

Foreword

Constitutionalization and the regulation of transnational firms

The constitution of governance in the global sphere has transformed dramatically in the past half century. Governance, at whatever level of social organization it takes place, refers to the system of authoritative rules, norms, institutions and practices by means of which any collectivity, from the local to the global, manages its common affairs. Historically, States were the sole constituent and constitutive units of global governance. They were the rule makers. They were also the subjects of the rules they made. International law applied to them and only through them to other actors – whether individuals, companies, or armed factions – and States were the enforcers of those rules, when they were willing to and capable of enforcing them. Globalization has changed that. States now share governance in the global sphere with other self-constituting actors that have global reach. This book explores how and why this has occurred, and what the implications are for dealing with global challenges – be they climate change, realizing human rights or the capacity of States themselves to pursue a wide range of issues in the public interest.

Perhaps nowhere is this transformation more pronounced than in the realm of corporate globalization, the focal point of this book. This is the realm inhabited by some 80,000 multinational corporations, many with hundreds of subsidiaries and affiliates, and millions of suppliers around the world. States made corporate globalization as we know it today possible, through privatization, liberalization, offshoring, providing enforceable investor protections, and the commercialization of sovereignty itself – not merely routine competition for foreign investment, but also deliberately creating havens for avoiding corporate taxation, regulation and transparency.

A number of underlying legal principles fundamentally shape the political status and roles of multinationals today, whether as subjects or sources of governance. These principles stem from the early days of corporate or company law, in some cases going back to the nineteenth century, originally intended to facilitate capital formation among natural persons. They include attributing legal personhood to corporations, thereby enabling the corporate entity itself to own property, enter into contracts, and to sue and be sued; limiting the liability of shareholders to the extent of their investments; and permitting one corporate entity to own another while still being construed as separate and distinct legal persons. Twenty-first century corporate globalization is built on these principles from a distant past and an entirely different economic reality.

For analytical purposes it is necessary to distinguish between our everyday image of a multinational corporation and its legal structure. We think of Exxon, GE, Siemens, Unilever, Sinopec, Google, Coca-Cola, Toyota, Novartis, SAB Miller and so on down the list of well-known names as *one* company, with unity of command, operating under a single global vision and strategy, optimizing its worldwide operations for efficiencies, market share and profits.

We are not wrong to think this. Those entities do exist in the everyday world of economic activity. But they don't exist as such in the legal world. In legal terms, each unit of a global corporate group is a separate legal entity, subject to the laws of the jurisdiction in which it is incorporated. Hence Jean-Philippe Robé insists that the first step in fully understanding the multinational in relation to governance issues is to differentiate between the single *economic* entity that organizes and controls its entire global activities, which he suggests we call the *multinational firm* or *enterprise*, and the complex clusters of individual *legal entities* held together through equity relationships and bundles of contracts that make up the corporate group. Domestic law for the most part governs only the individual legal entities operating within the separate jurisdictions, not the single global economic organization. International law barely recognizes the existence of multinational enterprises at all; indeed, a number of scholars go so far as to describe it as invisible.

The disjuncture between economic and legal entities provides multinational enterprises with sources of considerable power vis-à-vis other and typically more localized stakeholders, including States. This includes the instrumental power of, for example, coordinated global lobbying and mobilizing political support; the structural power that is inherent in making locational decisions or being able to transfer risk and obligations onto other parties; and the discursive power of framing and defining policy issues in a manner consistent with their interests. Thus, multinational enterprises have become a significant *constituent* unit in global governance.

Even more important, multinationals have become a *constitutive* unit in global governance by virtue of the authority they exercise. They exercise authority through the private law of contracts, the new *lex mercatoria,* which can affect workplace conditions, the welfare of communities and environmental practices in more jurisdictions than there are UN member States – and which can be more effectively enforced than the typical UN resolution and convention. Moreover, multinational enterprises exercise authority in relation to States themselves through binding international arbitration provisions in investment agreements. These give multinationals legal standing to sue States for damages, not only in cases of expropriation without prompt and adequate compensation, but also if the economic equilibrium that existed when the investment was made was upset through policy measures that an arbitration panel might construe as uncompensated regulatory takings, which can include progressive labor regulations, human rights standards and environmental requirements. International arbitration panel judgments are enforceable in the domestic courts of the more than 150 States that have ratified the Convention on the Recognition and Enforcement of Foreign Arbitral Awards, also known as the New York Convention.

That is what the contributors to this volume mean when they say that the constitution of governance in the global sphere has been transformed. They also use the term "constitution" in two other ways.

The first is that the global governance role of multinational enterprises has become "constitutionalized" in the sense that it has acquired an existential basis apart from States' discretion. At the foundation of this status, as Robé elaborates, are private property rights and freedom of contract – sacrosanct and codified in the liberal societies in which they first emerged as constitutional prerogatives of autonomous natural persons. Today they form the authoritative basis for the agglomeration of worldwide multinational enterprises as legal persons. Crucially, even States that have no political liberal institutions domestically, such as China, have been obliged to adhere to this transnational authority structure in order to participate on equal terms in the global economy, as when they accede to the World Trade Organization (WTO), for example, or sign up to the international investment regime. Of course, host States have a significant say in the day-to-day operations of multinational enterprises. Compliance with applicable laws is a formal requirement, though it is not always rigorously enforced. The State can require the multinational to take on local joint venture partners. It may require the company to obtain all manner of permits for its legal license to operate. It negotiates the payments the company must make in taxes and royalties. It can refuse access to particular sites. Competition authorities regulate mergers and acquisitions – and so on. Such State-based constraints on the extended enterprise's authority to conduct its own affairs across and within States are but limited incursions into the foundational principles of private property rights and freedom of contract. They do not challenge the constitutive principles themselves.

Yet another way the term "constitution" is used by the contributors to this book is in asking the question whether – and if so how – it might be possible to subject the self-constituting multinational enterprise to global constitutional constraints that more clearly express the needs of people and planet, rather than the narrow pursuit of economic gain. All are agreed that a single "global constitution" is impossible to achieve in practice and is undesirable if not frightening on normative grounds. Beyond that, a number of options are explored. They range from efforts to construct interlocking State-based international administrative and judicial bodies; trying to put the genie back in the bottle through national legal changes coupled with transnational cooperation; learning to live with global constitutional pluralism; and injecting what Robé calls "micro-devices" into the existing systems of governance, national and international, public and private, intended to move them in the desired direction. These options are meant to be invitations to further thinking and debate, not as preferred or mutually exclusive alternatives.

I was asked to write this Foreword because, in addition to my academic work on closely related subjects, I have held UN leadership positions in two initiatives that explicitly recognize this transformation in global governance as they seek to advance the People and Planet agenda. One is the UN Global Compact, the other the UN Guiding Principles on Business and Human Rights. Both help to illustrate some of the theoretical arguments in subsequent chapters.

The Global Compact was launched by then UN Secretary-General Kofi Annan in June 2000; at the time I served as his Assistant Secretary-General for Strategic Planning. It was established to pursue two complementary objectives: to mainstream within the business community ten principles drawn from UN declarations and conventions in the areas of human rights, labor standards, environmental precaution and anticorruption; and to encourage business support for broader UN goals, such as poverty reduction. The Global Compact had no intergovernmental mandate to regulate. Instead, it was designed as a platform to engage business. It does this by providing a learning forum (identifying and sharing dilemmas and best practices); promoting public/private partnerships; and generating innovative spin-offs that then acquire lives of their own, such as the Principles for Responsible Investment, which now involves more than 1,300 investment institutions with $45 trillion in assets under management, committed to including environmental, social and governance criteria in their investment decisions and to being active investors.

Today, the Global Compact is the world's largest corporate citizenship initiative, with 8,000 business and 4,000 nonbusiness participants (labor, civil society, academic institutions and even cities), as well as national networks in more than eighty countries. Critics like to point out that it lacks an enforcement mechanism – but that assumes it was intended to regulate or police. In contrast, its contribution is in establishing, connecting and supporting communities of practice; expanding cognitive and institutional horizons among firms and other stakeholder groups; and normalizing corporate responsibility discourse, particularly in emerging markets and developing countries, including the BRICS, where the UN brand opens doors more readily than private sector or civil society initiatives alone. In short, the Global Compact is a real-world example of what Robé calls "micro-devices", intended to promote a more social conception of the firm within the business community itself.

The second initiative is the UN Guiding Principles on Business and Human Rights. It builds on but goes well beyond the Global Compact. Attempts to subject multinational enterprises to an overarching international treaty instrument go back to the 1970s. Each has failed. The most recent instance focused specifically on human rights. It was called the Norms on Transnational Corporations and Other Business Enterprises with Regard to Human Rights ("Norms"), and was drafted by an expert working group of a subsidiary body of the UN Commission on Human Rights, the institutional predecessor of today's Human Rights Council. The Norms would have imposed human rights duties on business enterprises directly under international law, whereas international law typically imposes duties on States, which are then free to ratify (or not) the legal instrument and incorporate its provisions into domestic law. The Norms were vigorously opposed by business and most States, but had strong support in the human rights advocacy community. At its 2004 session, the Commission declined to adopt the text, pointedly noting in a resolution that it "has not been requested by the Commission and, as a draft proposal, has no legal standing." But governments felt under enough pressure to keep the issue on the agenda, so in 2005 the Commission requested the UN Secretary-General to appoint a Special Representative to start the process over again. Kofi Annan appointed me to the post. My initial mandate was modest: to "identify and clarify" prevailing standards and best practices in the area of business and human rights, to elaborate the meaning of the concepts "corporate complicity" in human rights abuses as well as "the corporate sphere of influence", and to make recommendations.

In June 2011 the Human Rights Council unanimously endorsed a set of thirty-one Guiding Principles (GPs) that I proposed, each with commentary elaborating its meaning and implications for law, policy and practice. They were developed through nearly fifty international consultations involving business, civil society, workers organizations and governments; voluminous research reports; and pilot projects. The GPs are the first authoritative guidance the United Nations has issued for States and business enterprises on their respective obligations in relation to business and human rights, and it marked the first time the UN human rights machinery "endorsed" a normative text on *any* subject that governments did not negotiate themselves. What accounts for this reception?

The GPs are based on the recognition that corporate conduct at the global level today is shaped by three distinct governance systems. The first is the traditional system of public law and governance, domestic and international. Important as it is, by itself it has been unable to do all the heavy lifting on this and many other global policy challenges. Indeed, formal State-based multilateralism has become harder, not easier, in the past decade. The second is a system of civil governance involving stakeholders affected by business enterprises and their representatives, employing various social compliance mechanisms such as advocacy campaigns, lawsuits and other forms of pressure, but also partnering with companies to induce positive change. The third is corporate governance, which internalizes elements of the other two as constraints, risks and opportunities. While the doctrine of separate legal personality may govern asset partitioning by multinational enterprises, risk management and the identification of strategic opportunities tend to be conducted on an enterprise-wide basis.

The process of developing the GPs involved participants from each of these governance systems; it was an instance of polycentric governance. The intellectual and policy challenge was to try to formulate an authoritative basis whereby the three forms of governance systems become better aligned in relation to business and human rights, compensate for one another's shortcomings and begin to play mutually reinforcing roles, out of which cumulative change can evolve over time.

To foster that alignment I drew on the different discourses and rationales that reflect the different social roles the three governance systems play in regulating corporate conduct. Thus, for States the emphasis in the GPs is on the legal obligations they have under the international human rights regime to protect against human rights abuses by third parties, including business, as well as policy rationales that are consistent with, and supportive of, meeting those obligations. For businesses, beyond compliance with legal obligations, the GPs focus on the need to manage the risk of involvement in human rights abuses. For affected individuals and communities, the GPs stipulate ways for their further empowerment to realize their right to remedy.

Pulling these elements together, the GPs rest on three distinct – but what I hoped would become dynamically interrelated – pillars:

1 The State *duty to protect* against human rights abuses by third parties, including business, through appropriate policies, legislation, regulation and adjudication;
2 An independent corporate *responsibility to respect* human rights, which means that business enterprises should act with due diligence to avoid infringing on the rights of others and to address adverse impacts with which they are involved;
3 Greater access by victims to *effective remedy*, judicial and nonjudicial.

The GPs encompass all internationally recognized rights, and apply to all States and all business enterprises. They do not by themselves create new legally binding obligations for business, but derive their normative force through the strong endorsement by States and other key actors, including business itself.

The relatively swift and widespread uptake of the GPs is the direct result of the polycentric process whereby they were developed and endorsed by stakeholder groups and the Human Rights Council. Elements are being implemented by individual governments (through national action plans; their role in implementing the complaints procedure under the OECD Guidelines for Multinational Enterprises, which now recapitulate the GPs' formulation of the corporate responsibility to respect human rights virtually verbatim; and in other discrete legal and policy measures, including guidance that China has issued for the overseas operations of its mining companies); by the European Union (for example, through a new mandatory non-financial reporting requirement for multinationals domiciled in EU member States); the International Finance Corporation (through its revised sustainability framework and performance standards); ASEAN (whose Intergovernmental Commission on Human Rights is drawing on the GPs in its own work); the African Union (in relation to the Africa Mining Vision); the International Organization for Standardization (through ISO 26000, laying out social responsibility criteria for all organizations); and the Equator Principles Banks (which provide three-fourths of private international project financing). The General Assembly of the Organization of American States has endorsed the GPs. Ever-increasing numbers of companies report that they are bringing their internal management and oversight systems into greater alignment with the GPs. Workers organizations as well as global and local NGOs are using the GPs as legal and policy advocacy tools. The International Bar Association, UK Law Society and American Bar Association are promoting the GPs' incorporation into the legal profession, including through law firms' client advisory work. These are but the most visible examples; others undoubtedly exist.

The two component elements of the GPs that have enjoyed the most rapid uptake are human rights due diligence by companies, and expanding the role of nonjudicial grievance mechanisms, including at the operational or site level established by or otherwise involving companies. The reason is simple. At least in principle, each of the three main stakeholder groups has an interest in making these provisions work, even though their rationales for doing so may differ. For States, promoting or requiring human rights due diligence and grievance mechanisms by multinationals serves the duty to protect; for firms, they are a means to manage stakeholder-related risk; and for affected individuals and communities they offer the prospect of reducing the incidence of corporate-related harm while also serving as one possible source of remedy where it occurs. I expect this kind of dynamic interaction to continue to drive change.

In sum, the GPs illustrate both the concept and the process of polycentric governance, as well as providing another example of micro-devices intended to have multinational enterprises take into account and manage their actual and potential human rights harm. They have triggered a wide range of cascading effects, including in the domain of hard law.

A core argument advanced in this book is that conventional social science understandings of both constitutionalism and of the multinational enterprise are inadequate to fully grasp the ongoing transformation in global governance, and that traditional modes of global governance are inadequate to meeting pressing people and planet challenges. All need to be reimagined and new approaches developed through informed practice. No comprehensive – let alone final – word is possible at this time about how to do that. Nevertheless, the authors advance the agenda enormously by pointing in, and exploring, promising intellectual and policy directions.

John Gerard Ruggie

Introduction

In the concluding remarks of his Foreword, John Ruggie states that "a core argument advanced in this book is that conventional social science understandings of both constitutionalism and of the multinational enterprise are inadequate to fully grasp the ongoing transformation in global governance, and that traditional modes of global governance are inadequate to meeting pressing people and planet challenges". This is indeed the task that the contributors to this book have set for themselves: Let's face reality and try understanding and explaining in renewed terms what is happening to us. The world governance system is going through a major mutation and we just can't keep on using schemes of analysis that do not match reality. Obviously, the existing World Power System is constituted of States and institutions derived from them – but a key to the understating of this power system is that in its constitution, in both a dynamic and static sense, one also finds firms: global, multinational firms. They have played an instrumental role in the coming about of this new power system, and they have to be understood as being part of it. They are holders of power to be made accountable for it, not just bystanders abiding by the rules made by others.

The contributors to this book, coming from a wide variety of horizons, have differences in their approaches and conclusions – but they all share a sense of urgency in the need to develop new analytical tools.

Their contributions are being presented in three parts. The first one "deconstructs" the relationship between firms and power. The second one addresses the concept of constitutionalization as such. The third one explores the application of the concept of constitutionalization to the firm.

Part I: Firms and power

In the first part of this book, four contributions offer a renewed analysis of power or, more appropriately, of the multiplicity of powers being exercised in the context of a globalized economy within which the largest enterprises, the "multinationals", play a driving role.

Jean-Philippe Robé's contribution, at the beginning of this first part, offers a meticulous description of the redistribution of powers that occurred in the movement towards the globalization of the world economy. This redistribution is not a mere decomposition of the structures within which powers are being exercised; it is also a recomposition within which multinational firms hold, due to their lack of legal identity, specific advantages while States, forced to compete among themselves, sometimes go as far as selling their sovereignty. This "World Power System", within which one cannot distinguish the public capacity of action (eroded) and private powers (enhanced) requires the development of a new framework of analysis. Robé proposes to describe and interpret it as a constitutional system, which requires putting aside many ideas taken for granted on the notion of constitution, and in particular its link with the historical process of State building. One of the strengths of this analytical method is to shed light on the importance of the relationships that firm powers have with powers and public institutions that have been historically constitutionalized. Robé then shows what the process of constitutionalization of firm power already encompasses.

In order for this process to consolidate and preserve freedoms of choices, which is required to protect individual liberties and advance collective interests, a series of micro-devices must be developed to serve as a reminder of this necessity. These devices, which Robé presents, require decentralized initiatives, actors sensitive to the stakes and able to take them into account, and judges aware of the new role that is increasingly theirs.

In the following contribution, Paddy Ireland proposes a detailed study of the power of today's financial elite, noting *in passim* that it derives its wealth from the "efforts of others". He draws the genealogy of this financial power, following the thread of the successive evolutions in the understanding of what a corporation is and of its relationship with its shareholders. The history he traces underlines a first major movement, one that progressively led to the retreat of an impersonal vision of the corporation that did not serve as a screen for its shareholders to a more personified perception of the corporation that ends up being presented as a real person, able to have its own purpose, integrated within social life. In this movement, the hybrid position of the shareholder – part creditor with the guarantees and limited liabilities attached and part owner, with control prerogatives –, is made apparent. It is by using these last prerogatives that, starting in the 1970s, a financial elite started to develop.

Ireland shows the origin and vulnerabilities of this power, which mainly come from the fact that the value of the share is mostly derived from the anticipation of future income streams. This vulnerability is at the origin of requests made to the States and to international organizations to ensure "investor protection".

Ireland then shows the extent of the limitations States impose on themselves and the rise of policies implemented in response to the exigencies of financial power. It is this set of devices that evidences the existence of a "neo constitutionalism" in today's world with no virtuous linkage to democracy.

The contribution closes with a proposal to re-personify power in order to recognize that it is being exercised in the name and in the interest of the financial elite.

In the following contribution, Ronen Palan proposes his analysis of the power being exercised within and by corporations and shows how fruitful it is to understand tax strategies in a globalized economy.

The analysis presented draws on the distinction between the "legality" of the corporation and economic logic. It is this distinction, and the behaviors it allows to understand while making them possible, which gave rise to techniques of tax optimization that are essential to interpret the rise of the offshore world. Palan illustrates both the use being made of this distinction and the invention of tax optimization techniques. He also shows that a rigorous analysis of ownership and control helps understanding why it is the ownership of shares that is essential to find out and study certain choices made by controlling shareholders.

In a deeper sense, these distinctions give a key to the evolution of today's capitalism.

Elsa Peskine and Stéphane Vernac, in the fourth contribution to this part, plead for a change in the referential system of analysis of private powers, of their growth and their possible regulation. Private power cannot be ignored anymore. It must be faced to become the instrument, or the object, of its own regulation.

Peskine and Vernac show that this movement has already started, but that it needs to be studied, brought to light and encouraged. It is in its early stages, when there is correction – mostly made by judges – of the abnormal use of the power of one company over another. This regime depends on the understanding of what the limits to normality are and of their displacement.

A change takes place when a genuine legal regime of the organization appears. The two authors identify various instances of such a change, in particular in the field of employment relationships, with, for example, the allocation of obligations to a company that is not the employer or in the evolution of the notion of employer itself.

Part II: The concept of constitutionalization

In Part II, four authors address the concept of constitutionalization as such.

Gunther Teubner's contribution envisages the future of constitutionalism and concentrates on one question: Will the constitutional rules for enterprises be part of the constitutions of the world of States or will they be part of a societal constitutionalism? In his view, one must free oneself-from the fascination with the architecture of the nation-state and instead understand that we are witnessing the constitutionalization of a multiplicity of autonomous subsystems of world society. His analysis addresses the focus of this book from a wider perspective in which the issue of constitutionalism goes way beyond tackling the power of multinational firms. In his perspective, the issue of constitutionalization in global society is raised not only with regards to the global economy, but also vis-à-vis science, technology, education, the media and public health. In all these subsystems, constitutional issues arise. Teubner's approach to transnational societal constitutionalism addresses the gradual development of the constitutionalization of this multiplicity of autonomous subsystems in world society.

An example illustrates the position. With enterprises' codes of conduct, we are witnessing an evolution that shows that, although they have been decried as mere exercises in public relations, these codes in fact have brought about real changes. The key factor has been the pressures of learning. Here, although the pressures exercised by States played their role, they are only a part of a larger process of inter-organizational power: the pressures of protest movements, NGOs, trade unions, nonprofit organizations and public opinion have proved to be just as effective. There is accordingly nothing voluntary in the adoption and effectiveness of these codes. As Teubner concludes, the autoconstitutionalization of the enterprise comes from external and diverted learning pressures removed from the world of the States.

Jean De Munck addresses the mutation of the notion of constitution. Historical constitutions have unified the principles of rational law with the existence of particular nations and have led to a territorial configuration of democracy. But orthodox constitutionalism suffers from four shortcomings. It concentrates on the nation-state and on the protection of the individual against State power. As a consequence, it remains blind to the abuses of private powers. It is linked to a restricted version of (*representative*) democracy when what is needed most now is both *deliberative* and *participative* democracy. Finally, it is linked to a limited concept of human rights. With orthodox constitutionalism, the State System is a given and is not part of the problem. With the analysis of Teubner and Robé developed in this book – which De Munck qualifies as "transformationist" – the constitution as an institution is the instrument of the differentiation between State and society, but with an important twist from the classical understanding: The constitution also empowers private individuals and corporations. Multiple normative spheres can therefore coexist precisely because of the constitution. With globalization, something new happens: Constitutionalism moves at the same time into the transnational context *and* into the private sector. Taking the issue of the development of civil constitutions seriously implies identifying civil sovereignties alongside political sovereignties.

For De Munck, what is at stake is the diffusion of human rights and of superior values throughout civil society. In this regard, societal constitutionalism renews the approach to the relationship between law and society, is adjusted to the requirements of globalization, and renews our concepts of democracy and of human rights.

Véronique Champeil-Desplats' contribution is a sobering reminder that for professional constitutionalists, the linking of the concepts of State and constitution is such that they have become inseparable. In this respect, she considers that the opportunity to think about the constitution – or even constitutionalization – outside of the State is quite reduced. She shows that although originally the word "constitution" and the particular power structure called the "State" were quite separated, they became progressively linked – so much so that, for Hans Kelsen, State and constitution are indivisible concepts. Does it make sense then to redifferentiate the two? And what would be the costs?

There are four potential approaches to proceed with such a differentiation: adopting a structural approach, for which the issue is power structuring per se; developing an institutional approach in which legal ordering, "constitutionalizing", is inherent to the pluralistic existence of numerous institutions; adopting a contractualist approach "à la Habermas"; or finally addressing the issue via an axiological approach in which the questions are not only *who* has competence and *how* to make use of it. The core of the matter is the content, the *what,* the normative content.

But then come the downsides of these potential uses of the term "constitution" or "constitutionalization". If all agree that one centralized constitution or constitutionalization can hardly be envisaged, is it preferable to have constitutional pluralism? Does it not run the risk of dissolving the concept of constitution itself? Also, isn't the pluralistic approach to constitutionalism putting too much faith in judges to "make it happen"? Then of course appears the classical question: Who takes care of the caretakers? Beyond this, does it not lead to further confusion in publicizing the private and privatizing the public? Champeil-Desplats concludes by even questioning the purpose of such an initiative. We may be living a time in which an even more comprehensive renewal of legal thought is required.

Larry Catá Backer concludes Part II with a very rich chapter on the evolution of corporate bodies from their *incarnation* (their perception as separate, existing body corporate), to their *ensoulment* (the infusion of normative values in these corporate bodies) to their *ministry* (the guidance of their autonomy).

Backer distinguishes four schools in the constitutionalization movement: global constitutionalism, which pursues the construction of one organized world order; transnational constitutionalism, trying to distil core principles from the various constitutional traditions to use them as meta-constraints applicable to States only; polycentric constitutionalism, which differentiates political constitutionalism applicable to political organs while societal constitutionalism applies to non-state actors; finally, World Power System (WPS) constitutionalism, which posits the WPS as a constitutional system having evolved from State constitutions into a complex and "unsystematic system" combining States and, inter alia, enterprises.

Both global and transnational constitutionalisms remain on the trajectory of a society of States and ignore enterprises. Societal constitutionalism and WPS constitutionalism instead are both trying to catch up with "facts on the ground" – and both confront the fact that social sciences are encased within the analytical structuring of the State System. But while WPS analysis concentrates on the impact of global economic enterprises on the power system, polycentric constitutionalism embraces all subsystems of society and is content with societal governance as an alternative to law. WPS constitutionalism, instead, is attempting to bring back enterprise management into the framework of law via superior constitutional obligations in the exercise of power. Implicitly but necessarily, the "demos" of the enterprise is extended from shareholders to stakeholders.

Finally, in a move from the study of constitutionalism to constitutionalization, Backer confronts the issue of ministry and of how the new ideologies of constitutionalization try to construct a new synthesis on which a more comprehensive community can be built. In this respect, WPS constitutionalism is relatively simple and might provide implementing mechanisms that do not require a great conceptual leap. One key feature of the future of constitutionalism is that it will need to be compatible with the customs and expectations of key stakeholders to make it easier for both enterprises and States to discipline themselves in world society.

Part III: The concept of constitutionalization applied to the firm

Constitutionalization is not a wish. The normative phenomena it encompasses are already at play. The concept of constitutionalization is a change in perspective allowing the presentation of micro-devices, found in States', supranational or private legal orders, which institute and channel the power of firms and, in particular, of multinational firms. The analysis of these micro-devices, through the constitutional prism, leads to numerous lessons and warnings.

To start with, the essence of a constitution is to make it possible to oppose fundamental rights to the power being exercised. In his chapter, Sheldon Leader analyzes the requirements that any process of constitutionalization requires in connection with the protection of fundamental rights. In this respect, two challenges must be met to guarantee the protection of fundamental rights confronted to the power of multinational firms. The first challenge is to define the arrangements among State or "external" norms, deemed to guarantee the protection of fundamental rights, and private or "internal" norms, included within firm constitutions. The combination among these norms can take several forms and can lead to the (auto)exclusion of State law. As an example, Leader describes stabilization clauses in investment agreements, via which the State undertakes not to apply new laws or treaties it may ratify after the execution of a contract. A second challenge requires determining the mode of enforcement of fundamental rights. How is it possible to ensure the coexistence among fundamental rights and economic ones? Is access to justice sufficiently open to ensure that fundamental rights are effective? Who can legitimately participate in the taking of firms' decisions?

From the various paths followed to face these two challenges, Leader provides a mapping of firms' accountability. He distinguishes three approaches to accountability that may be used towards the constitutionalization of private powers. "Strategic accountability" puts the emphasis to the attainment of the firm's objectives, while admitting that fundamental rights must be taken into account or at least that their breach should be redressed. External and internal norms are strictly separated. Fundamental rights are protected to the extent they do not prevent reaching the strategic objectives of the organization. A second approach ("Equitable accountability") ensures a greater integration of fundamental rights in the firm's activities. Private and public norms do not ignore one another anymore; they combine. Beyond that, fundamental rights can be exercised in such a way that they can be protected when they are affected by the pursuit of economic objectives. A more radical, third approach to accountability ("Ultimate accountability and constitutional principles") reverses the perspective. It leads to a reformulation of the firm's objective by taking into account the various "interests" affected. At the deeper level, the fundamental question is to determine why the firm is being created. According to Leader, this perspective should place employees at the heart of the process of constitutionalization. It is to them that the firm should be accountable.

Applying the process of constitutionalization to firms then requires grasping the enrichment of the relationships among State and private legal orders. In this respect, a French parliamentary initiative, proposing to impose to large firms a duty of awareness ("*devoir de vigilance*") represents a "constitutional moment" of private power in the views of Antoine Lyon-Caen and Tatiana Sachs. The proposed plan of awareness goes way beyond the legal person and encompasses all those who are within the sphere of influence of the dominant corporation. Of course, this technique is not new and precedents can be found in international fora and in the practices of transnational firms. What is more original, however, is that it is State statutory law that forces enterprises to adopt norms to prevent serious health or environmental damages and breaches of fundamental rights. The sanctions this can lead to in the State legal order will be determined in contemplation of the norms the firm created for itself. One witnesses here a micro-device of constitutionalization that evades the pure State referential system and combines public and private norms.

The internal organization of private firms is another aspect of the process of constitutionalization. This is the case, in particular, for the status of the firm manager, where one can find signs of the constitutionalization of private powers. According to Charley Hannoun, the rules on "Say on pay" allow testing the constitutionalization hypothesis by evaluating the power play among the various interests affected: those of the shareholders, of the managers, of the employees, and, more generally the stakeholders. For Hannoun, controlling the managers' compensation by the shareholders may strengthen the position of the manager as a mere agent of the shareholders and have the paradoxical effect of contributing to the return of agency theory. The process of constitutionalization could be enriched by a "Say on pay" extended to the stakeholders and, in particular, employees and their representatives. The rise of the social responsibility of the firm could encourage this movement and lead to a model of "welfare firm".

Finally, tax rules are a major instrument in the relationship among multinational firms and States. States have lost part of their fiscal sovereignty. Can they get it back? Christian Chavagneux addresses this sensitive question. The OECD action plan to address "Base Erosion and Profit Shifting" illustrates one attempt to constitutionalize the transnational firms' tax power. For the first time in a century, the State community has initiated a coordinated effort to define taxation rules applicable to multinational firms in a globalized economy. It has attempted, in particular, to correct the disconnection between the jurisdiction where profits are taxable and the jurisdiction where the activity generating them is being performed. Multinational firms are not passive in this effort to rewrite tax rules and try to be part of the rewriting process. A silent but exacerbated power play is taking place among States and multinational firms to (re)gain tax sovereignty.

* * *

As a postscript to this introduction, the editors of this book would like to acknowledge the support of the Collège des Bernardins in the endeavor that led to this publication. For several years, the Collège des Bernardins provided funding and hospitality to the participants in this collective enterprise. The apex was the seminar held on June 19 and 20, 2014 when all the contributors to this book were invited by the Collège des Bernardins to meet in the magnificent thirteenth-century Cistercian building hosting the Collège at the heart of Paris. A special thanks is owed to Baudoin Roger and Olivier Favereau, the co-chairs of the research department in the social sciences at the Collège. This book is also theirs. Beyond his constant and much-appreciated intellectual support, Baudoin Roger has shown an exceptional ability at what amounts to nothing less than herding cats: coordinating the contributions of fifteen authors with busy schedules in different parts of the world.

Finally, we would like to acknowledge the greatest contribution of the Collège des Bernardins in this effort. It provided means for the advancement of one of our greatest assets: our absolute freedom of thought.

Jean-Philippe Robé, Antoine Lyon-Caen,
Stéphane Vernac

Part I

Firms and power

1 Globalization and constitutionalization of the World Power System

Jean-Philippe Robé

The effective operation of the economy evidences the globalization of a power system in which the largest enterprises (the so-called multinationals) play a driving role that is hard to conceptualize with classical analytical tools. Globalization, as a historical process, has moved the locus of power by reducing the ability of "public" authorities (i.e. States and public international organizations) to act effectively and by granting more autonomy to certain "private" powers (those of the largest enterprises and of various investment funds). This has taken place progressively without any grand plan or any official institutionalization. The power system has evolved by itself and analytical tools are missing to describe and analyze what will be designated in this chapter as the "World Power System" that is taking shape as a consequence of this evolution. The challenge is to conceptualize this new power system.

The general thesis developed here is that via no formal institutionalization, no single international treaty, the World Power System has now become a "constitutional system".

The notion of constitution is traditionally attached to the State.[1] But it can be thought about in a pluralistic manner, both in a *territorial* sense (which is now a classical way of thinking about the European Union,[2] for example) and in a *de-territorialized* sense. Enterprises, in particular, can be thought about at the same time as *political orders* (it is within them that partially common and partially conflicting interests are being conciliated as a matter of principle) and as *legal orders*.[3]

The "constitutionalization" process of the various types of powers operating in the global economy has been at work for a very long time. One of the challenges of the globalization of the World Power System is to find ways to have an impact on this process of self-institutionalization (constitutionalization). For this purpose, a series of micro-devices has

1 See Arthur S. Miller, "The Global Corporation and American Constitutionalism: Some Political Consequences of Economic Power", *Journal of International Law & Economics*, 6, p. 235 (1972); Sol Picciotto, "The Control of Transnational Capital and the Democratization of the International State", *Journal of Law and Society*, 15(1) pp. 58–76 (1988) and, from the same author, "Constitutionalizing Multilevel Governance?" *I.CON*, 6(3&4), pp. 457–479 (2008); Jean-Philippe Robé, "Multinational Enterprises: The Constitution of a Pluralistic Legal Order", in *Global Law Without a State*, G. Teubner (ed.), Hanover, NH: Dartmouth (1997), pp. 45–77 and "Enterprises and the Constitution of the World Economy", in *International Corporate Law*, 2, Fiona Macmillan (ed.), Oxford: Hart Publishing (2003), pp. 45–64. See also the detailed review by Thomas Cottier & Maya Hertig, "The Prospects of 21st Century Constitutionalism", *Max Planck UNYB*, 261(7), pp. 261–328 (2003).

2 See Joseph Weiler's pioneer research, "The Community System: The Dual Character of Supranationalism", *Yearbook of European Law* 1, p. 267 (1981).

3 See Jean-Philippe Robé, "L'entreprise comme institution fondamentale de l'échange marchand", in *L'activité marchande sans le marché, Colloque de Cerisy*, Armand Hatchuel, Olivier Favereau & Franck Aggeri (eds.), Paris: Presse des Mines (2010), pp. 91–110.

been imagined and will be presented at the end of this chapter. Via their virtuous circle effects, they could contribute to a consolidation of the self-constitutionalization of the World Power System and improve the taking into account, by the various subsystems of power within the World Power System, of the interests and individual rights at stake.

The scheme of analysis proposed here offers a new field for research, enabling to think globalization in a new way. It seeks to identify various means to accompany globalization's development so as to make it more compliant with the wishes and needs of the people, society and the natural environment. It is still very open and is likely to benefit from multiple enrichments coming from other fields of study (such as corporate social responsibility, for instance, which currently suffer from a lack of proper conceptualization).[4]

I will present the analysis of the process of globalization of the World Power System in Section 1. I will show the very substantial role played by enterprises in the globalization of the power system and in the numerous challenges it presents. In Section 2 I will explore one possible route to restore some equilibrium in the operation of the World Power System by applying to enterprises themselves the constitutional idea developed to subject States to constitutional norms and procedures. The main point is that since we have successfully managed to subject States' operations to constitutional constraints, why not develop a similar framework for the management of global firms? Since all this may seem quite theoretical with no teeth, a few micro-devices that could help in reorienting the self-constitutionalization of the World Power System are presented in Section 3.

1. Globalization of the World Power System

Globalization challenges the analyses conducted within classical social sciences. Being mainly the outcome of enterprises acting on a global scale, while enterprises do not have any official existence in law or as political institutions, globalization challenges the traditional way of understanding the political and legal structure of today's global society. Although scholars may not always be aware of it, classical approaches in the social sciences implicitly treat society as if it were operating within one single State. Often unconsciously, society is taken as if it were always operating under the State's umbrella. In fact, if such analyses can be valid in the context of relatively closed societies, they are not pertinent for the understanding of a globalizing society that they fail to explain in a satisfactory manner. They treat whatever is "inter-national" as something marginal, secondary, coming "after" a dominant, "internal" analysis.[5] In their very existence, social sciences remain anchored in the State System – and they are deceiving themselves with the illusion of "interdisciplinary approaches", when what is at stake are the disciplines *themselves* and their borders, which are nothing but a distant by-product of States borders.[6]

This challenge to classical social sciences could be good news: It could open the way to a *scientific* analysis of the actual operation of the power system by forcing to place oneself-at

4 See Jean-Philippe Robé, "La responsabilité sociale des entreprises", *Revue de droit du travail*, pp. 413–415 (2010).

5 On the historicization of social sciences as a consequence of globalization, see Ulrich Beck, *Pouvoir et contre-pouvoir à l'heure de la mondialisation*, Paris: Champs, Essais (2003). For an analysis aiming to integrate the "global" and "national" elements, see Michel Beaud, *Le système national mondial hiérarchisé*, Paris: AGALMA, La découverte (1987).

6 See on this aspect, Jean Philippe Robé, "Les Etats, les entreprises et le droit – Repenser le système monde", *Le Débat*, 161(septembre–octobre), pp. 74/87 (2010).

the only level of analysis where there are *no external factors anymore*: the World Power System.

A. Diagnosis: Deconstructing/reconstructing power structures

There has been a historical process of deconstruction-reconstruction (decentralization/reconcentration) of power in favor of "business firms" (enterprises) via business corporations.

1. Deconstruction

(A) Today, the largest enterprises are organizations that control centers of production and of distribution of products and services, communication and trade networks, via resources they control and by producing and distributing on a worldwide basis. The resources they use obviously include natural resources, labor and capital. But among the resources used by enterprises, one also finds *law*. This is the case for the legal instruments used to structure enterprises' business activities, whether these instruments are legitimate ones (e.g. corporate and contract law instruments) or not (e.g. opportunities provided by tax havens, bank secrecy). Beyond that, enterprises operating on a global scale are presented with a series of "regulatory environments" to choose from. These legal environments, created by the various States, offer more or less protection to the various interests present on States' territories, and are therefore more or less attractive for the localization of the various activities conducted by firms. Some are attractive for production; some are attractive as financial centers; some are attractive for distribution, and so on.

A point of vocabulary: "Multinational"[7] no longer qualifies a noun; it became a noun in itself. But by using the word "multinational", what are we referring to? A multinational *corporation*? A multinational *company*? Even though authors use these terms very imprecisely (this is mainly a result of the widespread confusion between the notions of "enterprise" and "corporation";[8] more on that later), the word "multinational" designates a multinational *enterprise*. The word "company" lacks precision and there is no such thing in law as multinational *corporations*. There exist *international* corporations (these are corporations created by international public law treaties, such as the corporation that operates the Mont Blanc tunnel between France and Italy), but this is not the type of organization we are dealing with here.

A "multinational" is an enterprise. It is an economic organization producing goods or services, having structured its business activities on the territory of numerous States. To do so, a corporation, used to legally structure the enterprise, may create branches or representation offices outside of the territory of its State of origin. A multinational enterprise can be structured using a single commercial corporation, a single legal entity, as neither the branch nor the representation office is granted legal personality – but it is usually at the very early stages of its international development that an enterprise is structured in this fashion. In most cases, even in the early stages, the *corporate structure* of a multinational enterprise is that of a *group of corporations*.

In most cases, the parent corporation holds all or part of the shares issued by other corporations incorporated on the territory, and created under the laws, of other States than the parent

7 We should rather use "transnational" but it is not in common use.

8 On this confusion and its numerous consequences, see Jean-Philippe Robé, *L'entreprise et le droit*, Paris: Presses Universitaires de France (1999), reprinted in *Le temps du monde de l'entreprise*, Paris: Dalloz (2015).

corporation's State of origin. The corporate structure may be very complex, including sub-subsidiaries, cross-holdings, joint-ventures, and so on, but it is always the same mechanism that is at work: Via direct or indirect control over a sufficient portion of the shares issued by the subsidiaries or by sub-subsidiaries, one single economic organization can be created and managed. The parent corporation being incorporated in a specific State, oxymorons such as "American multinationals" or "Japanese multinationals" are used to designate these enterprises. This is precisely where the complexity begins: Each subsidiary is a legal entity with its own legal personality, its own legal representatives, its own assets, its own financial statements, its own contractual partners, its own torts (if it commits any) and contractual liabilities, and its own creditors and debtors. The *group* of corporations does not have any legal existence *as such*. It does not constitute a different legal entity, additional to that of the subsidiaries, to which anything can be imputed. Yet, it is thanks to this group of corporations that a unique *enterprise*, a unique *organization* coordinated by a *single management team*, exists in reality, although it does not exist as such in the legal system.

One should therefore make no confusion between the notions of "multinational" and of "group". "Multinational" refers to the economic organization. "Group" refers to the corporate structure that allows the economic organization (the "enterprise") to operate in the legal system, and each subsidiary within the group is granted legal personality in the various legal systems (State legal systems) in which the "multinational" enterprise carries out its activities. The group merely corresponds to the enterprise's *corporate* structure. It is far from covering the great legal complexity of a multinational enterprise's *legal* structure, which goes far beyond its *corporate* structure and involves many suppliers, employees, subcontractors, franchisees, and so on, and (sometimes) clients, which are all third-parties vis-à-vis the companies constituting the corporate group. The boundaries of the enterprise go well beyond the perimeter of the group's subsidiaries.

Being an *organization* (i.e. an institutional arrangement of assets and people over which a form of power is exercised) the enterprise's limits can be found where its effectiveness in organizing its business activities reaches its limit.[9] What is organized by the enterprise is part of the enterprise. What is not organized by it (i.e. what is merely *purchased* or *sold*) is not part of the enterprise. One then realizes that employees, probably franchisees and often subcontractors too, belong to the enterprise for at least part of their activities – although they, of course, do not form part of the group of companies that is the *corporate* structure of the enterprise. They are legally only contracting parties to one of the group's subsidiaries, but they are certainly part and parcel of the enterprise.

The consequences of the de facto existence of the enterprise (here, of the "multinational" enterprise) as an organization and of its inexistence *in law* are endless. For instance:

a) Contracting partners to a subsidiary enter into agreements with a particular subsidiary only and do not have, in principle, any right against the other companies of the group. It is the case for all contractual partners including employees, who deal only with the

9 For more details on this question, see Robé, note 8, p. 49 and Jean-Philippe Robé, "Conflicting Sovereignties in the World Wide Web of Contracts – Property Rights and the Globalization of the Power System", in *Soziologische Jurisprudenz, Festschrift für Gunther Teubner*, Graf-Peter Calliess, Andreas Fischer-Lescano, Dan Wielsch & Peer Zumbasen (eds.), Berlin: De Gruyter Recht (2009), pp. 691–703. For a pragmatic approach, see Jean-Guy Belley, Le contrat entre droit, économie et société, Québec: Les éditions Yvon Blais Inc (1998). See also Charley Hannoun, Le droit et les groupes de sociétés, Paris: LGDJ (1990) and Peter T. Muchlinski, Multinational Enterprises & The Law, Oxford: Oxford University Press (2007).

subsidiary's local management and assets; they benefit from local laws only. Subordinates are in fact subordinated to other subordinates, while the ultimate decision makers remain unreachable locally.

b) The law applicable to each subsidiary is the one of the State where the subsidiary is incorporated. Thus, a single organization (the multinational enterprise) may choose to establish part of its activities in specific legal environments. Such an opportunity explains the relocation of businesses: An activity existing in an "expensive" legal environment (i.e. with imperative norms imposing the internalization of negative externalities into production costs) can be relocated in a less "expensive" legal environment (in which negative externalities are supported wherever they fall or are internalized to a lesser extent). Nevertheless, the activity is still carried out by the *same enterprise*, within one *single power structure*, one *single organization*. The multinational enterprise's ability to relocate its business activities throughout the world and the resulting – positive or negative – consequences introduces competition among States for the creation of a legal environment favorable to enterprises (and those who control them). States become *market players* and take part in the economic competitive game since their *legal systems* have become a *product* – or even a *service* – that multinational enterprises use to their best advantage.

c) *Intra-enterprise* exchanges are perceived as *inter-national* ones when crossing State borders – but the analysis of States statistics should be reinterpreted in order to take into consideration the reality of economic exchanges. The "globalization of the economy" corresponds in fact mostly to a phenomenon of "globalization of enterprises".[10] For each enterprise, what appears to the external world as "international trade" is, in fact, trade *internal* to enterprises. It takes place *outside of the market*. Contracts are effectively entered into between the various subsidiaries involved to document the economic exchanges among them. However, although legally speaking the contracts are entered into between distinct legal entities, it is the *same economic organization* that is *at both ends* of the contract. Corporate law lays out constraints on what can be done with the contract, as corporate officers usually have a duty to manage the company (and thus to enter into agreements) in compliance with the "corporate interest" of the entity on behalf of which they act. Yet one knows that in reality they can hardly resist their superiors' orders. One can guess that the terms of the agreements (such as a license providing for the payment of royalties, sales providing for the payment of prices, loan agreements providing for the payment of interests, and so on) will most probably not be the same as those negotiated by two distinct parties defending their own interests with no other consideration in mind. Therefore, a large part of international trade takes place *within* organizations, is *organized trade* and is *not market exchange*. The amount of the royalties, the interest rates or the prices paid do not result from market competition. They are not the outcome of negotiations between autonomous market participants. They are set by the organization (the enterprise, the firm) itself. They are *administered*. For the main part, international economic exchanges are *administered* by "private organizations". They are *not* the outcome of market competition. *It is essential to master this fact to understand globalization, which is far from being a globalization of "markets"* It is the globalization of a complex power system within which enterprises play a key role.

10 Julius DeAnne, *Global Companies and Public Policy: The Growing Challenge of Foreign Direct Investment*, London: Royal Institute of International Affairs, Pinter Publishers (1991).

d) Competition among States' legal systems reaches a climax with tax laws, mainly because of the widespread practice of "transfer prices": The prices of the products or services exchanged among the group subsidiaries do not correspond to "market prices" and can therefore be increased or decreased compared with production costs depending on the advantages or disadvantages resulting from localizing gains or losses under any specific jurisdiction. This is a consequence of the phenomenon described in paragraph c). A multinational enterprise can quite easily locate its profit and gains in low-tax jurisdictions; it merely needs to acknowledge the profits or gains generated by the enterprise within the accounts of the subsidiaries located in these "favorable" States' jurisdiction. Let's see how with a simple example.

Let's assume product X is produced by subsidiary A in country A and sold to subsidiary C located in country C. The corporate tax rate is 40% in both countries A and C. Producing product X costs 20€ and it can be sold 100€ to consumers in country C. Whatever the price paid (from 20 to 100€) by subsidiary C to subsidiary A for product X, the tax cost will be the same: (100–20)X40% = 32€.

Now let's assume subsidiary A does not sell product X to subsidiary C, but instead to subsidiary B located in country B. In country B, the local corporate tax rate is 10%. If subsidiary A sells product X for 30 to subsidiary B, which then sells it for 90 to subsidiary C, the total corporate tax paid will be ((30−20) × 40%) + ((90−30) × 10%) + ((100−90) × 40%) = 4 + 6 + 4 = 14€.

As a consequence, the effective corporate tax rate borne by the group/enterprise in our example is 17.5% (as opposed to 40% without involving subsidiary B); and the State collecting the highest amount of tax is the only one having no initial involvement in this trade and having the lowest corporate tax rate. Country B collects 6€ when both countries A and C collect only 4€, and country B collecting 6€ is costing countries A and C 24€. Of course, this is the result of the assumptions made, but it shows the type of outcome the administration of prices by firms can lead to. Also, one needs to understand that there is no need for product X to go through country B: It just needs to be sold via subsidiary B, delivery being made directly from subsidiary A to subsidiary C. Of course, through such tricks, most of the statistics relating to international trade are simply irrelevant and classical notions about "comparative advantage" are also totally irrelevant.

Moreover, intellectual property assets – trademarks, patents – used by the enterprise can be located among the assets of a subsidiary established in a low-tax State (such as the country B of our example). The subsidiary owning these incorporeal rights will then receive royalties from all the other subsidiaries making use of these rights. These payments will decrease the local profits (royalties are treated as expenses): Profits are then "relocated" in a jurisdiction with less or no taxes.

The same can be done again with "management services" provided by a subsidiary which will just happen to be located in a low tax jurisdiction. *Ad libitem* . . .

e) The structuring of international trade can end up being completely distorted due to certain States' opportunistic positioning on the *world market for legal norms*. Certain States in fact *trade their sovereignty*. They use their sovereignty to adopt norms that have *no other purpose* than *distorting* international economic exchange *to their advantage*. The localization of a segment of economic exchange can be motivated by purely legal

> considerations. It is completely absurd – and fundamentally false – for statistics to "evidence" that the Cayman Islands are the fifth largest financial center in the world. This is true in a virtual world only, where one single building (Ugland House) is the home to 18,857 companies' headquarters (as of March 2008).[11] It is also because of legal distortions that Luxemburg "hosts" more banks than Switzerland, which itself counts more banks than dentists.[12] The activities of all these companies, banks and funds are not at all conducted offshore in these accommodating jurisdictions. They are conducted onshore, in the main financial centers of the world. Along the same line, the Cayman Islands, the British Virgin Islands, Bermuda and Bahamas together shelter more than 52% of the world's hedge funds (thanks to numerous common law "efficiencies" applicable to the legal hub they compose with the City of London). Some argue that this percentage reaches "only" 35%, while others claim that it amounts to 80%.[13] No one really knows, and this is actually part of the problem. In addition to the fact that with such opacity, interconnections with organized crime is guaranteed. With allegedly more than US$12,000 billion fueled in the real economy via these funds, this phenomenon is no longer marginal. It is a major component of globalization.[14]

These examples show that multinational enterprises, along with the funds owning an increasingly larger part of their shares, benefit from a large degree of organizational autonomy and can choose from a large menu of legal devices offered by States willing to benefit from a globalizing economy. Combined with the great variety of resources multinational enterprises control, which is due to the fact that their corporate structures are potentially eternal and can concentrate both real and financial capital with no other limit than their efficiency at doing so or competition law, such autonomy unsettles the official power structure centered on the "State System". States' sovereignty, which guaranteed States' autonomy *among them*, now turns *against them* because of the spreading of a competitive game that *both* opposes and links States to enterprises.[15] The States' capacity to produce international law to rebalance the system is completely undermined as they face a problem of collective action that has never been faced at such a level before. A great part of States' resources – even for powerful States – comes from their "offer" on the global market for legal norms. The very possibility for States to pursue an efficient action in the context of classical analyses of law is challenged. This explains attempts to develop "soft law"[16] on a voluntary basis; or, on an even more voluntary basis, to get the largest enterprises adhere to the "Global Compact"[17] under

11 Ronen Palan, *The Offshore World – Sovereign Markets, Virtual Places and Nomad Millionaires*, Ithaca, NY: Cornell University Press (2003, 2006), p. 241.

12 Ibid., pp. 3–4.

13 Ronen Palan, Richard Murphy & Christian Chavagneux, *Tax Havens – How Globalization Really Works*, Ithaca, NY: Cornell University Press (2010), p. 6. Hedge funds detained, in 2011 first trimester, US$ 2,000 billion. www.hedgefundresearch.com/index.php?fuse=press&1301697974

14 Ibid, pp. 4–5.

15 John Stopford, Susan Stange & John S. Henley, *Rival States, Rival Enterprises – Competition for World Market Shares*, Cambridge: Cambridge University Press (1991).

16 The literature on soft law is voluminous. For references, see in particular Larry Catá Backer, "Polycentric Governance in the Transnational Sphere: Private Governance, Soft Law, and the Construction of Public-Private Regulatory Networks for States and Transnational Corporations", *Indiana Journal of Global Legal Studies*, 17(1), pp. 101–166 (2011).

17 Georg Kell & John Gerard Ruggie, "Global Markets and Social Legitimacy: The Case for the 'Global Compact'", *Transnational Corporations*, 8(3), pp. 101–120 (1999). John Gerard Ruggie was UN Secretary-General's Special Representative for Business and Human Rights.

the aegis of the UN Secretary-General.[18] Whatever their effectiveness (and they have some), these theoretical and practical attempts highlight the inability of the classical legal and political systems to answer the questions raised by the globalization of the economy.

When one analyzes the impact of the globalization of enterprises on the power system, "corporate governance" takes on a new dimension. Far from triggering purely "private" questions, in the sense that the interests at stake would be only those of private stakeholders, *the entire constitution of the World Power System* is in fact challenged by the globalization of enterprises. The *delusion* that we are living in *market economies* contributes to neglecting intra-enterprise global trade, the resulting changes in power allocation and their impact on States, the State System, society at large and the natural environment. It is one of the consequences of the insufficient analysis of "private" powers as "powers" and of their insufficient submission to constitutional norms.[19]

In effect, States are still perceived as being in a position of sovereign power when they are confronted with these "private" powers. Control over a territory remains the basis of State authority, and locating a business activity on a territory results in granting jurisdiction to the State over this activity. Yet enterprises' de-territorialization reduces States' leeway towards these organizations, which have the capacity to escape from States' (territorial) jurisdiction. On one hand, there are other sources of authority than control over a territory (for instance the control over numerous "property rights") that result in the creation of powerful organizations leading States to compete among themselves and forcing them to produce legal norms serving these interests. On the other hand, the territory and the population on it impose heavy constraints for State power holders towards demands for greater protection of the interests adversely affected by globalization: those of the people left behind due to reduced employability on the global employment market, which expels them from the job market; those of the natural environment destroyed by the increased competition among states to host polluting activities; those of unstable and out-of-control financial markets due to financial black holes resulting from offshore finance and tax-havens, and so on.[20] While protective demands from the population remain at high levels, public budgets (both State and social) are drawn into a race to the bottom in terms of taxation to attract locally the accounting acknowledgment of revenues and profits. This probably explains at least in part the successes of city-states (Hong Kong, Singapore, Dubai) in the global economy. What is the perfect combination today for a Head of State? Governing a small territory and a small population – just enough not to lose being qualified as a "sovereign State", which requires an effective government, a population and a territory – and adjusting the use of one's sovereignty to the demands of "the market" (in fact, of firms).

Whereas globalization creates wealth that could be partly allocated to compensate its victims, enterprises' legal structures combined with the structure of the State System contribute

18 T. Berns, P.-F. Docquir, B. Frydman, L. Hennebel & G. Lewkowicz, *Responsabilité des entreprises et corégulation*, Brussels: Bruylant (2007) and particularly Benoît Frydman, "Stratégies de responsabilisation des entreprises à l'ère de la mondialisation", pp. 1–36.

19 John Kenneth Galbraith, *The Economics of Innocent Fraud – Truth for Our Time*, Boston: Houghton Mifflin Company (2004), for whom it is a *fraud* to describe our economy as a "market economy". See also Antoine & Gérard Lyon-Caen, "La doctrine de l'entreprise", in *Dix ans de droit de l'entreprise*, Paris: Librairie Technique, pp. 601-611 (1978).

20 See a comprehensive research by Palan, note 11 and Palan *et al.* note 13. See also Ronen Palan, "Tax Havens and the Commercialization of State Sovereignty", *International Organization*, 56(1), pp. 151–176 (2002) and Nicholas Shaxson, *Treasure Islands – Tax Havens and the Men Who Stole the World*, London: The Bodley Head (2011).

to avoiding taxing a large proportion of the generated wealth. As a result, the wealth produced is concentrated in increasingly fewer hands.[21] Whereas there is a growing need for greater public action to internalize the costs generated and to compensate those left behind, the public debt crisis becomes a structural problem.[22]

"Historical" sovereignties (i.e. States' sovereignty) are being challenged by enterprises that are now in a position to introduce competition among the judicial, social and tax systems implemented throughout history to ensure the cohesion of the various interests present in society – as long as such society was organized in relative autonomy on States' territories.[23] Globalization challenges the whole power system, which notably includes States, and public international organizations created by States and enterprises, and it is this combination that needs to be reshuffled.

(B) Understanding the current situation requires a better understanding of the history of our shared power system. In a nutshell,[24]

a) The power system focused on the "State System" was institutionalized in the mid-seventeenth century. Under this system, formalized by the Westphalia treaties of 1648, States are equal in the international legal order and recognize each other as masters of the organization of their own *internal* affairs. With the eighteenth- and nineteenth-century liberal revolutions, these internal affairs were progressively structured around the institutions needed for the operation of a market society with instruments such as the definition of strong property rights, contractual freedom and the right of free enterprise. On the international level, States have reached the greatest sovereignty they could obtain; on the internal level, individuals have been granted the greatest autonomy possible. The internal order shifted from a hierarchical, holistic, corporatist and organized society[25] to a society of autonomous individuals, free and equal (in rights), free to build the society they yearn for thanks to their property rights and the agreements they enter into among themselves.[26]

   In this fashion, the absolute sovereignty granted to States in the international order was decentralized in favor of the "private" sector in the internal order, allowing for almost absolute social and individual autonomy. As a matter of principle, property rights and contractual freedom[27] pull all arrangements and agreements entered into

21 Joseph E. Stiglitz, "Of the 1%, by the 1%, for the 1%", *Vanity Fair*, May (2011), available at www.vanityfair.com/society/features/2011/05/top-one-percent-201105

22 Some studies assess that offshore finance and tax havens represent from US$255 to US$300 billion tax loss *per year*, Palan *et al.*, note 13, p. 63.

23 Gabriel Ardant, *Histoire de l'impôt*, Livre I, De l'antiquité au XVII & Livre II, Paris: Fayard (1971, 1972); and Gabriel Ardant, "Financial Policy and Economic Infrastructure of Modern States and Nations", in *The Formation of National States in Europe*, C. Tilly (ed.), Princeton: Princeton University Press, pp. 164–242 (1975).

24 For a summarized presentation, see Robé, note 8.

25 François Olivier-Martin, "La France d'ancien régime, État corporatif", *Annales de droit et de sciences politiques*, 5, p. 690 (1937); "Le déclin et la suppression des corps en France au XVIIIe siècle", in *Études présentées à la Commission Internationale pour l'Histoire des Assemblées d'États*, 2, Louvain: Bureau du recueil, Université de Louvain (1937), p. 149 and his *Histoire du droit français des origines à la Révolution*, C.N.R.S. (1992) (1948 Edition).

26 François Ewald (ed.), *Naissance du Code civil*, Paris: Flammarion (1989).

27 Morris R. Cohen, "Property and Sovereignty", *Cornell Law Quarterly*, 13, p. 8 (1933); Robert L. Hale, "Coercion and Distribution in a Supposedly Non-Coercive State", *Political Science Review*, 38, p. 470 (1923) and

among autonomous individuals out of the State's scope of action.[28] In a liberal society, a State's absolute sovereignty on the *international* level turns out to be no more than a competence of *exception* in the *internal* order: Everything that is not prohibited or regulated is authorized.[29] Individuals' liberties are in principle *unlimited*, whereas State powers are *limited.*[30] Such a system arose from European history,[31] and from centuries of social, political, economic and legal evolutions that took place in this small part of the world. Born in Europe, adapted to the United States,[32] this structure of social relations was then exported through colonization,[33] and then by international institutions created after the Second World War.[34] Political decolonization led European powers to leave South America, Africa and Asia – but the legal colonization of the State System remained.

b) At the same time, this basic pattern has undergone a silent and long-hidden cataclysm, which only became easily noticeable with globalization: The massive introduction of limited liability corporations in the legal system, starting in the nineteenth century, has completely disrupted the balance of powers *and the constitutional structure of the power system itself*. The concentration of productive property rights within corporate structures started shifting the power structure in States' *internal* orders: the concentration of *property rights* on assets led to their reconstruction into *powers*. From rights of autonomy designed to protect individuals' autonomy, they became sources of heteronomy. They enabled the creation of private power structures (enterprises, notably) to which individuals became increasingly subjected. As a consequence, States had to adapt. From "night-watchmen States", which imposed only the respect of property rights and the compliance with contractual obligations, they moved to becoming "welfare states" attempting to correct the negative consequences of the unbalanced social relations created by the surge of corporate structures concentrating wealth, assets and contracts. One of the main reasons explaining this disruption lays in the fact that large enterprises developed within individualistic societies with no legal recognition of their existence as organizations, as a form of coordination of assets and of the individuals using them. These enterprises entered the legal world through *corporations*, which have legal personality and can be used to concentrate under one ownership structure various economic resources. The *enterprise's* lack of legal existence (as an organization) and the fact that its entry into the legal world has been made possible through the commercial corporation (or a group of corporations) resulted in a widespread confusion between the words and concepts of "enterprise" and "corporation" and led to numerous misunderstandings in social sciences. The worst of these developments is the so-called agency theory that is the basis of the current legal models of "corporate governance". The disastrous

"Force and the State: A Comparison of 'Political' and 'Economic' Compulsion", *Columbia Law Review*, 35, p. 149 (1935).

28 De Vareilles-Sommières, "La définition et la notion juridique de propriété", *R.T.D.C.*, p. 443 (1905).

29 Carl Schmitt, *Théorie de la Constitution,* Paris: Presses Universitaires de France(1989), p. 286.

30 *Ibid.* p. 296.

31 Carl Schmitt, *Le nomos de la terre,* Paris: Presses Universitaires de France (1988, 2001).

32 Schmitt, *supra* note 29, pp. 171 and 182–183.

33 Bertrand Badie, *L'État importé – L'occidentalisation de l'ordre politique*, Paris: Fayard (1992).

34 John Gerard Ruggie, "International Regimes, Transactions, and Change: Embedded Liberalism in the Postwar Economic Order", *International Organization*, 36(2), pp. 379–415 (1982).

consequences of this widespread erroneous theory are endless.[35] The inexistence of the firm as a positive legal concept is also the reason why legal scholars did not develop any widely acknowledged theory of the enterprise,[36] the sole adequate theory analyzing the enterprise as an autonomous legal order in competition/cooperation which the State's own legal order.[37] It is with such a pluralistic legal theory that one can develop an accurate description and analysis of the structure of the power system at the World Power System's level.[38] However, the development of a legal theory of the enterprise has been hindered by legal positivists' approaches to law. For them, law is inherently a production of the State and the idea that an enterprise could be a legal order in itself is anathema.[39] There are minority pluralistic approaches acknowledging the existence of legal orders on different levels than that of the State, whether on subnational or supranational levels or as intertwined legal orders[40]– but they haven't led, so far, to an understanding of the World Power System as a pluralistic power system. The State power system – and this is a key point – is at the origin of a *knowledge system* (about law, here) that hinders the understanding of globalization.

c) Faced with the rise of the power of enterprises and the resulting negative externalities, States, each in a position to react towards their *national* economies in the original liberal constitutional scheme, started producing *substantive law*, both normative and regulatory, protecting impacted interests through labor laws, social security laws, consumption laws, environmental laws, and so on. Given industrial damages, the evolution of tort law led everywhere to a reduced role played by *fault* and the emphasis was put on the notion of *risk*.[41] Numerous administrative agencies have been created to co-manage different aspects of the enterprise's life.[42] We then witnessed a true constitutional revolution of the State's role, one of its most significant expressions being the evolution of the US Supreme Court case law that, after having invalidated most of the laws adopted during the first New Deal, had to yield to the second one.[43] However, this evolution took place on a *national* basis, and therefore on a *territorial* basis. Even the difficult adventure of the European integration is territorially based, and thus geographically limited.

35 See Robé note 8. See also Daniel Bachet, *Les fondements de l'entreprise,* Ivry-sur-Seine : Les éditions de l'atelier (2007).

36 Jacques Le Goff, "Entreprise et institution ; retour sur un débat crucial", in *Les acteurs de l'histoire du droit du travail,* Jean-Pierre Le Crom (ed.), Rennes: Presses Universitaires de Rennes (2004), pp. 83–104.

37 Jean-Philippe Robé, "L'ordre juridique de l'entreprise", *Droits,* 25, p. 163 (1997); Nikitas Aliprantis, "L'entreprise en tant qu'ordre juridique", in *Le droit collectif du travail. Etudes en hommage à H. Sinay,* N. Aliprantis et F. Kessler (eds.), Francfort: Peter Lang (1994), p. 185.

38 See Robé, note 3.

39 Bruno Oppetit clearly stated: "state positivism as an ideology cannot put up with other approaches. Legal positivism cannot tolerate any pluralistic approach", in Bruno Oppetit, "La notion de Source du droit et le droit du Commerce International", *Archives de philosophie du droit,* vol. 27, pp. 43–53, 47 (1982).

40 The institutional theory is a pluralistic theory, cf. Eric Millard, "Hauriou et la théorie de l'institution", *Droit et Société,* 30/31, pp. 381–412 (1995) and "Sur les théories italiennes de l'Institution", in *Contrat ou institution: un enjeu de société,* B. Basdevant et M. Bouvier (eds.) Paris: LGDJ (2004), pp. 31–46. Santi Romano developed a theory of legal pluralism and, in particular, the interesting concept of "relevance"; see *L'ordre juridique,* Paris: Dalloz (1975) (1st edition 1917–1918, 2nd edition 1946).

41 René Savatier, "Le gouvernement des juges en matière de responsabilité civile", in *Recueil E. Lambert,* Glashütten im Taunus: Verlag Detlev Auvermann KG, vol. 1, pp.453–466 (1938) LGDJ.

42 Robé, note 8, p. 74 et seq.

43 Robert G. McCloskey, *The American Supreme Court,* Chicago: The University of Chicago Press (1960).

d) Because of State competition in the production of norms (via their legal and regulatory measures internalizing (or refraining from internalizing) the negative externalities generated by corporate activity), the globalization of the economy, which is the result of the globalization of enterprises, has shifted the instable balance of powers between official institutions (States and international organizations) and non-official ones (enterprises). Globalization puts in jeopardy what some have called the "Fordist compromise". Globalization has led to the surge of "private" powers, of the power of *enterprises*. But these powers and the heteronomy they generate remain analyzed from a "private" standpoint. Yet, the globalization of the power system now challenges the constitutional revolution of the "welfare state" itself.

2. *Reconstruction*

The recombination of the parcels of power decentralized via the property rights and liberties protected by liberal constitutions occurred as a consequence of what can be termed the "corporate counterrevolution".[44] The absolutism of property rights having an *erga omnes* effect in connection with the use of goods, designed to protect the individual against all forms of power, fostering his or her autonomy and limiting the scope of heteronomy,[45] has been concentrated through business corporations, to the benefit of those who control them or set their objectives.

One main complexity deriving from globalization is that enterprises are unofficial institutions, with no legal recognition of their existence as such. They do not exist in positive law (in the acknowledged official legal system), but it would be impossible for them to exist as they do without positive law as it is. They can live their very peculiar existence as *non-existing* institutions *thanks to* the law, *because of* the law. Indeed, enterprises take advantages of the legal personality of corporations and of the laws limiting shareholders' liability to concentrate assets and, eventually, enterprises end up exercising the strong autonomous prerogatives of the owner without owning anything – since they have no legal existence.

This is indeed the legal situation. Enterprises *do* exist as effective organizations but are *nobody's property* and *own nothing* – and they are *not liable* for any of the negative consequences of their very peculiar mode of existence.

2.1. THE SUPERIOR ADVANTAGES OF CORPORATIONS OVER INDIVIDUALS

Corporations hold (almost) the same rights as individuals do, but they enjoy advantages that individuals cannot have.[46] For instance:

a) An individual owns a single set of assets and liabilities, and all his or her assets are at stake in each of his or her actions. In addition, an individual's death leads to taxation and redistribution among the heirs. As a consequence, the capacity to develop an enterprise

44 Robé, note 8, pp. 61–71.

45 In the United States, see James W. Ely Jr., *The Guardian of Every Other Right – A Constitutional History of Property Rights* (2nd edition), New York/Oxford: Oxford University Press (1998).

46 See Jean-Philippe Robé, "The Legal Structure of the Firm", *Accounting, Economics, and Law*, 1(1, Article 5): www.bepress.com/ael/vol1/iss1/5, pp. 1–86 (2011).

that can outlive its creator is limited without having recourse to appropriate legal instruments (especially limited liability corporations, in our modern legal system).

b) Just like an individual, a corporation has a single set of assets and liabilities. However, the corporation's existence can potentially be eternal. This gives the corporation an ability to accumulate capital that no individual can do by him- or herself. Once a corporation is used to structure a business, the entrepreneur's death leads only to the redistribution of the shares among the heirs. All the assets and contracts entered into by the corporation remain stable. Once "incorporated", the enterprise is not immediately impacted by the vicissitude of physical life and, in particular, the death of its founders or directors.

c) A company's assets can also include shares issued by other corporations.[47] Groups of companies can be created in this fashion. This is particularly important, as one key characteristic of corporations is that they have a separate legal personality and their shareholders enjoy limited liability: The shareholders' liability is limited to the amount of the initial value of their shares. Each company within the group is contractually bound to various stakeholders of the enterprise: employees, other suppliers, distributors, and so on. The activity resulting from the contractual network structured around each subsidiary of the group is integrated in the larger activity of the enterprise as a whole, yet each contractual partner has (as a matter of principle) only one corporation of the group as counterparty. The structure of the network of contracts, on which the operation of a *single* enterprise relies, is legally speaking fragmented into various subnetworks, isolated from each other. The risks created by the business activity of each subsidiary are thus isolated within a specific legal entity although they may actually be the result of the larger operations of the enterprise.

d) The internationalization of enterprises results in the continuation of their organizational unity above State borders, but their legal organization is scattered in subset of contracts centered on subsidiaries operating in various legal and regulatory environments. As most of *inter-national* economic exchange is in fact *intra-enterprise* exchange, since it takes place among the various corporations of the group that are the enterprise's corporate backbone, enterprises are able to put public legal orders (States) in competition by shopping among the most favorable legal environments for each part of their activities: countries with low labor cost for production, countries with low taxation rate to locate the accounting acknowledgement of the wealth generated by the enterprise's activities, bank secrecy for activities demanding the highest degree of discretion; and so on. Many States, especially those with scarce natural or human resources, position themselves on the market for legal norms by offering a favorable legal environment for specific activities, whether legitimate or not, enabling them to grasp part of the wealth created globally, even if it is detrimental to global society and its natural environment. Obviously, the less material and human resources a State has, the more it is encouraged to foster *legal* localization (as opposed to *real* localization) under its jurisdiction and thus to monetize one of the only asset it has: its sovereignty. Solving problems generated by the World Power System will inevitably require addressing the strategic use that some States are making of their sovereignty as these States do not bear all the costs associated with their production of facilitating norms and thus artificially create for themselves a taxable basis and the means for their existence.

47 This was forbidden for a long time, until New Jersey – which was thus called the "traitor state" – allowed it in 1889.

2.2. RESPONSIBILITY AND PROPERTY RIGHTS

It is within the enterprise – as an organization – that decisions are being made regarding the use of the assets controlled via the firm's corporate structure. However – and this is a crucial point – the enterprise does not own any of these assets. With the development of large enterprises structured using groups of corporations, a sort of reconfiguration of property rights into power took place. No individual owns the enterprise as an organization; and, as an organization lacking legal existence, the enterprise *owns nothing* and is thus *never accountable for anything*. It has to cope with the consequences of decisions made within its organization to a certain extent, but only through the forms of accountability created by the official legal system – which, as far as the enterprise is concerned, come down to a potential allocation of liability to the various corporations used to legally structure the enterprise. The enterprise may thus allocate the risks it takes and creates by strategically locating subparts of its activities in specific legal entities and legal environments.

Inside an enterprise, no individual owns the assets used: neither the corporate officers nor the shareholders do. Only the corporations of the group of corporations own productive assets that may generate liabilities. However, the origin of the power exercised in and by the enterprise derives from the ownership of real assets. The enterprise, as an organization exercising the powers conferred by ownership actually hides behind the legal entities used, which own the physical assets granting power but that no individual possesses.[48]

Therefore, as a matter of principle, no individual is responsible for the use of corporate assets. Property rights, along with the legal liabilities their use may generate, can be attributed to *legal* entities only. But neither the enterprise (nor the group of companies) nor any individual – except, by way of exception, when *de jure* or *de facto* officers have committed a fault or in case of "piercing of the corporate veil" – can be held accountable.[49] As a governance institution, the enterprise makes use of property rights without entitlement or correlative responsibility.

The development of large business corporations has *de facto* led to the transformation of *property rights* initially allocated to individuals into *powers* exercised by enterprises. In this regard, one key characteristic of property rights must be introduced into the analysis: Property rights do not grant control over *goods* only. They give authority over individuals via the control they grant over the *access to goods* (and therefore to production and distribution *facilities*). Property is a form of autonomous power. It was *not* delegated by the State in the sense that the State can take it back: It has been *constitutionally decentralized via the acknowledgment of property rights.*[50] Desirable or not, there is no possibility of turning back: This would require fundamental changes in the basic tenets of our social system, which is virtually impossible given the global spreading of this mode of structuring society. Thanks to competition among enterprises and States, the World Power System granted enterprises with non-delegated prerogatives, i.e. a power over individuals that States cannot capture. As a consequence, we can speak of "private" sovereignty today. The idea is not to turn it into "public" sovereignty tomorrow (this is neither possible nor desirable) but rather to have these sovereignties abide by the rule of law. The suggestion is to have them governed by the legal principles of a society that cares about respecting individuals' rights,[51] with institutions designed to protect their common interests.

48 See Jean-Philippe Robé, "L'entreprise en droit", *Droit et société*, 29, p. 117 (1995); Robé, note 8 and, more recently, note 46. See also Christophe Clerc, "La légitimité du pouvoir actionnarial", in *A quoi servent les actionnaires?*, Jean-Philippe Touffut (ed.), Paris: Albin Michel (2009), pp. 17–46.

49 Robert B. Thompson, "Piercing the Veil Within Corporate Groups: Corporate Shareholders as Mere Investors", *Connecticut Journal International Law*, 13, p. 379 (1999).

50 See Cohen, note 27.

51 See Lawrence M. Friedman, *Total Justice*, New York: Russell Sage Foundation (1985).

B. The sources of perversion of the World Power System

There are at least two sources of perversion in the present operation of the World Power System deriving from the surge of corporations in legal systems constitutionally structured prior to their development. The first one is that private law legal entities are (almost) treated like individuals by the legal system, and the second one is that enterprises are widely perceived as being owned by shareholders.

1. Individuals and legal entities are treated equally by the legal system

In the traditional analysis of the constitutional system, prerogatives (the ability to make decisions) are exercised differently whether they belong to the *public* or the *private* sphere. In the public sphere, prerogatives must be exercised in an *objective* manner, for the defense and promotion of common interests, of the common good. In the private sphere, prerogatives are *subjective* rights of autonomy (absolute property rights, contractual autonomy) granted to *individuals*, real persons, to allow them to pursue their own private ends.

The private/public distinction, however, is valid only in a closed or relatively closed power system. Individuals can be granted autonomy only if the undesired outcomes of their *autonomous* actions can lead to the possibility of corrective, *heteronomous*, regulation ensuring the protection of other individual rights or common interests. In this construction, the existence of a public authority is needed to internalize negative externalities generated by individuals in the pursuit of their own private interests and to provide or protect "public goods". Of course, this goes directly against the tenets of neoliberalism, which today has the upper hand – but this is the very basis of the liberal dichotomies: subjective *property rights* v. objective *power*; *contracts* designed by the parties themselves with only *inter partes* effects v. *laws* adopted democratically applicable to all; financing via the collection of *prices v.* financing via the collection of *taxes*, and so on. Individualism and social and market autonomy can exist only if, faced with negative consequences deriving from the game of interpersonal exchanges, the possibility for democratic normative interventions exists *in reality*, and not only *in theory*.

The initial liberal constitutional system, developed to further individuals' autonomy, was conceptualized without taking into consideration (for obvious reasons) what would happen once corporations are introduced into the system. The introduction of corporations and large enterprises took place progressively as a consequence of State competition in the market for norms.[52] Without much thinking about the consequences, the legal prerogatives granted to corporations were aligned on those granted to individuals. Treating legal entities as if they were individuals led to the corporate counterrevolution. "Private" organizations have managed to concentrate rights initially granted to individuals, and have thus turned into power systems without being accountable for their actions. This is how enterprises have become autonomous *legal* orders creating their own norms of *heteronomy* imposed upon individuals. Eventually, this is how enterprises also became *political* orders competing with States in connection with the allocation of wealth.

The fundamental error in treating corporations like people goes on. Recently, in its *Citizens United* decision of January 21, 2010,[53] the US Supreme Court waived the limits to the financing of national political campaigns by corporations, invoking the First Amendment on

52 For more details, see Robé, note 8 p. 54 et seq.

53 Supreme Court of the United States, *Citizens United v. Federal Election Commission*, www.supremecourt.gov/opinions/09pdf/08-205.pdf

the freedom of speech.[54] In his dissenting opinion, Justice Stevens remarked that in 1816, Thomas Jefferson had already warned against the danger that corporations represented for the Republic,[55] emphasizing the fact that their difference with human beings should be plain for all to see. He noted, however, that the Court's majority opinion drew no conclusion out of it at all – and this despite the fact that companies have no consciousness, beliefs, feelings, thoughts or desire; they are mere fictions used to organize human activities. They are not part of the "We, the People", by whom and for whom the Constitution was written.[56]

This confusion between individuals and legal entities is, however, widespread and this is the first main source of perversion in the operation of our existing legal system – but worse is to come.

2. *A perversion amplified by a peculiar scholarly perception of the power relationships within an enterprise*

The common understanding of business corporations is that they are a contractual alliance among shareholders, directors and officers – and corporations/firms (the difference is rarely made) are thought about as being *owned* by shareholders. The consequences for the governance of enterprises are devastating. Whereas the managers of large enterprises should be in a positon to exercise the prerogatives they have with enough leeway to allow them to fulfill their duties as "Enterprise Men" (the functional equivalent of *statesmen*),[57] they are forced and/or enticed instead to manage enterprises in the sole interest of the shareholders.[58]

54 President Obama immediately commented on the decision: "With its ruling today, the Supreme Court has given a green light to a new stampede of special interest money in our politics. It is a major victory for big oil, Wall Street banks, health insurance companies and the other powerful interests that marshal their power every day in Washington to drown out the voices of everyday Americans. This ruling gives the special interests and their lobbyists even more power in Washington – while undermining the influence of average Americans who make small contributions to support their preferred candidates. That's why I am instructing my Administration to get to work immediately with Congress on this issue. We are going to talk with bipartisan Congressional leaders to develop a forceful response to this decision. The public interest requires nothing less". Then, in his "State of the Union" address: "Last week, the Supreme Court reversed a century of law to open the floodgates for special interests – including foreign companies – to spend without limit in our elections. Well, I don't think American elections should be bankrolled by America's most powerful interests, and worse, by foreign entities. They should be decided by the American people, and that's why I'm urging Democrats and Republicans to pass a bill that helps to right this wrong".

55 "I hope we shall . . . crush in [its] birth the aristocracy of our monied corporations which dare already to challenge our government to a trial of strength and bid defiance to the laws of our country"; see p. 36 of his opinion.

56 Ibid., pp. 75 and 76.

57 After the Copenhagen summit failure in December 2009, Unilever CEO Paul Polman, stated: "The failure of governments to produce a comprehensive agreement should not be taken as an excuse for inaction. . . . business can do a lot without help from the politicians. . . . Tackling with this urgency and priority makes good business sense. . . . Wherever you look, it's a no brainer. . . . A political agreement in Copenhagen would have been helpful . . . But even without a formal framework, business can still do a great deal". See "Redefining Business Success", paper presented at the Economist Third Annual Sustainability Summit "After Copenhagen: How can business face the Climate Change Challenge", London, February 25, 2010. In the words of Steven Pearlstein, "real business leaders don't just sit there and accept a competitive dynamic, let alone a dysfunctional one that is likely to result in a bad outcome for everyone. They figure out a way to change that dynamic". See Steven Pearlstein, "Just One Real Leader, and We Could Have Avoided This Mess", *The Washington Post*, December 12, 2008.

58 In Davos, in 2010, SAP's CEO stated: "It is time to talk about stakeholder value, not shareholder value. This will be a hard transition for many chief executives because they are not trained to do that. It will be tough but we have to do it". See *The Times*, January 29, 2010.

This view is supported by misconceptions generally shared in classical social sciences – economics in particular:

a) It is often alleged that shareholders own enterprises. But shareholders own only the shares issued by one or several corporations serving as the enterprise's corporate structure. When analyzing shareholders' true prerogatives and limited liability, their property rights over the *shares* cannot be considered as granting them a property rights over the *enterprise*.[59] Shareholders have prerogatives over the enterprise via their ownership of the shares issued by the corporation used to legally structure it, but they do not own the enterprise.
b) This common mistake was developed by the promoters of the so-called agency theory (on which all "corporate governance" theses rely): Corporate officers are presented as the shareholders' *agents* who should only seek to maximize shareholders' interests, i.e. maximize the present value of the shares. In this perspective, they should not worry about the negative externalities generated in the process: These can allegedly be internalized by each contractual partner during contract negotiations or via mandatory norms or regulations, and therefore it is up to the contractual partner or the State or States acting in common to take care of these negative externalities.[60]

   Such an analysis, which relies on the existence of a perfect contractual and legal environment, is obviously misconceived and inappropriate to describe the reality of our global society.[61] Globalization challenges the possibility of such a division of functions between "public" and "private" spheres when applied to large enterprises, which do not operate in a closed legal system. All liberal dichotomies between private/public law, legal heteronomy/contractual autonomy, power/property rights, politics/economy, tax/prices, and so on are totally devoid of meaning in a global society in which "private" organizations fulfill public functions while "public" organizations compete for the localization of businesses.[62]

* * *

With globalization, and in particular the globalization of *firms*, we need to think differently. Generally speaking, the language and the concepts used to think about the enterprise have long been the notions of contract, agency, property and individual, which are all *private law* instruments and which indeed enabled enterprises to develop, but which, at the same time, have been hiding the true organizational category to which they belong. The concept of "enterprise" has long been hidden behind these private law devices, to such an extent that even legal scholars have given up the idea of developing a legal theory of enterprises.[63] For

59 Jean-Philippe Robé, "A qui appartiennent les entreprises?", *Le Débat*, 155, p. 32 (2009). And Robé, note 46.

60 See Milton Friedman, "The Social Responsibility of Business Is to Increase Its Profits", *The New York Times*, pp. 32–33, 122, 126 (September 13, 1970); and Michael C. Jensen & William H. Meckling, "Theory of the Enterprise: Managerial Behavior, Agency Costs and Ownership Structure", *Journal of Financial Economics*, 3(4), p. 305 (1976) and Jean Tirole, *The Theory of Corporate Finance*, Princeton: Princeton University Press (2006).

61 See Robé, note 46.

62 See Peer Zumbansen, "The Evolution of the Corporation: Organization, Finance, Knowledge and Corporate Social Responsibility", *CLPE Research Paper*, 06/2009 5(1) (2009), p. 39.

63 See, for instance, Le Goff, note 36.

instance, enterprises are not subject to any property right and yet the concept of property is permanently used to explain their functioning. The enterprise is a place where power is exercised, and yet it is (almost) never thought about as a political institution.[64]

Classical categories of analyses have led to the division of knowledge relating to enterprises; they need to be rearticulated, which is hard to do within the existing understanding of positive law, economy and political science. The content of these fields of knowledge remains based on the assumption that an effective "States System" exists. A "national methodologism" bias in the social sciences has led to the conceptualization of global "society" as the horizontal coexistence of national societies.

To think about globalization, one needs to refer to other categories of thinking that historically have fallen into the scope of public law, such as power, common interests and control. Throughout history, we managed to frame State power (by submitting it to the rule of law) via constitutions. Why would it not be possible to "constitutionalize" other forms of power that are an integral part of the World Power System? Why not constitutionalize enterprises' exercise of power? Far from being out of the constitutional scope, as previously underlined, the power exercised within and by enterprises is in reality *the core* of the global liberal constitutional system, extended via multilateral treaties, as it relies on property rights and contractual autonomy, which are two prerogatives widely protected by liberal constitutions. Since the enterprise is neither an individual nor the property of any one of them, the enterprise lacks any legitimacy to exercise the property rights it controls in total autonomy; it is not even legitimate for it to do it for the benefit of one sub-part of its "stakeholders" since none of them *owns* the enterprise. Prerogatives exercised within an enterprise are not those of an "owner" whose autonomy should be protected; rather, they are those of a "holder of powers" (thanks to constitutional provisions) for which we should seek to ensure that these prerogatives are exercised in compliance with the enterprise's self-defined purposes while respecting individuals' rights and affected interests.[65]

2. The constitutional idea applied to the enterprise

In its traditional understanding, a constitution is the fundamental law of a State that defines, on one hand, individuals' rights and liberties and, on the other hand, the organization and the division of public powers into (usually) three branches of government: the executive, the legislative and the judiciary. In its modern sense, the constitution may be perceived in a historical perspective as the text organizing the separation of powers that include, *prior* to the separation among executive, legislative and judicial powers, the definition of a "private"[66] sphere, via the definition of a set of fundamental protective rights for individuals, and a "public" sphere with prerogatives that aim at fulfilling common interests (the common good).

There is currently no "global constitution" in the sense that there is no single text or series of texts proclaiming that such a constitution exists. There is, however, a global power system composed of "public" and "private" components, which has constitutional origins rooted in the various States' positive constitutions and in international treaties. This system

64 See, however, March, "The Business Enterprise as a Political Coalition", *Journal of Politics*, 24, p. 662 (1962) and Isabelle Ferreras, *Gouverner le capitalisme?*, Paris: Presses Universitaires de France (2012).

65 Some theories have been drawn on non-State power; see Emmanuel Gaillard, *Le pouvoir en droit privé*, Paris: Economica (1985).

66 See in particular the sources quoted in note 28. See also Carl Schmitt, note 29 pp. 263–266.

is effective; in a way, a global constitutional system is already in place, at least partially. It is certainly not coherent, all-encompassing and neatly structured. But a power system beyond States and markets and official international organizations does exist.

When applied to the World Power System, the notion of "constitution" must be thought about anew, taking into consideration the particular form of constitution of the liberal State by tracing the consequences of the concentration of rights originally designed for individuals (via property rights and contractual freedom) into enterprises having a global scope of action.[67]

Our analysis differs from certain current attempts to develop a constitutional theory free of any reference to the nation-state.[68] To the contrary, we associate enterprises' power with constitutional systems of powers recognized as such. Enterprises' power is of course not yet recognized as constitutional power – and yet, it originates from, and is nurtured by, positive constitutional norms. It is precisely these strong rights, initially designed for *individuals*, that are now concentrated within *organizations*, which integrate enterprises within the positive system of exercise of power. The form of legal pluralism to which our analysis leads cannot be separated from the peculiar mode of structuring liberal society. It is inherently linked to liberal society and to the position of the State as having only a *residual* jurisdiction.[69] This could remain hardly visible until globalization; it can hardly be ignored anymore: Enterprises exercise a power that results from their control over assets, of which no individual is either

67 See in particular Neil Walker, "The Idea of Constitutional Pluralism", *Modern Law Review*, 65, p. 317 (2002) and "Taking Constitutionalism Beyond the State", *Political Studies*, 56, p. 519 (2008). See also Kate and Terry Macdonald, "Non-Electoral Accountability in Global Politics: Strengthening Democratic Control Within the Global Garment Industry", *European Journal of International Law*, 17(1), pp. 89–119 (2006) and "Democracy in a Pluralist Global Order: Corporate Power and Stakeholder Representation", *Ethics and International Affairs*, 24(1), pp. 19–43 (2010).

68 For instance, Gunther Teubner refers to Internet law, which would be constitutionalized not by State or public constitutions but by civil ones; see Gunther Teubner, "Global Private Regimes Neo-Spontaneous Law and Dual Constitution of Autonomous Sectors in World Society", in *Globalization and Public Governance*, Karl-Heinz Ladeur (ed.), Aldershot: Ashgate (2004), pp. 71–87, Gunther Teubner, "Societal Constitutionalism: Alternatives to state-Centered Constitutional Theory", in *Transnational Governance and Constitutionalism*, Christian Joerges, Inger-Johanne Sand & Gunther Teubner (eds.), Oxford: Hart Publishing (2004), pp. 3–28, Gunther Teubner, "Fragmented Foundations: Societal Constitutionalism Beyond the Nation State", in *The Twilight of Constitutional Law: Demise or Transmutation*, Petra Dobner & Martin Loughlin (eds.), pp. 327–41 Oxford: Oxford University Press (2009) and Gunther Teubner, "A Constitutional Moment? The Logics of 'Hit the Bottom'", in *After the Catastrophe: Economy, Law and Politics in Times of Crisis*, Poul F. Kjaer, Gunther Teubner & Alberto Febbrajo (eds.), Oxford: Hart Publishing (2011).

69 We therefore face the dilemma raised by Bruno Oppetit: "If one wants to be intellectually rigorous regarding these spontaneous rules . . . one immediately faces the following dilemma: either one takes into account the weaknesses of the legal positivism dogma and rejects such so-called spontaneous law into the field of facts, or even into the non-legal field . . . or one proceeds to a complete inversion of the sources and decides to start, not with the absolute and exclusive characteristic of the principle of legality, but with the pluralism of sources". See Oppetit, note 39, p. 53.

In reality, legal pluralism is an integral part of legal liberalism by the definition of a sphere of private autonomy, and therefore finds its source in these particular positive norms such as the declaration of rights that are integrated into positive constitutions. However, one does not find oneself in the position of a "weak" pluralism as identified by John Griffiths, as the legal orders spontaneously created are *not* integrated into the State's legal order. See "What is Legal Pluralism?", in *Journal of Legal Pluralism*, 24, p. 1–55 (1986). See also Leopold Pospisil, "Legal Levels and Multiplicity of Legal Systems in Human Societies" *The Journal of Conflict Resolution*, XI(1), pp. 2–26 (1967).

For a condensed theoretical analysis, see Alf Ross, "Sur les concepts d''État' et d''organes d'État' en droit constitutionnel", *Droits*, 23, p. 131 (1996).

the owner or liable for, but which existence is guaranteed by the global constitutional apparatus, i.e. the combination between national constitutions and certain international treaties that have internationalized this particular way of structuring power.[70]

This global "constitutional system" finds its origins in the institutionalization, starting in the seventeenth century, of the "State System". In this perspective, State sovereignty is only one of the norms of the World Power System.[71] It is common knowledge that it is only in a second stage that liberal State constitutions have been adopted at the States' level. These constitutions are constitutions in the classical sense. The partial internationalization of this constitutional structuring of power was first achieved on a *bilateral* basis via commercial treaties following the model of the 1860 Cobden-Chevallier treaty (which Nussbaum describes as an "international bill of rights"[72]), and following the Second World War, on a *multilateral* basis. Its first component (the principle of self-regulation of society by individuals via contractual autonomy and property rights) was notably internationalized with the Bretton Woods treaties and, more specifically, with the GATT (which provided for the means of extension of the rules of a market society with the multilateral application of the principles of nondiscrimination, national and most favored nation treatments, and so on.).[73] Yet the implementation of its second component, the "organizational" side that was supposed to occur via the creation of the "International Trade Organization", aborted with the US Congress's refusal to ratify the Havana Charter, mainly due to its awareness of the loss of sovereignty it would lead to. The "private" liberal component of the constitutional system of power allocation was thus extended at the international level with no international "public" organizational counterweight in a position of handling the interests negatively impacted by the development of international economic exchange and with no institution able to ensure the protection of the world's public goods.

Progressively, all States had to abide by these rules to benefit from the advantages deriving from the participation in this ultra-dominant system of economic exchange.[74] Even States that had no *political* liberal institutions adopted such a "private" power structure to be in a position to participate in the global economic exchange system. This indeed created new issues as the lack of globalization of the liberal political way of structuring "political" power led to certain anomalies (as is the case for China for instance), which are problematic for an orderly operation of the World Power System.

In any case, because of the globalization of the constitutional principles of self-organization of society, human activities have been structured on a global scale within enterprises thanks to constitutional *norms*, independent from the existence (or the lack thereof) of a "World State" positioned to play the role of a public counterpower. This is mainly due to the prerogatives that were initially granted by the constitutions of national States to individuals

70 See in particular Danny Nicol, *The Constitutional Protection of Capitalism*, Oxford: Hart Publishing (2010).

71 Philip Allott also uses the concept of "international constitutional law" to refer to sovereignty. See "The Concept of International Law", *European Journal of International Law*, 10, pp. 31–50 (1999).

On the evolving concept of sovereignty, for our subject matter, see Kanishka Jayasuriya, "Globalization, Law and the Transformation of Sovereignty: The Emergence of Global Regulatory Governance", *Indiana Journal of Global Legal Studies*, 6, p. 425 (1998–1999).

72 Arthur Nussbaum, *A Concise History of the Law of Nations*, New York: Macmillan (1961), p. 203. See also W.O. Henderson, *The Genesis of the Common Market*, London: Frank Cass & Co. Ltd. (1962).

73 J. Tumlir, "Economic Policy as a Constitutional Problem", *Fifteenth Wincott Memorial Lecture*, Occasional Paper no. 70, London: Institute of Economic Affairs (1984).

74 A competing world economy was organized under radically different concepts and totally incompatible with the liberal world economy between 1949 and 1991 under the name of "Comecon".

only, States limiting themselves via the recognition of absolute property rights and contractual freedom.

(A) The process of constitutionalizing corporate power, first of all, requires being aware of the enterprise's position in the World Power System:

a) The enterprise – with its peculiar existence as an effective economic organization lacking legal existence as such[75] – needs to be conceptualized as a subsystem of powers integrated into a wider system of powers.
b) The issues of corporate governance are not merely private ones. They relate to the functioning of the power system *as a whole*, now on a global scale.
c) The "constitutionalization of the exercise of power" does not aim at setting the purposes to be pursued by enterprises; on the contrary, the constitutionalization project partly aims at guaranteeing the *a priori* indetermination of enterprises' purposes. There is no need, and it would be a mistake, to set from the outside of enterprises the purposes they should seek, such as, for instance, the maximization of profits. It is not the case in law,[76] and it should not be.[77] The making of profits is (should be) only one of numerous management constraints: The capital contributed to the corporation/firm must be compensated, but this compensation is not a purpose in itself. It is only a means to the various ends enterprises may pursue.
d) How can we guarantee the indetermination of enterprises' purposes? Although it is more and more challenged, proponents of agency theory have found a way to finalize the exercise of power in almost all of the largest enterprises. On the basis of a faulty agency theory, enterprises are to be managed in the interest of their shareholders only, who are misrepresented as being their "owners". Built on the misleading approximation that shareholders own enterprises, agency theory results in treating the enterprise's directors as mere *agents* whose one and only mission is to manage the enterprise in a way to maximize the profits of *principals*. The constitutionalization project may notably be understood as the implementation of obstacles to the determination of purposes imposed by only one segment of the enterprise's constituents. The constitutionalization process would seek to protect enterprises' and their members' opportunity to choose by granting fundamental rights to their members and a (procedural) space for discussion on these choices.

(B) We are now living in a power system in which the dominant ideology regarding firm management (agency theory) requires directors and officers to follow the indications given by the compass of the shareholders' interests; the protection of the other interests affected by the enterprise's activity is thus being transferred to public institutions, and therefore to institutions having a *territorial basis*. Even if such a system of allocation of roles may have

75 Robé, note 8.

76 E.g. Lynn A. Stout, "Why We Should Stop Teaching Dodge v. Ford", *UCLA School of Law, Law & Econ. Research Paper series*, Research Paper No.07–11. See also Robert N. Anthony, "The Trouble with Profit Maximization", in *The Firm as an Entity – Implications for Economics, Accounting and the Law*, Yuri Biondi, Arnaldo Canziani & Thierry Kirat (eds.), London/New York: Routledge (2007), pp. 201–215 and Yuri Biondi, "Governing the Business Enterprise: Ownership, Institutions, Society", *CLPE Research Paper*, 13/2009 5(3), pp. 1–6 (2009).

77 According to H. Arendt, *La condition de l'homme moderne*, Paris: Calmann-Lévy, coll. *Pocket Agora* (1983), any institution with a purpose that is likely to be imposed on men does not respect men's dignity. It is therefore important to limit its power to prevent it from carrying an imposed purpose.

worked in relatively closed economies (this is what is referred to as the "Fordist compromise", with all its imperfections), such a solution *cannot work* in an open economy with a system of globalized powers without a global State.

(C) Thinking about firm governance without the disturbance of an invented property right of shareholders over enterprises[78] offers new opportunities for the setting of the enterprise's objectives, which then become undetermined *a priori* and undeterminable from the outside, except with regards to fundamental principles of a "constitutional" nature: Enterprises must be managed according to their members' "common interest" while respecting non-members' interests that are being directly impacted; and they must respect their members' individual "fundamental rights".

In this perspective, enterprises must seek to achieve their contributors' common interest while complying with individuals' rights. In a globalized setting of competing States, it is not via national laws – and probably not via international treaties given the issues of collective action encountered – that such principles may be implemented. The only things that may be done from outside of the enterprises are:

a) Imposing compliance with *individuals'* rights (fundamental rights, adapted to the corporate context);
b) Ensuring appropriate proceduralization of the decision making process in the *common* interest defined as the "enterprise's interest", with appropriate procedures of contestability available to the individuals (or their representatives) subject to the consequences of these decisions; and
c) Imposing a duty to take into account interests located *outside* of the enterprise (e.g. social and environmental interests) when *directly* impacted. The qualification of this impact as *direct* is essential as the enterprise is not a political institution handling the *general* common interest. However, in order to ensure that negative externalities are taken into consideration in *major* corporate decisions, it is paramount to account for the direct social and natural environment consequences of these decisions.

* * *

In a nutshell:

a) We start from a conception of the constitutional apparatus of exercise of power integrating "public" and "private" spheres in a *single system* of allocation of prerogatives.

   The constitution, in the narrow conception, organizes a system of exercise of *public* prerogatives that are *objective* and should pursue the fulfillment of common interest. This is the traditional notion of power. It is within this framework that the State is organized and that its limits of action are set – this particular topic being at the core of the positions taken by competing political parties seeking to obtain votes from voters.

   The constitution also relies on a definition of private prerogatives, which are *subjective* and are not powers strictly speaking, but rather property rights and freedoms. These prerogatives, initially intended/reserved to individuals allow for the self-constitution of social life in a non-organizational setting (life in society, in a context of self-determination by individuals, whether alone or together, of their chosen personal

78 See Robé, notes 8 and 46.

or collective objectives). These "private", subjective, prerogatives form a part of the constitutional system.

The main dichotomies between public law/private law, heteronomy/autonomy, law/contract, hierarchy/equality, taxes/prices, politics/economy, and so on, are derived from this basic scheme.

b) Due to the development of large enterprises structured using corporate law, a reconfiguration of property rights into powers progressively took place. No individual owns the enterprise as an organization. Assets used by the enterprise are owned by legal fictions (business corporations). Securities are the only assets on which individuals' property rights are exercised. However, these property rights cannot be construed as property rights over the enterprise *itself*.

Such a "private" reconfiguration of property rights led to new structures of exercise of *powers* that have a *constitutional origin* but lack any *positive legal existence*.

c) In the meantime, the aforementioned basic constitutional scheme has progressively been "internationalized" (via, for example, the Bretton Woods institutions).[79] The inclusion of a State and its economy in the global economic system required adhering to these institutions. A State willing to participate in the "global market" – which can exist only thanks to these treaties – had no choice. Yet the rules imposed by these treaties limit States' normative autonomy.

Thus, States have found themselves integrated into a system of exercise of power on a supra-constitutional level with no need to create a "global State". In order to safeguard an appearance of sovereignty, there is a play on words between international public law and international constitutional law. When adhering to the Bretton Woods multilateral treaties, which define rules applicable to all State signatories and imposing the existence of a domestic "market" economy, a State is deemed to express its sovereignty and not to alienate it. However, when the rules of a treaty in effect impose to a State a peculiar way of organizing its internal economy, the "institutional" dimension (adherence to a set of rules governing life in common) prevails over the "contractual" dimension (an agreement among equals restricted to a limited subject matter).

d) Enterprises are in a position to make States compete among each other. The equal sovereignty granted to each and every States allows the adoption of "free rider" strategies, which is exactly what certain States do (e.g. tax and regulation havens, which position themselves in a strategic way on the global market for law by answering to enterprises' demand and thus attracting taxable income).

e) We are living in a global system of exercise of power (the World Power System) that globally functions on a "private" mode (the fulfillment of private interests) rather than on a "public" one (the fulfillment of common interests). States are "privatized" by being lured by the competition system, forcing them to reduce the level of protection (of employees, of the environment, and so on) granted by their laws. Enterprises' power are "privatized" to the benefit of one class of stakeholders (as a consequence of the "agency

79 For instance, being included in the GATT system was not possible for economies that were not "market economies"; see for instance, Patterson, "Improving GATT Rules for Nonmarket Economies", *Journal of World Trade Law*, 20, p. 185 (1986) and Kennedy, "The Accession of the Soviet Union to GATT", 21, *Journal of World Trade Law* pp. 23–39.

theory", which lacks legal basis but that is at the heart of the existing rules of "corporate governance"), which benefit from the reduction of norms internalizing externalities and put States in competition to obtain such reduction.

f) The proposal is to reflect on the self-constitutionalization processes operating in the institutions exercising power in the World Power System and, first of all, in enterprises, in order to "publicize" all the institutions exercising power.

Prior to analyzing a few of the suggested micro-devices to reach this objective, we must insist on the need for States to clarify what is the appropriate use of sovereignty in a global economy and to police improper uses. As noted earlier, State sovereignty is, in the analysis developed in this chapter, only one of the norms of the World Power System. The concrete content of the notion of sovereignty is not necessarily frozen in time,[80] and we are now the witnesses of what can be qualified as a reduction of State sovereignty in various fields. In the present state of the World Power System, we are witnessing a twofold movement of *internationalization of constitutional law* and of *constitutionalization of international law*; this movement should be increased. Given the strategic use of their sovereignty by certain States, it is necessary that norms applicable to States be developed to reduce what can generally be framed as "abuses of sovereignty". The World Power System should be analyzed as a global constitutional system in which the constitutionalization of enterprises' power is required in the absence of an unachievable and undesirable "global State". It also requires having a coherent understanding of the notion of State sovereignty in the context of a global economy. The G20 set the elimination of "tax havens" as a top priority, which is going to be difficult considering the integration of "offshore" into "onshore" finance.[81] However, it is urgent to challenge the strategic and almost commercial use of certain State sovereignties in the tax or financial fields. But the creation of "macro-devices" leading to such a result, required for the operation of a more harmonious World Power System, will undoubtedly amount to a very difficult reformulation of State sovereignty requiring exemplarity and leadership.

3. Means of action and a few micro-devices

The goal of the suggested micro-devices is to favor a self-constitutionalization of the largest enterprises so as to ensure their integration into the World Power System in a way that diminishes competition among States and have enterprises "take into account" the consequences of their *political* choices in the allocation of the resources they control.

The few micro-devices rapidly analyzed hereunder are by no means a complete list of the available devices. They are introduced as illustrations of the methods that remain available to influence the evolution of the power system in a positive way.

A. *First of all, corporate governance and firm governance must be distinguished*

The existence of the shareholders' property rights over the shares issued by corporations is *not* challenged by our analysis, but one must take into account one of the changes introduced

80 On the origin and evolution of the meaning of this notion, see in particular Antonio Truyol Serra, "Souveraineté", *Archives de Philosophie du droit*, vol. 35, p. 313 (1990).

81 See Palan, note 11.

by modern finance. Shareholders are supposed to be risk takers in the legal structuring of enterprises. In theory, the compensation allocated to other contributors to the enterprise is mainly *set by contracts* while the shareholders' compensation varies and is a *residual* after the prior compensation of other contributors (shareholders are the most subordinated creditors). This is formally true in case of liquidation – but the financialization of the economy often leads to a reversal of this logic: Profit rates are not a *residual* outcome; quite the opposite, they are a *given*, a constraint imposed from the outside of the enterprise to which all the other production factors are being subjected.

Be that as it may, while developing an analysis aiming at providing new foundations to capitalism rather than destroying it, it is important to keep, within the firm's organization structure, an authority able to sanction directors and officers who do not fulfill the duties of their offices. There is a need for a system designed to discipline the holders of prerogatives within the enterprise. This disciplinary function is fulfilled today by shareholders, which makes sense but only to the extent that they effectively hold a residual position. The difficulty is to define a system of rules and accountability preventing shareholders from *hijacking* enterprises' power to their sole benefit, a system granting sufficient powers to corporate officers to run the enterprise while "taking into account", in the strict sense of the expression, costs generated by the enterprise's activity that should be reflected in the *prices* of products and services sold on the market. We all know that in the context of a global economy, the market alone is not sufficient as the lack of a global authority leads to a deficit in norms and to the fact that the *costs* generated by a business activity are not all translated into the level of *prices*. Not all of the negative externalities are internalized by the existing political system, which is an anarchy leading to the unfortunate fact that individuals' rights and common goods are insufficiently protected.

Consequences must be drawn from the fundamental difference that exists between a *corporation* and an *enterprise*. Governance of the former is not equivalent to governance of the latter.[82] Corporate directors and officers are bound by particular fiduciary duties[83] towards the corporation and its shareholders because of the shareholders' position as the most subordinate creditors in case of liquidation. But the mere compliance with these fiduciary duties does not embrace all of the duties imposed on the *enterprise's* managers towards all the other stakeholders and affected interests. The enterprise's manager occupies his or her office because he or she was appointed as corporate officer and should be provided with the means to fulfill that role: to manage the enterprise pursuant to the *enterprise's interest*, in accordance with the *common* interest of the contributors of resources to the firm and not with the partial interest of any specific category of stakeholders.[84]

82 For an analysis of the governance of the commercial corporation in constitutional terms, see Stephen Bottomley, "From Contractualism to Constitutionalism: A Framework for Corporate Governance", *Sydney Law Review*, 19, pp. 277–313 (1997) and also *The Constitutional Corporation – Rethinking Corporate Governance*. Aldershot, England: Ashgate Publishing (2007).

83 On the notion of "fiduciary duties", see generally "The Report of the Task Force of the ABA Section of Business Law Corporate Governance Committee on Delineation of Governance Roles & Responsibilities", of the American Bar Association dated August 1, 2009. Corporate officers must make their decisions in the company's best interests in compliance with their duty of loyalty and due diligence. Their duty of loyalty forbids them to contract with themselves or to take advantage of an opportunity belonging to the company and due diligence requires for them to (a) make their decisions on an informed basis, (b) act in good faith and (c) act in the honest belief that the decision is made in the company's best interest (which differs from the one of shareholders). Similar notions exist in the corporate laws of other countries.

84 Gérard Couturier, "L'intérêt de l'entreprise", in *Écrits en l'honneur du Professeur Jean Savatier*, Pierre Couvrat (Ed.), Paris : Presses Universitaires de France, pp. 143–156 (1992).

Contrary to the result obtained by the promoters of agency theory – which resembles a true *abuse of power* – there is a need to reduce the pressure imposed by shareholders on firm governance. Since agency theory is misconceived and results in heavy consequences in terms of social costs, consequences must be drawn and first of all there should be a disconnection between the compensation of those in position of power within the enterprise and the so-called creation of "shareholder value". There are several ways to do so, either by strongly taxing stock options or their economic equivalent (the allocation of free shares, for example) or by forbidding them. Such a movement is already under way.

The disconnection between the incentive system and the interests of one segment only of the stakeholders made, the scope of the directors' and officers' fiduciary duties should be broadened. Procedures have been implemented in order to ensure compliance with the fiduciary duties owed to shareholders. There are both known and recognized fiduciary duties that derive from the existence of the corporation as a legal instrument having an independent legal existence: A corporate officer must act in furtherance of the corporate interest, in good faith, and must never put his or her own personal interest before the one of the company he or she runs. There is no need to challenge these fiduciary duties, which are and remain justified in corporate law.

Nonetheless, other fiduciary duties must be recognized to improve the ability to take into account other interests affected within and by the enterprise.[85] These are all the fiduciary duties deriving from the existence of the *enterprise* as a locus of power in which unilateral decisions made by the corporate officers/managers have a direct impact on individuals or on natural or social interests.

B. The management of the enterprise

The managers' incentive system relying on their compensation should be based on the creation of "true" value and not on "shareholder value". To do so, the accounting of the consequences of the enterprise's activity should be improved, by taking corporate accounting as it is as a starting point and yet enhancing it by the taking into account of those impacts that are not translated into a price paid by the companies of the group and integrated into production costs via the price system.

a) To make a decision, managers of the enterprise need proper accounting systems to evaluate the performance of the enterprise they run.

   The current accounting systems have been developed from the shareholders' sole point of view[86] and therefore create many issues. They allow evidencing the creation of "shareholder value" (profits) without any creation of "added value".[87]

85 See the pioneer analysis by Robert C. Clark, "Agency Costs versus Fiduciary Duties", in *Principals and Agents: The Structure of Business*, John W. Pratt & Rochard J. Zeckhauser (eds.), Boston: Harvard Business School Press (1985), pp. 55–80. See also Robé, note 46.

86 See in particular Jacques Richard, "Une comptabilité sur mesure pour les actionnaires", *Le Monde Diplomatique*, November 26–27, 2005 and "Comment la Comptabilité modèle le capitalisme", *Le Débat*, 161, pp. 53–64 (2010). See also Paul-Louis Brodier, "Les comptes de l'entreprise ne sont pas faits pour elle", *L'Expansion Management Review*, pp. 109–114 (September 1996).

87 I do not use this expression in its accounting meaning, according to which "added value" equals to the value of goods and services produced minus the value of intermediary consumption plus commercial margins (value of goods sold "as is" minus their purchase value).

For instance:

a. Let's take the case of the relocation of a profitable activity to increase the profits generated by the firm's activity by taking advantage of the new location of the activity in an environment with low employment costs. The costs associated with the closing down of the initial production site are in part borne by the corporation that is legally accountable for the closing down (it pays termination indemnities, a social plan, and so on.). It will also be borne by the former employees, by social security institutions (paying employees revenues of substitution), by local communities (impacted by the drop in taxable revenue and the need to jugulate inferred social problems), by subcontractors (whose activity is reduced), by other suppliers, by the local economic environment, and so on. However, only the group of companies created to be the corporate structure of the enterprise within which the decision was made – and its shareholders – is going to take advantage of the reduction in costs resulting from the relocation of the activity in a low-cost environment. With a proper accounting of all of the direct costs (and benefits) generated by such a decision, certain relocation of activities would remain socially beneficial and "relocation" is not a bad thing *per se*. But some of them would *no longer* be beneficial.
b. Let's take the case of the relocation of a polluting activity in an environment with lower environmental norms. Prior to the relocation, pollution costs are internalized into production costs and, *in fine*, into the prices paid by the consumers for the goods or services provided by the firm. What would otherwise be an *externality* is *internalized* into *prices* by *legal norms*. After the relocation, prices are lower (as they do not integrate such cost), profits are higher (if the entire reduction in costs does not translate into a decrease in prices), but the pollution now impacts the natural environment. For some pollutants with no dangerous effects in the long run or on the local community (pollution in a desert zone for instance) there may be arguments in favor of such relocation that consist of a more balanced use of natural resources. For pollution with global effects (CO_2 emissions, for example) regardless of where they are produced, the generated profits *do not correspond to any creation of value*. They are only the accounting counterpart of an "externalization" of costs on the natural environment. The profits result from the creation of externalities in a location where the existing legal system does not force the internalization of this cost of production – and we all "pay" for the generation of this cost by bearing the consequences, such as climate change.

   There is a need to develop accounting systems accounting for the creation of *added value* (and not merely "shareholder value") by consolidating the *direct* impact of firms' decisions on stakeholders and on the social and natural environments.

c. Beyond this, it is necessary to screen "creative" financial instruments. Some of them, – made legitimate in the name of "financial innovation" – are doing nothing else than disrupting the enterprises' economic activity and do not contribute in the creation of *any value*. When such is the case, one should not be misled by the ideological use of the expression "financial innovation". Its mere purpose is to create legitimacy by referring to the notion of "creativity". In fact, the financial sector's role is to finance enterprises; enterprises are not at the service of any resources contributors, equity contributors included. Since certain financial products can have serious noxious effects, we should treat them in the same manner we treat *drugs*. Before drugs are authorized to enter our bodies, they usually need to obtain an authorization from an administration (such as the Food and Drug Administration, or FDA) in charge of checking their positive effects and of balancing them with their potential negative ones. The same should be done with new financial products: They should be entitled to enter into our financial system only after a similar weighting of their pluses and minuses. No one would imagine getting rid of the FDA's prior approval because it reduces "drug innovation". Should "financial innovation" be more protected?

b) The idea is not to discourage personal initiative, innovation and the creation of new products or services. Again, the ambition of the method proposed is not to upset our economic system but to make its operation more compliant with social and environmental demands, in a context in which traditional political actors are losing their (territorial) power. The purpose of the suggested micro-devices is to ensure that activities and innovation creating *added value* are the only favored ones. Destructive innovation (such as alleged "financial innovation") should no longer be rewarded.

   a. The accounting system on the basis of which decisions are made must be enriched. Studies assessing social and environmental impact should be performed and the *direct* costs generated by the decisions shall be assessed and *taken into account.* This is done today to assess the relevance of public action; why not doing the same to assess the relevance of major decisions made by large enterprises?
   b. A generalization of "triple bottom line" accounting would integrate the assessed impact of social and environmental consequences of the enterprise's activity. Furthermore, any significant change in the enterprise's organization should be subject to a prior study assessing its social and environmental impact. To do so, we can take advantage of the existence of a very few large audit firms that are able to develop the necessary expertise to assess the impact of major corporate decisions and spread worldwide "best practices".

c) One can imagine, as an additional development, that the profits acknowledged by corporate accounting may only be distributed to shareholders in the lowest limit of either the generated profit or the creation of added value. "Shareholder value" would then correspond to "added value".

   We would thus remove the current motivation to create "shareholder value" without any parallel creation of "added value" by virtue of the sole externalization of costs on social or natural environments.

d) One can go as far as recommending that managers' variable compensation based on the creation of *added value* should *not* be taxed, or only limitedly so. The community would largely benefit from the added value created, and the motivation to create added value would have a virtuous effect upon society and the natural environment would benefit.

   Such a tax incentive to the creation of added value would also have the advantage of silencing those who would not fail to criticize the proposed reforms by claiming that they are nothing more than a new version of "collectivism".[88] It is often asserted that the

88 For instance, Jensen considers that if "the interests of participants in the firm other than shareholders can generally be adequately protected by contract and regulation . . . the interests of equity investors in the firm . . . cannot be adequately protected by contract", and if we do not force the directors to defend this sole interest, it would

removal of stock options or their taxation would lead to a leakage of talents. In this area as well, the competition among States is raging – but loosing so-called talents generating negative externalities is not necessarily a bad thing. To the contrary, measures fostering innovation that create added value by removing taxes on related bonuses would have the beneficial effect to *attract* talents able to create "real" added value and not merely "shareholder value".

C. Shareholders' prerogatives and their limits

As far as the appointment and dismissal of corporate directors is concerned, the prerogatives granted to the shareholders' assembly should be upheld.

However,

a) shareholders should be compensated only if "real" added value is created, otherwise such value may only be the accounting result of cost externalization;
b) shareholders should not be granted the right to dismiss a corporate officer only because he or she makes decisions integrating the costs generated by the production of goods and services into their prices;
c) we can imagine protective devices for directors if the compensation of the capital at risk (equity) is, for instance, higher than the average compensation in the same sector of activity, and/or if it is superior to the compensation rate of the debt plus a risk margin;
d) shareholders' limited liability should not survive to cases in which they abuse their prerogatives within the enterprise,[89] i.e. when they prevent directors and officers from taking into account direct costs generated by the enterprise's activity on the social and natural environment;
e) shareholders' limited liability is legitimate provided it is not abused to generate costs that, once externalized, translate into profits. The privilege associated with limited liability is not justified if the appropriate procedures of decision making, adapted to the enterprise's activity, are not implemented and result in decisions harmful to the affected interests;
f) the rationale behind the "business judgment rule" should be expanded: The idea is not to sanction the consequences of all bad business decisions. What would be sanctioned is the lack of implementation of the appropriate *procedures of decision making* to take into account the interests directly affected by decisions having harmful consequences. The sanction could affect either the management level or the shareholder level if the management has been prevented from implementing the necessary procedures or from taking into account the identified costs.

lead "managers and directors to invest in their favorite projects that destroy firm-value whatever they are . . . without having to justify the value destruction . . . just as in the failed communist and socialist experiments of the twentieth century". Michael C. Jensen, "Value Maximization, Stakeholder Theory and the Corporate Objective Function", *Business Ethics Quarterly*, 12, pp. 235–256, 244 (2002).

89 Even Hansmann and Kraakman propose this; see Henry Hansmann & Reiner Kraakman, "The End of History for Corporate Law", *Georgetown Law Journal*, 89, pp. 439–468 (2001).

D. The role of the judiciary

The judiciary is in a particular position to contribute to the constitutionalization of the World Power System.

It may play this role for two main reasons:

a) There can be no accountability in the exercise of power if there is no associated sanction. But sanctions, or the allocation of damages, can only be enforced by the institution having the monopoly of legitimate violence on a territory: the State. In order to access to the redistribution capacity States have, due to their monopoly of legitimate physical coercive prerogatives, one or the other of its institutions having the ability to proceed with such redistribution must be activated. The judiciary is – potentially, and provided that standing criteria are extended – the locus of State power which is the most readily accessible to citizens and may therefore be the place for rational and ordered debates on duties and responsibilities. It is in a position to draw consequences of the real allocation of power in the World Power System and may therefore be a driving force for a self-constitutionalization of power holders.

b) It is mainly via the judiciary that States have progressively been subjected to the rule of law and that the constitution has become the text that effectively protects individuals against power abuses. Courts have managed to turn States into "States governed by the rule of law"; i.e. States acting by the law and subject to the law). It falls on them to continue along the same line by turning all the institutions of power into "powers of law".

   The judiciary could play a key role in the constitutionalization of the institutions of the World Power System. This is not surprising: It is indeed the US Supreme Court that truly created the US system of federal government as it exists nowadays, with a generalized control of the constitutionality of public norms and action. In Europe, the Court of Justice of the European Community played a fundamental role in the production of a European legal order.[90]

   We can also refer to the historical role played by the French Conseil d'Etat in the development of the rule of law in France and to many similar national histories.

c) The judiciary has played an essential role everywhere in submitting power to law. Understanding the enterprise as an institution of power that is not subject to a strictly private, thus *subjective*, rationale opens a wide field of possibilities for judges to subject managers to the duty to act in furtherance of the *objective* purposes to be pursued in the exercise of these prerogatives.[91] The judicial recognition of liabilities in case of breach of extended fiduciary duties offers a wide field for judicial action and possible evolutions in the case law.

   We can also imagine granting more effectiveness to the rule pursuant to which no one can contradict himself-to the detriment of others (rule of estoppel) in order to give more effectiveness to unilateral undertakings made in the management of the enterprise.

90 Costa/ENEL decision, Recueil, 1964, pp. 1159–1160. It is also in the context of the European Community that the term "constitutionalization" was used to describe the process according to which the Court of Justice of the European Community transformed the treaties under way.

91 There is no need to wait for a "global state above States", cf. Julie Allard & Antoine Garapon, *Les juges dans la mondialisation – La nouvelle révolution du droit*, La République des Idées, Paris: Seuil (2005), p. 24. The question really is "Who governs? Where does the authority lay?"; ibid. p. 93. It is also because the answer to these questions leads to conclude that there are deterritorialized powers beyond the reach of legislation that judges must perform a duty of domestication of power.

d) It would be possible to start from local issues and to then distil solutions via a cumulative process of generalization (a *bottom-up* approach) notably via risk insurance.[92] It could lead, for instance, to impose a better proceduralization of decision making processes. Global insurance companies would thus play an essential role in the spreading of best practices, which could be set as a prerequisite before insuring risks and their improvement would be a factor reducing insurance premiums. This is how environmental accountability operated and led to the generalization of double-hull oil tankers, for example.

e) In terms of legislative methodology, the Statute against corruption adopted in the United Kingdom (the UK Bribery Act of April 2010) uses a very interesting approach that could be duplicated in other fields. The key measure of this Act is the implementation of an offence for *failing to prevent bribery*. Indeed, any legal entity that "conducts its business, *even only part of it*, in the United-Kingdom" and of which one of the "associated persons" (whether an employee, a subsidiary or a representative) is responsible for committing an act of corruption or an attempt to corrupt is exposed to an (unlimited) fine except – and this is the essential aspect – if the legal entity can demonstrate that it had implemented and used "adequate procedures" designed to prevent such acts from those "associated persons". Guidelines were published by the British Ministry of Justice in April 2011,[93] pursuant to which procedures are deemed adequate (1) if they are proportionate (to the activities and risks of the enterprise), (2) if they are derived from a regular and documented analysis, (3) if they are complemented with regular verifications and audits on "associated persons", (4) if they are communicated internally and outside of the enterprise (for instance via training), (5) if they are periodically controlled and revised, and (6) if they are part of a visible and univocal undertaking by the management (i.e. "tone at the top"), who have to clearly forbid any form of corruption. It falls under the responsibility of each enterprise conducting part of its business activity on the territory of the United Kingdom to implement "adequate procedures" to prevent the perpetration of acts of corruption. The procedures depend on the specific business activity of the enterprise and can be specified in details only *by the enterprise itself*. It is implicitly recognized that the enterprise cannot be held liable for *any* act of corruption. However, the enterprise is granted all powers to implement appropriate procedures to fight against any misuse of the resources it controls in view of corrupting and can only be exonerated from its potential liability by demonstrating an effective implementation of "adequate procedures". Here, we have an illustration of a particularly interesting new way of legislating. One could imagine extending it to other fields, such as the prevention of environmental damages, the protection of human rights, the abuse of tax havens, and so on. This legislative method amounts to a certain form of recognition of the enterprise's integration in a World Power System in which a State may adopt norms leading to *better firm governance* – without imposing compliance with *material* norms – wherever they operate. In the process, other States' practices are also impacted. State law is thus used to ensure that the enterprise has better firm governance practices, including outside of the considered State's territory. By doing so, better public governance (of other States) is also promoted.

92 We would thus reproduce the circular role of the evolution of insurance law on the evolution of tort law. See in particular, Lawrence M. Friedman (1985), *Total Justice*, New York: Russell Sage Foundation.

93 Available on the following link: www.justice.gov.uk/publications/bribery-bill.htm

f) The identified fields (there are certainly many others) on which a reflection should be led include, inter alia:

- The role of NGOs in the creation of information and action, notably judicial information and action in case standing – the ability to seize courts of legal issues – would be made more flexible. However, it will be paramount to ensure some sort of accountability for the NGOs as well to avoid harassment practices or even extortion attempts.
- Taking into account the existence of the large enterprise as an organization existing on a global scale, rules of jurisdiction may be developed to lead to some sort of "universal jurisdiction" for courts having jurisdictions over the locations where decisions are being made. Indeed, if enforcement powers are territorially bound, commanding power is not, as highlighted by the UK Bribery Act detailed in Section (e) hereabove.
- Granting standing in a more flexible manner probably requires reflecting on the appropriate degree to which affected interest should be hurt to be granted standing. In numerous fields, the standing granted to shareholders or the associations they create could be extended to other contributors of resources to the enterprise or their representative institutions. We could imagine, for instance, that the Workers' Council found in many European jurisdictions would be granted the right to go to court, or to launch an alert procedure in case of suspicion of misuse of corporate assets. It is impossible today because employees are treated as third parties to the *corporation*, which is legally accurate. However, they are not third parties to the *enterprise* and the misuse of the equity resources made available by shareholders affects them as well.
- Criminal prosecution: There again, we could imagine an extension of standing. Shareholders are not the only ones to be impacted by the misuse of assets. Other creditors, including employees, are directly impacted too.
- The possibility for "class actions", in a form that would avoid their significant flaws, should probably be extended further.
- One may also think about the possibility of bringing actions for unfair competition when competitors do not integrate all the direct costs they generate into the "triple bottom line" accounting of their activities.
- An enterprise that is aware of the existence of negative externalities resulting from its activities that are not handled due to a collective action problem at the State level could be bound by an obligation to handle them via the production of norms within professional organizations to create a "leveled playing field". Such an attempt could, in part, exonerate it from liability or, to the contrary, be the origin of liability for enterprises refusing to participate, in case of future damages.
- We can also imagine nurturing the information available on products by using QR codes or similar technological devices. The consumer buying a product actually "buys" the entire normative system that led to its production.[94] By enhancing the available information (governance rules of the enterprise producing the product, place of production, adherence to charters, to the principles of the Global Compact,

94 Robé, note 9, pp. 858–859, and Robert B. Reich, *Supercapitalism – The Transformation of Business, Democracy and Everyday Life*, New York: Alfred A. Knopf (2008).

and so on.) we would enable consumers to promote an *enhanced competition*, which would not be reduced to a competition on *prices* that do not integrated all costs, by taking into account *production conditions*.

There is a whole new set of reflection to be carried on, by placing ourselves in the ambitious context of a reflection on the constitutionalization of the various institutions of power operating in the World Power System. However, such an analysis remains realistic as it aims at taking the world as it is today and favoring its institutional development in line with a shared history that is far from being over.[95]

Bibliography

Aglietta, Michel & Antoine Reberioux (2004). *Dérives du capitalisme financier*, Paris: Albin Michel.

Aliprantis, Nikitas (1994). L'entreprise en tant qu'ordre juridique, in *Le droit collectif du travail. Etudes en hommage à H. Sinay*, N. Aliprantis et F. Kessler (éds.), Francfort: Peter Lang, p. 185.

Allard, Julie & Antoine Garapon (2005). *Les juges dans la mondialisation,* La République des Idées, Paris: Seuil.

Allott, Philip (1999). The Concept of International Law, *European Journal of International Law*, 10, pp. 31–50.

American Bar Association (2009). *The Report of the Task Force of the ABA Section Of Business Law Corporate Governance Committee On Delineation Of Governance Roles & Responsibilities*, August 1, 2009.

Arendt, Hanna (1983). *La condition de l'homme moderne*, Paris: Calmann-Lévy, coll. Pocket Agora.

Avi-Yonah, Reuven (2005). The Cyclical Transformation of the Corporate Form: A Historical Perspective on Corporate Social Responsibility, *Delaware Journal of Corporate Law*, 30, p. 767.

Bachet, Daniel (2007). *Les fondements de l'entreprise*, Ivry-sur-Seine: Les éditions de l'atelier.

Backer, Larry Catá (2011). Polycentric Governance in the Transnational Sphere: Private Governance, Soft Law, and the Construction of Public-Private Regulatory Networks for States and Transnational Corporations, *Indiana Journal of Global Legal Studies*, 17(1), pp. 101–166.

Balassa, B. (1961). Toward a Theory of International Economic Integration, *KYKLOS*, 14, p. 1.

Balassa, B. (1962). *The Theory of Economic Integration*, London: Allen & Unwin.

Beaud, Michel (1987). *Le système national mondial hiérarchisé*, Paris: AGALMA, La découverte.

Beck, Ulrich (2003). *Pouvoir et contre-pouvoir à l'heure de la mondialisation*, Paris: Champs, Essais.

Beck, Ulrich (2008). Reframing Power in the Globalized World, *Organization Studies*, 29(5), pp. 793–804.

Belley, Jean-Guy (1998). *Le contrat entre droit, économie et société*, Québec: Les éditions Yvon Blais Inc.

Berman, Harold J. (1983). *Law and Revolution*, vol. 1 "The Formation of the Western Legal Tradition", Cambridge: Harvard University Press.

Berman, Harold J. (2003). *Law and Revolution*, vol. 2 "The Impact of the Protestant Reformations on the Western Legal Tradition", Cambridge: Harvard University Press.

Berman, Paul Schiff (2004). From International Law to Law and Globalization, *Columbia Journal of Transnational Law*, 43, p. 485.

Berman, Paul Schiff (2006–2007). Global Legal Pluralism, *Southern California Law Review*, 80, p. 1155.

Berman, Paul Schiff (2007). A Pluralist Approach to International Law, *The Yale Journal of International Law*, 32, p. 301.

95 Contrary to the triumphal announcement by Henry Hansmann and Reiner Kraakman in their article, "The End of History for Corporate Law", *Georgetown Law Journal*, 89, pp. 439–468 (2001), in which they argue that agency theory gives all the keys to corporate law and corporate governance.

Berns, T., P.-F. Docquir, B. Frydman, L. Hennebel & G. Lewkowicz (2007). *Responsabilité des entreprises et corégulation*, Bruylant: Bruxelles.
Biondi, Yuri (2009). Governing the Business Enterprise: Ownership, Institutions, Society, *CLPE Research Paper*, 13/2009, 5(3), pp. 1–6.
Biondi, Yuri, Arnaldo Canziani & Thierry Kirat (eds.) (2007). *The Firm as an Entity – Implications for Economics, Accounting and the Law*, London: Routledge.
Blackett, Adelle (2000–2001). Global Governance, Legal Pluralism and the Decentered State: A Labor Law Critique of Codes of Corporate Conduct, *Indiana Journal of Global Legal Studies*, 8, p. 401.
Bobbio, Norberto (1984, 1991). *Il futuro della democrazia*, Torino: Einaudi.
Bobbio, Norberto (1985). *Stato, Governo, Società. Per una teoria generale della politica*, Torino: Einaudi.
Bottomley, Stephen (1997). From Contractualism to Constitutionalism: A Framework for Corporate Governance, *Sydney Law Review*, 19, pp. 277–313.
Bottomley, Stephen (2007). *The Constitutional Corporation – Rethinking Corporate Governance*, Aldershot: Ashgate.
Bowles, Samuel & Herbert Gintis (1983). The Power of Capital: on the Inadequacy of the Conception of the Capitalist Economy as "Private", *The Philosophical Forum*, 14, p. 225.
Braudel, Fernand (1979a). *Civilisation matérielle, économie et capitalisme, XVe–XVIIIe siècles*, vol. 1 "Les structures du quotidien: le possible et l'impossible", Paris: A. Colin.
Braudel, Fernand (1979b). *Civilisation matérielle, économie et capitalisme, XVe–XVIIIe siècles*, vol. 2 "Les jeux de l'échange", Paris: A. Colin.
Braudel, Fernand (1979c). *Civilisation matérielle, économie et capitalisme, XVe–XVIIIe siècles*, vol. 3 "Le temps du monde", Paris: A. Colin.
Braudel, Fernand (1985). *La dynamique du capitalisme*, Paris: Arthaud.
Brethe De La Gressaye, Jean (1938). *La corporation et l'État (histoire et doctrine)*, Archives de philosophie du droit et de sociologie juridique, p. 78.
Brethe De La Gressaye, Jean (1939). *Les transformations juridiques de l'entreprise patronale*, Droit social, p. 2 à 5.
Brethe De La Gressaye, Jean (1953–1954). *La discipline dans les entreprises, les syndicats et les professions organisées*, Archives de philosophie du droit.
Brewster, Kingman Jr (1959). The Corporation and Economic Federalism, in *The Corporation in Modern Society*, Edward S. Mason (ed.), Cambridge: Harvard University Press, p. 72.
Brodier, Paul-Louis (1996). Les comptes de l'entreprise ne sont pas faits pour elle, *L'Expansion Management Review*, September, pp. 109–114.
Cappelletti, Mauro (1986). Repudiating Montesquieu? The Expansion and Legitimacy of "Constitutional Justice", in *Noi si mura, Selected Working Papers of the European University Institute*, Werner Maihofer (ed.), Badia Fiesolana, Florence: European University Institute, p. 191.
Carbonnier, Jean (1986). Gurvitch et les juristes, *Droit et société*, 4, p. 347.
Carbonnier, Jean (1994). *Sociologie juridique*, Paris: Presses Universitaires de France.
Cary, William L. (1974). Federalism and Corporate Law: Reflections upon Delaware, *The Yale Law Journal*, 83, p. 663.
Centre Des Jeunes Dirigeants D'entreprise (1996). *L'Entreprise au XXIe siècle*, Paris: Flammarion.
Cerny, Philip C. (1995). Globalization and the Changing Logic of Collective Action, *International Organization*, 49(4), p. 595.
Clark, Robert C. (1985). Agency Costs versus Fiduciary Duties, in *Principals and Agents: The Structure of Business*, John W. Pratt & Rochard J. Zeckhauser (eds.), Boston: Harvard Business School Press, pp. 55–80.
Clerc, Christophe (2009). La légitimité du pouvoir actionnarial, in *A quoi servent les actionnaires?*, Jean-Philippe Touffut (ed.), Paris: Albin Michel, pp. 17–46.
Coase, Ronald H. (2007). Accounting and the Theory of the Firm, in *The Firm as an Entity – Implications for Economics, Accounting and the Law*, Yuri Biondi, Arnaldo Canziani & Thierry Kirat (eds.), London: Routledge, pp. 82–91.

Cohen, Morris R. (1933). Property and Sovereignty, *Cornell Law Quarterly*, 13, p. 8.

Coleman, James S. (1991). Natural Persons, Corporate Actors, and Constitutions, *Constitutional Political Economy*, 2, p. 81.

Conard, Alfred F. (1973). An Overview of the Law of Corporations, *Michigan Law Review*, 71, p. 621.

Conard, Alfred F. (1982). Federal Protection of the Free Movement of Corporations, in *2 Courts and Free Markets – Perspectives from the United States and Europe*, T. Sandalow & E. Stein (eds.), Oxford: Clarendon Press, p. 363.

Conybeare, John A.C. (1980). International Organization and the Theory of Property Rights, *International Organization*, 34, p. 307.

Cottier, Thomas & Maya Hertig (2003). The Prospects of twenty-first Century Constitutionalism, *Max Planck UNYB*, 261(7), pp. 261–328.

Couturier, Gérard (1992). L'intérêt de l'entreprise, in *Ecrits en l'honneur du Professeur Jean Savatier*, Pierre Couvrat (ed.), Paris: Presses Universitaires de France, pp. 143–156.

Cox, Robert W. (1976). Labor and the Multinationals, *Foreign Affairs*, 54, p. 344.

Cox, Robert W. (1981). Social Forces, States and World Order, *Millenium*, 10(2), pp. 126–155.

Cox, Robert W. (1987). *Production, Power and World Order*, New York: Columbia University Press.

Cox, Robert W. (1996). *Approaches to World Order*, Cambridge: Cambridge University Press.

Cox, Robert W. (1997). Democracy in Hard Times: Economic Globalization and the Limits to Liberal Democracy, in *The Transformation of Democracy? – Globalization and Territorial Democracy*, Anthony McGrew (ed.), Cambridge: Polity Press, p. 49.

Dan-Cohen, Meir (1986). *Rights, Persons and Organizations: A Legal Theory for Bureaucratic Society*, Berkeley: University of California Press.

Danielsen, Dan (2010). Local Rules and a Global Economy: An Economic Policy Perspective, *Transnational Legal Theory*, 1, pp. 49–115.

Deanne Julius (1991). *Global Companies and Public Policy: The Growing Challenge of Foreign Direct Investment*, Royal Institute of International Affairs, London: Pinter Publishers.

Despax, Michel (1957). *L'entreprise et le droit*, Paris: LGDJ.

Despax, Michel (1982). L'évolution du rapport de subordination, *Droit Social*, p. 11.

Despax, Michel (1992). L'évolution du droit de l'entreprise, in *Ecrits en l'honneur du Professeur Jean Savatier*, Pierre Couvrat (ed.), Paris: Presses Universitaires de France, p. 97.

Despax, Michel (1994). Droit du travail et droit de l'environnement, *Droit et Ville*, 34, p. 9.

Dumont, Louis (1977). *Homo-aequalis – Genèse et épanouissement de l'idéologie économique*, Paris: Gallimard.

Dumont, Louis (1978). La conception moderne de l'individu, *ESPRIT*, 2, p. 12.

Dumont, Louis (1983). *Essais sur l'individualisme*, Paris: Seuil.

Elias, Norbert (1939, 1969, 1975). *La dynamique de l'Occident*, Paris: Calmann-Lévy.

Elias, Norbert (1991). *La société des individus*, Paris: Fayard.

Ely, James W., Jr (1998). *The Guardian of Every Other Right – A Constitutional History of Property Rights*, 2nd edition, Oxford: Oxford University Press.

Evan, William M. (1961). Organization Man and Due Process of Law, *American Sociological Review*, 26, p. 540.

Evan, William M. (1962). Public and Private Legal Systems, in *Law and Sociology*, W. M. Evan (ed.), New York: The Free Press of Glencoe, p. 165.

Ewald, François (1986a). *L'État providence*, Paris: Grasset.

Ewald, François (1986b, 1996). *Histoire de l'État providence – Les origines de la solidarité*, Paris: Grasset.

Ewald, François, ed. (1989). *Naissance du Code civil*, Paris: Flammarion.

Favereau, Olivier (2000). La procéduralisation du droit et la théorie économique, in *Démocratie et procéduralisation du droit*, Philippe Coppens et Jacques Lenoble (eds.), Bibliothèque de la faculté de droit de l'Université catholique de Louvain, Bruylant: Bruxelles, p. 155.

Frankel, Tamar (1983). Fiduciary Law, *California Law Review*, 71, p. 795.

Freeland, Robert F. (2009). The Social and Legal Basis of Managerial Authority, *Enterprises et histoire*, 57, pp. 194–217.

Freeman, R. Edward, Jeffrey S. Harrison, Andrew C. Wicks, Bidhan L. Parmar & Simone De Colle (2010). *Stakeholder Theory – The State of the Art*, Cambridge: Cambridge University Press.

Friedman, Lawrence M. (1985). *Total Justice*, New York: Russell Sage Foundation.

Friedman, Milton (1970). The Social Responsibility of Business Is to Increase Its Profits, *The New York Times*, September 13, pp. 32–33, 122, 126.

Frug, Gerald (1980). The City as a Legal Concept, *Harvard Law Review*, 93, p. 1075.

Frydman, Benoît (2007). Stratégies de responsabilisation des entreprises à l'ère de la mondialisation, in *Responsabilité des entreprises et corégulation*, Bruxelles: Bruylant, p. 1.

Galbraith, John Kenneth (2004). *The Economics of Innocent Fraud – Truth for Our Time*, Boston: Houghton Mifflin Company, translated from *Les mensonges de l'économie – Vérité pour notre temps*, Paris: Grasset.

Gierke, Otto Friedrich von (2008). *Les théories politiques du Moyen Age*, Paris: Dalloz (Réimpression de Sirey 1914).

Gilissen, J., Ed. (1972). *Le pluralisme juridique*, Brussels U.L.B.

Gilpin, Robert (1987). *The Political Economy of International Relations*, Princeton, NJ: Princeton University Press.

Gilpin, Robert (2000). *The Challenge of Global Capitalism. The World Economy in the twenty-first Century*, Princeton, NJ: Princeton University Press.

Gilpin, Robert (2001). *Global Political Economy – Understanding the International Economic Order*, Princeton, NJ: Princeton University Press.

Gomez, Pierre-Yves (2009). *L'entreprise dans la démocratie – Une théorie politique du gouvernement des entreprises*, Bruxelles: De Boeck.

Granovetter, Mark (1985). Economic Action and Social Structure: The Problem of Embeddedness, *American Journal of Sociology*, 31, pp. 481–510.

Griffiths, John (1986). What is Legal Pluralism?, *Journal of Legal Pluralism*, 24, pp. 1–55.

Gurvitch, Georges (1931a). *Le temps présent et l'idée du droit social*, Paris: Vrin.

Gurvitch, Georges (1931b). Les idées maîtresses de Georges Hauriou, *Archives de philosophie du droit et de sociologie juridique*, 1, p. 155.

Gurvitch, Georges (1933). Droit naturel ou droit positif intuitif ?, *Archives de philosophie du droit et de sociologie juridique*, 7, p. 55.

Gurvitch, Georges (1940). *Eléments de sociologie juridique*, Paris: Aubier.

Hale, Robert L. (1923). Coercion and Distribution in a Supposedly Non-Coercive State, *Political Science Review*, 38, p. 470.

Hale, Robert L. (1935). Force and the State: A Comparison of "Political" and "Economic" Compulsion, *Columbia Law Review*, 35, p. 149.

Hannoun, Charley (1990). *Le droit et les groupes de sociétés*, Paris: LGDJ

Hauriou, Maurice (1910, 2010). *Principes de Droit Public*, Paris: Dalloz.

Hauriou, Maurice (1925). La théorie de l'institution et de la fondation (essai de vitalisme social), *Cahiers de la nouvelle journée*, 4, p. 89.

Hauriou, Maurice (1933, 1986). *Aux sources du droit – Le pouvoir, l'ordre et la liberté*, Bibliothèque de Philosophie politique et juridique, Textes et documents, Caen: Université de Caen.

Henderson, W.O. (1962). *The Genesis of the Common Market*, London: Frank Cass & Co. Ltd.

Hirst, Paul (1988). Associational Socialism in a Pluralist State, *Journal of Law and Society*, 15, p. 139.

Hirst, Q., ed. (1993). *The Pluralist Theory of the State – Selected Writings of G.D.H. Cole, J.N. Figgis, and H.J. Laski*, London and New York: Routledge.

Hobhouse, L.T. (1913). The Historical Evolution of Property in Fact and in Idea, in *Property, Its Duties and Rights*, Bishop of Oxford (ed.), London: Oxford University Press, p. 1.

Hobhouse, L.T. (1994). *Liberalism and other Writings*, Cambridge: Cambridge University Press.

Hodgson, Geoffrey M. (2002). The Legal Nature of the Firm and the Myth of the Firm-Market Hybrid, *International Journal of the Economics of Business*, 9(1), pp. 37–60.

Horwitz, Morton (1981–1982). The History of the Public/Private Distinction, *University of Pennsylvania Law Review*, 130, p. 1423.

Horwitz, Morton (1985). Santa Clara Revisited: The Development of Corporate Theory, *West Virginia Law Review*, 88, p. 173.

Ireland, Paddy (1996). Capitalism without the Capitalist: The Joint Stock Company Share and the Emergence of the Modern Doctrine of Separate Corporate Personality, *Legal History*, 17(1), pp. 40–72.

Ireland, Paddy (1999). Company Law and the Myth of Shareholder Ownership, *The Modern Law Review*, 62, pp. 32–57.

Ireland, Paddy (2008). Limited Liability, Shareholders Rights and the Problem of Corporate Irresponsibility, *Cambridge Journal of Economics*, 34(5), pp.837–856.

Ireland, Paddy (2009). Financialization and Corporate Governance, *Northern Ireland Legal Quarterly*, 60(1), pp. 1–34.

Jayasuriya, Kanishka (1998–1999). Globalization, Law and the Transformation of Sovereignty: The Emergence of Global Regulatory Governance, *Indiana Journal of Global Legal Studies*, 6, p. 425.

Jensen, Michael C. (2002). Value Maximization, Stakeholder Theory and the Corporate Objective Function, *Business Ethics Quarterly*, 12, pp. 235–256.

Jensen, Michael C. & William H. Meckling (1976). Theory of the Firm: Managerial Behavior, Agency Costs and Ownership Structure, *Journal of Financial Economics*, 3(4), p. 305.

Kantorowicz, Ernst H. (1984). *Mourir pour la patrie*, Paris: Presses Universitaires de France.

Kantorowicz, Ernst H. (1989). *Les deux corps du Roi* (1957, traduction française1989), Paris: Gallimard.

Kinley, David (2002). Human Rights, Globalization and the Rule of Law: Friends, Foes or Family?, *UCLA Journal International Law & Foreign Affairs*, 7, p. 239.

Kirchgassner, Gerhard (1994). Constitutional Economics and Its Relevance for the Evolution of Rules, *KYKLOS*, 47, p. 321.

Lane, Frederic C. (1950). Force and Enterprise in the Creation of Oceanic Commerce, *The Tasks of Economic History, Supplemental Issue of the Journal of Economics History*, X, pp. 19–30.

Lane, Frederic C. (1958). Economic Consequences of Organized Violence, *Journal Economics History*, 18, p. 401.

Le Goff, Jacques (2004). Entreprise et institution; retour sur un débat crucial, in *Les acteurs de l'histoire du droit du travail*, Jean-Pierre Le Crom (ed.), Rennes: Presses Universitaires de Rennes, pp. 83–104.

Lyon-Caen, Antoine (2010). Le pouvoir entre droit du travail et droit des sociétés, *Revue de Droit du Travail*, September, pp. 12–17.

Lyon-Caen, Antoine & Gerard Lyon-Caen (1978). La doctrine de l'entreprise in *Dix ans de droit de l'entreprise*, Paris: Librairie Technique, p. 601.

Macdonald, Terry & Kate Macdonald (2006). Non-Electoral Accountability in Global Politics: Strengthening Democratic Control Within the Global Garment Industry, *European Journal of International Law*, 17(1), pp. 89–119.

Macdonald, Terry & Kate Macdonald (2010). Democracy in a Pluralist Global Order: Corporate Power and Stakeholder Representation, *Ethics and International Affairs*, 24(1), pp. 19–43.

Madeuf, Bernadette (1986). Du paradoxe à l'auto-organization: pour une nouvelle approche de l'économie mondiale, *The Review*, 9, p. 573.

March, James G. (1962). The Business Firm as a Political Coalition, *Journal of Politics*, 24, p. 662.

Martin, Xavier (2003a). Fondements politiques du Code Napoléon, *R.T.D. Civ., avril/juin*, p. 247.

Martin, Xavier (2003b). Mythologie du Code Napoléon – Aux soubassements de la France Moderne, Bouère: Editions Dominique Martin Morin.

McCloskey, Robert J. (1960). *The American Supreme Court*, Chicago: The University of Chicago Press.

McGrew, Anthony (ed.) (1997). *The Transformation of Democracy? – Globalization and Territorial Democracy*, Cambridge: Polity Press.

Millard, Eric (1995). Hauriou et la théorie de l'institution, *Droit et Société*, 30/31, pp. 381–412.

Millard, Eric (2000). Deux lectures critiques d'Alf Ross, in *Théories réalistes du droit*, O. Jouanjan (ed.), Strasbourg: Presses Universitaires de Strasbourg, pp. 9–14.
Millard, Eric (2004). Sur les théories italiennes de l'Institution, in *Contrat ou Institutions: un enjeu de société*, B. Basdevant and M. Bouvier (eds.), Paris: LGDJ, pp. 31–46.
Miller, Arthur S. (1960). The Corporation as a Private Government in the World Community, *Virginia Law Review*, 46, p. 1539.
Miller, Arthur S. (1968a). *The Supreme Court and American Capitalism*, New York: The Free Press.
Miller, Arthur S. (1968b). Toward the "Techno-Corporate" State? – An Essay in American Constitutionalism, *Villanova Law Review*, 14, p. 1.
Miller, Arthur S. (1972). The Global Corporation and American Constitutionalism: Some Political Consequences of Economic Power, *Journal of International Law & Economics*, 6, p. 235.
Miller, Arthur S. (1976). *The Modern Corporate State: Private Governments and the American Constitution*, Connecticut: Greenwood Press.
Miller, Arthur S. (1978). Toward Constitutionalizing the Corporation, *West Virginia Law Review*, 80, p. 187.
Millon-Delsol, Chantal (1992). *L'État subsidiaire. Ingérence et non-ingérence de l'État: le principe de subsidiarité aux fondements de l'histoire européenne*, Paris: Presses Universitaires de France.
Moore, Mark T. & Antoine Reberioux (2010). Corporate Power in the Public Eye: Re-Assessing the Implications of Berle's Public Consensus Theory, *Seattle University Law Review*, 33, p. 1109.
Muchlinski, Peter T. (2007). *Multinational Enterprises & the Law*, Oxford: Oxford University Press.
Nicol, Danny (2010). *The Constitutional Protection of Capitalism*, Oxford: Hart Publishing.
Nonet, P. & P. Selznick (1978). *Law and Society in Transition – Toward Responsive Law*, New York: Octagon Books.
Nussbaum, Arthur (1961). *A Concise History of the Law of Nations*, New York: Macmillan.
Olivier-Martin, François (1973a). La France d'ancien régime, État corporatif, *Annales de droit et de sciences politiques*, 5, p. 690.
Olivier-Martin, François (1973b). Le déclin et la suppression des corps en France au XVIIIe siècle, in *Etudes présentées à la Commission Internationale pour l'Histoire des Assemblées d'États*, Louvain: Bureau du recueil, Université de Louvain, pp. 2, 149.
Olivier-Martin, François (1992). *Histoire du droit français des origines à la Révolution*, Paris: CNRS (réédition de 1948).
Oppetit, Bruno (1982). La notion de source du droit et le droit du commerce international, *Archives de philosophie du droit*, vol. 27, pp. 43–53.
Palan, Ronen (2002). Paradis fiscaux et commercialisation de la souveraineté de l'État, *L'Economie Politique*, 3, pp. 79–97.
Palan, Ronen (2002). Tax Havens and the Commercialization of State Sovereignty, *International Organization*, 56(1), pp. 151–176.
Palan, Ronen (2003, 2006). *The Offshore World – Sovereign Markets, Virtual Places and Nomad Millionaires*, Ithaca, NY: Cornell University Press.
Palan, Ronen (2010). International Financial Centers: The British-Empire, City-States and Commercially Oriented Politics, *Theoretical Inquiries in Law*, 11, pp. 149–176.
Palan, Ronen, Richard Murphy & Christian Chavagneux (2010). *Tax Havens – How Globalization Really Works*, Ithaca, NY: Cornell University Press.
Pearlstein, Steven (2008). Just One Real Leader, and We Could Have Avoided This Mess, *The Washington Post*, December 12.
Perroux, François (1954, 1990). *L'Europe sans Rivages*, Grenoble: Presses Universitaires de Grenoble.
Picciotto, Sol (1988). The Control of Transnational Capital and the Democratization of the International State, *Journal of Law and Society*, 15(1), pp. 58–76.
Picciotto, Sol (2008). Constitutionalizing Multilevel Governance?, I.CON, 6(3&4), pp. 457–479.
Polanyi, Karl (1944, 1983). *La grande Transformation*, Paris: Gallimard, Bibliothèque des Sciences Humaines.

Polman, Paul (2010). *Redefining Business Success*, Paper presented at the Economist Third Annual Sustainability Summit "After Copenhagen: How Can Business Face the Climate Change Challenge", London, February 25.

Pospisil, Leopold (1967). Legal Levels and Multiplicity of Legal Systems in Human Societies, *The Journal of Conflict Resolution*, XI(1), pp. 2–26.

Reich, Robert B. (2008). *Supercapitalism – The Transformation of Business, Democracy and Everyday Life*, New York: Alfred A. Knopf.

Renard, Georges (1935). *De l'institution à la conception analogique du droit*, Archives de philosophie du droit et de sociologie juridique, pp. 81–145.

Renard, Georges (1939). *La philosophie de l'institution*, Paris: Sirey.

Renard, Georges (1963). *L'institution – Fondement d'une rénovation de l'ordre social*, Paris: Flammarion.

Repetto, R. (1992). Accounting for Environmental Assets, *Scientific American*, 266(6), pp. 64–70, June, trad. fr. *La comptabilisation des ressources naturelles*, in Pour la science, n°178, août (1992).

Richard, Jacques (2005). Une comptabilité sur mesure pour les actionnaires, *Le Monde Diplomatique*, November 26–27.

Richard, Jacques (2010). Comment la Comptabilité modèle le capitalisme, *Le Débat*, 161, pp. 53–64.

Robé, Jean-Philippe (1995). L'entreprise en droit, *Droit et société*, 29, p. 117.

Robé, Jean-Philippe (1997a). Multinational Enterprises: The Constitution of a Pluralistic Legal Order, in *Global Law Without a State*, G. Teubner (ed.), Aldershot: Dartmouth, pp. 45–77.

Robé, Jean-Philippe (1997b). L'ordre juridique de l'entreprise, *Droits*, 25, p. 163.

Robé, Jean-Philippe (1999). *L'entreprise et le droit*, Paris: Presses Universitaires de France.

Robé, Jean-Philippe (2003). Enterprises and the Constitution of the World Economy, in 2 *International Corporate Law*, Fiona Macmillan (ed.), Oxford: Hart Publishing, pp. 45–64.

Robé, Jean-Philippe (2009a). Conflicting Sovereignties in the World Wide Web of Contracts – Property Rights and the Globalization of the Power System, in *Soziologische Jurisprudenz, Festschrift für Gunther Teubner*, Graf-Peter Calliess, Andreas Fischer-Lescano, Dan Wielsch & Peer Zumbasen (eds.), Berlin: De Gruyter Recht, pp. 691–703.

Robé, Jean-Philippe (2009b). A qui appartiennent les entreprises ?, *Le Débat*, 155, p. 32.

Robé, Jean-Philippe (2009c). Responsabilité limitée des actionnaires et responsabilité sociale de l'entreprise, *Entreprises et histoire*, 57, pp. 165–183.

Robé, Jean-Philippe (2010a). L'entreprise comme institution fondamentale de l'échange marchand, in *L'activité marchande sans le marché, Colloque de Cerisy*, Armand Hatchuel, Olivier Favereau & Franck Aggeri (sous la direction de), Presse des Mines, pp. 91–110.

Robé, Jean-Philippe (2010b). La responsabilité sociale des entreprises, *Revue de droit du travail*, pp. 413–415.

Robé, Jean-Philippe (2010c). Les États, les entreprises et le droit – Repenser le système-monde, *Le Débat*, 161, pp. 74–87.

Robé, Jean-Philippe (2011). The Legal Structure of the Firm, *Accounting, Economics, and Law*, 1(1, Article 5). www.bepress.com/ael/vol1/iss1/5, pp.1–86.

Roberts, Simon (2005). After Government? On Representing Law Without the State, *Modern Law Review*, 68, p. 1.

Romano, Santi (1975). *L'ordre juridique*, Paris: Dalloz (1ère édition 1917–1918, 2ème édition 1946).

Ross, Alf (1996). Sur les concepts d'" État" et d'"organes d'État" en droit constitutionnel, *Droits*, 23, p. 131.

Ruggie, John Gerard (1982). International Regimes, Transactions, and Change: Embedded Liberalism in the Postwar Economic Order, *International Organization*, 36(2), pp. 379–415.

Ruggie, John Gerard (1983). Continuity and Transformation in the World Polity: Toward a Neorealist Synthesis, *World Politics*, 35(2), pp. 261–285.

Ruggie, John Gerard (1993). Territoriality and Beyond, *International Organization*, 41(1), pp. 139–174.

Sassen, Saskia (2000). Territory and Territoriality in the Global Economy, *International Sociology*, 15(2), pp. 372–393.

Sassen, Saskia (2001). *The Global City*, 2nd edition, Princeton, NJ: Princeton University Press.
Sassen, Saskia (2002). Locating Cities on Global Circuits, *Environment and Urbanization*, 14, pp. 13–30.
Sassen, Saskia (2006a). *Territory, Authority, Rights – From Medieval to Global Assemblage*, Princeton, NJ: Princeton University Press.
Sassen, Saskia (2006b). *Critique de l'État – Territoire, Autorité et Droits, de l'époque médiévale à nos jours*, Paris: Editions Démopolis.
Sassen, Saskia (2007, 2009). *La globalisation. Une sociologie*, Paris: Gallimard.
Saussois, Jean-Michel (2006). *Le capitalisme sans répit*, Paris: La Dispute.
Savatier, Jean (1965). Du domaine patriarcal à l'entreprise socialisée, in *Mélanges offerts à René Savatier*, Paris: Dalloz, pp. 863–881.
Savatier, Jean (1974). Les groupes de sociétés et la notion d'entreprise en droit du travail, in *Etudes de droit du travail offertes à A. Brun,* Paris: Librairie sociale et éconmique, pp. 527–546.
Savatier, Jean (1982). Pouvoir patronal et direction des personnes, *Droit Social*, 1, p. 3.
Savatier, René (1938). Le gouvernement des juges en matière de responsabilité civile, *Recueil E. Lambert*, Glashütten im Taunus: Verlag Detlev Auvermann K.G., vol. 1, pp. 453–466 (1ère éd. LGDJ).
Schmitt, Carl (1988, 2001). *Le nomos de la terre*, Paris: Presses Universitaires de France.
Schmitt, Carl (1989). *Théorie de la Constitution*, Paris: Presses Universitaires de France.
Seavoy, Ronald E. (1982). *The Origins of the American Business Corporation (1784–1855) – Broadening the Concept of Public Service During Industrialization*, Westport, CT: Greenwood Press.
Seidl-Hohenveldern, Ignaz (1987). *Corporations in and under International Law*, Cambridge: Cambridge University Press.
Selznick, Philip (1963). Legal Institutions and Social Control, *Vanderbilt Law Review*, 17, p. 79.
Selznick, Philip (1968). Law – The Sociology of Law, *International Encyclopedia Social Science*, 9, p. 50.
Selznick, Philip (1969, 1980, 1983). *Law, Society and Industrial Justice*, New York: Russel Sage.
Slaughter, Anne-Marie (1997). The Real New World Order, *Foreign Affairs*, 76, p. 183.
Slaughter, Anne-Marie, Andrew S. Tulumello & Stephan Wood (1998). International Law and International Relations Theory: A New Generation of Interdisciplinary Scholarship, *American Journal of International Law*, 92, p. 367.
Slaughter Burley, Anne-Marie (1993). International Law and International Relations Theory: A Dual Agenda, *American Journal of International Law*, 87, p. 205.
Snyder, David V. (2007). Molecular Federalism and the Structures of Private Lawmaking, *Indiana Journal of Global Legal Studies*, 14, p. 419.
Snyder, Francis (1999). Governing Economic Globalization: Global Legal Pluralism and European Law, *European Law Journal*, 5(4), pp. 334–374.
Stein, Eric (1979). Treaty Based Federalism, *University of. Pennsylvania Law Review*, 127, p. 897.
Stevenson, Russell B. Jr (1979). The Corporation as a Political Institution, *Hofstra Law Review*, 8, pp. 39–62.
Stone, Alec (1994). What Is a Supranational Constitution? An Essay in International Relations Theory, *The Review of Politics*, 56(3), pp. 441–474.
Stone, Christopher (1972, 1996). *Should Trees Have Standing? And Other Essays on Law, Morals and the Environment,* Oxford: Oxford University Press.
Stone, Christopher (1975). *Where the Law Ends – The Social Control of Corporate Behaviour*, New York: Harper & Row.
Stone, Christopher (1982). Corporate Vices and Corporate Virtues: Do Public/Private Distinctions Matter?, *University of Pennsylvania Law Review*, 130(6), pp. 1441–1509.
Stone, Christopher (1985). Public Interest Representation: Economic and Social Policy Inside the Enterprise, in *Corporate Governance and Directors' Liabilities*, Hopt, K.G. & G. Teubner (eds.), Berlin: De Gruyter, p. 122.
Stopford, John, M., Susan Strange & John S. Henley (1991). *Rival States, Rival Firms – Competition for World Market Shares*, Cambridge: Cambridge University Press.

Supiot, Alain (1985). Groupes de sociétés et paradigme de l'entreprise, *Revue Trimestrielle de Droit Commercial et de droit Economique*, 38, p. 621.

Supiot, Alain (1994). *Critique du droit du travail*, Paris: Presses Universitaires de France, Coll. "Les voies du droit".

Teubner, Gunther (1988). Enterprise Corporatism: New Industrial Policy and the "Essence" of the Legal Person, *American Journal of Comparative Law*, 36, p. 130.

Teubner, Gunther (1991). Unitas Multiplex: Corporate Governance in Group Enterprises, in *Regulating Corporate Groups in Europe*, D. Sugarman & G. Teubner (eds.), Nomos Verlagsgesellschaft: Baden-Baden, p. 67.

Teubner, Gunther (1993a). The "State" of Private Networks: The Emerging Legal Regime of Polycorporatism in Germany, *Brigham Young University Law Review*, p. 553.

Teubner, Gunther (1993b). *Le droit, un système autopoïétique*, Paris: Presses Universitaires de France, Coll. "Les voies du droit".

Teubner, Gunther (1993c). The Many-Headed Hydra: Networks as Higher-Order Collective Actors, in *Corporate Control and Accountability – Changing Structures and the Dynamics of Regulation*, Joseph McCahery, Sol Picciotto & Colin Scott (eds.), Oxford: Clarendon Press, p. 47.

Teubner, Gunther (1993d). Piercing the Contractual Veil? The Social Responsibility of Contractual Networks, in *Perspectives of Critical Contract Law*, Thomas Wilhelmsson (ed.), Dartmouth: Aldershot, pp. 211–238.

Teubner, Gunther (1994). *Droit et Réflexivité. L'auto référence en droit et dans l'organization*, Paris: LGDJ.

Teubner, Gunther (1997). Braking Frames: The Global Inter-"Play" of Legal and Social Systems, *The American Journal of Comparative Law*, 45, pp. 149–169.

Teubner, Gunther (1997). *Global Law without a State*, Dartmouth: Aldershot.

Teubner, Gunther (2002). Hybrid Laws: Constitutionalizing Private Governance Networks, in *Legality and Community*, Robert Kagan, Martin Krygier & Kennet Winston (eds.), Berkeley: Public Policy Press, pp. 311–331.

Teubner, Gunther (2004a). Global Private Regimes: Neo-Spontaneous Law and Dual Constitution of Autonomous Sectors in World Society, in *Globalization and Public Governance*, Karl-Heinz Ladeur (ed.), Aldershot: Ashgate, pp. 71–87.

Teubner, Gunther (2004b). Societal Constitutionalism: Alternatives to State-Centered Constitutional Theory, in *Transnational Governance and Constitutionalism*, Christian Joerges, Inger-Johanne Sand & Gunther Teubner (eds.), Oxford: Hart Publishing, pp. 3–28.

Teubner, Gunther (2009). Fragmented Foundations: Societal Constitutionalism Beyond the Nation State, in *The Twilight of Constitutional Law: Demise or Transmutation*, Petra Dobner & Martin Loughlin (eds.), Oxford: Oxford University Press, pp. 327–341.

Teubner, Gunther (2010). Self-Constituting TNCs? On the Linkage of "Private" and "Public" corporate Codes of Conduct, *Indiana Journal of Global Legal Studies*, 18, pp. 617–638.

Teubner, Gunther (2011). A Constitutional Moment? The Logics of "Hit the Bottom", in *After the Catastrophe: Economy, Law and Politics in Times of Crisis*, Poul F. Kjaer, Gunther Teubner & Alberto Febbrajo (eds.), Oxford: Hart Publishing. Electronic copy available at: http://ssrn.com/abstract=1592465.

Teubner, Gunther & Alberto Febbrajo (eds.) (1991–1992). *State, Law and Economy as Autopoietic Systems, European Yearbook in the Sociology of Law,* Milan: Giuffré.

Thompson, Robert B. (1999). Piercing the Veil within Corporate Groups: Corporate Shareholders as Mere Investors, *Connecticut Journal of International Law*, 13, p. 379.

Tilly, Charles (1975). Reflections on the History of European State-Making, in *The Formation of National States in Western Europe*, Charles Tilly (ed.), Princeton: Princeton University Press, p. 38.

Tilly, Charles (1990, 1992). *Contrainte et capital dans la formation de l'Europe – 990–1990*, Paris: Aubier.

Tilly, Charles (1993). *Les révolutions européennes*, Paris: Seuil – Collection "Faire l'Europe".

Tilly, Charles (2000). La guerre et la construction de l'État en tant que crime organisé, *Politix*, 13(49), pp. 97–122.
Tirole, Jean (2006). *The Theory of Corporate Finance*, Princeton: Princeton University Press.
Trubek, David M. (1987). Consumer Law, Common Markets and Federalism: Introduction and General Concepts, in *Consumer Law, Common Markets and Federalism in Europe and the United States*, 1 T. Bourgoignie & D. Trubek (eds.), pp. 1–25, vol. 3 of *Integration Through Law – Europe and the American Federal Experience*, M. Cappelletti, M. Secombe & J. Weiler (general eds.), Berlin: De Gruyter.
Truyol Serra, Antonio (1990). Souveraineté, *Archives de Philosophie du droit*, vol. 35, p. 313.
Tumlir, Jan (1984). *Economic Policy as a Constitutional Problem*, Fifteenth Wincott Memorial Lecture, Occasional Paper no. 70, London: Institute of Economic Affairs.
Tumlir, Jan (1986). GATT Rules and Community Law – A Comparison of Economic and Legal Functions, in *The European Community and GATT*, M. Hilf, F. G. Jacobs & E.-U. Petersmann (eds.), Kluver: Deventer, the Netherlands, p. 1.
Vareilles-Sommieres (1905). Marquis de, La définition et la notion juridique de propriété, *R.T.D.C.*, p. 443.
Walker, Neil (2002). The Idea of Constitutional Pluralism, *Modern Law Review*, 65, p. 317.
Walker, Neil (2008). Taking Constitutionalism Beyond the State, *Political Studies*, 56, p. 519.
Walzer, Michael (1983). *Spheres of Justice – A Defense of Pluralism and Equality*, New York: Basic Books.
Zumbansen, Peer (2006). The Parallel Worlds of Corporate Governance and Labor Law, *Indiana Journal of Global Legal Studies*, 13, pp. 261–315.
Zumbansen, Peer (2009). The Evolution of the Corporation: Organization, Finance, Knowledge and Corporate Social Responsibility, *CLPE Research Paper*, 06/2009, 5(1), pp. 1–40.

2 The corporation and the new aristocracy of finance

Paddy Ireland

"The test [of a security] is whether the scheme involves an investment of money in a common enterprise with profits to come solely from the efforts of others".

Securities and Exchange Commission v. W.J Howey Co
(US Supreme Court, 1946)[1]

1. Corporate power, the distribution of wealth, and the *Howey* test

This chapter was prompted by a number of disparate things that struck me as connected in important but not necessarily readily apparent ways.

The first prompt was a series of articles by well-known academics and journalists published in *The Guardian* in December 2014 under the banner "Taming Corporate Power". The term "corporate" was deployed, as it often is in everyday usage, to denote not all incorporated business firms but the large public corporations that dominate many fields of productive activity. Pointing out that "of the top 175 economic entities in the world in 2011, whole nations included, 111 were giant corporates", an editorial lamented the rise and rise of "a source of power that has grown beyond democracy's reach".[2] Much of what was said was familiar: Ever since the emergence of growing numbers of joint stock companies (JSCs) – the precursors of today's large public corporations – in the mid-nineteenth century and particularly since the rise of the corporate economy in the early twentieth century, the power of corporations has been a source of ongoing debate and concern. The financial crisis and its aftermath have simply brought the issue to the fore once more, highlighting the economic and political power of corporations. Not only were some of them deeply implicated in the crash, they have since successfully acted to block radical reform. To add insult to injury, as States have tried to handle the resulting fiscal problems by imposing "austerity" on their populations, they have continued to engage in aggressive and ostentatious tax avoidance. When added to their lobbying activities, it sometimes seems as if corporations are not merely "beyond democracy's reach" but in control of what little is left of it.

In the *Guardian* articles, corporate power was portrayed, as it usually is, as essentially *impersonal*, as power that is exercised, as Ted Nace puts it, not by "a someone" but by "a

1 328 US 293 (1946), per Murphy J.

2 The *Guardian*, December 12, 2014. The contributors included George Monbiot, Prem Sikha, Aditya Chakrobortty & Larry Elliott.

some*thing*".[3] There is a common sense tendency to see and experience corporate power as power that is exercised for and by a "disembodied entity", an "autonomous, self-directed economic being",[4] rather than as power that is exercised for and by particular individuals or social groups. This isn't to say that it isn't recognized that corporations act through flesh-and-blood human beings. On the contrary, corporate acts are quite often "personified" or "personalized" by reference to corporate agents, especially senior managers. Indeed, since the financial crisis considerable attention has been focused on the activities and behavior of corporate executives. It is to say, rather, that when they aren't seen as using their power in a purely self-interested manner, these flesh-and-blood individuals tend to be seen as exercising it on behalf of a separate, impersonal corporate entity rather than on behalf of other flesh-and-blood human beings. It is not difficult to identify the sources of these perceptions. Impersonality is inherent in large, bureaucratic organizations of this sort. These perceptions are also, however, in part the product of the separate *legal* personality of the corporation – of its constitution as a property-owning legal person that, in the words of L.C.B. Gower, is "completely separate" from its (flesh-and-blood) shareholders.[5] Paradoxically, therefore, our experience of corporate power as *impersonal* is in part the result of the *personhood* of the corporation – of its constitution as a separate legal person, which has in certain key respects been cleansed of flesh-and-blood human beings. Corporations are *de-personified legal persons* that we experience as "things".

The second prompt was the publication in March 2014 of the English translation of Thomas Piketty's sprawling book, *Capital in the Twenty-First Century.* The book, which generated a remarkable amount of comment and debate in both academia and the media, traces the trends in income and wealth inequality in the developed capitalist world over the last two hundred or so years and seeks to account for them in terms of certain structural features of capitalism.[6] Thus Piketty claims at various points to have identified (Marx-like) capitalism's "logic of accumulation", its "fundamental forces" and its "central contradiction". The strength of the book doesn't really lie in its theorizing, however: Despite the praise the book has received, Piketty's theorizing has attracted considerable criticism, including from many on the left.[7] It lies, rather, in the data it presents about the changing distribution of income and wealth.[8] This data has not only been meticulously gathered, but is also disconcerting, putting detailed

3 Ted Nace, *Gangs of America*, San Francisco: Berrett-Koehler (2003), p. 3.

4 Gregory Mark, "The Personification of the Business Corporation in American Law", *University of Chicago Law Review*, 54, pp.1443, 1445 (1987).

5 L.C.B. *Gower's Principles of Modern Company Law* (9th edition), London: Sweet & Maxwell, (2012), pp. 35–38.

6 Thomas Piketty, *Capital in the Twenty-First Century,* Belknap: Harvard University Press (2014). Since its publication in English the book has been the subject of numerous reviews in academic journals and newspapers, leading some to ascribe to him the status of "rock-star economist": See "Lessons from a Rock-star Economist" by Gillian Tett, *Financial Times*, April 25, 2014.

7 See, for example, David Harvey's review: http://davidharvey.org/2014/05/afterthoughts-pikettys-capital/

8 Piketty himself-uses the terms "capital" and "wealth" interchangeably as if they were perfectly synonymous: *supra* note 6, p. 47. Generally, when it is used by inequality researchers, the term "wealth" is used to denote the value of everything a person or household owns, minus any debts – so-called net worth. For the purposes of studying wealth distributions, however, economists tend to define wealth in terms of marketable assets – real estate, shares (stocks), bonds and the like, excluding consumer durables, like cars and TVs, because of their relative illiquidity. Some economists, like Edward Wolff, deploy a concept of "non-home wealth" to refer to these forms of wealth, excluding homes. Most "non-home wealth" is financial, so it is often referred to as "financial wealth", corresponding roughly to what I refer to here as "financial property": See G. William Domhoff, "Wealth, Income and Power": www2.ucsc.edu/whorulesamerica/power/wealth.html

empirical flesh on what many long suspected: Income and wealth inequality have grown significantly in recent decades.

Piketty argues that the trajectories of income and wealth distribution have been broadly similar across the developed capitalist world over the last century or so, following a U-shaped pattern. At the beginning of the twentieth century levels of inequality were very high, but they began a steady fall from around 1910 before starting to rise again in the 1970s. There was at the same time what Piketty calls a "great inequality reversal" between Europe and the United States. On the eve of the First World War, the income share of the top decile in most European countries stood at 45–50%, whereas in the United States it stood at about 40%. Between 1914 and the 1950–60s, however, in Europe the income share of the top decile fell sharply to around 30%; in the United States it fell less sharply to around 30–35%. Since then, the share of the top decile has risen to 35% in Europe (slightly less in continental Europe; slightly more in the United Kingdom) and to nearly 50% in the United States. Piketty attributes the "explosion" in income inequality in the United States in large part to the "supersalaries"' going to the "supermanagers" of the new executive class.[9] The trajectory of wealth inequality has been broadly similar.[10] For much of the twentieth century the trend was downward, but in recent decades wealth inequality has risen quite markedly, with wealth becoming more concentrated not only in the upper decile but in the upper percentile and upper fractions of the upper percentile. Thus in the United States in the decades before 1914, the wealth share of the top decile stood at about 70–80%. By the 1950–1960s it had fallen to around 50–60% but has subsequently climbed again to over 70%. During the same period the wealth share of the top 1% rose from under 30% to around 35%.[11] Wealth inequality in pre–First World War Europe was even more extreme, with the wealth share of the top decile standing at nearly 90% in most European countries and more than 90% in the United Kingdom. By the 1950–60s, however, the top decile's share had fallen dramatically to less than 60%, with particularly steep drops in inequality in the post-war period. Since then wealth inequality has risen once more. In the United Kingdom, for example, recent decades have seen the wealth share of the top 10% increase from just over 60% to nearly 70%, and the share of top 1% increase from just over 20% to just under 30%. In France the share of top 10% has increased from 60% to 63%, and the share of top 1% from 21% to 25%.[12] In all these societies, the bottom half of the population has always owned less than 10% of national wealth, and generally less than 5%. In recent decades, the share of the "super-rich", those at the apex of the upper percentile (the top 0.1%), has increased even more dramatically.[13] As Paul Krugman says, the current era really is "a new Gilded Age or *Belle Epoque*".[14]

Despite crude attempts to dub him a Marxist or neo-Marxist, Piketty is no uber-radical anti-capitalist. On the contrary, although the book's title clearly references Marx, Piketty

9 Piketty, *supra* note 6, pp. 294–303, 315–320, 336–376. For a brief summary of Piketty's findings, see Thomas Piketty & Emmanuel Saez, "Inequality in the Long Run", *Science*, 344 (May 23, 20, 2014, issue 6186), pp. 838–843.

10 Wealth inequalities tend to be higher than income equalities. The top decile have typically enjoyed between 60–90% of total wealth, but only 30–50% of total income. In similar vein, the income share of the least rich half of the population has usually been between 20–30%, much higher than their wealth share, which has typically been less than 5%.

11 Piketty, *supra* note 6, pp. 347–350.

12 Ibid., pp. 339–347.

13 Ibid., pp. 432–439.

14 Paul Krugman, "Why We're in a New Gilded Age", *New York Review of Books*, May 8, 2014.

has little sympathy with – or, it would seem, knowledge of – Marx's ideas.[15] It is clear, for example, that Piketty's conception of "capital" is very different from Marx's: For Piketty, capital is not only synonymous with "wealth", but it also is a "thing", a view that Marx derided. The book has nevertheless raised hackles on the right, inducing near apoplexy in certain quarters. The problem is, of course, that although Piketty is at pains to make it clear that his meticulously assembled statistics should be seen as rough guides rather than precise measures, his empirical findings about growing income and wealth inequality are for many intrinsically threatening. Moreover, as some critics are discovering to their cost, they are not easy to refute. The *Financial Times* launched an assault only to be met by a typically measured, but nevertheless very firm, response from Piketty that independent commentators have since broadly backed.[16] Indeed, others have endorsed Piketty's findings, most notably perhaps Edward Wolff in the United States and Tony Atkinson in the United Kingdom; some more recent work even suggests that Piketty may have understated the levels of wealth concentration in the United States.[17] In a further provocation, Piketty suggests that the increases in inequality "cannot be reduced to purely economic mechanisms", to "natural, spontaneous processes", or to the operation of meritocratic market mechanisms. The history of the distribution of wealth, he says, has "always been deeply political" and the "resurgence of inequality after 1980 is due largely to the political shifts of the past several decades". Moreover, he argues that with inherited wealth coming to dominate wealth amassed from labor, the concentrations of wealth and capital that have emerged are "potentially incompatible with the meritocratic values and principles of social justice fundamental to modern democratic societies", and that in the absence of radical remedial action, these inequalities are likely to become more acute in the future, consolidating the anti-democratic "patrimonial" capitalisms that have begun to emerge. The *rentier,* he argues, is the "enemy of democracy".[18] In concluding the book, Piketty offers some tentative proposals for reform, among them more progressive taxes and a global wealth tax, though he concedes that his proposals for reform are utopian and unlikely to be politically achievable. It is not difficult to see why the book made such a splash in the United States and the United Kingdom, the intellectual heartlands of neoliberal financial capitalism.

The third prompt was the decision of the US Supreme Court in *Securities and Exchange Commission v. W.J. Howey Co* in 1946. *Howey* was concerned with whether a particular

15 See, for example, Piketty, *supra* note 6, pp. 227–230. See also "I don't care for Marx", Piketty Interview, *New Republic*, May 5, 2014.

16 The *Financial Times'* Chris Giles alleged that the book was marred by errors that were "sufficiently serious to undermine Piketty's claim that the share of wealth owned by the richest in society has been rising", particularly in relation to the United Kingdom: http://blogs.ft.com/money-supply/2014/05/23/data-problems-with-capital-in-the-twenty-first-century/?Authorised=false. Piketty posted a measured but ultimately dismissive response (http://piketty.pse.ens.fr/files/capital21c/en/Piketty2014TechnicalAppendixResponsetoFT.pdf), which has since been endorsed by a number of commentators. The economist Howard Reed, for example, trawled through Giles's work and concluded not only that Piketty's wealth inequality series "fits the pattern of underlying changes in wealth inequality much better than the Giles series" but that Giles makes "a very serious error in his . . . handling of the UK data": www.theguardian.com/news/datablog/2014/may/29/piketty-chris-giles-and-wealth-inequality-its-all-about-the-discontinuities?view=desktop

17 See, for example, Anthony Atkinson & Salvatorre Morelli, *Chartbook of Economic Inequality*, ICINEQ, Working Paper 234, 2014, A. B. Atkinson, "After Piketty" *British Journal of Sociology*, 65, p. 619 (2014); Edward Wolff, Emmanuel Saez & Gabriel Zucman, *The Distribution of US Wealth, Capital Income and Returns Since 1913* (March, 2013): http://gabriel-zucman.eu/files/SaezZucman2014Slides.pdf

18 Piketty, *supra* note 6, pp. 20–27, 415–424.

investment contract was within the definition of "security" for the purposes of federal securities law. The test, Justice Murphy held, writing the majority opinion, was "whether the scheme involves an investment of money in a common enterprise with profits to come *solely from the efforts of others*".[19] Since then, the "*Howey* test", as it has come to be known, has been consistently affirmed,[20] although the requirement that the profits come "solely" from the efforts of others has been relaxed.[21] Indeed, it is possible that the test was on the mind of that leading theorist of corporate law, Mitt Romney, when he responded to a campaign trail heckler who suggested that tax revenues might be raised by increasing taxes on corporations rather than people. "Corporations", Romney fired back, "are people, my friend". When it was suggested that this confused individuals and legal entities – a view summarized by a bumper sticker saying "I'll believe corporations are people when Texas executes one"[22] – Romney explained that corporations are people because "everything corporations ultimately earn goes to people". What Romney didn't say was that this meant they went primarily to the financial property–owning elite identified by Piketty, Wolff and others. Nor did he say that these earnings came "from the efforts of others".

This chapter argues that the growing concentration of financial property ownership amongst the wealthiest in society, together with the (re)concentration of these owners in financial institutions and the liberalization of financial markets, has seen the emergence of a powerful "new aristocracy of finance" – a reconfigured financial elite. This elite, it suggests, is able, mainly through its activities in these markets, to exercise growing power not only over corporations, but over States and societies. The rise of the ideas of "shareholder value" and, more recently, "austerity" are emblematic of this. Moreover, concerted efforts are being made to entrench the power of this financial elite by providing its property with quasi-constitutional protections that insulate it from democratic interventions that affect its value. This is manifested in the emergence of a constitutionalizing project,[23] of a "new constitutionalism", and the growing prioritization by States and international agencies of "investor protection" as a policy goal – a goal that, because of the peculiarities of financial property, requires the strict delimitation of democracy. While the growing *wealth* of this elite is only too evident,[24] however, the economic and political *power* it is able to exercise is not always immediately apparent because it is obscured by the forms it takes and the mechanisms through which it operates. Ordinary people tend to feel subject not so much to the power of other people but to the power of

19 328 US 293 (1946) at 298–299, emphasis added. The court, recognizing "the countless and variable schemes devised by those who seek to use the money of others on the promise of profits", decided to define security broadly. Post *Howey*, discussion has centered not so much on the correctness of the test but on the specific meaning of one or other of its component parts.

20 In *United Housing Foundation Inc. v. Forman*, for example, the US Supreme Court argued that "the essential attributes that run through all the Court's decisions defining a security . . . is the presence of an investment in a common venture premised on a reasonable expectation of profits to be derived from the entrepreneurial or managerial efforts of others": 421 US 837 (1975) at 852, per Powell J.

21 See Miriam Albert, "The *Howey* Test Turns 64", *William & Mary Business Law Review*, 2, p. 1 (2011).

22 A string of US states and cities have passed resolutions calling for the overturning of the *Citizens United* decision and/or the abolition of corporate personhood: See http://united4thepeople.org/ and also https://movetoamend.org/, with its "We the people, not we the corporations" slogan.

23 On the distinction between constitutionalization as "project" and constitutionalization as "critique", see David Schneidermann, "A New Global Constitutional Order", in *Research Handbook on Comparative Constitutional Law*, Rosalind Dixon & Tom Ginsburg (eds.), Cheltenham: Edward Elgar (2010), pp. 189–210. This article seeks to describe certain aspects of the constitutionalization project as part of a process of critique.

24 See, for example, the April 26, 2015 *Sunday Times* "Rich List", which suggests that the total wealth of the richest 1,000 individuals and families in Britain has doubled in the last ten years to £547 billion.

impersonal "things" – like corporations and the impersonal forces of "the market". If we wish to understand the growing social power of the new aristocracy of finance, therefore, we need not only to re-personify corporate power and recognize it as power that is being exercised primarily on behalf and in the interests of a small financial property–owning elite, but to re-personify these impersonal "things". In other words, we need look behind the reified and de-personified forms taken by financial property, the corporation and "market forces", and seek to bring back into focus their social relational dimensions.

The chapter proceeds as follows. It begins by exploring the historical shift, central to our contemporary perception of corporate power as impersonal, from a conception of the joint-stock business corporation as a *personified legal person* – a separate legal entity composed of its shareholders merged into a single body – to a conception of the business corporation as a *de-personified legal person* – a separate legal entity *cleansed* of shareholders, a "thing". It suggests that this shift was a product of the processes whereby shareholding in JSCs came to take on a purely *rentier*, money capitalist form and whereby the share emerged as a Janus-faced, hybrid legal form which mixes rights *in rem* with rights *in personam*. This has enabled shareholders to retain some of the key proprietary privileges of owners ("insiders") at the same time as they enjoy the responsibility- and liability-free privileges of creditors ("outsiders").[25] The chapter argues that as a result of this hybridity the rise of the JSC and money capitalist shareholding contained both "socializing" and "financializing" tendencies capable of leading corporations and corporate governance in very different directions. Thus, what we see historically is an initial period in which corporations, especially in the United States and Germany, were dominated by high finance, followed by a period in which the power exerted over corporations by *rentier* shareholders and financial institutions diminished, prompting the emergence of more "socialized" forms of governance. During this period corporations were less closely identified with their shareholders and the separate personality of the corporation was taken more seriously, creating a more capacious and "socialized" sense of corporate purpose. Beginning in the 1970s, however, with the reconcentration of share ownership, liberalization of financial markets and enhancement of shareholder rights, the shareholding class, operating in financial markets, has vigorously reasserted its power in and over corporations using the residual proprietary rights attached to shares. This has led to a (re)financialization of corporate governance, exemplified in the idea of "maximizing shareholder value". The chapter argues that, predictably, (re)financialized corporate governance has not only proved productively damaging, but has contributed to the distributional shifts documented by Piketty and others. It has also seen corporations come in certain important respects to be much more closely identified with their shareholders, something which has "de-socialized" ideas about corporate purpose. The chapter moves on to argue that the power of this financial elite – partially hidden behind intangible property forms such as shares and bonds, and behind the seemingly impersonal forces of the financial markets – is not immediately visible but is clearly reflected in the emergence of "investor protection" as one of the main policy goals of both States and international agencies. Against this backdrop, it explores the peculiar nature and vulnerability of the intangible financial

25 Shareholder rights are defined in part by statute and in part by the terms of the share issue and by the company's constitution. What I describe here is the common position. See Paddy Ireland, "Corporate Schizophrenia: The Corporation as a Separate Legal Person and as an Object of Property" (Forthcoming); Jongchul Kim, "Identity and the Hybridity of Modern Finance", *Cambridge Journal of Economics*, 38, p. 425 (2014); Jongchul Kim, "The Trust is Central to Understanding of Modern Banking, Business Corporations, and Representative Democracy", *Journal of Economic Issues*, XLIX, p. 271 (2015).

property that lies at the heart of the wealth and power of the new aristocracy of finance, and the policy demands that these property forms make. It concludes by examining the rise of the "new constitutionalism" and its impact on democracy.

2. The corporate person

I am going to begin my examination of the origins of our current conception of the corporation as a de-personified legal person with an article published in 1923 by Harvard law Professor E. H. Warren. In it Warren complained about the linguistic skills of nineteenth-century English "legislators, pleaders and judges". They had, he wrote, "never been strong on corporation grammar", "persistently call[ing] a corporation "they". The context was a discussion of asset ownership in early English JSCs. When a JSC was *un*incorporated, Warren argued, there was "no legal unit distinct from the associates" and the company's assets were therefore the "joint-stock of the associates". When the company incorporated, however, the "assets became the property of the corporation, and were not held by *it* with others". Despite this (for Warren) obvious truth, in the early English cases the assets of incorporated JSCs "were. commonly spoken of as though they were the assets of the members and not of the corporation". The judges and lawyers did not seem to appreciate that once incorporated a JSC became a property-owning legal entity, an "it' "completely separate" from its shareholders.[26]

Contrary to Warren's suggestion that in the absence of incorporation there could never be a "legal unit distinct from the associates", business associations had long had a limited legal existence separate from that of their constituent members as a result of the process of "affirmative asset partitioning" whereby the property of business associations, incorporated and unincorporated, came to be treated as a separate estate shielded to some degree from the creditors of the members of the firm as individuals.[27] This established "the firm' as a separate entity, but only to a limited extent. It did not prevent the firm from being identified with its members, seen as an aggregate of individuals, and referred to as a "they". Nor did it

26 E. H. Warren, "Safeguarding the Creditors of Corporations", *Harvard Law Review*, 26, p. 506 (1923).

27 Affirmative asset partitioning is distinguishable from the "defensive" asset partitioning associated with limited liability. In relation to incorporated JSCs, affirmative asset partitioning was achieved by the simple application to them of the principles developed in relation to non-commercial corporations, and meant (as it still does today) that the right to liquidate the company was confined to the company's creditors, the personal creditors of the shareholders having only the right to seize the latter's shares. In relation to partnerships lacking corporate status and separate personality, affirmative asset partitioning was achieved judicially and took a weaker form: The personal debtors of bankrupt partners could force a dissolution of a partnership, but their claims on the latter's assets were (as they still are today) subordinated to those of the partnership's own creditors. See Henry Hansmann & Reinier Kraakman, "The Essential Role of Organizational Law", *Yale Law Journal*, 110, p. 387 (2000); Henry Hansmann & Reinier Kraakman, "Organizational Law as Asset Partitioning", *European Economic Review*, 44, pp. 807– 817 (2000); Henry Hansmann, Reinier Kraakman & Richard Squire, "Law and the Rise of the Firm", *Harvard Law Review*, 119, p. 1333 (2006); Joshua Getzler & Mike MacNair, "The Firm as an Entity Before the Companies Acts", in *Adventures of the Law*, Paul Brand, Joachim Jacobs & Kevin Costello. (eds.), Four Courts Press (2005), pp. 267–293. As Hansmann & Kraakman point out, while it is possible to try to achieve some degree of defensive asset partitioning (limited liability) through contract, affirmative asset partitioning "cannot feasibly be created by contract", but requires the promulgation of a rule of law: See Paddy Ireland, "Property and Contract in Contemporary Corporate Theory", *Legal Studies*, 23, p. 453 (2003). The ability of firms to become separate entities even in this limited sense, however, was and is limited wherever the firm's creditors are not confined to the members property but can go beyond it to reach the members themselves: See S. J. Stoljar, *Groups and Entities*, Canberra: ANU (1973), pp. 79–87.

prevent the firm's assets from being seen as the property of its members. Warren's comments reflected a very different idea of the incorporated company as a *de-personified* legal person that had been conceptually cleansed of its flesh-and-blood shareholders and thereby rendered "completely separate" from them. It was this conception of the corporation as a reified, "disembodied entity" that underlay Warren's emphasis on the fact that corporate assets are *wholly* owned by the corporate entity and are "not held by *it* with others"; and it is this conception of the corporation as a thing (an "it") that underpins our experience of corporate power as fundamentally *im*personal. The rise of this conceptualization of the incorporated business firm was reflected in the growing tendency in the early twentieth century – a tendency noted by Harold Laski a few years before Warren – to "personalize" the corporation and to treat it not only grammatically as an individual but as a de-personified "it", as a "real" entity with an existence quite independent and separate from that of its shareholders.[28] Indeed, since Warren's time and especially in the last couple of decades, the "personhood" of corporations has in certain respects been enhanced and the analogies drawn between corporations and flesh-and-blood people extended.[29] Corporations have come in certain contexts to be treated more and more as if they really are akin to real human beings. This tendency to anthropomorphize the corporation is most obvious, perhaps, in the development of the idea that corporations are "citizens", an idea that corporations themselves have promoted, not least because it helps them to lay claim to ethicality, to human rights, and, in the US context, further constitutional protections.[30] Indeed, corporations are increasingly being addressed in these terms. In the United States, this was exemplified by the recent Supreme Court decision in *Citizens United v. Federal Election Commission,* in which the court waived the limits placed on corporations in financing national political campaigns on the grounds that they were protected by the First Amendment on freedom of speech.[31]

3. From the personified to the de-personified corporate person

Warren was nevertheless right that during the eighteenth and for much of the nineteenth century English lawyers and judges did identify incorporated companies with their shareholders and did regularly refer to them as "they". He was wrong, however, to attribute this to grammatical or conceptual error on their part, and wrong to assume that this problem was confined to the English. As Merrick Dodd noted in his book on the history of American business corporations, published posthumously in 1954, in the early nineteenth-century American judges

28 Harold Laski, "The Personality of Associations" *Harvard Law Review*, 29, pp. 404–405 (1916). "Personalize" was Laski's term. I use the term "personify" in this article.

29 As Ruth Bloch & Naomi Lamoreaux point out in the context of a discussion of the application to corporations of the Fourteenth Amendment to the US constitution, it is important not to overstate the extent to which corporations have been treated as akin to natural persons. They note that during the late nineteenth and early twentieth centuries, the US Supreme Court drew careful distinctions among the various clauses of the Fourteenth Amendment, applying some parts of it, in particular those involving property rights, to corporations (or, more accurately, to the persons composing them), but declining to apply other parts to corporations, such as the privileges and immunities clause: "Corporations and the Fourteenth Amendment", paper prepared for the Tobin Project Conference on Corporations and American Democracy.

30 In the United Kingdom, this development has been explored in some detail by Grahame Thompson, who has explored the ways in which corporations around the world have come to be viewed as not just legal persons but citizens: See *The Constitutionalization of the Global Corporate Sphere*, Oxford: Oxford University Press (2012).

31 *Citizens United v. Federal Election Commission*, 558 US 310 (2010).

also "frequently refer[red] to a corporation as 'they' rather than it".[32] Naomi Lamoreaux has since confirmed this: "During the early nineteenth century, . . . [American] judges invariably referred to partnerships in ways that focused attention on the people who made them up rather than on the enterprises as entities . . . [and] during this early period, judges often referred to corporations in the same way they did partnerships".[33] Only in the mid-late nineteenth century (in the United Kingdom) and late-nineteenth and early twentieth centuries (in the United States) did there emerge a de-personified conception of the corporate entity as a reified property-owning legal person – an "it" "completely separate" from, and conceptually cleansed of, its shareholders. As Lamoreaux says, references to corporations "with singular verbs and nouns" gradually "came to dominate, and the plural constructions that typified the first half of the century gradually disappeared". Moreover, "the particular verbs used often implied that the entities had human capacities or qualities". As she observes, this was not the case with partnerships, which continued to be paired with plural verbs and pronouns.[34]

Warren's view was rooted in the "essentialist" belief that the creation of an autonomous, property-owning legal entity radically separate from its shareholders was inherent in the act of incorporation. For him the problem was that English legislators and judges struggled to grasp this and tended to identify corporations, partnership-style, with their members, hence their references to them as "they". Others have shared this "essentialism". In the United Kingdom, for example, L. S. Sealy argued that the introduction of general incorporation led to the substitution of a "metaphysical being" for a "collective organism", but that only "in due course" was the "jurisprudential significance of this change . . . recognized".[35] In a similar vein L.C.B. Gower asserted that it was "not until *Salomon v. Salomon & Co Ltd* at the end of the nineteenth century" that the implications of corporate personality "were fully grasped even by the courts" and the "independent legal personality of the company" clearly established, since which time "the complete separation of the company and its members has never been doubted".[36]

History suggests, however, that rather than lawyers and judges struggling to grasp the "true" meaning of incorporation in the business context, understandings of the nature of the corporate entity and its relationship to shareholders *changed* over time. In the eighteenth and for much of the nineteenth century, the incorporation of a JSC was *not* seen as bringing into existence a fully autonomous, property-owning legal person "completely separate" from its shareholders. On the contrary, in both incorporated and unincorporated JSCs, shareholders were regarded as the owners in equity of the company's assets, and shares regarded as equitable interests in those assets.[37] Incorporation created a separate legal entity, but this entity was seen as the company's members merged into a single, legally distinct body. In the words of one contemporary writer, an incorporated company consisted of "several individuals, united

32 E. M. Dodd, *American Business Corporations until 1860*, Cambridge, MA: Harvard University Press (1954), 66. Dodd also notes that at the same time that they used the plural pronoun to describe a corporation, they stressed that the corporation was a single and separate legal person.

33 Naomi Lamoreaux, "Partnerships, Corporations and the Limits on Contractual Freedom in US History", in *Constructing Corporate America*, Kenneth Lipartito & David B. Sicilia (eds.), Oxford: Oxford University Press (2004), pp. 44–45.

34 Ibid.

35 L. S. Sealy, *Cases and Materials in Company Law* (5th edition), London: Butterworths (1992).

36 Gower, *supra* note 5 (4th edition) (1979), pp. 97, 100. The same assertions are to be found in the 2012 (9th edition), edited by Paul Davies & Sarah Worthington, *supra* note 5, pp. 35–38.

37 See Paddy Ireland, "Capitalism Without the Capitalist: The Joint Stock Company Share and the Emergence of the Modern Doctrine of Separate Corporate Personality", *Journal of Legal History*, 17, p. 40 (1996).

in such a manner, that they and their successors constitute but one person in law, a person distinct from that of any of the members, though made up of them all".[38] This underlay the regular references to corporations as "they". By 1923, when Warren was writing, however, there had been a shift from a conception of the corporate entity as a *personified* (separate) legal person (a "they") to a conception of the corporate entity as a *de-personified* (separate) legal person (an "it"). What underlay this shift?

A clue is to be found in one of the differences between the United States and the United Kingdom: What is called "corporate law" in the United States is called "company law" in the United Kingdom. This difference is usually treated as purely terminological and it is true that the subject matters of company law and corporate law are now basically the same. But the historical origins of the difference are revealing. Both "corporate law" and "company law" were nineteenth-century creations, the first books on which were published at around the same time: Joseph Angell and Samuel Ames's *The Law of Private Corporations Aggregate* appeared in 1832, Charles Wordsworth's *The Law Relating to Railway, Bank, Insurance, Mining and Other Joint Stock Companies* followed in 1836.[39] However, they were rather different in orientation and approach. Like both corporate and company law texts today, Angell and Ames's treatise was organized around the corporate *legal* form, embracing all businesses with corporate status. Nowadays, of course, this means firms of all economic types, from large multinationals to medium-sized firms to small corner shops, all of which can (and do) become incorporated companies. In the eighteenth and for much of the nineteenth century, however, the term "company" was an abridgement of "joint stock company", and as the title of his book suggests, Wordsworth's "company law" was concerned with the law relating to JSCs. Crucially, JSCs were distinguished not by their *legal* status but by their *economic* natures: At this time, some JSCs were incorporated, but many were not. Organized around the JSC *economic* form rather than the corporate legal form, Wordsworth's book encompassed all JSCs, incorporated and *un*incorporated, reminding us that "company law" developed as a body of law designed for application to JSCs. Indeed, so too, in essence, did American "corporate law".[40]

4. The joint stock company and *rentier* investment

The distinguishing characteristics of JSCs were outlined by Adam Smith in *The Wealth of Nations* when he contrasted them with the "private copartneries" that dominated productive activity at this time.[41] The ideally typical "private copartnery" or partnership was based around a small number of closely related individuals who were active participants in the firm. In law, this was reflected in the principles of mutual agency (whereby partners could bind

38 J. W. Smith, *A Compendium of Mercantile Law* (3rd edition), London: Saunders & Benning (1843), p. 81.

39 Joseph Angell & Samuel Ames, *Treatise on the Law of Private Corporations Aggregate* (1st edition), Boston: Hilliard, Gray, Little & Wilkins (1832); Charles Wordsworth, *The Law Relating to Railway, Bank, Insurance Mining, and Other Joint Stock Companies* (1st edition), London: Butterworth (1836; 2nd edition, 1837).

40 The situation was more complicated in the United States, where capital was less abundant and individual states more willing to grant corporate privileges to facilitate the formation of firms that would foster development. However, the close link between incorporation and JSCs remained: See Angell and Ames, *supra* note 39, pp. v–vi.

41 Adam Smith, *Wealth of Nations*, Indianapolis: Liberty Fund (1776, 1982), R.H. Campbell, A.S. Skinner & W.D. Todd (eds., vol. 2, 731–758. The section on JSCs appeared in the 3rd edition, published in 1784, though the material probably existed in draft from as early as 1774: See John Rae, *Life of Adam Smith*, New York: Kelley, (1965), p. 362.

one another), joint asset ownership (whereby partners were the joint owners of the partnership property), and joint and several unlimited liability. For inactive "investors" who opted to become partners rather than creditors in search of better returns than those available from government debt and usury-capped loans, the unlimited liability of the law of partnership was a problem. However, the prevailing view was that partners should be active and that by ensuring that success was rewarded and failure penalized, unlimited liability not only accorded with the natural principles of justice and the laws of the market, but operated in the public interest by ensuring that firms were run productively and efficiently: In Britain, the "partnership system of commerce" was widely seen the foundation of economic success.[42]

By contrast, the ideally typical JSC was based around a capital fund and had many more members. Moreover, most of these members were inactive, their interest in the firm being largely, if not wholly, financial. The "proprietors" of JSCs, Smith wrote, "seldom pretend to understand anything of the business of the company; . . . and give themselves no trouble about it, but receive contentedly such half yearly dividend or yearly dividend as the directors think proper to make to them".[43] As this suggests, JSCs were vehicles not only for productive activity, but also for *rentier* investment. In a JSC, Marx later wrote, "the actually functioning capitalist" is transformed "into a mere manager, [an] administrator of others people's capital" and the "owner of capital [transformed] into a mere owner, a mere money capitalist".[44] Or as *The Times* put it, the JSC was "a system of dormant partners" in which "the sole bond of connection between the proprietors is money".[45] It followed that JSCs were characterized by a separation of ownership and management, and by (more or less) freely transferable shares. Indeed, it was the size, nature and changing character of their memberships that made the possession by JSCs of corporate privileges so desirable.

Smith believed that JSCs composed of inactive *rentier* shareholders and run by directors who were managing "other people's money" were inevitably less efficient than private copartneries and bound to be characterized by "negligence and profusion". He did not think that their formation should be encouraged and argued that they should be granted "exemptions from the general law" (such as limited liability) only when certain conditions were met: where the capital required was beyond the capacity of a private partnership; where the risks were unusually great; where the operations of the business could be reduced to a routine; and where there was an identifiable public benefit.[46] These ideas about the limited legitimate scope of the JSC shaped both public opinion and State policy well into the nineteenth century. As late as 1840, *The Times* was drawing on Smith to denigrate JSCs. JSC shareholders, they complained, wanted to make money from money, to "enjoy the profits of trade consistently with the luxury of being sleeping partners", to "share in the profits of trade without knowledge of trade, or any education in it; without abilities, without character, without any attention or exertion". *The Times* concluded that shareholding was "a means or making money in idleness" and that JSCs were "inconsistent with the solid and proper principles of trade" and "contradict[ed] the proper principles of partnership".[47] The persistence

42 See Ireland, "Limited Liability, Shareholder Rights and the Problem of Corporate Irresponsibility", *Cambridge Journal of Economics*, 34, p. 837 (2010).

43 Smith, *supra* note 40, vol. 2, p. 741.

44 Karl Marx, *Capital*, vol. 3, London & Moscow: Lawrence & Wishart (1973), p. 436.

45 *The Times*, November 9, 1840.

46 Smith, *supra* note 41, vol. 2, pp. 757–758.

47 *The Times*, October 9, 1840; October 22, 1840. There was, the article added, "only one more quality wanting to make the morsel wholesome as well as tempting" to the idle *rentier* – limited liability.

of such views meant that throughout this period corporate privileges were granted only sparingly, forcing many JSCs to operate as unincorporated concerns, hence the scope of Wordsworth's book.[48] It is nevertheless clear that from their inception JSCs were associated with, and linked to, corporate status and privileges, even if not all JSCs were able to secure them. When incorporation and limited liability were made freely available in the mid-nineteenth century, the link became even stronger. Thereafter, not only were nearly all JSCs legally obliged to incorporate, for many years only JSCs did so. The result was that in the business context the JSC and the corporate legal form became more or less co-extensive. It was only towards the end of the nineteenth century, with the rise of the so-called private company, that the link was broken. Thereafter, "company law" came to encompass not only JSCs but all incorporated firms, irrespective of their economic natures.

5. The changing nature of JSC shareholding

History shows that the shift from a personified to a de-personified conception of the corporate entity and the emergence of the modern doctrine of separate corporate personality occurred in the second half of the nineteenth century when company law and corporate law were closely associated with the JSC economic form and, indeed, being developed to accommodate it. Crucially, this conceptual change also occurred during a period in which the nature of the JSC was itself undergoing significant change. It is to these changes, which were economic as well as legal in nature, that we need to look if we wish to understand the emergence of the de-personified conception of the corporate person.

In empirical reality, in the late eighteenth and early nineteenth centuries the line between the private partnership and the JSC was less clear than Smith's analysis suggested. Many firms resembling Smith's JSC emerged: they had relatively large memberships, a separation of ownership and management, and relatively freely transferable shares. Some of these firms were incorporated, some not. Many of them, however, were not "pure" JSCs but more in the nature of "extended partnerships" whose shareholders had, by choice, more than a purely financial interest in the firm.[49] Indeed, even if they aspired to pure *rentier* status, shareholders in these concerns faced significant obstacles, most notably the absence of a developed market for JSC securities and the continuing legal restrictions on and impediments to share transfers. The result was that shares simply weren't the liquid assets they are today, and there remained important senses in which shareholders were tied to companies. These material realities were reflected in the tendency, which continued well into the nineteenth century, to regard *all* JSCs (incorporated and unincorporated) as types of partnership. In the jargon of the day, they were "public, rather than "private", partnerships – quantitatively rather than qualitatively different. They also found expression in the continuing depiction of shareholders as "partners" and continuing conceptualization of JSCs as aggregates of individuals – as personified legal persons ("theys"). It also found expression in the legal nature of shares: Throughout the eighteenth and early nineteenth centuries, shares in both incorporated an unincorporated JSCs were treated as equitable interests in the assets of companies. Shares represented "real", tangible capital. The second half of the century, however, saw the emergence of much "purer" JSCs and much "purer" money capitalist shareholding. These changes were underlain by

48 See James Taylor, *Creating Capitalism*, Woodbridge: Boydell & Brewer (2006).

49 See Mark Freeman, Robin Pearson & James Taylor, *Shareholder Democracies*, Chicago: University of Chicago Press (2012).

the emergence of railway companies, which needed to raise far more capital than previous JSCs and were populated by thousands (rather than tens or hundreds) of members, most of whom had a purely financial interest in the companies concerned. The rapid growth in pure *rentier* investment that resulted laid the foundations for the emergence for the first time of a developed market in JSC shares. As shares became liquid assets capable of being turned into money at any time, share capital, as Rudolf Hilferding later pointed out, was endowed "completely with the character of money capital".[50]

The changing character of shareholding generated major changes to the law relating to JSCs, some of them effected by the legislature, some by the judiciary. Their cumulative effect was to accommodate and protect the growing number of pure *rentier* investors. In this context it was not, perhaps, insignificant that more and more of the lawmakers themselves, legislative and judicial, were becoming members of the *rentier* shareholder class. The legislative changes, and in particular the introduction of incorporation by registration and general limited liability, are well-known. However, a series of judicial changes were also made to the law of partnership as it applied to JSCs. The 1840s, for example, saw the abandonment of the partnership doctrine of mutual agency[51] and the reformulation of the doctrine of ultra vires:[52] both changes sought to protect shareholders and to make *rentier* investment in JSCs more secure. The shares of both incorporated and *un*incorporated JSCs were also reconceptualized to reflect the changing nature of shareholding and to facilitate transferability. By the middle of the century shares had ceased to be regarded as interests in the assets of companies (and, therefore, potential interests in real estate) and come instead to be regarded as rights to profit, forms of intangible personal property.[53] This was the start of a very significant shift.

Originally, when JSCs were still seen as aggregates of individuals, JSC shares were seen, partnership-style, as shares (equitable interests) in the company's assets (including, potentially, real estate) and also as shares in the contracts the company had entered into. Because contractual burdens couldn't be assigned without the consent of the other contracting party, JSC shares couldn't be transferred without statutory authority.[54] When they were legally detached from the company's assets, however, shares became, in essence, mere bundles of contractual and statutory rights with no direct connection to any tangible "things".[55] Ironically, this disconnection of shares from the company's assets, including any real property owned by the company, made them easier to transfer and, in that sense, more thing-like – and

50 See Ireland, *supra* note 37. On the tendency of capital to seek liquidity, see Lorraine Talbot, "Why Shareholders Shouldn't Vote", *Modern Law Review*, 76, p. 791 (2013). See also Rudolf Hilferding, *Finance Capital*, London: Routledge (1909, 2007), p. 109.

51 See *Burnes v. Pennell* (1849) 2 HLC 497.

52 See *Colman v. E Counties Railway* (1846), 10 Beav 1.

53 See *Bligh v. Brent* (1837) 2 Y&C 268; *Watson v. Spratley* (1854) 10 Ex. 222.

54 See *Duvergier v. Fellows* (1828), in which Best CJ explained that the attempt to create transferable shares without public authority was not so much illegal as legally impossible. When it was said that shares were to be transferable, it had to mean "that the assignee was to be placed in the precise situation that the assignor stood in before the assignment; that the assignee was to have all the rights of the assignor, and to take upon him all his liability". In fact, however, "the assignee [could] join in no action for a cause of action that accrued before the assignment", for such rights of action continued to "remain with the assignor, who, notwithstanding he has retired from the company, will still remain liable for every debt contracted by the company before he ceased to be a member": See 5 Bing 248.

55 Relating mainly to dividends, winding up and voting. The rights are determined, like contractual rights, mainly by the terms of the share issue and by the company's constitution, though some of them are conferred by statute: See Sarah Worthington, "Shares and Shareholders: Property, Power and Entitlements: Part 1", *Company Lawyer*, 22, p. 258 (2001).

property-like – though the problem of the nonassignability of the contractual burdens attaching to them remained and could be satisfactorily resolved only by statutory declarations that they (and the burdens attaching to them) were transferable.[56] On one hand, therefore, shares began to look in certain important respects less like the rights *in rem* of partners – "insiders" who retain ownership of a firm's assets and continue to carry the responsibilities and liabilities that went with this – and more like the rights *in personam* of creditors, "outsiders" who transfer ownership of their assets and cede responsibility and liability in return for a bundle of contractual rights and regular money payments. On the other hand, although they were now bundles of contractual and statutory rights disconnected from the company's assets, shares were becoming ever more easily transferred, both in law and practice, thereby increasingly acquiring the thing-like qualities of "property". By mid-century, there were now two quite different pieces of property: the tangible assets (wholly) owned by the company, and the shares owned by shareholders. With this, even *un*incorporated JSCs began to acquire, in certain important respects, a legal existence quite separate from that of their (share-owning) shareholders. *All* JSCs were being constituted, in a much fuller sense than before, as separate, asset- and property-owning legal persons.

As part of these processes, JSC shareholders were also reconceptualized, coming increasingly to be depicted as passive "investors" rather than active "partners", as finance-providing "money capitalists" rather than asset-owning "industrial capitalists".[57] Although for many years policy makers continued to assume, or hope, that shareholders would play a role in monitoring managers, the articles of companies and the emerging body of "company law" increasingly recognized that they stood outside the company and the process of production. This was reflected in the gradual transfer from shareholders to directors of the rights traditionally associated with "ownership".[58] *The Times* picked up on this as early as 1840, remarking that companies had become "means of making money" not only "in idleness" but "in compulsory idleness", for in "public partnerships" of this sort, "the proprietors are excluded from . . . control and all intimate knowledge is kept back from them", something they saw not as a risk but "accepted as a privilege".[59] By this time, however, the earlier belief that money (and, therefore, finance) was essentially and inherently unproductive was waning, as was the shadow of disrepute that surrounded the practices whereby money made money. Marking this, in 1856, one year after the introduction of general limited liability, the usury laws were finally repealed.

By the closing decades of the century, the law on JSCs had deviated so much from the principles of partnership that "company law", previously regarded as a branch of the law of partnership, had come to be seen as an autonomous legal category in its own right.[60] In 1888 Nathaniel Lindley marked this by splitting his celebrated text on partnership into two

56 See *Duvergier v. Fellows* (1828) 5 Bing 248. See also John George, *A View of the Existing Law Affecting Unincorporated Joint Stock Companies*, London: Samuel Sweet (1825). Even then, the liabilities of the assignor to the company and its creditors – even when capped by limited liability – tended to be extended for a specified time after the assignment. Under the Joint Stock Companies Act 1844, for example, the liabilities of former shareholders did not terminate on transfer, remaining in certain circumstances for a further three years: See 7 and 8 Vict c 110, s66.

57 In *Bligh v. Brent*, shareholders were explicitly conceptualized as providers of money.

58 See Freeman et al., *supra* note 48.

59 *The Times*, October 9, 1840.

60 See Paddy Ireland, "Property and Contract in Contemporary Corporate Theory", *Legal Studies*, 23, p. 453 (2003).

separate books: one on the law of partnership, the other on company law. Crucially, although JSC shareholders had by now relinquished most of the rights traditionally associated with "ownership", the share having become a limited bundle of rights, they had acquired the privilege of limited liability and retained their residual control rights: Even if they couldn't direct directors they could still dismiss them. This coupling of limited liability with residual control rights, generalized by the 1855–6 *Acts*, was controversial. It is not, for example, insignificant that many of the mid-nineteenth century advocates of limited liability argued not for the introduction of general limited liability but for something resembling the French *société en commandite*, a limited partnership in which in which passivity was a prerequisite of being given the privilege of limited liability. In *sociétés en commandite*, the liability of passive *rentier* (or 'special') partners was limited, but that of active, managing (or "general") partners was not. Limited liability was given to investors only on the condition that they remained passive and inactive; their rights and powers in the firm and ability to intervene in management were strictly limited. If they became more actively involved, they lost their privileged status as "special" partners and became "general" partners subject to unlimited liability.[61] For the *rentier* investor in these firms, therefore, the price of limited liability was a further loss of control rights. The belief was that the risk of irresponsible behavior would be minimized by fixing those in control with unlimited liability and restricting the control rights of those with limited personal responsibility. While the *société en commandite* decoupled limited liability from control rights, the newly emerging corporate legal form, which has since spread around the world, combined them.[62]

6. The emergence of the de-personified corporate person

As the nineteenth century progressed, then, JSC shareholders became ever more detached from the companies in which they held shares, conceptually, legally and in economic reality. As this happened, the separate existence of "the company" – its degree of separate legal personhood – grew. This gradual shift from a personified to a de-personified conception of the corporate person was exemplified by a subtle change in the wording of the Companies Acts. The Joint Stock Companies Act 1856 permitted seven or more persons to "form *themselves*" into an incorporated company, implying that the company was made *of* them, that the shareholders *were* the company. By contrast, the Companies Act 1862 permitted seven or more persons to "form a company", implying that the company was an object external to them, a "thing" made *by*, but not *of*, them. It was not, however, until the final decades of the century that the concept of "the company" was completely cleansed of shareholders and fully reified.

For much of the nineteenth century, shares were not only conceptualized as interests in the assets of companies but carried high denominations and were only partly paid up. The uncalled capital gave companies a ready source of additional finance and acted as a comfort to creditors, providing them with what the Americans called a "trust fund" upon which they could draw in the event of corporate bankruptcy. But the residual liabilities attached to shares also meant that links remained between shareholders and companies, and, indirectly, between shareholders and creditors. In the closing decades of the century, however, these links were all but severed as share denominations fell and the residual liabilities on shares

61 See Francis Troubat, *The Law of Commandatary and Limited Partnerships*, Philadelphia:, Kay (1853)

62 See Henry Hansmann & Renier Kraakman, "The End of History for Corporate Law", *Georgetown Law Journal*, 89, pp. 439–468 (2001).

were eliminated, a process that was once again facilitated by the courts and legislature.[63] The period between 1867 and 1885 was a "watershed in the demise of the prevalence of uncalled capital".[64] In the United Kingdom, by 1885 only about 32% of companies outside the banking, insurance and finance sectors had shares that weren't fully paid up; by 1913 this had fallen to just 5.4%. This development was largely attributable to "demand-side pressures from investors" and to the growing and increasingly prosperous middle classes demanding "safe equity" and a "diversified portfolio of readily marketable stocks".[65] Indeed, by the 1870s, the wealthier among them were already diversifying their holdings through investment trusts, spreading the remaining risk across a portfolio of investments. Having already delegated management of the company, they were now beginning to delegate management of their money.[66]

The result was that by the close of the century existing shares were no longer sources of additional capital for companies, and directors no longer had any need to check the financial wherewithal of new shareholders. Crucially, corporate creditors could now look only to the assets of companies to meet their debts: The liability links between corporations and shareholders, and between shareholders and creditors, had been severed. JSC shareholders really did now benefit from Smith's "total exemption from trouble and from risk". The de jure regime of limited liability had been turned into a de facto regime of no-liability, completely detaching shares from any remaining obligations, establishing them as freestanding, freely assignable bundles of contractual and statutory rights.[67] This laid the foundations for the emergence of the doctrine of separate corporate personality in its modern form, with its conception of the business corporation as a de-personified, property-owning legal person cleansed of and "completely separate" from its shareholders. Corporate shareholding now entailed ownership of an unencumbered, freestanding right to revenue, external to the process of production and entailing no liabilities or obligations, contractual or otherwise, to the company or third parties. Standing outside the company, shareholders now received their returns in the form (if not at the level) of interest, as a simple reward for owning money. They had become money capitalists, able (if they wished) to completely detach themselves from companies and to do so with minimal risk: All they stood to lose was the money they had spent on their shares.

These developments saw the rights of shareholders to direct management diminish and saw directors became agents of "the company" not of the shareholders.[68] Significantly, however, the retention by shareholders of their right to dismiss directors gave them the ability to exercise considerable power and influence over the now de-personified, property-owning legal entity. Indeed, their retention of this right was instrumental in giving rise to the idea that the company was an object of property that they "owned". This idea persists today and is reflected in the widespread treatment of the interests of "the company" as (more or less) synonymous with those of its (owner) shareholders. As a result, the corporation has come to be

63 See Seymour Thompson, *Treatise on the Liability of Stockholders in Corporations*, St. Louis: Thomas & Co. (1879).

64 Ibid.

65 See Graeme Acheson, John Turner & Qing Ye, "The Character and Denomination of Shares in the Victorian Equity Market", *Economic History Review*, 65, pp. 862–886 (2012).

66 See Arthur Scratchley, *On Average Investment Trusts*, London: Shaw & Sons (1875).

67 See Ireland, *supra* note 42.

68 Contrast *Isle of Wight Railway Co v. Tahourdin* (1883) 25 Ch. D 320 with *Automatic Self-Cleaning Filter Syndicate Co Ltd v. Cuninghame* [1906] 2 Ch. 34.

seen as both a de-personified property-owning legal *person* (a "real" entity) and an *object* of property that belongs to its shareholders. Although the legal basis for the idea of shareholder corporate ownership is slender – as we have seen, shareholders have relinquished most of the rights and obligations traditionally associated with ownership – it has become part of our everyday common sense and is of considerable ideological and practical significance, not least in legitimating shareholder primacy.[69] The result is a form of schizophrenia: For some (liability) purposes, companies and shareholders are regarded as "completely separate"; for other purposes, they are regarded as more or less synonymous. This schizophrenia can be traced back to the peculiar nature of corporate shareholding and the fact that shareholders possess an odd mix of rights *in rem* and rights *in personam.* They are, on one hand, "insiders" with proprietary control rights, able to insist that companies are run in their interests. On the other hand, they are "outsiders", who, like creditors (and unlike partners), have transferred ownership of their property to the company and are responsibility- and liability-free, standing only to lose the money they have invested. The Janus-faced nature of corporate shareholding underlies the difficulties company lawyers have defining the legal nature of the share.[70] It also lies at the heart of contemporary corporate irresponsibility, for it gives shareholders the power to ensure that directors run companies in their exclusive interests while at the same time enabling them to detach, like creditors, from companies with minimal risk. Shareholders and their institutional representatives are able to enjoy revenue rights without actually doing anything, and able to insist (as "owners") on the maximization of those revenues without having to worry about how they are generated, safe in the knowledge that, like creditors, they aren't legally responsible for corporate misbehavior and only their initial investments are at risk in the event of failure. As Harry Glasbeek says, corporate shareholders "have little financial incentive to ensure that the managers involved behave legally, ethically, or decently . . . [because] in law, [they] are personally untouchable".[71] This was, of course, only too evident in the recent financial crisis.

The significance of these developments grew with the rise of the private company and corporate groups. After the House of Lords held in *Salomon v. Salomon & Co Ltd* that even one-man companies were quite separate legal entities from their shareholders, more and more firms adopted the corporate legal form, enabling shareholders even in owner-managed forms to eliminate their liabilities.[72] The significance of the de-personified conception of the corporate entity grew still further as JSC enterprises began increasingly to take the legal form not of single corporations but of interconnected corporate groups. Although these "enterprises" were usually coordinated by a single management team – as they still are – the *Salomon* principle was applied to them and the companies in the group treated as separate legal entities. This has made it possible for firms to create layers of limited liability and to avoid taxes and press States into competing for their custom through the creation of favorable legal and regulatory environments. The rise of private and subsidiary companies has also served to fuel the

69 "The share gives the shareholder neither ownership of the company's assets nor ownership of the company as a 'thing' . . . If a company is truly a person at law, then it cannot also be a thing – there is a fundamental disjunction between the two": See Worthington, *supra* note 55, 258, 265. See also Paddy Ireland, "Company Law and the Myth of Shareholder Ownership", *Modern Law Review*, 62, p. 32 (1999); Todd Sayre, "The Myth of Shareholder Ownership and its Implications for Accounting": http://papers.ssrn.com/sol3/papers.cfm?abstract_id=1464148

70 See Ireland, *supra* note 25, note 67; Kim, *supra* note 25.

71 Glasbeek, *Wealth by Stealth*, Toronto: Between the Lines (2002), p. 129.

72 *Salomon v. Salomon & Co Ltd* [1897] AC 22. See also Paddy Ireland, "The Rise of the Limited Liability Company", *International Journal of the Sociology of Law*, 12, pp. 239 (1984).

myth of shareholder corporate "ownership". While in large public companies populated by detached *rentiers*, there is little or no *legal* or de facto basis for the idea that they are "owned" by their shareholders, in private and subsidiary companies the "ownership" claim often has considerable de facto substance, for in these companies although the "complete separation" of company and shareholders is legally very real for liability purposes, it is often entirely fictional in empirical reality so far as the control of corporate assets is concerned. The rise of private companies and of corporate groups has thus contributed to the entrenchment of the idea of shareholder corporate "ownership" in common sense, even in situations where it lacks de facto, as well as legal, substance.

7. The joint stock company: Towards socialization or financialization?

It was quickly recognized that the rise of the joint stock corporation in the second half of the nineteenth century had fundamentally altered the nature of capitalism. "Modern capitalist development", wrote Rudolf Hilferding in 1909, "can only be comprehended in terms of the ascendancy of the corporation and its causes".[73] Marx was among the first to explore the impact and significance of this phenomenon. It is clear that he saw it as embodying two rather different and conflicting tendencies. On one hand, it was evidence of the way in which the credit system, by facilitating an "enormous expansion of the scale of production and enterprises" beyond what was possible for "individual capitals", was accelerating the concentration and centralization of capital and thus the growing "socialization of production". The capital invested in JSCs, Marx claimed, was "directly endowed with the form of social capital (capital of directly associated individuals) as distinct from private capital", as a result of which JSCs assumed "the form of social undertakings as distinct from private undertakings". Marx also implicitly recognized the diminution of the shareholder to something resembling a creditor. Echoing Smith, he observed that in JSCs the "actually functioning capitalist" was transformed into "a mere manager, administrator of other people's capital", while the "owner of capital" was transformed into "a mere money capitalist", receiving his reward in the form of interest, "that is, as mere compensation for owning capital that now is entirely divorced from function in the actual process of production". For Marx, the rise of the JSC replaced individual private property with (a kind of) "socialized" property. It represented "private production without the control of private property" – the "abolition of capital as private property within the framework of capitalist production itself".[74]

This belief led him to argue that the rise of the JSC was "a self-dissolving contradiction which prima facie represent[ed] a mere phase of transition to a new form of production". There was, he argued elsewhere, a "contradiction between the general social power into which capital develops . . . and the private power of the individual capitalist". He thought, it seems, that the JSC rendered ever more "blatant" the tension between increasingly socialized production and continuing private appropriation. He implied that as management was handed over to "functionaries" the "owners" were rendered redundant and functionless, and could therefore be replaced by workers managing their own firms. This led him to argue that "the co-operative factories of the laborers . . . represent[ed] within the old form the first sprouts of the new". Within these cooperatives "the antithesis between capital and labor [wa]s overcome", though "at first only by way of making the associated laborers into their

73 Hilferding, *supra* note 50, p. 107.

74 Marx, *supra* note 44, chapters 23 and 27.

own capitalist, i.e. by making them use the means of production for the employment of their own labor". Cooperatives nevertheless showed "how a new mode of production naturally grows out of an old one". When the development of the material forces of production and corresponding forms of social production had "reached a particular stage . . . the capitalist stock companies, as much as the cooperative factories, should be considered as transitional forms from the capitalist mode of production to the associated one, with the only distinction that the antagonism is resolved negatively in the one and positively in the other". The JSC, Marx believed, was "a necessary transitional phase towards the reconversion of capital into the property of producers, . . . as the property of associated producers, as outright social property".[75]

On the other hand, Marx also saw that the rise of the JSC, with its detached *rentier* shareholders, contained within it the seeds of what we have come to call "financialization", linking its rise and the development of the credit system to the emergence of "money power" and a "new financial aristocracy". "Loanable money capital", Marx observed, was increasingly coming to be concentrated in and invested by banks in their "capacity of representatives of all money lenders". These banks, Marx argued, had become "the general managers of money-capital", the "representatives of social capital" – of "capital in general". This combination of small amounts of money, each in themselves "incapable of acting in the capacity of money-capital", into large masses was creating a "money power", a "financial oligarchy". So, while for Marx the rise of the JSC was evidence of the growing socialization of both production and credit, it had also contributed to the rise of "a new financial aristocracy" and "a new variety of parasites in the shape of promoters, speculators and simply nominal directors: a whole system of swindling and cheating by means of corporation promotion, stock issuance, and stock speculation".[76] The "enormous centralization" made possible by the credit system gave to "this class of parasites the fabulous power not only to periodically despoil industrial capitalists, but also to interfere in production in a most dangerous manner".[77] Elsewhere Marx linked this new "aristocracy of finance" to State debt. "All modern finance, the whole of the banking business", he argued, "is interwoven in the closest fashion with public credit", as "a part of their business capital is necessarily invested and put out at interest in quickly convertible public funds".[78] This, Marx observed, enabled this elite to exercise considerable power over the State. He also pointed out that when concentrated ownership of State debt was coupled with regressive systems of taxation that gathered revenues from taxes on basic staples rather than on income, it served to redistribute income upwards, enriching the financial aristocracy of bondholders at the expense of the laboring class.[79]

Implicit in these conflicting tendencies were, then, two rather different possible futures: one of increasing "financialization", already clearly visible and present; and one of increasing "socialization", present in a distorted form but as yet still largely latent. Which of these different tendencies would prevail? Was the rise of the corporate economy paving the way for domination by a "new financial aristocracy"? Or was it (ultimately) paving the way, as Marx

75 Ibid., chapters 23, 25 and 27.

76 Ibid.

77 David Harvey, *The Limits to Capital*, Oxford: Blackwell (1982), p. 287.

78 Marx, "The Eighteenth Brumaire of Louis Bonaparte" (1852): www.marxists.org/archive/marx/works/1852/18th-brumaire/.

79 Ibid. "The position of the aristocracy of finance [was] most strikingly depicted", Marx argued, "in a passage from its European organ, the *London Economist*", which in November 1851 declared: "The President is the guardian of order, and is now recognized as such on every stock exchange of Europe".

believed, for a transition to socialism? Over the course of the next century, the double-edged nature of the "corporate revolution" repeatedly came to the surface, finding vivid expression in the debates about the nature of the corporation and (what we now call) "corporate governance". As we shall see, the outcome turned in significant part on the ability, or otherwise, of shareholders to retain their residual ownership rights and to wield them effectively.

8. Financialization in the ascendancy

In the decades Marx's death, the number of JSCs grew, a development driven by the demands of modern industrial technology and by the increasingly desperate attempts of firms to suppress destructive overproduction and price-cutting competition. The years around the turn of the century saw not only the formation of numerous trusts and cartels but a merger boom in which large joint stock corporations came to dominate more and more key industries. Financial institutions lay at the heart of many of these arrangements. By the turn of the century the growing power of "high finance" was clear for all to see, especially in the United States and Germany. This was the period of "the first financial hegemony".[80] In the United States, financiers like J. P. Morgan arranged merger after merger and – using a mixture of voting trusts, debt and interlocking directorates – came to exercise de facto control over more and more corporations. The growing domination of this plutocratic financial and industrial elite (the so-called money trust) prompted the Pujo Committee investigations of 1912–3 and Louis Brandeis' celebrated attack on the American "financial oligarchy".[81] In Germany, banks led the way, prompting Rudolf Hilferding to develop his theory of "finance capital". Elaborating and building upon Marx's sketch of "the economics of the corporation", Hilferding analyzed the implications of what he saw as the growing domination of German industry by a small number of banks and the fusion of industrial and financial capital.[82]

Although he recognized the growing power and influence of high finance, however, Hilferding was one of a number of commentators who saw the rise of the corporate economy as evidence of the increasingly "social" character of production. There were different dimensions to this claim. It was based, first, on the sheer size and market power of these joint stock corporations, which was seen as endowing their activities, individually and collectively, with wider social significance, making it increasingly difficult to characterize them as purely "private" enterprises.[83] Their rise was leading to production that seemed to be coordinated not

80 Gerard Dumenil & Dominique Levy, *The Crisis of Neoliberalism*, Cambridge, MA: Harvard University Press (2011).

81 Louis Brandeis, *Other People's Money*, New York: Stokes & Co. (1912).

82 Hilferding, *supra* note 50, p. 114. The book was mostly written in 1905–6: see Jan Grietens, "Marxian and Non-Marxian Foundations of Rudolf Hilferding's Finance Capital", *History of Economic Thought*, 55, pp. 18–35 (2013). See also Karl Renner, *The Institutions of Private Law*, London: Routledge & Kegan Paul (ed.), with an introduction by Otto Kahn-Freund (1904, 1949).

83 This underlay Walther's Rathenau's idea of the "enterprise as such", itself a popularization of the ideas of Franz Klein. Rathenau argued that the shareholders of a firm like the Deutsche Bank could not be permitted suddenly to put the firm into voluntary liquidation because the bank had become an institution – an enterprise with a life of its own – which had to be preserved in the public interest: *Vom Aktienwesen, eine Geschaftliche Betrachtung* (1918). After Rathenau's death, the idea was championed by people such as Oskar Netter, who argued that when conflicts of interest arose between a company, its shareholders, and the public, it was the interest of the "enterprise as such" as an independent legal object that should prevail: See F.A. Mann, "The New German Company Law and Its Background", *Journal of Comparative Legislation and International Law*, 19, pp. 223–224 (1937).

by free markets but by corporate planning,[84] a development that later led to the emergence of ideas about "organized" and "monopoly" capitalism.[85] It was also based, however, on the changed nature of JSC shareholding and the growth in the volume of intangible financial property – ordinary shares, preference shares, corporate bonds and the like – which conferred on their holders not direct rights to and over tangible assets but rights to receive future revenues. The tangible productive assets of industry were now increasingly owned by corporate entities and managed by professional managers, with shareholders reduced, for the most part, to the status of passive and functionless holders of income rights. Hilferding noted the reduction of the shareholder to something resembling a creditor – shares, he said, represented "creditor's claims on future production" – and argued that the rise of the JSC and of "finance capital" was "establish[ing] social control of production" and "socialize[d] production to the extent that this [was] possible under capitalism".[86] The JSC and finance capital represented "an antagonistic form of socialization", "a fraudulent kind of socialism, modified to suit the needs of capitalism", in which "the control of social production remain[ed] vested in an oligarchy . . . a small number of large capitalist associations". He seems nevertheless to have seen this as progressive, arguing that "the socializing function of finance capital" had "facilitate[d] enormously the task of overcoming capitalism". Taking possession of "six large Berlin banks", he asserted, would enable one to take "possession of the most important spheres of large scale industry. . ." The key was "the struggle to dispossess this oligarchy".[87]

Although often written in a very different idiom, similar themes ran through the work of other commentators. In 1914 in *Drift and Mastery,* for example, the American journalist Walter Lippmann argued that technological advances and the rise of the professionally managed corporation, with its separation of ownership and management, was "sucking the life out of private property", "organizing [it] out of existence" While "in theory" the stockholder was one of the corporation's "owners", "the modern shareholder" was a "very feeble representative of the institution of private property", no longer having a productive role to play or any responsibilities to discharge: "the one qualification is the possession of some money and the desire for more". Shares were now "little more than claims to residual profits", and shareholders "transient" "absentee owners", who flitted "like . . . butterfl[ies] from industry to industry" with their liquid, mobile capital. "Deprived of their property rights", they were "being transformed into money lenders" with "a single motive". It was unrealistic to expect a "high sense of social responsibility" from them; it would be much better if they were formally reduced to the status of creditors. Lippmann went even further, however, arguing that socialization was already becoming a reality. There had been a discernible "change in business motives" and a "revolution in business incentives". Business and management were becoming "professions" akin to medicine, law and engineering in which "motives other than

84 From within the Marxist tradition, for example, the "revisionist", Eduard Bernstein, argued that the growing control exercised by these large corporations over productive activity was not only diminishing the cyclical instabilities and "anarchy" of competitive capitalist production, but also paving the way for an evolutionary (as opposed to a revolutionary) transition to socialism.

85 The term "organized capitalism" was first coined by Hilferding; the term "monopoly capitalism" is associated with the work of Paul Baran and Paul Sweezy. For a brief discussion, see John Scott, *Corporate Business and Capitalist Classes*, Oxford: Oxford University Press (1997), pp. 13–14, 24–25.

86 Hilferding, *supra* note 50, p. 110. Following Marx, Hilferding pointed out that the second (fictitious) capital was "an illusion . . . What really exists is the industrial capital and its profit", p. 111.

87 Hilferding, *supra* note 50, pp. 367–368. In the 1920s, Hilferding served on the German socialization commission and developed a concept of what he called "organized capitalism".

profit came into play". It was true that "control ha[d] passed *for the time being* into the hands of investment experts, the banking interests", but that control was already being challenged – not by the "decadent stockholders" but by "those most interested in the methods of industry: the consumer, the worker and the citizen at large".[88]

Not everyone, however, was as confident that the financial domination of industry was a temporary stop on the road to socialization. The American economist and sociologist Thorstein Veblen could see the progressive potential of the large corporation. "Machine industry", he wrote, demanded genuine "social" ownership and control and rendered the idea of individual property rights in the means of production hopelessly outdated; modern technology not only made a more "socialized" economy possible, it demanded it. But while the rise of the joint stock corporation had facilitated large-scale production and the full exploitation of technological advances, it had also seen "industry", the technical processes concerned with the efficient production of useful goods, fall under the control of "business" – by which Veblen meant financial interests more concerned with making money than things. The result was that industrial processes were being managed primarily not to enhance productive efficiency and maximize output, but to secure pecuniary gains for the owners of financial property.[89] "The financial community", Veblen argued, had taken over ownership of the country's largest corporations and thereby gained control of "the usufruct of [its] industrial system".[90] This operated against the best interests of the community, which lay in the "efficient management" of industrial enterprises and the "unhampered working out of the industrial system at its full capacity without interruption or dislocation".[91] The financial interests of "absentee" shareholder-owners obstructed productive activity and conspired against the full use of the "industrial arts".[92] Indeed, financial domination often led to the "conscientious sabotage" of industry, for larger profits were often to be had from financial manipulation and from obstructing production than from facilitating and maximizing it. Business, Veblen claimed, had become a parasitic growth on industry and the investment bankers and corporate financiers had become as restrictive of further economic development as the old landed elite.[93] Having little faith in class struggle as a way of realizing the possibilities inherent in modern industry and technology, Veblen struggled to see how these vested financial interests might be overcome.

9. Towards socialization?

By the 1920s, however, Veblen's pessimistic vision of continuing financial domination seemed at odds with the economic trajectory of society. The tensions between the financializing and socializing tendencies inherent in the JSC remained, but the latter appeared to be winning out. This was reflected in the growing number of commentators arguing that the residual control rights of shareholders should be either attenuated or abolished altogether,

88 Walter Lippmann, *Drift and Mastery*, Madison: University of Wisconsin Press, introduction by Walter Leuchtenburg (1914, 1985).

89 Thorstein Veblen, *Theory of Business Enterprise*, New York: Scribner (1904), pp. 77–78, 80.

90 Thorstein Veblen, *Absentee Ownership*, New York: Huebsch (1923), pp. 231–232.

91 Veblen, *supra* note 89, p. 78; Veblen, *The Vested Interests and the Common Man*, New York: Huebsch (1919), p. 93.

92 Veblen, *supra* note 91, pp. 93–113.

93 See Veblen, *supra* note 87. See also Joseph Dorfman, *Thorstein Veblen and His America*, New York: Viking Press (1934), pp. 227–228; Veblen, *supra* note 91, chapter 5.

and vested elsewhere. Veblen was among them. In his final book, *Absentee Ownership*, published in 1923, he continued to rail against the consequences of financial domination. "Business enterprise" and "particularly American business enterprise", he argued, "habitually looks to the short run", sacrificing long-term productive gains in favor of "an enhanced rate of earnings for the time being".[94] But by now Veblen's attack on finance was turning into a thoroughgoing attack on the Janus-faced legal position of shareholders. Echoing Lippmann, he began to question the legitimacy of the remaining proprietary rights of shareholders, arguing that the classic liberal justifications for absolute property rights simply didn't apply to passive, financial property. The new "absentee owners" of industry had delegated most of the traditional rights and obligations associated with ownership to managers, retaining only certain "rights and immunities". "Ownership" in the new corporate order had been "depersonalized" and "no longer carrie[d] its earlier duties and responsibilities". Corporate shareholders, he argued, now resembled bondholders rather than "real" owners. They were "anonymous pensioners", whose personal identities were irrelevant "even to the concern itself" and whose "sole effective relation to the enterprise [was] that of a fixed overhead charge on its operations". Foreshadowing *Howey*, he argued that they were the owners of rights to receive a "free income" drawn from "the . . . product of the underlying community".[95]

These views were echoed in the United Kingdom by Labor Party intellectuals R. H. Tawney and Harold Laski. In his influential 1920 book, *The Acquisitive Society*, Tawney castigated the inherently pernicious and parasitic nature of intangible financial property forms like the corporate share.[96] Like Veblen, he argued that the traditional justifications for private property rights were inapplicable to property forms of this sort, which divorced gain from service, and reward from work. Unlike rights to tangible personal possessions that could be defended as "indispensable to a life of decency and comfort" and as encouraging industry and initiative, these new intangible, passive property forms were "functionless". Indeed, they were positively dysfunctional, directing productive activity towards "acquisition" rather than "service to society". They dissipated creative energy, "corrupt[ed] the principle of industry", and distorted productive activity. To redirect industry along more productively rational and socially beneficial paths, Tawney proposed that shareholders be reclassified as creditors and their rights attenuated. This would release industry from financial domination, enable it to be reorganized in productively more functional ways, and allow management to be turned into a "profession" akin to medicine and law.[97] A few years later, Harold Laski made similar arguments in *Grammar of Politics*.[98]

Indeed, by this time some were arguing, like Lippmann, not only that corporate governance *should* be "socialized", but that it was gradually becoming so as a matter of empirical fact. These claims were based on various developments: the widening and dispersal of share ownership, the rise of the idea of corporate managers as "professionals" performing a (public) service rather than acting as simple profit maximizers, and the changing nature and declining power of investment banks. In the United Kingdom, Keynes was arguing as early as the mid-1920s that there was an inevitable tendency for "joint stock institutions, when

94 Veblen, *supra* note 90, p. 214.

95 Veblen, *supra* note 90, chapters 5 and 8.

96 R. H. Tawney, *The Acquisitive Society*, New York: Harcourt Brace (1920)

97 For an earlier expression of this idea, see Louis Brandeis, "Business – A Profession", *System* (October 1912), pp. 1–25.

98 H. Laski, *A Grammar of Politics*, London: Allen & Unwin (1925).

they [had] reached a certain age and size, to approximate to the status of public corporations rather than that of individualistic private enterprise". The "tendency of big enterprise to socialize itself", he suggested, arose when "the owners of the capital, i.e. its shareholders, are almost entirely disassociated from the management". At this point managers became more concerned about the stability and reputation of the institution than with profit maximization, and shareholders had to satisfy themselves with "conventionally adequate dividends". On this basis, Keynes dismissed the need for overt "socialization". There was, he claimed, "no so-called important political question so really unimportant, so irrelevant to the reorganization of the economic life of Great Britain as the nationalization of the railways. . . . The battle of socialism against unlimited private profit [was] being won in detail hour by hour" from within these large enterprises.[99]

In the United States, in his later work Veblen began to trace the growing depersonalization and bureaucratization of financial control, arguing that while this did not mark the end of the financial domination of corporations, it did mark an important change:[100] A "new order" not only of "absentee ownership" but of "absentee management" was emerging.[101] Although investment banks, which had taken the lead in financing the war, continued to prosper in the 1920s, promoting mergers and combinations and using the holding company to carry pyramiding to new extremes, it was, as Paul Sweezy says, their "last hurrah".[102] During the course of the decade, equity ownership by individuals and institutional investors (primarily insurance companies) increased,[103] as did corporate self-financing, and with this "bargaining strength gradually shift[ed] . . . from the bankers in favor of the corporations".[104] "The relative abundance of capital", observed Ellis Hawley, "coupled with the rise of new investment houses, the growth of direct investments, and the ability of large corporations to finance their own expansion from corporate surpluses, . . . undercut the finance capitalists, shifted power to a new managerial elite, and produced situations where the industrialist rather than

99 J. M. Keynes, *The End of Laissez-Faire*, London: Hogarth Press (1926).

100 See Veblen, *The Engineers and the Price System*, New York: Harcourt Brace (1921) and Veblen, *supra* note 90.

101 Malcolm Rutherford, "On Trusts and Technostructures: Veblen, Berle and Means, and Galbraith", *International Journal of Social Economics*, 19, p. 271 (1992). Commenting on developments in the same period, Galbraith noted the remarkable rapidity with which ownership of US corporations had passed from the personal to the impersonal: See Becht & de Long, "Why Has There Been So Little Block Holding in America?", in *A History of Corporate Governance around the World*, Randall Morck (ed.)., Chicago: University of Chicago Press (2007), p. 615.

102 Paul Sweezy, "Investment Banking Revisited", *Monthly Review*, 33(10), p. 9 (1982). Sweezy's knowledge of investment banking was personal: his father was a Wall Street banker, a vice president of First National Bank of New York headed by George F Baker, a close partner of J.P Morgan & Co.

103 William Z. Ripley reported that there were only 4.4 million shareholders in the US in 1900, but 14.4 million by 1923: *Main Street and Wall Street*, Little, Brown (1927). Leslie Hannah says that it is hard to trace more than half a dozen or so US corporations that numbered their stockholders in above four figures in 1900, but that by the 1930s several had six-figure totals: "The Divorce of Ownership from Control from 1900 Onwards: Recalibrating Imagined Global Trends", *Business History*, 49, p. 404 (2007).

104 Paul Sweezy, "The Decline of the Investment Banker", *Antioch Review*, Spring 1941, reprinted in Sweezy, *The Present as History*, New York: Monthly Review Press (1953), pp. 191–202. As "the grip of American owning families faltered", Hannah argues, the "retreat from personal capitalism" in the 1920s US was "remarkably fast': "The Divorce of Ownership from Control. . ".. On the ways in which the economic crises of the inter-war years and the rise of National Socialism in Germany served to reduce the influence over industry of finance, see George Edwards, *The Evolution of Finance Capitalism*, New York: Longmans (1938), pp. 107–117; see also Anon, "The Destruction of Capitalism in Germany", *Foreign Affairs*, 15, p. 595 (1937).

the banker could call the tune".[105] The shattering effects of the crash and subsequent depression further weakened the power of the banks: Investment banking was, Sweezy says, their "special victim".[106] As the evidence grew that the power exercised not only by investment banks but also by shareholders was waning,[107] the idea that managers were acquiring significant discretionary power gained ground. "The great mass" of American industry, Robert S. Brookings argued in 1925, had been "almost unconsciously converted from a management based on an intensely personal ownership to a management based on an ownership widely distributed and therefore almost entirely impersonal".[108] The small investor found it "practically impossible . . . to keep in touch with, and exercise any intelligent control over, management". However, while the "internal pressure from the stockholders [on managers] had decreased", the "external pressures" on them from trades unions, politicians and the public had increased, creating new trends and objectives in corporate management. "The more completely management [was] separated from ownership", Brookings argued, "the more it comes to be regarded as the representative of all the cooperating parties and conflicting interests, and not simply of stockholders". Management was thus coming to "occupy the position of trustee" with a duty to ensure that both stockholders and labor received "fair returns". Indeed, he suggested, "stockholders were as a rule content with a reasonable but reliable return".[109] The contemporary business commentator Mary Follett agreed: "management, not bankers nor stockholders" was coming to be seen to be "the fundamental element in industry".[110] "Financial sovereignty" the journalist Lincoln Steffens concluded in 1931, was "passing from the banks to the management of industry – the management, not the ownership".[111] The growing detachment and disempowerment of the shareholder was, it seemed, turning the corporate tide in the direction of socialization.

This was, of course, precisely what Merrick Dodd argued in his famous debate with Adolf Berle. In contesting Berle's defense of shareholder primacy, Dodd observed that the great majority of the shareholders in large joint stock corporations were *rentiers* with little resemblance to traditional owners, and argued that corporations were increasingly becoming *social* or *public* institutions, not mere private enterprises. On this basis it was clearly arguable that directors should, as a normative matter, be required to take account of the interests of employees, consumers, creditors and society as a whole, not just of shareholders. Indeed, Dodd argued, this was already happening. "Public opinion" was making "substantial strides in the direction of a view of the business corporation as an economic institution which has a social service as well as profit-making function". Tapping into these ideas, some corporate managers, such as Owen D. Young and Gerard Swope of the General Electric Company, were arguing that managers were "no longer attorneys for stockholders" but "trustees of an

105 Ellis Hawley, *The New Deal and the Problem of Monopoly*, Princeton: Princeton University Press (1966), p. 305.

106 Sweezy, *supra* note 102.

107 See Sweezy, *supra* note 104.

108 Robert Brookings, *Industrial Ownership: Its Economic and Social Significance*, New York: Macmillan (1925), p. viii. Brookings was the founder of the Brookings Institution.

109 Brookings, *supra* note 108, pp. 21–25, 76. According to Brookings, stockholders were "as a rule content with a reasonable but reliable return".

110 Mary Follett, "How Must Business Management Develop in Order to Possess the Fundamentals of a Profession?", in *Business Management as a Profession*, Henry Metcalf (ed.), Chicago: Shaw & Co. (1927), pp. 73 at 78.

111 Lincoln Steffens, *The Autobiography of Lincoln Steffens*, New York: Harcourt, Brace (1931), p. 869. Steffens was a "muckraking" journalist and leading critic of high finance.

institution" who owed obligations to employees, customers and the general public as well as to shareholders: Their job was "to administer wisely and fairly in the interest of all". Dodd's message wasn't that the shareholder interest was now being ignored – far from it – but that managers, liberated to a significant degree from both market imperatives and shareholder control, had considerable discretion and were using it to balance the interests of different groups: They weren't under intense pressure to maximize shareholder returns, at least in the short term. Dodd added that this "socialization" of the corporation was perfectly defensible if you took seriously the separation of "the corporation" from its shareholders and the existence of the former as a genuinely separate legal person with interests of its own,[112] an idea that, as Berle and Means later noted, had already found expression in Europe in the notion of the "enterprise as such".[113]

Berle and Means, of course, added empirical weight to the idea of growing management power and it is clear from his exchanges with Dodd that Berle sympathized with the more "socialized" conception of the corporation Dodd was advocating. Berle did not feel, however, that mechanisms had yet been developed to impose a broader "scheme of responsibilities" on managers. In these circumstances, and fearing abuse of power, it was, he argued, better to stick with and, indeed, strengthen the existing fiduciary techniques for controlling managerial power associated with shareholder primacy.[114] His objections to Dodd were thus more pragmatic than principled. Like Dodd, he recognized that the changing character of the shareholder and the corporation justified greater "socialization", and in the final section of *The Modern Corporation and Private Property* he and Means drew on the radical critiques of Veblen, Tawney and Laski to explore these issues. The modern corporation, they argued, had "dissolved the [private] property atom" in which possession and control were united, undermining the applicability of the "traditional logic" of profit and property. Corporations now involved two forms of property: one *active*, the tangible assets owned by the corporation and controlled by the managers; the other *passive*, the intangible revenue rights, "liquid, impersonal, and involving no responsibility", owned by the shareholders. Reduced to a "mere recipient of the wages of capital", they argued, the modern corporate shareholder was now "not dissimilar in kind from the bondholder or lender of money" – and the modern corporation had to be recognized as qualitatively different from the traditional, small, "private" enterprise. It had a "quasi-public" character. It followed that it might no longer be appropriate to view shareholders as "owners" (other than of shares) or to view corporations as objects of property. The "corporate revolution", they concluded, had raised "legal, economic and social questions" of considerable importance, the "greatest" of which was "in whose interests should the great quasi-public corporations . . . be operated?"[115]

In the final chapter of their book, Berle and Means outlined some possible answers. The first entailed sticking with the traditional logic of property and insisting that corporations be run in the exclusive interest of their shareholders "despite the fact that [they] ha[d] ceased to have power over or accept responsibility for the active property". The second entailed giving the controlling managers "free rein"' to use their powers as they wished, though this was

112 See E. Merrick Dodd, "For Whom Are Corporate Managers Trustees?" *Harvard Law Review*, 45, p. 1147 (1932).

113 This idea was popularized by Walther Rathenau.

114 Adolf Berle, "For Whom Corporate Managers Are Trustees", *Harvard Law Review*, 45, p. 1365 (1932).

115 A. A. Berle & G. C. Means, *The Modern Corporation and Private Property*, New York: Macmillan (1932). Berle's work is permeated by "Veblenite echoes": See D. M. Wright, "The Modern Corporation – Twenty Years After", *University of Chicago Law Review*, 19, p. 662 (1951–52).

thought likely to encourage the emergence of a plundering "corporate oligarchy". The third involved abandoning the ideas of shareholders as "owners" and corporations as private property, and developing a "new concept of the corporation" as a social institution. In becoming functionless *rentiers* shareholders had "surrendered the right that the corporation should be operated in their sole interest" and "released the community from the obligation to protect them to the full extent implied in the doctrine of strict property rights". The community was now entitled "to demand that the modern corporation serve . . . all society" and that various groups be "assign[ed] . . . a portion of the income stream on the basis of public policy rather than private cupidity"; shareholders should get only "a fair return" on their capital.[116]

10. Socialization in the ascendancy: The rise of managerialism

The decline in financial power did not prevent popular belief in the existence of an industry-dominating "money trust" persisting well into the 1930s. Some "continued to think in terms of 1912" and still saw "Money Power . . . as the chief enemy".[117] But by the outbreak of the Second World War, it was clear that the direct domination of industrial capital by finance, which some had seen as a more or less permanent state of affairs, had, for the time being at least, come to an end.[118] In the decades after the war, the idea that ownership and control had been separated took hold and became the basis of "managerialist" theories not only of the corporation but of capitalism as a whole. Many thought that, taken together, the replacement of competition by monopoly and oligopoly and replacement of market coordination by planning, the weakening of high finance, effective disempowerment of *rentier* shareholders and the rise of professional managers was leading to more "socialized" corporations. Liberated in significant part from both shareholder control and market imperatives, managers now had considerable discretion and were no longer bound to profit maximize. "Is it not time", asked L.C.B. Gower in 1955, "to recognize that shareholder democracy, with its exclusive emphasis on the profit-making element in corporate activity, has a slightly old fashioned ring?"[119] Within a few years, the American economist Carl Kaysen was arguing that corporate management "no longer [saw itself as] the agent of proprietorship seeking to maximize return on investment", but as "responsible to stockholders, employees, customers, the general public, and, perhaps, most important, the firm itself as an institution". The modern corporation, he concluded, was "a soulful corporation".[120] By the 1960s, it had become common, even in Britain, for the representatives of business "to declare that industry owes duties

116 Berle & Means, *supra* note 115, Book IV, Chapter IV.

117 Hawley, *supra* note 105, p. 305. William O Douglas, for example, who played a pivotal role in financial regulation in the US in the 1930s as commissioner and chair of the SEC, continued to liken the institutions of high finance to "termites" who fed off industrial enterprises: *Democracy and Finance*, New Haven, CT: Yale University Press (1940). In fact power had begun seeping away before that.

118 Sweezy, *supra* note 104, p. 195. In Germany, the rise of Hitler and the National Socialists saw what Edwards describes as the "triumph of industrial capital", *supra* note 101, p. 114. Following the collapse of the banking system in 1931, the power of the state over financial institutions grew, culminating in such significant transfers of power away from shareholders that some commentators thought it the end of German capitalism: See Edwards *supra* note 104, p. 117.

119 Gower, "Book Review of Emerson & Latcham's *Shareholder Democracy*", *Harvard Law Review*, 68, p. 927 (1955).

120 Carl Kaysen, "The Social Significance of the Modern Corporation", *American Economic Review*, 47, pp. 313–314 (1957).

to employees, consumers and the nation as well as to shareholders".[121] The corporate interest was becoming less closely identified with the shareholder interest, and corporate power, it seemed, was being exercised in a more socially sensitive and responsible manner. This was the era of the "socially responsible corporation".

The claims of the managerialists did not go unchallenged. Broadly speaking, two rather different critiques of managerialism emerged. The first accepted the decline in shareholder power and the rise of managerialism, but argued that managers were exercising their new-found power and discretion in a self-interested way: The managerialism that had emerged was selfish and "sectional" rather than socialized and "non-sectional".[122] The second denied the loss of shareholder financial control, arguing that the dispersal of shareholdings had actually made it possible for minority interests to wield disproportionate power. Here they echoed Hilferding, who had argued that the "financial techniques" of the "joint-stock system", which by now included the use of parent-subsidiary arrangements, had facilitated huge concentrations of economic power.[123] During this period, much empirical research was carried out into the alleged separation of corporate ownership and control, focusing (inter alia) on the ways in which financiers could impose their will on enterprises and managers using intercorporate relations, interlocking directorships and the like. Some insisted that financial control remained real.[124] "The control of corporations", argued Victor Perlo in the 1950s, "is more and more centralized in knots of financial power".[125] Much of this research purported to show that the level of shareholding required for effective strategic control by minorities was much lower than often thought, and that minority control was widespread.[126] This led to attempts to distinguish "legal" or "nominal" ownership (which was dispersed) from "control" and "effective" or "social" ownership (which was concentrated).[127]

Although this research yielded different findings and conclusions, it suggested that some of the more extreme claims of managerial autonomy were unsustainable: "Finance" in its various forms continued to influence corporate managers and corporate behavior. But with the benefit of hindsight, it is hard to deny that corporate practices and behavior – and the social outcomes they generated – were rather different from today. In general terms, and riding roughshod over the undoubted and significant jurisdictional differences, Edward Herman probably got it about right when he argued that "management control" was a reality, but was "constrained".[128] Although one must be careful not to overstate, therefore, there is clear evidence that during this period corporate governance *was* more "socialized" than it had been before and has been since. Indeed, it is not insignificant or coincidental that the decline

121 Gower, *supra* note 5, 1979 ed., p. 578.

122 Theo Nichols dubbed this "sectional managerialism", contrasting it with the "non-sectional" managerialism of mainstream managerialism: See Nichols, *Ownership, Control and Ideology*, London: Allen & Unwin (1969).

123 Hilferding, *supra* note 50, Chapter 7, pp. 118–119.

124 See, for example, Michel De Vroey, "The Separation of Ownership and Control in Large Corporations", *Review of Radical Political Economics*, 7, p. 1 (1975). For a brief discussion of some of the literature refuting the separation of ownership and control thesis, see Lorraine Talbot, *Critical Company Law*, Abingdon, Oxford: Routledge Cavendish (2008), pp. 139–145.

125 Victor Perlo, *The Empire of High Finance*, New York: International Publishers (1957), p. 15.

126 Strategic control was distinguished from operational control. On this, see Charles Bettelheim's models of ownership: *Economic Calculation and Forms of Property*, London: RKP (1976).

127 However, there was little agreement about the proportion of shares needed to generate "control": See Scott, *Corporate Business and Capitalist Classes*, pp. 23, 30, 42–55.

128 Edward Herman, *Corporate Control, Corporate Power*, Cambridge: Cambridge University Press (1981); see Scott, *supra* note 127, p. 51.

in the power wielded by shareholders and the more "socialized" corporate governance that marked the "managerialist" era corresponded with the post-war heyday of social democracy, the welfare state, relatively strong trade unions, Keynesianism and *les trentes glorieuses*—and with the fifty-year or so period identified by Piketty and others as one in which income and wealth inequality in the advanced capitalist world narrowed quite substantially. Nor is it insignificant that this was a period in which the existence of the corporation as legal persons radically separate from their shareholders was taken increasingly seriously – and not just for liability purposes. During this period the corporate interest really did come widely to be seen as something rather different from the interests of its shareholders.[129]

Despite the seeming progress of socialization in practice, however, some continued to argue for formal alterations to the corporate legal form to make it better reflect the "true" nature of the corporate shareholder as a passive *rentier*, more creditor than owner. They advocated further formal juridical disempowerment and their relegation to the status of preferred creditors. Control rights, they suggested, should be dispersed amongst different groups, including employees.[130] In light of what seemed like the gradual triumph of "socialization", however, others argued that as corporate shareholders had been de facto disempowered, there was no need to risk provoking a political reaction by attenuating shareholder rights or nationalizing more industries. It simply wasn't necessary. The process of socialization, it was believed, could be continued without making radical changes to the corporate legal form. Managers simply needed to be nudged and educated to act in a socially responsible manner. Indeed, many argued that it was not only were corporations being socialized so too was capitalism as a whole. A more socialized capitalism – what Berle called a "people's capitalism" – was emerging. Some went even further and argued that capitalism was being transcended: We were moving towards a post-capitalist society.[131]

11. Resurgent finance: The rise of the shareholder value corporation

As it turned out, they were mistaken. Amidst a resurgence of financial power, recent decades have seen shareholders and their institutional representatives, armed with their residual control rights, reassert their power over corporations. Central to these processes has been the demise of Bretton Woods, the liberalization of financial markets, and the reconcentration of previously dispersed financial property owners in institutions. Investment management – the management of *rentier* money capital – has emerged as a global industry characterized by intense competition not only between institutions but also within them. Typically assessed on their quarterly performance, money managers are under constant pressure to enhance the market value of the financial property (assets) in their portfolios. The result in the corporate

129 However, the English courts stubbornly clung on to this view: See *Parke v. Daily News* Ltd. [1962] Ch 927.

130 There was "no reason", argued Bill Wedderburn, "not to equate [the shareholder's] position with that of a well secured creditor"; the law should "not treat the shareholder as a 'proprietor' entitled to control": See K. W. Wedderburn, *Company Law Reform*, London: Fabian Society (1965); George Goyder expressed a similar view in *The Responsible Company*, Oxford: Blackwell (1961). Ideas about re-classifying shareholders as types of creditor were not confined to the left: See Bayless Manning. This was the period within which ideas about worker participation and industrial democracy began to reemerge.

131 On the United Kingdom, see C.A.R. Crosland, *The Future of Socialism*, London: Jonathan Cape (1956); Ralf Dahrendorf, *Class and Class Conflict in Industrial Society*, Stanford: Stanford University Press (1959). On the United States, see Howard Brick, *Transcending Capitalism*, Ithaca: Cornell University Press (2006).

context is that directors, although not under a legal duty to maximize shareholder value,[132] have been placed under severe market pressure to do so. Failure to meet the expectations of money managers and the growing army of security analysts[133] renders corporations vulnerable to takeover and managers vulnerable to negative assessment and removal by those who feel more "value" could be extracted.[134] As Grahame Thompson says, "even the largest global firms can be stalked by activist investors – hunted by private equity or sovereign wealth funds seeking added shareholder value extraction. . . . Few companies – however large or internationalized – are immune from the threat of takeover".[135] The focus on share price has, of course, been encouraged and reinforced by the rise of neoliberal (and shareholder value) ideology and new forms of executive remuneration involving share options and other performance-related bonuses. Aimed at realigning the financial interests of managers with those of shareholders, these new modes of remuneration have forged a less-than-holy alliance between high finance and the executive class, contributing to and facilitating the controversial executive "supersalaries" that Piketty sees as exacerbating growing income inequality, particularly in the United States. It is important not to forget, however, that just as money managers are subject to intense competitive pressures, so too are corporate managers: Managing the share price (getting it up and keeping it there) is as much an externally imposed (market) imperative as it is a matter of personal advantage and choice.

As this suggests, financial power today is not exercised in the same way as it was during the "first financial hegemony," when it tended to be exercised directly by financial institutions *within* corporations and operated at the level of the individual company. In the new finance capitalism of the early twenty-first century, financial power is predominantly exercised from *without*, through the arms-length mechanism of the (stock) market in whose constant shadow executives now work. It is an incredibly effective form of power that combines concentration with mobility and liquidity. De-personalized and ubiquitous, it operates at the level of the corporate sector as a whole. The result has been a transformation of corporate governance and a dramatic shift from the situation in the 1960s and 70s when firms were,

132 See Lynn Stout, *The Myth of Shareholder Value*, New York: Berrett-Koehler (2012); Worthington, *supra* note 55, doubting whether acting in the interests of the company means acting in the interests of shareholders, pp. 262–263.

133 With institutions clamoring for information upon which to base their investment decisions, in recent years security analysts have grown in number and importance: See Ezra Zuckerman, "The Categorical Imperative: Securities Analysts and the Illegitimacy Discount", *American Journal of Sociology*, 104, p. 1398 (1999); "Focusing the Corporate Product: Securities Analysts and De-Diversification", *Administrative Science Quarterly*, 45, p. 591 (2000). This has served to divert the attention of managers from simple profitability to "meeting the estimates" for profitability used by these analysts: Share prices have to be protected at all costs. This has been reflected in the increased concern shown by corporations with earnings and performance management, in the marked increase in earnings preannouncements and in the implementation of investor relations programs aimed at keeping the expectations of analysts in line with the firm's own forecasts.

134 Beginning in the early 1980s, there emerged a growing number of specialist takeover firms that were prepared to borrow heavily in order to gain control of corporations, which were then "restructured", their presumptive income streams recapitalized and their securities resold at a profit. After dwindling during the downturn of the late 1980s and early 1990s, debt-financed purchases of public companies of this sort – so-called leveraged buyouts – had a second coming. By the early years of the new century, new actors – private equity firms – were regularly taking medium-sized public companies or divisions of large corporations private before restructuring them and selling them on. On the leveraged buyouts of the earlier period, see Doug Henwood, *Wall Street*, London: Verso (1997), pp. 265–285; for an accessible account of the way in which today's private equity firms operate, see Robert Peston, *Who Runs Britain?*, London: Hodder & Stoughton (2008), chapters 2 and 3.

135 Thompson, *supra* note 30.

by their own accounts, relatively insulated from investor preferences, to a situation in which they are intensely sensitive to the assessments of financial market participants and signals emitted by the markets themselves. Corporate strategies have become increasingly tied to a narrowly financial view of how firms should be run in which maximizing stock price trumps other goals. The result has been a shift from a "managerial" to an "investor capitalism", and the rise of highly financialized corporate cultures and modes of governance.[136] This has not been confined to Anglo-American jurisdictions, for the gospel of shareholder value has gradually extended its tentacles to places such as Germany and Japan.[137] With this, as Rakesh Khurana says, the image of the ideal executive has been transformed "from one of a steady, reliable caretaker of the corporation and its many constituencies to that of a swashbuckling, iconoclastic champion of shareholder value". "The ideals of professionalism", established in American business schools in the 1920s and aimed at creating "a managerial class that would run America's large corporations in a way that served the broader interests of society rather than the narrowly defined ones of capital and labor", have been swept away, relegating managers to the status of "hired hands".[138]

Unsurprisingly, with managers downsizing, outsourcing, engaging in share buybacks, distributing a larger proportion of profits as dividends and striving to raise share prices, the main beneficiaries of the new financialized forms of governance have been shareholders and financial property owners. In the 1980s in many OECD countries the share of national income accruing to financial institutions and *rentier* owners of financial property began to rise[139] as corporations abandoned earlier policies of "retain and invest" in favor of policies of "downsize and distribute".[140] In the United Kingdom, for example, there was a marked upward shift in payouts from 13–20% in the 1980s to 20–35% in the 1990s and 2000s.[141] Further financial gains for *rentiers* came in the form of higher share prices – and although some of these were wiped out by the financial crash of 2007–8, prices have since recovered. The rise of the shareholder value corporation has, then, contributed directly to the growth in income and wealth inequality documented by Piketty. It has also fostered a return to the pre-managerialist days when corporations were closely identified with their shareholders – at least for the purpose of determining corporate goals. For liability and misfeasance purposes, of course, corporations and their shareholders continue to be regarded as "completely separate".

136 See, for example, Michael Useem, *Investor Capitalism*, New York: Basic Books (1996).

137 There is a considerable literature on "convergence": See, for example, Joseph McCahery, Luc Renneboog & Piet Moerland. (eds.), *Corporate Governance Regimes: Convergence and Diversity*, Oxford: Oxford University Press (2002); Gerald Davis & Christopher Marquis, "The Globalization of Stock Markets and Convergence in Corporate Governance", in *The Economic Sociology of Capitalism*, Richard Swedberg & Victor Nee (eds.), Princeton: Princeton University Press (2005); Ronald Dore, "Japan's Conversion to Investor Capitalism", in *Corporate Governance and Managerial Reform in Japan*, High Whittaker & Simon Deakin (eds.), Oxford: Oxford University Press (2009), pp.134–162.

138 Rakesh Khurana, *From Higher Aims to Hired Hands: The Social Transformation of American Business Schools*, Princeton: Princeton University Press (2007), pp. 3–4, 20.

139 Gerald Epstein, "Introduction", in *Financialization and the World Economy*, Gerald Epstein (ed.), Cheltenham: Edward Elgar (2005), pp. 3–6; Gerard Dumenil & Dominque Levy, "Costs and Benefits of Neoliberalism: A Class Analysis", in Epstein (ed.), ibid., p. 23; Gerald Epstein & Arjun Jayadev, "The Rise of Rentier Incomes in OECD Countries" (2005), ibid., p. 42.

140 William Lazonick & Mary O'Sullivan, "Maximizing Shareholder Value: A New Ideology for Corporate Governance", *Economy & Society*, 29(1), p. 13 (2000).

141 Julie Froud, Sukhdev Johal, Adam Leaver & Karel Williams, *Financialization and Strategy: Narrative and Numbers*, London: Routledge (2006), pp. 68, 87–88.

Moreover, in recent decades concerted efforts have been made to universalize the shareholder-oriented, stock-market-based forms of corporate governance found in the United Kingdom and the United States. The East Asian crisis of 1997–8 saw international financial institutions (IFIs), led by the World Bank and the IMF, try to quell the growing volatility of the international financial system by developing standards in areas considered important for macroeconomic and financial stability – standards against which the practices of particular countries could be regularly measured and assessed.[142] Although they purport to allow for differences between jurisdictions, the "universal" standards on corporate governance developed by the OECD and World Bank seek to normalize a broadly Anglo-American shareholder-oriented model of the corporation.[143] Compliance with the OECD's *Principles of Corporate Governance*, as with all the standards, is formally voluntary but the signals that would be sent to the international financial community by noncompliance (and their impact on a country's Standard & Poor debt rating) mean that compliance is, in reality, more or less compulsory if capital flight and investment strikes are to be avoided. With the World Bank policing the implementation of the standards on a regular basis, the OECD *Principles* have become a formidable disciplinary mechanism, entrenching shareholder-oriented models of corporate governance around the world.

Despite the criticisms that have been levelled at it, shareholder value maximization has been vigorously defended not only by those who directly benefit from it financially, but also by many academics. The traditional justification for shareholder primacy is, of course, that corporations belong to and are "owned" by their shareholders and should, therefore, be run in their interests. Significantly, however, in recent decades the academic supporters of shareholder primacy have tended to downplay the "ownership" claims of corporate shareholders, in recognition perhaps of the fact that the legal basis of this claim is rather thin.[144] They have instead developed alternative, consequentialist justifications centering on the claim that shareholder primacy and the pursuit of shareholder value benefit society as a whole by furthering economic efficiency (the optimal allocation of resources) and ensuring that aggregate social wealth is maximized. In other words, we all *indirectly* benefit from it. I'm not going to explore this dubious claim here. Suffice it to say that there is considerable evidence that contemporary financialized corporate governance is productively damaging for very similar reasons to those laid out by Veblen a hundred years ago. Indeed, since the financial crash of 2007–8, which cast serious doubts over the economic wisdom of pursuing shareholder value maximization, even some of its erstwhile champions have questioned it as a goal.[145]

142 The IFIs refer to these as the Reports on the Observance of Standards and Codes (ROSCs). Participation in the ROSCs is "voluntary", though refusal to submit to these practices is inevitably seen as sending negative signals to the international financial and investment communities.

143 See Susanne Soederberg, *The Politics of the New Financial Architecture*, London: Zed Books (2004).

144 A number of commentators have used A. M. Honore's analysis of the "legal incidents" of ownership to examine the ownership claims of corporate shareholders and concluded that they possess very few of Honore's ownership rights: See John Kay, "The Stakeholder Company", in *Stakeholder Capitalism*, Gavin Kelly, Dominic Kelly & Andrew Gamble. (eds.), London: Palgrave Macmillan (1997). In response to the "ownership problem", some theorists, anxious to defend shareholder primacy and aware of the threat posed to this principle by recognizing the separate legal existence of the corporate entity, have sought to eliminate the corporation as a separate legal person by developing so-called nexus-of-contracts theories of the corporation that seek to reestablish shareholders as the owners of the corporation's assets: See Paddy Ireland, "Defending the Rentier: The Reprivatization of the Public Company", in *The Political Economy of the Company*, J. Parkinson, A. Gamble & G. Kelly (eds.), Oxford: Hart (2001).

145 Most notably, Jack Welch, former CEO of General Electric, famously declared shareholder value maximization to be a "dumb idea", having seemingly pursued it for many years.

12. The distribution of financial property ownership

The advocates of shareholder primacy have, however, made a second related claim that I would like to explore in a little more detail. With the growth of such things as private pensions, they argue, financial property ownership has spread and been "democratized", with the result that more and more people *directly* benefit from the maximization of shareholder value. The empirical findings of Piketty and other researchers into inequality cast serious doubt on this claim. It is clear that despite the spread of direct and indirect financial property ownership, financial wealth remains very heavily concentrated amongst the wealthiest decile and has become even more so in recent decades.[146] As we have seen, Piketty shows that the concentration of capital and wealth ownership amongst both the top 10% and the top 1% of the population has risen significantly since the 1970s and 80s. In the United States the share of the top 10% rose from just over 60% to about 72%, and the share of the top 1% from just below 30% to just over 35%. During the same period in the United Kingdom the wealth share of the top 10% rose from just over 60% to 70%, and the share of the top 1% from just over 20% to just under 30%. Edward Wolff paints a broadly similar picture in his analysis of the US Federal Reserve's triennial Survey of Consumer Finances (SCF), arguing that the wealth share of the top 1% in the United States rose sharply in the 1980s, levelled out during the 1990s and fell sharply around the turn of the century, since which time it has steadily risen: By 2010 the top 1% accounted for 35.4% of total wealth.[147] Moreover, Wolff shows that what he calls "non-home" wealth – meaning, in essence, financial wealth – is even more heavily concentrated. In the United States in 2010, he reports, the share of financial (non-home) wealth of the richest top 1% stood at 42% and the share of the top 20% at over 95%.[148] In 2010, the richest 1% of households held about 50% of all outstanding stock, financial securities, trust equity and business equity, and 36% of non-home real estate; the top 10% accounted for 85–90% of stocks, bonds, trusts, business equity and non-home real estate. In relation to stock ownership specifically, the 2010 SCF shows that "the richest 10% of households accounted for 81% of the total value of these stocks"; it also shows that there has been a fall in the proportion of US households owning corporate stock (directly and indirectly) to 47% from its 52% peak in 2001.[149] Wolff concludes that "in terms of wealth or income, substantial stock holdings have still not penetrated much beyond the reach of the rich and the upper middle class".[150] The findings of the 2013 Survey suggest that these trends

146 The rise of institutional investors – and especially of widely held pension funds – had made the structure of financial property ownership (and thus beneficial ownership) much murkier that it used to be, as much larger proportions of the population have an indirect stake in financial property.

147 Wolff's top 1% have a net worth of 46.6 million or more; the next 9% have a net worth of between about $900,000 and $6.6 million: See Edward N. Wolff, "The Asset Price Meltdown and the Wealth of the Middle Class", August 26, 2012: www.colorado.edu/AmStudies/lewis/1025/incomestudy2012.pdf

148 Wolff, *supra* note 147. See also Domhoff, *supra* note 8. It is worth noting that the concentration of financial property ownership amongst the very wealthy contributes to income inequality, as a substantial proportion of their income does not come directly from "work". Domhoff reports that only 19% of the income reported by the 13,480 individuals or households making over $10 million came from wages and salaries. Piketty confirms that "a very substantial and growing inequality of capital income since 1980 accounts for a about one-third of the increase of income inequality in the US", *supra* note 6, p. 300.

149 The holdings of most of these stock-owning households are modest: Only 22% owned stocks worth $25,000 or more.

150 Wolff, *supra* note 147. Wolff's analysis also suggests that the concentration of ownership of "financial securities" is even greater than the concentration of stock ownership, with the wealthiest 1% accounting for 64%.

have continued, with a further decline in the proportion of households owning stock directly and indirectly.[151]

Sandy Hager has recently added further empirical flesh to the pictures painted by Wolff and Piketty in his work on the ownership of US public debt. Before Hager's research, in the absence of detailed empirical evidence, there was considerable disagreement about whether ownership of the US public debt was concentrated in relatively few hands (the "bondholding class")[152] or, as some argued, was widely spread.[153] Hager's research seems to have settled the argument. Using the 2010 SCF, Hager shows that the level of concentration of US government bond ownership is very high, and that in the last three decades "there has been a massive concentration in the distribution of federal interest towards the top one percent".[154] During this period, ownership of federal bonds, and thus receipt of interest payments from the State, has become concentrated in the hands of three groups: foreign investors, whose holdings have mushroomed in the last half century, rising from less than 5% in the 1960s to around 50% today; corporations, whose share has fallen from about 40% to 30%; and households, whose share has fallen from about 30% to about 15%.[155] The top 1% of households own nearly 69% of the declining but still significant household share, and in recent years the corporate share has rapidly concentrated in the largest 2,500 corporations. Having held steady at around 65% for many years, the share of these corporations has risen rapidly in the last three decades to stand at more than 80% today. It has, moreover, concentrated in large corporations in the FIRE sector (finance, insurance and real estate).[156] Crucially, the dominant corporate owners of the public debt are not, as in the past, "traditional" intermediaries such as banks, but institutional investors. Some of these institutions, like pension funds, are, of course, widely owned, and "broad swathes of the population" have an indirect stake in the public debt they own.[157] However, the share of the public debt held by pension funds has fallen sharply from 14% in the mid-1980s to 6% in 2014, while the share held by mutual funds, characterized by ownership that is much more heavily concentrated amongst the very wealthy, has risen to around 10%.[158] This leads Hager to conclude that there is "still

151 Jesse Bricker, Lisa Dettling, Alice Henriques, Joanne Hsu, Kevin Moore, John Sabelhaus, Jeffrey Thompson . . . Richard Windle., "Changes in US Family Finances from 2010 to 2013: Evidence from the Survey of Consumer Finances", *Federal Reserve Bulletin*, 100 (September 2014), pp. 1–41.

152 This term was first coined by Henry Carter Adams: See *Public Debts: A Study in the Science of Finance*, New York: Appleton (1887).

153 Wolfgang Streeck observes that no one seems to know who the holders of public debt are, though "we know the names of a few large funds that specialize in the government bond market, like Calpers and PIMCO (Public Investment Management Company)": See *Buying Time*, London: Verso (2014), p. 82.

154 Sandy Brian Hager, "What Happened to the Bondholding Class? Public Debt, Power and the Top One Per Cent", *New Political Economy*, 19, p. 173 (2014).

155 Though Hager points out that a substantial proportion of gross US public debt is actually held by the government itself (linked to various government trust fund accounts). From the 1940s until the late 1980s, the intragovernmental share stood at around 10%; it has since grown to just over 30%: See Sandy Brian Hager, *Public Debt, Ownership and Power*, PhD, Toronto: York University (2013), pp. 105–106.

156 The share of the largest corporations grew rapidly after the financial crisis, probably because federal government debt was seen as a safe haven. In this context, institutional investors have replaced traditional banks intermediaries as the dominant owners. See Gillian Tett, "Elite's Grip on US Bonds Lays Bare Fiscal Divide", *Financial Times*, November 15, 2013, summarizing Hager's research.

157 Sandy Brian Hager, "Public Debt as Corporate Power", *Working Papers (Capital as Power)*, 2015/01, p. 3 (2015): www.capitalaspower.com/2015/01/no-201501-hager-public-debt-as-corporate-power/.

158 Hager, *supra* note 157, p. 11. The top 10% (in terms of wealth) held only 15% of total pension fund assets in 2010 (up from 8% in 1983), whereas they held 47% of the total assets of mutual funds (up from 40% in 1983).

a powerful bondholding class in the United States, one whose power has augmented rapidly over the past three decades".[159]

13. The new aristocracy of finance

The concentration of share ownership amongst the (very) wealthy clearly undermines claims that share ownership has been democratized and that shareholder value maximization directly benefits most of us. Quite apart from the doubts that many have expressed about whether the pursuit of shareholder value maximization operates for the long-term benefit of shareholders, most ordinary people have, at best, only very modest holdings and reap little benefit from the distribution of a larger proportion of corporate surpluses to shareholders or from rising share prices. On the contrary, for many workers the pursuit of shareholder value has meant job losses (not least amongst the middle classes), relentless downward pressure on wages, and declining terms and conditions of work.[160]

The same elite financial-property-owning groups have been the main beneficiaries of growing public debt. Hager's analysis shows that a significant proportion of the interest payments paid by the US government on its debt finds its way to the wealthiest in society, although the class redistributive effects of this are murkier than they used to be. In Marx's time, the tax system did little if anything to redistribute downwards from the wealthy, and public debt therefore served as an upward mode of redistribution, shifting resources from the ordinary tax-paying citizen to the interest-receiving financial elite.[161] Since then, the tax system has become more progressive and social spending has risen, making it harder to work out who the ultimate beneficiaries of State borrowing and spending are. It is clear, however, that in recent years, as wealth – and especially financial wealth – has become more mobile and able to avoid (or evade) taxes, fiscal competition has grown and States have struggled to raise sufficient revenues to cover their social expenditures. The result is that they now fund a large part of their spending through further borrowing – from those with money to invest – rather than through taxation. As Wolfgang Streeck says, the "tax state" has become the "debt state".[162] The result, he suggests, is that governments now have to satisfy two "electorates': On one hand, the *Staatsvolk*, the "general citizenry" with the right to vote in elections; on the other, the *Marktvolk*, the "people of the market", the *rentier* class who invest in financial

159 Hager, *supra* note 154, p. 177.

160 Financialized corporate governance has led to the "hollowing out" of many corporations through downsizing, reengineering, outsourcing and the like. In the words of one commentator, the "serial restructuring" that has accompanied the worship of shareholder value has "elevate[d] breach of implicit stakeholder contract into a guiding principle of management": See Froud *et al.*, *supra* note 138, p. 100. That the more privileged members of the working class in the developed world gained as owners of modest amounts of financial property – gains that in many cases have now been all but erased – they often lost in other ways. The emergence of a "neoliberal order under the aegis of finance" has contributed to the destruction of the old compromises and social alliances; to deregulation followed by re-regulation in financial interests; to higher unemployment and downward pressure on wages (whose real growth has slowed and, at times, stagnated); to reductions in job security; to the dismantling of social protection systems; to higher income and wealth inequality (testaments to the growing share of the social product accruing to the owners of financial property in the form of dividends and interest); to the "financialization" of everyday life; and to unpredictable currency fluctuations, reckless capital movements, growing financial instability and to what now looks like a financial crisis of major proportions.

161 Hager, *supra* note 155.

162 See note ibid., p. 14. Streeck, *supra* note 153, p. 72.

property and cast their votes in financial markets.[163] With States financially dependent on the latter, "finance capital" has emerged as "a second people – a *Marktvolk* rivalling the *Staatsvolk*", which states have to satisfy for their own survival. Drawing an explicit parallel with corporate governance, Streeck suggests that creditors have risen "to become a second constituency of the modern state" in a way which is "strikingly reminiscent of the emergence of activist shareholders in the corporate world under the "shareholder value" doctrine of the 1980s and 1990s".[164] As Streeck's notion of two electorates suggests, the power of this new financial oligarchy goes well beyond its ability to shape the distribution of wealth. It wields enormous political as well as economic power. In short, what we have seen in recent decades is the emergence of a "new aristocracy of finance" – a power bloc comprising those at the top of the wealth and income hierarchy in whom financial property ownership is concentrated, their institutional representatives, the executive class, and a range of financial intermediaries[165], prominent among them what Jeffrey Winters has called the "agents of wealth defense" – a reference to the army of well-paid skilled professionals – lawyers, accountants and the like – employed by the wealthy to protect their property and incomes.[166] In this context we need to re-personify not only corporate power in terms of these groups, but the seemingly impersonal market forces through which they operate and to which corporations, States and individuals are increasingly subject.

14. The nature of financial property

In recent years, one of the main ways in which the influence of this new aristocracy of finance over policy has been manifested is in the prioritization of "investor protection" as a goal. To fully understand the significance of this, not least its impact on democracy, we need to explore the nature of financial property in a little more detail. The growth in the volume of financial property in the eighteenth and nineteenth centuries was inextricably linked to the rise of capitalism and development of an increasingly sophisticated credit system.[167] Since then financial property has become one of – if not *the* – most important form(s) of property in the modern world. But it is a peculiar because it is intangible: There is no tangible "thing", no tangible object to which the property rights directly relate. This is most obvious with government bonds, but, as we have seen, it is also true of JSC shares, for they confer no direct proprietary interest in the company's assets on their holders. Financial property is composed, in essence, of rights to receive income streams – dividends, interest payments and the like. It involves investments of money in intangible "things" that make more money.[168]

163 Streeck, *supra* note 153, p. 80.

164 Streeck, *supra* note 154, 79, 84.

165 See Froud *et al.*, *supra* note 141; Ismael Erturk, Julie Froud, Sukhdev Johal, Adam Leaver & Karel Williams, "General Introduction", in *Financialization at Work*, Ismael Erturk, Julie Froud, Sukhdev Jonal, Adam Leaver & Karel Williams (eds.), London: Routledge (2008), p. 1; Peter Folkman, Julie Froud, Sukhdev Jophal and Karel Williams, "Working for Themselves?: Capital Market Intermediaries and Present Day Capitalism", *Business History*, 49, p. 552 (2007), pointing how a diverse bunch of financial intermediaries – corporate advisors and service providers, securities analysts, hedge fund operators, private equity firms, city lawyers and the like – have also reaped significant financial benefits from the "economy of permanent restructuring" that has emerged. These are the groups who have played a key role in generating a finance-oriented corporate culture in which everything is for sale if the price is right.

166 See Jeffrey A. Winters: www.newleftproject.org/index.php/site/article_comments/wealth_defence

167 These developments generated a dazzling variety of new forms of property: See Morton Horwitz, *The Transformation of American Law 1870–1960*, Oxford: Oxford University Press (1992), p. 150.

168 It was because the revenues accruing to money capital seemingly presupposed no production at all (M-M1) that Marx considered it to be the most fetishistic form of capital of all.

The US Supreme Court has provided some clues as to what this obscures, for as we have seen, under the *Howey* test a financial instrument is a "security" for the purposes of federal securities law if it "involves an investment of money in a common enterprise with profits to come *solely from the efforts of others*".[169] The test is strikingly revealing of the social nature and class dimensions of financial property. Indeed, the class dimensions of public debt, also obscured behind these reified property forms, were recently highlighted by Streeck when he suggested that the conflict between the *Marktvolk* and the *Staatsvolk* in relation to public debt is "derivative of the conflict between wage-earners and profit-makers".[170] Although the revenues received by financial property owners tend to be seen as emanating from the "things" they own – a view reflected in Piketty's treatment of capital as synonymous with wealth and as a "thing" – financial property (money) isn't autonomously productive. The revenues accruing to it are rooted in social relations: They come from "the efforts of others".

Financial property has not always been seen in this reified, de-personified way, however. Historically, revenue rights were classified in law as rights *in personam* rather than as rights *in rem*; they were regarded, in other words, as personal rights against other (specific) people rather than as rights to "things"; and as *choses in action* rather than *choses in possession* – as rights enforceable only by taking legal action, not by taking physical possession. They were originally seen, in other words, as what James Penner calls "personality-rich", as relations between particular people; they lacked the "personality-poor" qualities and "thingness" of "property". As such, they could not be assigned. As Penner explains, because *choses in action* are rights arising from personal dealings, "it is natural not to think of either of the parties to such special relationships as substitutable by other people".[171] By the eighteenth century, the category *choses in action* covered instruments as diverse as bills, notes, checks, government stock and JSC shares, all of which were conceptualized as rights personal to the parties bound by the obligation and generally considered to be nonassignable and incapable of being independent forms of freely alienable property.[172] At common law they could not even be stolen. "Bonds bills and notes, which concern mere choses in action", Blackstone explained, "were . . . at the common law held not to be such goods whereof larciny [sic] might be committed; being of no intrinsic value, and not importing any property in possession of the person from whom they are taken".[173] Legislation was required to take them outside the scope of this rule.[174] Gradually, however, some of these *choses in action* – JSC shares amongst them – "changed their original character and [became] very much less like merely personal rights of action and very much more like rights of property".[175] What had previously been seen as a legal relation between people began to take the form of a relation between people and things – "property".

169 328 US 293, per Murphy J. The case still represents the leading attempt by the US Supreme Court to define the nature of a security. It was affirmed in *United Housing Foundation Inc. v. Forman*, 421 US 837 (1975), and in *Landreth Timber Co v. Landreth*, 471 US 681 (1985).

170 Streeck, *supra* note 153, pp. 90–91.

171 In making this argument, Penner was drawing on the work of Wesley Hohfeld: See Penner, "The Bundles of Rights Picture of Property", *UCLA LR*, 43, pp. 802 (1996).

172 William Holdsworth, *A History of English Law* (2nd edition), London: Methuen (1937), Vol VII, p. 516. The difficulties surrounding the assignment of JSC shares at this time was precisely a reflection of their contractual character; of the *in personam* nature of many of the rights and obligations that constituted them, and of the perception of them as arising out of personal dealings and as inseparable *from particular people.*

173 William Blackstone, *Commentaries on the Laws of England* (1765–9), Vol IV, Chapter 17.

174 See, for example, 2 George II, c.25, dealing with South Sea bonds, bank notes and East India bonds, amongst other things.

175 Holdsworth, *supra* note 172, p. 543.

What changed the character of the JSC share? As we have seen, the processes whereby shares came to be seen as intangible revenue rights with no direct connection to the assets of companies were complex. Economically, the driving forces were the growth of pure *rentier*, money capitalist shareholding, the emergence of a developed share market and the commercial desire to render shares as freely transferable as possible. The emergence of a developed market made shares increasingly liquid assets and enabled them to acquire a capital value of their own quite separate from the value of the company's assets; their transferability was also enhanced by a series of legal changes.[176] The result was that although shares were disconnected from the assets of companies and became, at one level, more contractual in nature, they also became increasingly exchangeable bundles of rights and, as such, came to possess property-like qualities. They were increasingly treated and felt like autonomous objects of property-like "things". The elimination of the remaining residual liabilities attaching to them completed this process, rendering them unencumbered, personality-poor, fully exchangeable and liquid bundles of rights. As James Penner says, although the *personam* origins of shares still assert themselves in certain circumstances – and even now there are still some who question their status as "property"[177] corporate shares have acquired "the character of property", of freely assignable rights *in rem* "only contingently related to any particular person' and separable from any particular individual or "owner".[178]

Crucially, extensive legal interventions are needed not only to constitute these intangible income rights as objects (of property) but also to preserve their value. Lacking inherent exchange value as useful physical objects, financial property is unusually vulnerable. This vulnerability stems from the fact that its value is derived not from the properties of a tangible object but from the expectation that it will attract money payments *in the future*. In the case of corporate shares, this is reflected in the fact that while the value of the tangible assets of companies tends to remain relatively stable, share values often fluctuate alarmingly as perceptions of their future earning power change. As a result, there are often substantial differences between the market and book values of companies, between the value of their tangible assets and their value of their shares on the stock exchange. The fact that share values are based on *expectations* about *future* returns is a further problem, for it renders them unusually vulnerable to manipulation, fraud and speculation. To protect their integrity, therefore, a wide range of legal and other interventions are needed to try to eliminate deceit and swindling, and to ensure that the market value of shares reflects with reasonable accuracy their future income-generating potential. This is reflected in the many and varied sources of the rules protecting investors found in company, security, bankruptcy, takeover and competition laws, as well as in stock exchange regulations and accounting standards.

The vulnerability of intangible financial property extends beyond this, however. As its value is derived from anticipated *future* revenues, it is potentially affected by any changes

176 Thus, as we have seen, incorporating Acts regularly declared company shares to be personal and transferable, and judicial decisions held them to be rights to profit, not equitable interests in the assets of companies, disconnecting them from any real estate owned by companies.

177 See, for example, Robert Pennington, *Company Law* (6th edition), London: Butterworths (1990), pp. 56–57, 135–136; Robert Pennington, "Can Shares in Companies Be Defined?", *Company Lawyer*, 10, p. 144 (1989).

178 The *personam* nature of intangible forms of property sometimes reasserts itself "when things go awry" and their holders, inter alia, "launch shareholder suits": See Penner, *supra* note 171, p. 813. It also frequently reasserts itself in the context of many private companies whose shares are not freely transferable and whose underlying *personam* nature is only too evident. On this see *Ebrahimi v. Westbourne Galleries* [1973] AC 360, and the jurisprudence surrounding section 994 of the UK Companies Act 2006.

in the processes through which the income streams are generated. It is unusually vulnerable, in other words, to everything from changes in labor and corporate laws to changes in health and safety regulations and trade and taxation policies, from changes in the balance of political and class power to changes in particular markets as well as in general economic conditions. All of these things potentially have an impact on the size and reliability of the income streams concerned. As a result, to paraphrase Robert Hale, the owners of financial property are reliant upon large number of people "conduct[ing] themselves in a manner advantageous to [them]" and continuing to do so indefinitely into the future.[179] Investment abroad is particularly risky as it is vulnerable to local political change and instabilities, and to the vagaries of changes in host State laws.[180] The integrity of financial property therefore requires not only corporate employees and managers but governments and, indeed, societies as a whole to behave in particular ways. It therefore requires measures aimed at preserving the social conditions and practices responsible for ensuring a continuing flow of returns, and, ideally, the imposition of significant constraints on policy makers. As Streeck shows, this is as true of government debt as it is of corporate shares and bonds. In short, preserving the value of financial property means exerting control over the future.

Government bonds are attractive to *rentiers* because they offer fixed rates of return which, being paid by an immortal debtor – the people of a nation-state – are theoretically guaranteed. As long as the State has the capacity to levy sufficient taxes to meet the interest payments, government bonds are secure. In recent years, however, for a variety of reasons – ranging from an ageing population and the growing demand for State-provided services to the financial consequences of the crash and the socialization of the (private) losses, to the growing difficulties States are encountering in raising taxes, especially from wealthy individuals and corporations – many States have been forced to borrow more and more to cover their expenditures. Potentially, this "state poverty" is, as Streeck says, good for investors, offering them "a golden outlet" to invest their money profitably by enabling them to access the wealth produced by "the efforts of others" – but this is the case only "so long as the state's capacity to repay its creditors can be relied upon". The financial crash of 2007–8 has raised the indebtedness of some States to such levels that their creditors are no longer sure that the governments concerned will be able to meet their future obligations. The result is that "lenders seek far more than in the past to protect their claims by exerting influence on government policies". In recent decades, institutions such as the IMF, World Bank and ECB have demanded significant changes to government policies as preconditions of further lending. As Streeck says, "the main aim of lenders" is "to ensure that, in the event of a crisis", the claims of the investors "take precedence over those of *Staatsvolk* – in other words that debt service gets priority over public services".[181] As the people of Greece are currently discovering, "austerity" entails prioritizing the payment of interest on debts over social and human needs. This should not, of course, come as a surprise: The interests of the *Marktvolk* are very different from those of the *Staatsvolk*. It is, as the *Howey* test reminds us, the difference between the interests of investors in securities and the interests of those whose efforts produce the profits.

179 Robert Hale, "Value and Vested Rights", *Columbia Law Review*, 27, p. 523 (1927).

180 David Schneiderman, *Constitutionalizing Economic Globalization*, Cambridge, UK: Cambridge University Press (2008), p. 26.

181 Streeck, *supra* note 153, pp. 78–79, 86. Crucially, unlike the *Staatvolk*, the *Marktvolk* –who are investors, not citizens – "are bound to national states purely by contractual ties. Their rights vis-à-vis the state are of a private rather than a public character, deriving not from the constitution but from the civil law", p. 81.

The new "aristocracy of finance" has been able to intensify its demands, of course, precisely because of the power it is now able to wield in global financial markets. As Streeck says, "debt states" have subjected themselves and their activities "to the control of creditors in the shape of the 'markets'". The *Marktvolk* may not be able to vote out a government, but they can sell their bonds or decline to buy new issues, and governments are only too aware that if they do this, the interest rates on their future debt issues will rise. Interest rates "are the 'public opinion' of the *Marktvolk*". Just as maintaining share price has become an imperative for corporate managers, so preserving the trust and confidence of the *rentier* financial elite has become an imperative for governments, narrowing their perception of what is politically possible. Just as corporate managers have become subject to the power exercised by financial property owners in financial markets, so too have States. Just as capital markets have transformed corporate governance, so credit markets are transforming democracy. The imperative of "shareholder value" has been joined by the imperative of "bondholder value".[182]

15. The capitalist Magna Carta: Investor protection and the new constitutionalism[183]

There are, however, differences between the two types of investment. Finance has control over any new investments in State debt. Using its right to withhold, it is in a position to insist on alterations to government spending and policy as preconditions of new lending. But what about existing investments, investments that have already been made in, for example, corporate shares or plant and equipment where rates of return are potentially higher but aren't guaranteed or fixed in advance? In a world in which more and more key productive resources are in private hands, States are desperate to attract investment in order to create jobs. As we know, this has led them to try to provide corporate, labor, welfare, environmental and tax regimes that are attractive to investors (so-called good investment climates). But there is always a risk that the citizenry, the *Staatsvolk,* will rebel and make demands – like higher wages, improved labor and environmental standards, and enhanced levels of social spending – that threaten to lower profitability and the market value of existing revenue rights. What can be done if States won't voluntarily desist from implementing such measures? The "states of advanced capitalism have to be constructed in such a way", writes Streeck, "that they earn the enduring trust of the owners and movers of capital, by giving credible guarantees at the level of policy and institutions that they will not intervene in 'the economy' – or that, if they do, it will only be to protect and enforce market justice in the shape of suitable returns on capital investments. A precondition of this is the neutralization of democracy".[184]

In recent decades new techniques have been developed to try to protect investors from the political threats posed by democracy, central amongst them the development of a "new constitutionalism" aimed at giving investments protection from policy changes that might lower their value. What we have seen is not only the implementation of measures aimed at facilitating the free flow of goods, services, capital and persons across borders, but also the emergence of an ensemble of laws and institutions aimed at offering quasi-constitutional protection to foreign investments, especially those made by corporations. Actively promoted and developed by the leading OECD countries, this new "investment rules regime"

182 Streeck, *supra* note 153, pp. 78–81.

183 "The Capitalist Magna Carta", *Time Magazine*, 70(18), p. 67, October 28, 1957.

184 Streeck, *supra* note 153, p. 62.

encompasses legal and quasi-legal agreements, the institutionalization of standards and domestic constitutional changes of the traditional sort. It is most clearly evident, however, in the gradual emergence of a complex, transnational network of rules for the protection of foreign direct investment. These rules are embodied in a variety of legally binding agreements: bilateral investment treaties (nearly 3,000 in number), a range of regional investment and trade agreements such as NAFTA, and, at the multilateral level, things such as the agreement on Trade-Related Investment Measures (TRIMs).[185] This "investment rules regime" is aimed at protecting property, which tends to be conceptualized in this context as (like the share) a right to future profit.[186] The goal of the regime is to restrict the ability of States to adopt policies that threaten to diminish investors' "anticipated future returns" without paying compensation by locking them into a "rule of investment law" that protects investors from legislative and administrative action that impairs or might impair their investment interests.[187] The rules constituting the regime, negotiated away from the public gaze by technocrats, often amidst intense corporate lobbying, look likely soon to be joined by Transatlantic Trade and Investment Partnership (TTIP), the controversial partnership currently being negotiated between the European Commission and the US government.

There are many different aspects to this regime, but one of the most important is the way in which it seeks to compel States to provide compensation not only for the outright physical expropriation (nationalization) of property but for the adoption of policies that have the effect of reducing the revenues likely to accrue to property in the future. So-called regulatory takings of this sort are regarded as tantamount to expropriation and widely seen as the most important part of the regime because of the restrictions they place on State policy.[188] With third-party investors increasingly being given standing to sue in domestic courts and international arbitration tribunals, States are now constrained not only by fears of capital flight but also by the threat of litigation arising out of the pursuit of economic and social policy objectives that negatively impact the "future anticipated profits" of investments. Since 2000, hundreds of foreign investors have sued States, claiming damages for policies they claim have diminished or threatened to diminish their profits. Thus Philip Morris has brought actions against Australia for introducing plain packaging on cigarettes, claiming that it constituted an expropriation of their Australian investments[189] and against Uruguay for putting health warnings on cigarette packets, claiming that it devalued their cigarette trademarks and investments in the country.[190] The Canadian oil and gas corporation Lone Pine sued its own government through a US subsidiary after Quebec issued a moratorium on fracking.

185 See Schneiderman, *supra* note 180; see also David Schneiderman, "Investing in Democracy? Political Process and International Investment Law", *University of Toronto Law Journal*, 60, p. 909 (2010).

186 The European Union and the United States urge defining the term "investment" as broadly as possible to cover both tangible and intangible property so that it encompasses more or less anything with economic value.

187 See David Schneiderman, "Investment Rules and the Rule of Law", *Constellations*, 8, p. 521 (2001); Schneiderman, *Resisting Economic Globalization: Critical Theory and International Investment Law*, London: Palgrave Macmillan (2013); Schneiderman, "Constitutional Approaches to Privatization: An Inquiry into the Magnitude of Neo-Liberal Constitutionalism", *Law and Contemporary Problems*, 63, p. 106.

188 Other rules center on the idea of "nondiscrimination" and the principle that states should not distinguish, for regulatory purposes, between foreign and domestic investors. The principle of nondiscrimination rules out such things as rules calling for the use of local goods, labor or services.

189 The claim was made for an alleged breach of Article 6 of the 1993 Agreement between the Government of Australia and the Government of Hong Kong for the Promotion and Protection of Investments.

190 The claim was made under a bilateral investment treaty (BIT) between Uruguay and Switzerland, where Philip Morris has its headquarters.

The Swedish energy giant Vattenfall has twice sued Germany, first for imposing strict environmental conditions to limit the company's water usage and its impact on fish, and later for deciding to phase out nuclear power. Ecuador was recently ordered to pay $1.8 billion to Occidental Petroleum, a Houston-based oil corporation, after it stripped the company of an oil concession following a breach of contract, and El Salvador is trying to fend off a multimillion dollar suit lodged by an international mining company after refusing it permission to dig for gold on environmental grounds. The list goes on. TTIP, which seeks to eliminate the so-called non-tariff barriers to trade (most tariff barriers having already been negotiated away), would extend the regime still further, as the concept of "non-tariff barriers to trade" potentially encompasses everything from food standards to labor rights, and from safety regulations to environmental protection.

It is because of the extensive protections offered by this body of rules to property interests and its constraining effects on government policies that it has come to be described as representing a "new constitutionalism".[191] The aim of this "new constitutionalism" is to establish rules that protect foreign investments and then freeze them so that States cannot act in ways that undermine the value of existing property rights and interests.[192] In this way, States are bound far into the future, "whatever political combinations develop at home to counteract it". Punishing monetary disciplines seek to make resistance "difficult to sustain, if not futile".[193] The "new constitutionalism" thus operates to limit the range of viable policy and regulatory choices available to States. It strives to restrict the range of political possibility and to insulate key aspects of economic life from majoritarian politics and democracy. The formal institutions of democracy survive, but are hollowed out.

Indeed, recently, there have also been suggestions that investors might in the future seek quasi-constitutional protection for other forms of financial property. In December 2011, the *Financial Times* reported that a Madrid-based hedge fund, Vega Asset Management, was threatening to take legal action against officials negotiating Greece's debt restructuring if the losses they suffered on their binds became too great.[194] What had originally been considered "a ludicrous possibility" was becoming "all too real".[195] The following month, the *New York Times* reported that hedge funds were considering bringing an action for violation of bondholder rights in the European Court of Human Rights against Greece, whose government was considering passing legislation to force all private bondholders to take losses while exempting the ECB. Their argument was that it amounted to a violation of their property rights and, as such, of their human rights.[196]

191 The phrase was coined by Stephen Gill. See, for example, "New Constitutionalism, Democratisation and Global Political Economy", *Pacifica Review*, 10, p. 23 (1998). See also David Schneiderman, "Investment Rules and the New Constitutionalism", *Law & Social Inquiry*, 25, p. 772 (2000).

192 In Stephen Gill's words, the aim is to "provide political anchorage for capital in the long term . . . through political and legal mechanisms that are difficult to change": See Gill, "Globalisation, Market Civilisation, and Disciplinary Neoliberalism", *Millennium: Journal of International Studies*, 24, p. 399 (2001); Stephen Gill, *The Constitution of Global Capitalism.* Paper presented at the ISA Annual Convention, Los Angeles (2000).

193 Schneidermann, *supra* note 180, p. 6.

194 *Financial Times*, "Funds Threaten to Sue over Greek Bond Losses" December 21, 2011: www.ft.com/cms/s/0/c2943c1e-2bf4–11e1–98bc-00144feabdc0.html#axzz3XHO4l8df

195 See: www.zerohedge.com/news/greek-voluntary-restructuring-verge-collapse-hedge-fund-vega-threatens-sue-greece-excessive-hai

196 *New York Times*, "Hedge Funds may Sue Greece if it Tries to Force Losses" January 18, 2012: www.nytimes.com/2012/01/19/business/global/hedge-funds-may-sue-greece-if-it-tries-to-force-loss.html

The constitutionalization of rights is often seen as a positive development – as power-diffusing and as spreading liberal, egalitarian values and there is no doubt that the trend towards constitutionalization has been accompanied by what Hirschl calls "a craze for . . . judicial review". This has been welcomed by some academics and activists, but there are good reasons for doubting whether the trend towards constitutionalism and the rise of "juristocracy" in the investment context is really driven by a genuine commitment to growth, democracy, social justice or universal rights. As Hirschl says, it is more likely part of a "broader process whereby political and economic elites, while . . . profess[ing] support for democracy, attempt to insulate policymaking from the vicissitudes of democratic politics".[197] Indeed, one of the features of the new "investment rules regime" is its deployment of extra-judicial enforcement mechanisms. Thus one of the most controversial and contested aspects of TTIP has been its investor-State dispute settlement (ISDS) mechanism. International trade and investment treaties and agreements have long embraced ISDS mechanisms which eschew ordinary courts of law in favor of arbitration panels composed of senior (corporate) lawyers.[198] Pioneered in the late 1950s by a group of German businessmen led by Hermann Abs, the chairman of Deutsche Bank, ISDS mechanisms of this sort are not new. In recent decades, however, their number has grown rapidly. Indeed, it is the ISDS mechanisms embodied in TTIP that have generated much of the political opposition to it.[199] In this context, it is not, perhaps, insignificant that Abs saw the development of special international courts of arbitration as providing "a Magna Carta" for the protection of capital abroad.[200] As Colin Crouch suggests, however, these mechanisms are "not so much post-democracy as post-law".[201]

16. Conclusion: Re-personifying corporate power

In recent decades, shareholders – acting through their institutional representatives using the power conferred by the residual control rights attached to shares, operating mainly in financial markets, and in collusion with the executive class (the recipients of Piketty's "supersalaries") and a variety of financial intermediaries and "agents of wealth defense" – have managed not only to reassert the principle of shareholder primacy but also to engineer a transformation of corporate governance. This brought to an end a period in which corporations were less closely identified only with their shareholders and the separate legal personhood of the corporate entity was taken more seriously – a period in which corporations had come widely

197 Ran Hirschl, "The Political Origins of the New Constitutionalism", *Indiana Journal of Global Legal Studies*, 11, pp. 71–73, 105 (2004); see also Hirschl, *Towards Juristocracy: The Origins and Consequences of the New Constitutionalism*, Cambridge, MA: Harvard University Press (2004); and David Schneiderman, "Judging in Secular Times", 63 *Supreme Court Review* (2d), 63,, pp. 557–577 (2013).

198 States, in effect, confer on international organizations and other bodies powers that, when exercised by states themselves, would usually be referred to as "sovereign powers", rendering sovereignty itself a contestable concept: See Dan Sarooshi, *International Organizations and Their Exercise of Sovereign Powers*, Oxford: Oxford University Press (2005).

199 As I write (June 2015), a vote in the European Parliament on TTIP has just been postponed, ostensibly because there were too many proposed amendments.

200 "The Capitalist Magna Carta", *Time Magazine*, 70(18), p. 67, October 28 1957. See also Claire Provost & Matt Kennard, "The Obscure Legal System that Lets Corporations Sue Countries": www.theguardian.com/business/2015/jun/10/obscure-legal-system-lets-corportations-sue-states-ttip-icsid

201 See Colin Crouch, "Democracy at a TTIP"ing point: Seizing a slim chance to reassert democratic sovereignty in Europe: www.ippr.org/juncture/democracy-at-a-ttiping-point-seizing-a-slim-chance-to-reassert-democratic-sovereignty-in-europe

to be seen as social or quasi-social institutions and in which corporate governance was, to a degree at least, "socialized". It began an era in which the pursuit of "shareholder value" has come to dominate and the corporate interest has come once more seen to be seen as more or less synonymous with shareholder interest.[202] In these circumstances it is not only appropriate but necessary to *re-personify* corporate power and recognize it as power that is being exercised largely on behalf and in the interests of the financial elite that owns the great majority of corporate shares. Crucially, this elite now shapes how much investment occurs, in what sectors and in what locations, exercising enormous power over the material resources that are the lifeblood of society. It possesses what Winters calls "resource control".[203] What we have seen in recent decades, then, is not a Keynesian euthanasia of the *rentier* but a resurgence of *rentier* power.[204]

Collectively, the various groups that make up this elite represent a new aristocracy of finance. Operating in liberalized global financial markets, increasingly transnationally integrated, with no loyalty to place or community, they are able to exert power over governments and societies as well as over corporations. This has contributed not only to the reassertion of shareholder primacy and emergence of highly financialized and productively damaging forms of corporate governance, but also to growing income and wealth inequalities, financial speculation and instability, spiraling government debt, economic stagnation, and depleted and diminished democracies. Moreover, as we have seen, measures are being taken to try to entrench this power by providing financial property with quasi-constitutional protections and by setting liberalized financial (and other) markets in stone. At the present conjuncture, therefore, we need to engage not only in a re-personification of corporate power but in a more general process of re-personifying power. We need to look behind the separate personhood of "the corporation", behind the reified and de-personified forms taken by financial property and behind the seemingly impersonal forces of "the market". We need to stop "seeing through" these forms in the sense of using them as our eyes on the world, and to start "seeing through" them in the sense of penetrating them to bring into sharper focus the people and social relations underlying them.[205] Indeed, it is, one suspects, in part because of the light it threatens to cast on the social relations hidden behind wealth, and particularly financial wealth, that Piketty's book has met with such hostility from certain quarters. As the court in *Howey* observed, the revenues attracted by financial property are not the magical autonomous products of money: They come from the "efforts of others".

Challenging the entrenched power of this financial elite will not be easy, but it is important to remember that the (re-)emergence of global finance and global financial markets is, like the rise of joint-stock corporation, double edged. On one hand, it represents – and potentially pushes in the direction of – ever greater financialization, facilitating the continuing and growing private appropriation of productive surpluses. On the other hand, it is also an expression of the growing global integration of production and international division of labor – in other words, of growing "socialization" – and has the capacity to push still further in this direction in the future. This point is underlined by Jean-Philippe Robé in this volume. As he says, the modern corporate capitalist economy is a "market economy"

202 Some would, of course dispute whether the kind of (short-term) financialized governance that has emerged really operates for the (long-term) benefits of shareholders. They would argue that it represents unenlightened, rather than enlightened shareholder value.

203 Jeffrey A. Winters, *Power in Motion*, Ithaca: Cornell University Press (1996), p. 7.

204 The *rentier* has made "a powerful comeback": See Streeck, *supra* note 153, p. 77.

205 This is what Marx might have called "de-fetishisation".

in a limited sense only, for much of the international trade that is seen as the hallmark of globalization actually takes place between the corporations that make up the large multinational enterprises that dominate so much productive activity. It is intra-enterprise trade that is coordinated and regulated not by markets but by administrative planning. As Robé says, these enterprises – whose existence is barely recognized by law – use markets (and, indeed, create them) when it suits them, as when they are trying to reduce their labor costs and tax bills. They use and manipulate the corporate legal form and separate legal personality in a similar fashion.[206] What we have is what Hilferding might have called an "antagonistic" or "fraudulent" type of socialization.

It is also important to remember that the institutional arrangements that currently prevail – including the dominance of finance – are not the inevitable products of some all-powerful, irresistible, universal, market-based, beneficent, purely economic logic. As we have seen, historically the tensions between the socializing and financializing tendencies inherent in the corporation, with its detached hybrid owner-creditor shareholders, have been resolved in different ways at different times. These different outcomes have been determined as much by political decisions and their impact on prevailing institutional arrangements as they have by the economic logic of either capitalism or the market. These institutional arrangements are as much determinative of the economic logic and dynamic of societies as they are determined by them. Just as the first financial hegemony of the late nineteenth and early twentieth centuries was in significant part a product of the way that the corporate legal form was legally and politically constructed to accommodate and protect *rentier* investors, so the gradual drift towards more socialized corporations and governance was rooted in the inability of dispersed *rentier* shareholders effectively to exercise their residual control rights. This contributed to the mid-twentieth century reduction in inequality identified by Piketty and others. As we have seen, during this period, radical reform of the corporate legal form was mooted not implemented. We are now paying the price for the failure to grasp this nettle. In recent decades, the reconcentration of financial property owners in institutions, together with the liberalization of financial markets and enhancements to their rights (free movement, quasi-constitutional protections), has seen *rentiers* reassert the power conferred by their property rights with a vengeance. The mantra of "shareholder value maximization" may have lost some of its lustre since the crash, but there are few signs that corporate practices have significantly changed: The maximization of shareholder value may not be what the law requires, but it is still what "the markets" press managers to deliver.[207]

If the way in which the financial oligarchy has ridden the crash and emerged almost unscathed has made its power seem unchallengeable, we should not forget the peculiarities and vulnerabilities of the intangible financial property upon which this power is based. Its legal and institutional base is surprisingly fragile and contingent. Despite the efforts of supportive intellectuals to naturalize these institutional arrangements, to depict them as flowing from "ownership", or to make them seem like the outcomes of efficiency-enhancing economic forces rather than of political power, existing corporate rights-obligations structures are hard to justify – morally or consequentially. By granting income and control rights to *rentier* shareholders while allowing them to disclaim any responsibility for corporate liabilities or misfeasance, they positively encourage irresponsibility. They are crying out to be challenged, not constitutionally entrenched. Only when we do this can we begin to

206 Jean-Philippe Robé, "Globalization and the Constitutionalization of the World Power System," in this volume.
207 Stout, *supra* note 132; Worthington, *supra* note 55.

formulate viable strategies to loosen the grip of this elite, to eradicate the financialization and domination of enterprise by speculation, to reduce the irresponsibility that characterizes the contemporary corporate system, to resuscitate and revitalize our democracies, to reverse the growing inequalities documented by Piketty and others, and begin to realize the potential the corporation offers for more productive, efficient and socially responsible production.[208] We made these institutions and we can remake them.

208 For a discussion of some of the issues, see Lorraine Talbot, *Great Debates in Company Law,* London: Palgrave Macmillan (2014), chapter 7.

3 Corporate power in the global economy

An evolutionary perspective

Ronen Palan

In a highly influential book published in the early years of the Great Depression, two of Thorstein Veblen's students, Adophe Berle and Gardiner Means, employed his binary analytical framework to analyze the rise of corporate power (Berle & Means, 1932). Veblen distinguished between technological advance and know-how, or "industry" in his words, and the realm of business (Veblen, 1923). Business, he thought, hijacked societal advances and parceled out their benefits parochially, often retarding development by "withholding" innovation from society. Berle and Means argued that development in corporate law in the early twentieth century United States encouraged the further separation of ownership and control of companies. In an analysis that is reminiscent of Robé's work, they argue that corporate personalities formally owns a corporate entities, while shareholders own shares in the entity only and elect directors who control the company's activities. In Robé's words, ultimately no one owns the corporate entity.

Berle, Means, Tugwell and other members of first Roosevelt administration "brain trust" were not anti-business per se; their mission was to try to reform laws and policies to direct business energies towards societal goals. They understood that juridical reforms and not only regulatory amendments were key to their efforts. Post–second World War economics has abandoned, or so it appears, the historical work and reform-minded approach of the old school of evolutionary economics of Veblen and Commons and the principles of long-term economics in favor of the neoclassical synthesis that combines Keynes' short-term policy prescriptions within an orthodox framework. In doing so, it gave up on the essential tools of juridical and constitutional reforms.

It is perhaps not an accident that the project on constitutionalism returns to those "old" perennial questions that were hotly debated during the Depression era, on the role of enterprises and power. Like the old school of institutionalism, the project starts from a rigorous analysis of the legal foundations of the firm in order to pursue normative goals. The ultimate goal, as Christian Chavagneux observed in a previous meeting of the contributors to this volume at the Collège de Bernardins, amounts to nothing less than "rebooting" twenty-first economics and releasing it from its self-imposed shackles of the twentieth century's unfortunate synthesis.

I have a lot of sympathy with many of the core propositions of this project, which I understand as follows:

1 An international economy that traverses diverse sovereign territories behaves very differently from the world of abstract economics. Such an understanding is a defining characteristic of an approach that is called "international political economy".
2 The corporate world is having a decisive influence over an international system of opportunities, penalties and rewards. But conventional disciplinary arrangements of

politics, economics, law and the like are ill prepared to analyze corporate power in the international system.

3 A rigorous legal analysis of the nature and character of the actors in the world economy is an essential prerequisite for an analysis of their power and systemic influence of corporations and business.

4 Paradoxically, one of the mainstay of corporate power originates in the discrepancy between the "legal personality" corporate forms that are located within territorial boundaries of sovereign States, and economic personality of the firm, which consists of a string of companies located in various jurisdictions. That economic and strategic planning entity is often described confusingly as the "multinational enterprise", but it does not have clear status in law.

5 The articulation of international norms, laws and conventions that combines the fiction of the Westphalian State System with the fiction of the legal personality of the company amounts to a form of constitutionalization of the world economy that sustains power discrepancies, the growing gap between rich and poor, and the globally exploitative system.

This chapter discusses two important implications of the study of human expectations to the project on constitutionalism. First, I argue that Robé's distinction between the legality of the corporation and the economic logic of the firm has a very material consequence in the "real" world. It has emerged as a core tactical instrument of corporate tax avoidance and hence a core technique of power and control. Second, I argue that the theory of ownership – or rather the theory of lack of ownership of corporate personalities that emerges from this project – would lead us to question the stress that this project is placing on the firm as the locus of economic logic. The firm, I argue, is an intermediate institutional structure as well that is used by groups of people, which I call "controlling interests", whose legal obligation and a sense of social responsibility is even less well defined. I also argue with Veblen's notion of absentee owner and replace it with a concept of the absentee controller. The firm as an intermediate unit may serve certain logistical and organizational purposes, but the locus of the economic logic lies typically with individuals and families that use these firms as leverage for income-stream purposes. These are entirely beyond the regulatory realm.

1. OIE and corporate power

Capitalism is a decentralized system of resource allocation, leaving crucial decisions over savings and investments to private enterprises. Economic theories from Adam Smith onward provided a theoretical rationale for such system, but as enterprises grew in size to become large monopolies – many of which are controlled by powerful individual or families – the original logic of "classical" theories of economics appears less convincing. Corey, for instance, calculates that during the 1920s the J.P. Morgan group controlled about 26% of US assets, while the Rockefeller family controlled approximately 18% of the rest. In these circumstances, any theory that is predicated on the assumption that an economy that consists of a multitude of producers are competing for the favors of a multitude of consumers is unlikely to correspond with the observable world.

The question, then, becomes one of political economy: whether and how concentrated financial and economic power shapes the environment to advance its interests, and whether power concentration produces adverse systemic effects, such as lower economic growth, higher frequency of financial and economic crisis and so on. One line of research has tended to concentrate on the capacity of concentrated power to manipulate politicians or the political system to their own advantage, but this approach is of limited value to systemic theories, not least because economic groups are usually in competition with one another and often employ their political power one against the other (although they tend to unify against organized labor). Systemic theories or theories of long term economic growth have tended, instead, to challenge the assumption and methodologies of classical and neoclassical economics.

Among those, a school of thought known as "old institutional economics" (OIE), sometimes described as "the school of economics and law", has been particularly influential. OIE scholars strongly objected to the "scientific" turn in economics towards linear time frames. In John R. Commons' words, economics and political science are sciences of human expectation and hence are ultimately historical, as opposed to theories that emulate the sciences that have no intrinsic interest in the individual events of concrete reality.[1] Key ingredients in the science of human expectations are historically learned "habits of thought", rule-bounded behavior and expectation of future gains (or losses).

This approach helps to explain an important facet of corporate or economic power: the uncanny ability of economic power to arbitrate rule-bound environments to its benefit so that those rules that benefit economic power – such as ownership and control that is fully backed by the power of the State – are enforced (and in that sense economic power is leveraged), whereas rules that were devised to sustain State power but which are seen as costs, such as taxation and regulation, are avoided. To achieve that, economic power must be visible to those rules that benefit it, and at the same time invisible, to the extent that is possible, to those rules that do not.

2. The firm and the four dimensions of the sovereign space

Demsetz (1988) notes that classical theory was less concerned with competition, as often it is often thought, and more with decentralized order, which it opposes to the familiar order of its day (eighteenth century): centralized or top-down order. As a result, classical theory never developed a theory of the firm. A default position has evolved whereby firms are treated as utility-maximizing actors that respond to the price system. The theory works on the general principles of so-called *homo economicus*, a utility-maximizing individual, and assumes that corporate entities are instruments established to further advanced individual utility, and in addition, (at least until Coase), that the legal niceties of such incorporation laws and norms would be handled somehow instrumentally by those individuals.

It is generally believed that these utility-maximizing actors are profit oriented and would seek either to maximize profits or at the very least "beat the average" profitability in their respective sectors – but theory does not pay sufficient attention to the differences between the concepts of pre-tax and post-tax profit. The presumption is that pre- and post-tax positions are closely correlated, only that the post-tax position of an entity is simply its pre-tax minus the necessary tax that is paid to government. Post-tax profit can, in this perspective,

1 Commons was clearly influenced by Webber, Rickert and the debate on the difference between science and the social sciences that took place in late nineteenth century Germany. Oakes describes Rickert's position as follows: "Natural science is nomothetic. It has no intrinsic interest in the individual events of concrete reality. On the contrary, the individual datum is relevant to natural science only to the extent that it can be represented as a type. The interest of historical science, on the other hand, is idiographic. Here the purpose of knowledge is to comprehend the distinctive properties of the unique events itself. History is interested in a phenomenon not because of what it shares with other phenomena but, rather, because of its own definitive qualities" (Oakes, 1988, p. 44).

and given known statutory tax rates, be read off the pre-tax position. Since pre-tax and post-tax profits are behaviorally the same, they can be treated for all intent and purposes in the same way.

A third related of assumptions of orthodox thought relates to the boundaries between the national and the international sphere. Utility-maximizing firms do not care about national borders or the nationality of their locations, registrations or employees. National boundaries are simply facts of life that firms need to adapt to. From the firm's perspective, they are often seen as hindrance or "extra" costs. Firms would seek to locate wherever their market is, and would try and adapt to local conditions to the best they can. The assumption seems to be that transactions that directly or indirectly have cross-border implications are both marginal and do not affect the basic structure or goal of the firm.

This view, if it were ever true, is increasingly obsolete. As businesses operate in a world of notionally separate States, each with different treatments of different assets and income streams, the "bottom line", for companies, for all intents and purposes, is their post-tax position in the jurisdictions in which they operate. As businesses increasingly operate across multiple jurisdictional spaces (either directly or indirectly) they can and do structure their corporate organization, costs, expenses and financial transfers in such way as to minimize taxation. In conventional accounts, the world of States consists of political entities that are in control of landed territories, including adjacent waters, each of which are sovereign independent States and have a right to regulate businesses located, domiciled or licensed in their territories as well as to levy tax on them. From an international businesses perspective, the world consists of easily traversed diverging sovereign platforms, each of which offers a distinct bundle of regulatory, taxation and market attributes. There are no particular reasons why business would tend to ensure that activities are recorded, and hence tax is paid where income accrues, costs incurred or profits are made. On the contrary, business would aim to structure activities in such way that profits accumulate where tax is minimal, while expenses are recorded where subsidies and deductions are maximized. Tax is therefore integral to evaluating a spread, or how much above a risk-free rate a product must return. Modern systems of taxation have developed on the basis of a relatively simple world where corporeal property is exchanged in the provision of goods and services, where costs and income accrues and corporate entities have a recognizable national home. Taxation is typically levied on an entity at the point of assumed completion of the series of transactions (where the good or services are delivered). But two changes to economic activity have changed these assumptions. First, the growth of services sector activity has meant that more and more economic exchange occurs in or is based around incorporeal property, and these activities make locational, ownership and valuation issues far more fungible and mobile. Second, in the inherently incorporeal world of finance and commerce, these simple attributes of ownership, location and forms of capital can be unbundled, rearranged and relocated to achieve one of the following.

This is of course all well known, but the underlying principles for such behavior is not very well understood. As a result a gulf had emerged between theory that assumes that competition leads to ever-increasing efficiency in production and organization, and the practice of the corporate world that appears to invest considerable resources in activities, such as tax minimization, that do not seem to support the hypothesis.

In contrast to mainstream theory, OIE theory is highly legalistic in orientation. It centers, as Commons argued, on the concept of the transaction, or the point of exchange of property titles that may, or may not, be accompanied by an exchange of goods or services. Economic transactions take place, argues Commons, simultaneously in two spheres: the sphere of actual delivery of goods or services, and a legal sphere where the transfer of ownership takes place (Commons, 1959 [1924]). Crucially, OIE maintains that the latter determines the former. An economic analysis of the business world should start, therefore, with a rigorous analysis of the forms of transfers that are taking place, and of course, of the nature of legal nature of the contracting parties, in this case, corporations and firms. Such an analysis yields a different set of generalization of the corporate world.

The project at hand does exactly that: It is founded on the idea that the conventional view of firms in economic studies tends to conflate the ownership structures of assets (the capital) with institutions (such as multinational corporations) and furthermore conflates legal institutions (corporations) with economic units (firms). In the word of Robé,

> corporations are apart among the legal instruments used to legally structure firms. The reason for this is that they are treated by the legal systems as if they were "real" persons (with some adaptations), i.e. they can participate in the legal systems through the phenomenon of "juridical personality". They can own property, have debts, contract, sue and be sued in courts, get bankrupt, etc. – i.e. they can "function" in the economy like human beings because they are treated by the legal system as if they were "persons".
>
> (Robé, 2011, 11)

As "legal personalities", corporations are licensed by a sovereign entity to operate within an imagined four-dimensional national territorial space. The national space is four-dimensional because it contains the three physical dimensions of space (countries have a depth and a defined height, in additional to their territorial coverage) and it also defined in law, the a fourth dimension,. Crucially, different countries define that fourth dimension differently. In other words, countries project their sovereignty into a notional legal space that is conceived differently by different countries. As a result the projection of territorial sovereignty is not universal, giving rise to all sorts of loopholes and blind spots that are taken advantage of. Differences in conceptions of the fourth dimension of national space open the door to regulatory and fiscal arbitrage.

3. The legal foundation of the firm and tax avoidance

Robé insists that the economic unit, which may or may not operate through different jurisdictions, is not the corporation but an entity that he defines as "the firm". This is not a legal definition of the firm, but perhaps a convention that I am happy to adopt. Firms that wish to operate internationally must by their very nature organize themselves as a string of legal entities or corporations united through series of contractual relationships, some of which are visible and some not. Modern firms consist of many such corporations, at times numbering in the thousands. These firms are clearly important economic actors, but strictly speaking, they lack legal existence. In other words, legally speaking, there is no such thing as a "multinational corporation".

There is, therefore, a discrepancy between the legal status of the corporation and economic agency of the firm, a discrepancy that is viewed as of little consequence in standard economics – or the economics that does not distinguish between pre-tax and post-tax profit situations. But in the world of taxation, or the "real" world of economic action – a world that is concerned primarily with post-tax positions – the discrepancy has proven to be crucial and serves as the mainstay of so-called legal corporate tax avoidance. This important distinction between the legal corporation and the economic firm has been at the heart of my interpretation of the rise of the offshore world, with current aggregate financial assets estimated at between US$ 25–30 trillion. In essence, tax minimization techniques exploit a blind spot in revenues surveillance techniques that results from the differences between the economic control of firms and the legal foundations of territorially bounded companies. On one hand, companies are bound by national rules and regulations, and if those are shown to be duly observed, they are sufficient to raise companies above legal suspicions. Firms, on the other hand, are organizations that are put together by accountants, typically one of the Big Four accounting firms (Deloitte, PwC, Ernst and Young, KPMG), as strings of companies registered in different locations. Most household names firms typically span a number of territories and are used to link companies from different jurisdictions in such a way as to minimize their overall tax footprint. All the evidence suggests that considerable resources are spent on tax avoidance – and indeed, many corporate entities are created for no other purpose. The business of setting up such structures is highly profitable, estimated recently by a United Kingdom parliamentary committee to turn over US$ 55 billion.

Let us take the example of Apple Inc. The following is taken from a detailed study by the Levin Congressional Committee. It appears that Apple has created three offshore corporations that receive tens of billions of dollars in income, but that have no tax residence – neither in Ireland, where they are incorporated, nor in the United States, where the Apple executives who run them are located.

> Apple has arranged matters so that it can claim that these ghost companies, for tax purposes, exist nowhere. One has paid no corporate income tax to any nation for the last 5 years; another pays tax to Ireland equivalent to a tiny fraction of 1 percent of its total income.
>
> (The Permanent Subcomittee on Investigations, 2013, 3)

One of Apple's shell companies is Apple Operations International (AOI). AOI directly or indirectly owns most of Apple's other offshore entities. On one hand, under Irish law only companies that are managed and controlled in Ireland are considered Irish residents for tax purposes. Since AOI is incorporated – but not managed or controlled – in Ireland, it does not count as an Irish tax resident. Under US law, on the other hand, a company is generally taxed on the basis of where it is incorporated, not where it is managed and controlled. Since AOI is not incorporated in the United States, it is not tax resident in the United States either. AOI, therefore, is tax resident nowhere. In fact, AOI has no employees, either.

The second corporate shell set up by Apple in Ireland is Apple Sales International (ASI). ASI holds the economic rights to Apple intellectual property rights outside of the United States. From 2009 to 2012, its sales income amounted to US$74 billion. Similarly to AOI, the company is incorporated in Ireland but operated from the United States. ASI paid only a minimal amount of tax to Ireland. For example, in 2011 it paid US$10 million against US$22 billion in revenue. Apple's third subsidiary, Apple Operations Europe (AOE), sits between ASI and AOI. It, too, has no tax home.

Not unlike many firms of its kind, Apple is taking advantage of discrepancies in incorporation and tax residency rules between different countries. In other words, the United States and Ireland maintain divergent positions of their territorial boundaries in the fourth dimension discussed earlier. This divergence is arbitrated by Apple to achieve a rare and highly sought after position of having virtually no residence for tax purposes. Compared with more sophisticated techniques used by other household names, this is one of the simplest schemes of tax minimization, but one that makes full use of multi-jurisdictional tax arbitrage. Needless to say, it is all legal.

Legal techniques of tax arbitrage are taking advantage, therefore, of the discrepancy between the legal foundation of the corporation, the economic logic of the firm and the divergent projection of sovereign rules into the fourth dimension. Rather than view the discrepancy between the legal personality of the corporation and the economic rationale of the firm as a problem, firms have learned to take advantage by rearranging their legal presence in such way as to minimize taxation.

4. Ownership and control

Another important factor in the institutional makeup of contemporary capitalism was the innovations of the limited liability company, and more specifically, the holding company. The holding company was an innovation that took place more or less concomitantly in two separate countries in the late nineteenth century, the United States and the Netherlands. Further deregulation of corporate control took place in 1889, when New Jersey allowed the facility of company ownership of other companies. These institutional innovations produced an institutional infrastructure of corporate control that encouraged great concentration of capital funds of many investors under the control and management of small groups. Furthermore – and this is crucial to understanding the nature of modern capitalism – controlling groups typically have small stakes compared to the capital under management and control. In effect, these institutional structures serve, therefore, to leverage control under pyramidal structures.

There is barely conceptual literature on the holding company. An important exception is a study by Bonbright and Means published in 1932 (Bonbright & Means, 1932) as part of the background information of the Roosevelt administration brain trust. Bonbright and Means take note of the quick expansion in use of holding companies in the late 1920s. They argue:

> The public significance of the holding company, as distinct from the simple business corporation is twofold. In the first place, the holding company is the most effective device that has ever been invented for combining under a single control and management the properties of two or more hitherto independent corporations . . . holding company, perhaps more than any other legal device, is being used by business men as a means of avoiding various forms of social control.
>
> (Bonbright & Means, 1932, 5–6)

They continue,

> partly because it is protected from interference by our traditions of constitutional law, and partly because it often extends beyond the jurisdiction of any one state, the holding company has so far been largely, though not completely, exempt from the restrictions to which other business corporations have been subject.
>
> (Bonbright & Means, 1932, 6)

The holding company has a place of honor in the offshore world. It is the mainstay business of the offshore sectors of Ireland, Luxembourg, the Netherlands, joined now by a whole host of others such as Malta, the Cayman Islands and the like.

The pervasive use of the facility of the holding company leads to me to question the supposed centrality of the firm, as the economic unit, in this project's analysis. Indeed, we find a more complex typology of "actors" in modern capitalism that consists of corporations, firms, shareholders and what I would call "controlling interests". The concept of economic logic lies with this elusive controlling interest, which may prefer at times to sacrifice whole firms in support of its goals.

Robé follows Berle and Mean in differentiating between share ownership and corporate ownership. He argues that:

> shareholders do not own *firms* and nor do they own *corporations*: they own *shares* issued by corporations. The shareholders enjoy the privileges of the owner towards what they own: the shares. They don't and can't have these privileges towards the corporation having issued the shares. They own neither corporations nor firms; no one does.
>
> (Robé, 2011, 4)

In this analysis, there are two reasons to own shares, and each leads towards very distinct behavior. The first reason is to have access to any rise in share value and/or dividends. The second is to have seats on the firm's board in other to influence the firm's behavior.

If share ownership was traditionally intended to achieve the first goal – access to rise in share value and/or dividends – then, in time, business logic dictated against ownership. Ownership is an intermediate step towards speculative "investment" that has many disadvantages. It may be cumbersome in the sense that one has to pay brokerage fees, profit making is aligned with rise in share value and ownership "locks" money in less-liquid assets. In addition, many countries impose capital tax on increases in share value. But "investors" are interested in making profit, not in owning companies, and they prefer to make profits from both the rise and fall in the value of shares.

Firms, in turn, have shareholders who may be located in many jurisdictions in the world. There is a tendency now for a certain class of share ownerships to be "owned" for very short times (down to seconds or milliseconds) due to techniques such as high-frequency trading. Indeed, trade in stocks and shares has spawned its own – and far larger in terms of volume – parallel world of trading (or betting) on share movements (known as "financial derivatives"). For that purpose, a parallel world of financial derivatives has emerged, worth notionally in excess of US$600 trillion nowadays.

Clearly, the concept of "ownership" in these cases is a legacy term that does not capture what is going on. Investors in stock are not interested in property ownership as it is normally understood. This also shows that the relationship between ownership and profit making is not as straightforward as assumed.

Share ownership for the second goal is different altogether. It suggests that focusing on the firm may be misleading as well. Whereas economists are fond of concepts such as Pareto optimality, supply and demand curves, marginal utility and efficiency, business speaks in a language that is more familiar to students of international relations (like myself): the language of battles and war. Business literature is replete with military terms such as "tactics" and "strategy", "attack", "defense", "control", "competitive alliances", "secret negotiations" and so on.

A key strategy in this war is the use of leverage and pyramidal structures. The technique can work as follows (I am presenting the simplest structure): Let us take a firm, Firm A, currently capitalized at US$10 billion. Controlling interests can purchase 51% of shares in the company, or US$5 billion, to achieve control over the entire company (or a leverage of 1:2). Controlling interests can then create a holding company, Company B, preferably in the Netherlands or Ireland for tax purposes, and sell half of the shares of the of the US$5 billion holding company so that it maintains only 51% in that holding company. The controlling interests can also issue bonds, for say, US$3 billion in Company B, and then sell nearly US$1 billion of the holding company's stock in the market. At this stage, those controlling interests have invested effectively US$1 billion in order to control in effect a US$10 billion enterprise. They can then create another layer with another holding company, Company C, that may dilute holding by a factor of ten. By this stage, the three-tier pyramidal structure has a leverage of holding that reaches 1 × 100. Israel is now introducing laws to limit pyramidal structures to three tiers, down from the six or seven tiers that are the more typical of its oligarchic interests.

Such pyramidal structures are very common and serve to leverage control over great amounts of capital, combined with minimal investment. Although there is scant research on the subject, all the evidence suggests that firms, even very large firms, are sometimes used as pawns or "cash cows" by controlling interests in order to maintain such pyramidal structures. The firm may have an interest in survival, as economists believe, but controlling interests may have a different set of strategies and tactics that may, or may not, benefit the firm in the long run.

The analysis suggests that the powerful "actors" in the business world are neither firms nor corporations, nor even the majority of fleeting owners of various corporate structures, but the somewhat amorphous and legally confusing groups that I describe as "controlling ownership structures". These controlling ownership structures tend to operate through pyramidal share ownerships that are used to leverage their power within the corporate world. Such ownership structures are often in control of a great many firms, let alone corporations, and may choose to exercise their power through one legal unit controlling the rest (holding companies), or may devise complex sets of controlling units, located in various tax havens.

The result is a constitutional arrangement that is potentially very problematic for a number of related reasons:

1 Financial derivatives in effect severed the link between growth and profitability in the financial system (Wigan). As one can make money from shorting the market or a company, modern finance does not rely directly on economic growth.
2 Pyramidal structures sever the link between a production unit and its health. The assumption that the firm seeks to maximize utility or profit is no longer tenable.
3 The corporate world operates through a string of jurisdictions for tax avoidance purposes.

5. Conclusion

The direction that capitalism has taken in the twentieth is not necessarily one of increased concentration of ownership over assets, as is often assumed, but of concentration of control over existing or potential income streams and capitalization of future profits. Ownership can be seen as a double-edged sword: It brings certain benefits, but combines them with certain responsibilities. It makes business sense to try to hold on to the former without the latter.

Bibliography

Atkinson, G. (2009). Going Concerns, Futurity and Reasonable Value, *Journal of Economic Issues*, XLIII(2), pp. 433–441.

Berle, A. A. & G. C. Means (1932). *The Modern Corporation and Private Property*, New York: Macmillan.

Bonbright, J. C. & G. C. Means (1932). *The Holding Company: Its Public Significance and Regulation*, New York: McGrew Hill.

Commons, J. (1961). *Institutional Economics*, Madison: University of Wisconsin Press.
Commons, J. R. (1959 [1924]). *The Legal Foundations of Capitalism*, Madison: The University of Wisconsin Press.
Demestz, H. (1988). The Theory of the Firm Revisited, *Journal of Law, Economics & Organization*, 4(1), pp. 141–161.
Palan, R., R. Murphy & C. Chavagneux (2010). *Tax Havens: How Globalization Really Works*, Ithaca: Cornell University Press.
The Permanent Subcomittee on Investigations (2013). *Offshore Proft Shifting and the US Tax Code – Part 2 (Apple Inc.)*, Washington, DC: US Congress.
Veblen, T. (1923). *Absentee Ownership and Business Enterprise in Recent Times. The Case of America*, Boston: Beacon Press.
Weichenrieder, A. J. & J. Mintz (2007). *What Determines the Use of Holding Companies and Ownership Chains?*, Oxford: Oxford University Center for Business Taxation.

4 Powers and responsibilities in multimember organizations

Elsa Peskine and Stéphane Vernac

The development of the means of exercising power within organizations is challenging State law. For a long time focused on legal entities, State laws have been unable to grasp most of the manifestations of power in private organizations. This neglect has strengthened the independence and sovereignty of these powers, which take advantage of the borders between legal entities and between States.

Understanding how private powers emerge and overseeing these powers more effectively, is the perspective offered by the theory of constitutionalization of private powers. This school of thought assumes changing intellectual and institutional references.

On one hand, private powers should no longer be tied only to a person or a subject of law and to a single territorial and state framework. They are formed precisely where the law does not tackle them head-on, either because private powers are ignored by the law or because powers develop in the cracks of the law, such as partitioning between States, legal entities or branches of the law. On the other hand, alongside the State reference – the creation of a global State or a world constitution – micro-systems specifying the means for assigning responsibility reflect a change of reference.

This change of reference can be seen through the emergence of what we might call a "law of the organization". The law of the organization reflects a change in the perception of power and in the instruments for governance of these powers. Power is no longer ostracized, for it becomes itself an instrument of regulation. This regulation is not only State-based, since the organization is itself a creator of standards. In doing so, in order to control the exercise of these powers, the law of the organization enables State and private standards to be combined, or even to go as far as dispensing with the partitioning of State borders and branches of the law.

In many ways, observing the mechanisms of responsibility in employment law provides a particularly striking illustration of the first manifestations of this subtle change in reference and the development of a law of the organization. How does employment law tackle the various manifestations of power relating to employees? How does it organize the assignation of responsibilities when the employer is part of an organization?

Under French employment law, the category of employer can be used to identify both the party to the contract, the holder of specific managerial powers and someone who is obliged to comply with employment law.

Traditionally, only the employer is liable for obligations under employment law, excluding any other company within the group.[1] French judges have taken into account the development

1 Cass. Soc. January 13, 2010, 08–15.776, *Recueil Dalloz,* 2010. 1129, note B. Dondero; ibid. 2029, obs. J. Pélissier, M.-C. Amauger-Lattes, A. Arseguel, T. Aubert-Monpeyssen, P. Fadeuilhe, B. Lardy-Pélissier & B. Reynès,

of groups by redefining the space within which the employer's obligations are assessed. For example, the obligation of an employer to redeploy employees made redundant for economic reasons is implemented within a scope that extends beyond that of the contractual relationship: the group.[2] Other scopes are sometimes retained: The reason for the dismissal is assessed in light of what is known today by way of the business sector.

Therefore, although the independence of legal entities does not act as a barrier when redefining the spaces within which more extensive rights may be assessed, it does constitute an obstacle to any change in the model for assigning responsibility. Indeed, considering the employer as a point for assigning responsibility has reduced the latter to a sort of black box, even though it is shaped, influenced or even determined by other legal relationships with shareholders, backers, corporations, corporate officers and investors.[3] The employer is a legal personality – a natural person or legal entity – and capable, as such, of concluding contracts, forming capitalist relationships and being part of an organization.

The consequence of portraying employers in this way is the rejection, outside of the employment relationship, of relationships forged by the employer and of the effects of decisions taken by a group company or any other complex organization, which nevertheless are likely to affect employees.

However, change is under way, brought about by legal challenges, proposals for laws and academic research. Far from being outdated, there are now a number of improved pathways that allow employees of one company to find someone in another company within the same organization to take on certain obligations. The gap between the unitary assignment of responsibility and the sophistication of employer's organizational techniques means that we must redesign the traditional analytical framework. Faced with a group of companies or more generally a complex organization, the employment relationship can no longer be considered independently from the company power relationship that unites the employer with a third party. Furthermore, a new organization model undoubtedly emerges. This is formed by the interconnection of two legal relationships, a legal employment relationship between the employee and the employer and a legal corporate governance relationship, or more generally power relationships between two or more corporate legal entities, where one is the employer of the employee. The boundaries between internal and external relationships, traditionally defined by those of the legal entity, are therefore blurred. This does not mean that the employment relationship must be dependent on corporate relations and consequently on corporate law, but it must now rely on the corporate relationship to produce certain effects.

The development of the methods for assigning responsibility and the related thinking on organizations reflects a change of reference. In order to lift the veil of legal personality, conventional governance of inter-company relations requires that an abnormality is found in the power exercised by one company over another. The independence of the legal personality of the employer is infringed to such an extent that assigning obligations to the author of the infringement is admitted. However, this abnormality-based regulation, besides the fact that it does not tackle more decentralized types of organizations, falls short when it comes up against normalized powers in corporate groups. Indeed, this normalization leads, inexorably,

Revue de droit du travail p. 230 (2010), obs. F. Géa, *Droit social.* p. 774 (2010), obs. G. Couturier; see also, E. Serverin & T. Grumbach, "La saga Flodor", *Revue de droit du travail*, p. 693 (2009).

2 Art. L. 1233–4 of the French Labor Code.

3 S. Vernac, *Le pouvoir d'organisation. Au croisement du droit du travail et du droit des sociétés*, Thesis, Université Paris Ouest Nanterre La Défense (2012) (éditions LGDJ, forthcoming).

to the quasi-impossibility of regulating any abnormal exercise of power by a group company or any other legal party in the group. What emerges little by little is another mode of accountability for companies or decision makers in the organization that takes into account the inter-company power relationship independently of the excesses it reveals and is accompanied by a distribution of obligations to each of the parties involved. Note is therefore taken of a form of sophistication of the inter-company power relationships and of the fact that powers must be identified, regardless of its content and who wields it. More generally, these are the first steps towards what might constitute a genuine employment law of the organization. Produced by the connections between power, by their interlocking and their interdependence, the organization becomes a useful reference to regulate the supervisory power that structures it. It therefore allows understanding structured groups having changing boundaries, in particular, corporate groups or networks. The ruling of abnormal exercise of power (I), gradually complemented by the construction and juxtaposition of a law of the organization are (II) reveal a constitutionalization of private powers.

1. The law of abnormal exercise of power

Cases involving group companies are traditionally based on the sanction of the abnormal exercise of power exercised by a company over the management of the employer company (A). Today, this runs into an obstacle because the limits of abnormality have shifted (B).

A. The abnormal exercise of power

Two techniques may be deployed. The first is based on the misuse of power (1). The second requires the characterization of excess power (2).

1. Assignment and misuse of powers

Companies within a group are sometimes held liable for misconduct. The misconduct most commonly involves the age-old technique of misuse of power, consisting of the use of powers by their holder "for a purpose other than that for which they had been bestowed".[4] Strategies used by the groups to manipulate bankruptcy laws and employment laws are sanctioned. Imposing cessation of payments upon its subsidiary certainly allows the parent company to organize covering the social costs of restructuring[5] – granting salaries payment – whilst also creating an economic reason for redundancies.[6] In addition to manipulating and controlling motives, the misconduct also stems from the adverse consequences of the decision of a shareholder in the employer company.[7]

4 See, already in administrative law, Council of state November 24, 1875, Pariset, *Grands arrêts de la Jurisprudence Administrative*, no 1.

5 See in particular C. Parès, "Controverse: Cessation d'activité: l'immixtion du juge est-elle excessive?", *Revue de droit du travail*, p. 285 (2011).

6 A judgement of the court of appeal of Versailles on October 31, 2011 in a famous case, *Klarius*, delivered a perfect illustration of this strategy: The judges considered the cessation of activity of the subsidiary to only be a result of "strategic choices decided at group level" and "the deliberate will of the group companies to abandon the subsidiary" (Court of Appeal, Versailles, October 31, 2011, *Klarius*, Répertoire général n° 10/00578).

7 Such was the case in the judgements given on April 8, 2014 (Court of Cassation, social Chamber, April 8, 2014, 13–15.573 and 13–15470). The French Supreme Court noted that the decision was in the interests of the sole

Despite the success of liability claims, this action involves limits.[8] The false modernity on which these actions rely deserves to be remembered. Although liability claims have the virtue of authorizing employee claims against a company that cannot be characterized as co-employer, they actually presuppose highlighting the motives of the parent company[9] and allow ruling certain "borderline cases" only, for which the basic rules of morality[10] have been forgotten.[11] Above all, liability claims for misconduct do not avoid the need to search and identify the actual decision of the dominant company that led to the prejudice, unlike co-employment, which authorizes the action whenever exists a control by the parent company of the structure of its subsidiary.

2. *Assignment and excess of power*

Fraud and the fictitiousness of a company have formed the first manifestations of excess of power. These categories of corporate law have influenced judges, at least in the first instance, and have helped them in employment cases to exceed the independence of legal entities. Co-employment provides another exemplary illustration of this. By the requirement of an intermingling of interests, activities and leadership, it is in fact the loss of independence of the employer's legal entity that is required by the French Supreme Court so that a situation of co-employment might be established. This requirement is the result of various findings.

In the first place, the requirement of a loss of independence of the legal entity is reflected in an intermingling of interests. This appears less of an operational and independent criterion, and treated as such, and more of a justification for the abuse of legal personality[12] since, in precise terms, the independence of a legal entity assumes on the contrary that it follows a personal interest.[13] The judges go so far as to describe an employer company deprived of full independence as a "simple establishment . . . without real financial and management independence".[14] Co-employment thus condemns interference leading to the total loss of independence of a legal entity. Indeed, it is the abuse of the legal entity that must be characterized.[15] The result of a statement of co-employment then comes naturally enough, the co-employer becoming the debtor *in solidum* of the obligations that, in principle, are incumbent upon the nominal employer.

Second, more than the three-way intermingling, the intermingling of management seems to imply the statement of co-employment. What must therefore be noted is a convergence of evidence characterizing power exercised over the management of the employer company. On one hand, some evidence points to direct interference in employer management decisions, including when a dominant company defines the strategic choices of the employer company, including the termination of business activities. This is also the case when the dominant

shareholder of the employer company, had aggravated economic difficulties for the latter, and contributed to its bankruptcy and the loss of the jobs which resulted from it.

8 A. Fabre, "La responsabilité délictuelle pour faute au secours des salariés victimes d'une société tierce", *Revue de droit du travail*, p. 672 (2014, November).

9 Cass. soc. April, 3 1990, 87–44.904, unpublished, *Revue de jurisprudence sociale,* 1990/5, no. 354.

10 E. Gaillard, *Le pouvoir en droit privé*, preface G. Cornu, Economica, 1985, 202, p. 128.

11 P. Lokiec, "Contrat et pouvoir", *LGDJ*, 2002, in particular n 392. The author notes in addition that this control has long cohabited with the theory of the employer alone determining management decisions.

12 G. Auzero, *Semaine sociale Lamy* 2013, n 1600, p. 8.

13 Ibid.

14 Court of Cassation, Social Chamber, September 28, 2010, n 09–41.243 (unpublished).

15 G. Auzero, "La nature juridique du lien de coemploi", *Semaine sociale Lamy* 1600, p. 8 (2013).

company is responsible for administrative, accounting, financial, commercial, technical and legal management,[16] or even for the management of staff, at the company of the employer.[17] On the other hand, other evidence reveals the manifestations of power exercised over the management structures by the dominant company. For example, the latter sometimes manages recruitment, career development and executive bonuses, and exercises hierarchical control over them.[18] Similarly, the directors of the employer and subsidiary company are sometimes salaried employees of the parent company. In sum, statement of co-employment is only the sanction of the abnormal exercise of power.[19] It may be considered in terms of excess, in terms of deviation.

Controlling the power of the firm by referring to the abnormal exercise of power has now reached its limits, due to the normalization of power in corporate groups.

B. The shifting of the limits of abnormality

Several factors contribute to the phenomenon of normalization of power. First, while it defines the outer limits of abnormal power over the employer, case law recognizes the existence of the normal power of one company over another. It thus limits the characterization of a situation of co-employment by encouraging judges to see this situation as being "beyond the need to coordinate the economic actions of companies belonging to the same group and the economic dominance that this belonging may generate.[20] In other words, the concentration of power, specific to corporate groups, reveals no abnormality. The Court of Cassation recognizes the validity of techniques for delegating powers in groups. It accepts, for example, the employment contract relating to the exercise of a social mandate in a subsidiary company of the employer.[21] It also recognizes the validity of the delegation of powers within a group allowing a director of human resources of the parent company to dismiss an employee of a subsidiary company.[22] To this end, the Court of Cassation proves receptive to the development of techniques concentrating power in groups, the use of which is encouraged by the conclusion of agreements pertaining to the cash management, human resources, accounting, and so on.

In short, the rule of legal autonomy in a group is widely adapted today: It accepts the forms of coordination, control and dependency between companies of the same group. It is

16 Court of Cassation, Social Chamber, June 22, 2011 n 09–69.021 (unpublished), *Novoceram*, *Revue de droit du travail*, p. 634 (2011), obs. G. Auzero. According to the court, "responsibility for administrative, accounting, financial, commercial, technical and legal management of the BSA company was taken on by the Novoceram company, which also managed its staff, the executives of BSA only implementing decisions taken by Novoceram management as regards the management of staff and in industrial and technical fields".

17 Court of Cassation, Social Chamber, September 28, 2011, n 10–12.278, *Metaleurop*.

18 Court of Cassation, Social Chamber, September 28, 2011, prev. The judges highlighted that management staff should report regularly about their management, including in terms of incurring current expenditure.

19 P. Bailly, "Le coemploi n'est ni une 'baguette magique' ni une aberration juridique", *Semaine Sociale Lamy*, 1600, p. 11 (2013); G. Auzero, "Coemploi, le rappel à l'ordre de la Cour de cassation *Semaine Sociale Lamy*, 1645, p. 7 (2014).

20 Court of Cassation, Social Chamber, July 2, 2014, n 13–15.208 s. [P].

21 Court of Cassation, Social Chamber, October 2, 1991, *Klaine*, *Revue de Jurisprudence sociale* 1991/11, n 1252,; Court of Cassation, Social Chamber, October 6, 1993, *Bulletin civil* See, n 226, Moriaux, *Revue des sociétés*, 1994. 76, obs. B. Petit; *La semaine juridique*, 1994. I. 3746, n 10, obs. A. Viandier and J.-J. Caussain.

22 Court of Cassation, Social Chamber, January 19, 2005, *Bull. civ.* See, n 10; Soc. September 2009, *Bulletin civil*, See, n 191.

undoubtedly for this reason that the latest decisions relating to co-employment situations appear, to a large extent, to close the door to this characterization,[23] demonstrating the willingness of the senior judges to make co-employment an "exceptional situation".[24] Invoking an abnormality of power in a court in order to lift the veil of the legal entity is made increasingly difficult, at the end of a fairly traditional shifting of the limits of the abnormal. To some extent, co-employment itself sowed the seeds of its fading influence by being tied to the quest for an abnormality.[25]

These observations lead to an observation: the need to go looking for other technologies in order to hold the companies of a group accountable, following in the footsteps of social legislation of the organization.

2. The emergence of a law of the organization

Alongside rules penalizing the abnormal exercise of a power, others regulations urge us to rely on its exercise. As the power becomes standardized, the organization becomes a baseline for understanding these interlocking connections between powers and useful in controlling the power that it produces. Taking note of a particular normalization of power in organizations involves On one hand, reconsidering the reasons why – and the way in which – obligations are distributed among the companies of the organization (A) and on the other hand, identifying what would be the prospects and outlook of a law of the organization (B).

A. Pathways of accountability of companies within the organization

Rather than penalizing the abnormal exercise of power, the law sometimes takes note of the existence of an inter-company power to assign obligations to a company that is not the nominal employer. Multiple responsibility of the companies of a group does not, therefore, require an employer figure to be duplicated. Without making another legal entity debtor of all the obligations, the technique tends to create additional obligations, to assign them variably to various member companies of the organization and to express the responsibilities in case of breach of these obligations.[26] Complementarity of obligations (1) and expression of responsibilities (2) are the watchwords of the reasoning that unfolds.

1. Diversification of obligations

On several occasions, judges and legislators have assigned specific obligations to a parent company or contracting company, reinforcing those that fall to the subsidiary or the subcontractor. The multiplication of these obligations reflects the deployment of a real law of the organization, regardless of any considerations of abnormality.

23 See in particular, Court of Cassation, Social Chamber, December 18, 2013, 12–25.686 s.; Court of Cassation, Social Chamber, May 20, 2014, 12–20.527 (unpublished); Court of Cassation, Social Chamber, July 2, 2014, 13–15.208.

24 P. Bailly, "Le coemploi: une situation exceptionnelle", *La Semaine juridique, édition Social,* 46, p. 1441 (November 12, 2013).

25 E. Peskine, "Le coemploi sur la sellette?, Controverse avec J.-F. Cezaro", *Revue de droit du travail,* p. 663 (2014).

26 On the existence of distributive obligations in complex organizations, see E. Peskine, "Réseaux d'entreprise et droit du travail", *LGDJ* (2008), in particular p. 261; M. Kocher, "La notion de groupe d'entreprises en droit du travail", *LGDJ* (2013), in particular p. 365.

There are two kinds of obligation.

The first, imposed on the parent company, are intended for the employees or employee representatives of the subsidiary. The law thus creates an oblique legal link between the holder of corporate power and the employees of one of the companies. Such is the case when employees claim, on a noncontractual basis, a unilateral commitment of the parent company to the works council of the subsidiary.[27]

The second type of obligation is incumbent upon the parent company or the main company but will have the partner company as debtor. For example, article L. 2323 16 of the French Labor Code stipulates that when a restructuring project is likely to affect the volume of activity or employment of a subcontractor, "the contracting company shall immediately inform the subcontractor". Although the rule reflects on the relationship between employer and representative bodies – since the employer of the subcontractor must in turn inform its works council, or failing that, its employee representatives – this concerns first and foremost the relationship between the two partner companies. In the same sense, the law of July 10, 2014[28] provided for a duty of care by the contracting party in terms of the application of employment law. The contracting party is therefore required by the legislator to guarantee that certain rules of employment law are effectively applied once a work inspection officer has informed them of any breach. It is, moreover, a weak version of the duty of care involving no supervision or monitoring of the status of the subcontractor, but simply an obligation to act as soon as the public authority detects an offence and informs them of it. However, beyond this nuance, the effectiveness of certain legal and conventional provisions is given weight by the rapport established by the contractual terms of the subcontracting relationship. If the infringement relating to a lack of knowledge of the rules is due to the subcontractor, a particular infringement is created for failure to perform a specific duty of care that is attributable to him or her.

It is typically within this framework that there is a law, which is still under discussion, concerning the duty of care of parent companies and contracting companies[29] supported by various parliamentary groups following the collapse of the Rana Plazza building in Bangladesh in 2013, which caused the death of more than 1,100 textile workers. This text creates an obligation to set up a duty of care plan that is the responsibility of parent companies and contracting companies in respect to their subsidiaries or their subcontractors, and includes measures to identify and prevent the occurrence of risks in terms of human rights, fundamental freedoms, personal injury or environmental damage.

When qualifying a parent or contracting company, there are several possible grounds that may be cited, including, of course, the balance of power between the two entities or, more generally, the principal company's ability to influence.[30] Beyond that, however, the mere fact that a parent company or even a contracting company can be identified justifies the creation of a specific obligation, intended to ensure compliance by the nominal employer of its own obligations.

The examples cited are biased towards legal obligations, but the judge may also create specific obligations. For example, the Court of Justice of the European Union stated in a

27 Court of Cassation, Social Chamber, November 27, 2007, n 06–42.745, *Revue de droit du travail* 2008. 178, obs. A. Fabre.

28 Law of July 10, 2014, n 2014–790, aimed at combating unfair competition.

29 Draft law number 2578 pertaining to the diligence of parent companies and contracting companies, French National Assembly.

30 For more on justification, see n 41.

decision of September 10, 2009[31] that when a parent company makes a decision that forces its subsidiary to consider economic redundancies, the consultation procedure by the subsidiary must begin as soon as it has adopted the "strategic decisions of the parent company that compel the employer to consider collective redundancies" and must be closed before any "decision of the parent company that has the effect of compelling the subsidiary to terminate the contracts of the workers in question". Only the subsidiary, the employer, is bound to the duty to consult its representatives as is posed by the directive. However, the parent company is held, in a particular way, to an obligation to ensure that its subsidiary can consult its representatives in good time.[32] By some sort of variation of the useful effect of a rule, implied and additional obligations to the primary obligation, intended to put the employer in a position to perform his legal obligation, have been added to the obligations attributable to the nominal employer.

Ultimately, this technique allows the balance of power and interplay of influence to be taken into account between more sophisticated companies, which may be discreet or modest in size but that nonetheless exist. While the co-employment hypothesis assumes abnormal interference and total intermingling between legal entities, the balance of power, which authorizes various obligations to be assigned to companies of the same group, may be more discreet and highlighted by way of various techniques such as delegation of authority, the majority or unique shareholding, employment contracts concluded with a parent company by the manager of a company subsidiary, the designation of the representatives of the subsidiary by the parent company or the existence of a profitability target in investment contracts.[33] This attention to power in all its forms allows other types of power relationships – that may be less institutionalized, such as subcontracting relationships – to be considered. It is therefore not surprising that the technique of the distribution of obligations is becoming increasingly widespread in subcontracting relationships.

2. *Articulation of responsibilities*

The abundance of obligations are commensurate with the liabilities incurred in the event of breach of these obligations.

While the search for a co-employer naturally results in a united front between the companies for all of the obligations of employment law, the precise allocation of obligations authorizes some variations in the proposed sanctions. As each company holds separate obligations and duties, damages may be sought against each one for breach of its obligations. For example, nothing prevents the employees of the subsidiary from invoking a failure to uphold this inter-company obligation: first, because this breach is likely to establish the liability of the subsidiary in tort;[34] second, because employees suffer separate harm when the subsidiary fails to uphold its own obligations, including damages for loss of employment, for the loss

31 S. Vernac, "L'information et la consultation des représentants des travailleurs lors de la restructuration d'un groupe. À propos de l'arrêt Fujitsu Siemens", *Revue de droit du travail,* p. 285 (2010, May); see also F. Dorssemont & S. Vernac, "Les destinataires des règles communautaires d'information et de consultation en cas de licenciement collectif. À propos des arrêts Mono Car Styling et Fujitsu Siemens", *Revue de droit social* (Belgium), 3, édition La Charte, pp. 427–446 (2010).

32 Ibid.

33 S. Vernac, *Le pouvoir d'organisation. Au croisement du droit du travail et du droit des sociétés*, Thesis, Université Paris Ouest Nanterre La Défense (2012) (édition LGDJ, forthcoming).

34 Court of Cassation, plenary assembly, October 6, 2006, *Revue de droit des contrats*, p. 609 s (2007).

of a chance to keep a job, or to benefit from a job-safeguarding scheme, may constitute variations.[35] Nothing prevents us from considering that breaches of distinct obligations are likely to lead to the joint liability of the companies. Such is the sanction chosen for undeclared or illicit work, the contracting party being financially interdependent with its subcontractor of the payment including all taxes, duties and mandatory contributions, as well as penalties and increases when failing to fulfil its obligation to check that the formalities required by law have been observed by the co-contracting party.[36] The precise allocation of the obligations does not therefore necessarily mean that sanctions are assigned individually, but it does allow some variation.

These provisions illustrate another way to consider the responsibility of decision makers in multi-company organizations. Furthermore, they enable us to consider the organization as the result of two interrelationships: a corporate relationship to which obligations can be attached and an employment relationship.

The prospects of holding group companies accountable require the jurisdiction of – or the outlook for – a law of the organization to be laid bare.

B. The outlook for a law of the organization

Reference to the organization, and in particular the inter-company relationships that shape it, enriches the figure of the employer. The employer is no longer solely responsible for following employment law. Indeed, while the employer is, historically, the pivotal category of the regulations of employment law, the diversification of responsibilities and their debtors may well be the expression of a discreet paradigm shift. Could this be the return of the figure of the company manager? Is this not the prelude to a breakup of the category of employer, and the advent of a functional notion of employer? Understanding the jurisdiction of the law of the organization (1) helps to highlight the tests that must be overcome (2).

1. The meanings of a law of the organization

The exercise of power in companies has changed dramatically in recent decades. Hans Jonas showed in "Le principe responsabilité"[37] that power has shifted from one where the effects are felt in the here and now to a power of a different order of magnitude. The holder of power no longer shares the same temporal and geographic space as those affected by this power. In companies, the legal techniques for exercising power are, in truth, quite sophisticated. Corporate groups or networks are indeed arranged by a "power of organization"[38] that is separate from the line-management powers of the employer in that it is not exercised directly on employees but rather on the management of the employer company.

Accountability, in terms of employment law, is mainly attributed to the employer. In this regard, the virtual disappearance – during recodification of the French Employment Code in 2008 – of the concept of "company manager", which was replaced by that of "employer",

35 A. Fabre, "La responsabilité délictuelle pour faute au secours des salariés victimes d'une société tierce", *Revue de droit du travail*, p. 672 (2014, November).

36 Article L. 8222-1 of the French Labor Code.

37 H. Jonas, *Le principe responsabilité. Une éthique pour la civilisation technologique* (new edition), Paris: Champs Essais (1979, 2010).

38 S. Vernac, *Le pouvoir d'organisation. Au croisement du droit du travail et du droit des sociétés*, Thesis, Université Paris Ouest Nanterre La Défense (2012) (édition LGDJ, forthcoming).

only reinforced the centrality of the employer even if it also reestablished consistency across all of the regulations.

However, the emergence of the figure of the dependent employer inevitably creates a mismatch between the holder of power and the responsible subject. This engineering inevitably encourages us to reconsider the systems for allocating responsibilities.[39] The shift in power requires the causal link between misconduct and damage to be reconsidered, and accountability mechanisms to be renewed by establishing the presumption of misconduct, the presumption of liability of the holder of power,[40] and by identifying specific and implied obligations. Regardless of the content, the changes in techniques for allocating responsibilities – if they are to be recognized in employment law – call for new figures of management power to be identified. They therefore require the centrality of the category of employer to be dismantled.

In this regard, the ongoing debate regarding co-employment illustrates both the tensions caused by the transformations of power in the category of employer and the inadequacies of this category. A genuine "stepping stone that provides access to the parent company,[41] identifying a co-employer not only allows the latter to be deemed responsible *in solidum* of the nominal employer obligations but it can also result in obligations being assigned to the co-employer, such as the duty to put in place a scheme for safeguarding jobs.[42] The broad potential offered by the quality of co-employer, such as its ability to engage the responsibility of many groups, explains the backward step taken by the High Court in recent decisions.[43]

Challenging the centrality of the qualification of employer can follow two paths. The first is to assign obligations to a company or legal entity, regardless of its quality of employer, as shown in the emergence of the aforementioned obligations. The second would involve the breakup of the employer category. Breaking with a traditionally unified design, a functional concept of employer based on the identification of specific functions[44] could be suggested.

In a ruling made on October 21, 2010, the Court of Justice considered that a group company, to which employees were permanently assigned without being linked to it by an employment contract, should be regarded as a ceding undertaking within the meaning of directive 200/23. The Court of Justice noted that the directive does not deem it imperative to systematically give priority to the "contractual employer"[45] that "is not responsible for the economic activity of the economic entity transferred".[46] The Court of Justice explicitly

39 E. Peskine, "L'imputation en droit du travail", see above.

40 See in particular A. Lyon-Caen's seminar paper "Le droit du travail et le droit économique en mouvement face à la financiarisation et à l'organisation des groupes et entreprises à structure complexes", at the Maison des Avocats du Barreau de Paris, December 17, 2009; B. Grimonprez, "Pour une responsabilité des sociétés mères du fait de leurs filiales", *Revue des sociétés*, p. 715 (2009).

41 According to M.A. Mazeaud, "Le déploiement de la relation de travail dans les groupes de sociétés. Aspects de droit du travail", *Droit social* p. 738 (2010, July), in particular n 22.

42 *Court of cassation, Social Chamber*, June 22, 2011, n 09–69.021; see *Court of cassation, Social Chamber*, January 13, 2010, Dalloz 2010. 1129, note B. Dondero; *Revue du droit du travail* p. 230 (2010, April), obs. F. Géa; see also E. Serverin & T. Grumbach, "La saga judiciaire Flodor", *Revue de droit du travail* p. 693 (2009, December), Recueil Dalloz 2010 Pan. 2029, obs. B. Reynès.

43 Court of Cassation, Social Chamber, July 2, 2014, n 13–15.208 to 13–21.153. See J.-F. Césaro & E. Peskine, "Le coemploi sur la sellette", Controverse, *Revue de droit du travail*, p. 661 (2014, June).

44 J. Prassl, "L'emploi multilatéral en droit anglais. À la recherche du patron perdu", *Revue de droit du travail*, p. 236 (2014, April).

45 CJUE, October 21, 2010, *Albron Catering BV*, C-242/09, pt 25; H. Tissandier, "Transfert d'entreprise et groupe de sociétés: la reconnaissance de 'l'employeur non contractuel'", *Revue de droit du travail*, p. 35 (2011).

46 CJUE, October 21, 2010, *Albron Catering BV*, C-242/09, pt 29.

reestablished the quest for the "company manager", the term designating in this instance a noncontractual employer, responsible for the conduct of the activity transferred.[47] Ultimately, there lurks a functional view of the employer, depending on the legal prerogative called into question. From a functional perspective, qualification criteria for the employer would be distinct according to the employment law regulations to be applied. The criteria would thus adapt to the multiple and shifting forms of organization.

2. The challenges of a law of the organization

Several tests must be overcome in order for a law of the organization to become widespread.

An initial test involves eliminating the static conception of the organization and its stakeholders. The power that structures the organization is elusive. Its holder is not identifiable in advance. It can be a parent or grandparent company, a contracting company or a donor of funds, such as a bank or an investment fund. In addition, this power can circulate within the organization and target various decision making areas, so it is futile to firmly map out the outer limits of the organization. The organization is necessarily functional. Its boundaries cannot therefore be defined a priori, but depend precisely on identifying the power relationships in question, which therefore enables the organization to be reconstructed, even one that is paperless, international and dispersed.[48]

In addition, understanding internal organizational relationships requires some procedural adaptations. For example, the rights of employees in legal suits are very limited in commercial law. Should we not consider redefining the *locus standi* of employees in business law? Moreover, enabling employees to invoke inter-company relations assumes that they have sufficient information to be able to invoke the content. Apart from the progress made in the litigation of the forced production of items,[49] we must admit that inter-company relations still remain largely opaque. In addition to business confidentiality, knowledge of the existence of certain acts as well as their communication constitutes a serious obstacle to knowledge of the reality of internal relations within the organization. Adjusting the burden of proof could, in certain circumstances, remedy these shortcomings. A proposed law pertaining to the due diligence of parent companies and contracting companies[50] provides an interesting response in this respect, by establishing a presumption of misconduct. According to the text of the proposal, the applicant must prove the existence of power – a control relationship, a relationship of influence, a subcontracting agreement – in order to justify the applicability of this rule. Then it will be for the holder of the power to prove that he or she has taken all necessary and reasonable steps within his or her power to anticipate or prevent the occurrence of damage.

Finally, the law of the organization encourages us to reconsider the normative technique itself, and especially the combination of sources. In other words, it is the close

47 Ibid., pt 30.

48 C. Hannoun, "Notion et enjeux de la dématérialisation de l'entreprise", in *La dématérialisation de l'entreprise. Essai sur les dimensions immatérielles de l'entreprise*, C. Hannoun (coord.), L'Harmattan (2010), p. 11; "L'émergence de l'entreprise-marchandise", *Revue de droit du travail*, p. 22 (2010, January).

49 C. Parès, "La production forcée par voie judiciaire des informations dues au comité d'entreprise", *Droit ouvrier*, p. 170 (2010); S. Bernard, "Contentieux social et régime probatoire", *Droit ouvrier*, p. 187 (2010); T. Grumbach, "Tel est pris qui croyait prendre", obs. under Tribunal de grande instance, Paris, February 5, 2009, no 09/51089, *Revue de droit du travail*, p. 250 (2009, April).

50 Draft law number 2578 pertaining to the diligence of parent companies and contracting companies, French National Assembly.

complementarity between State and private standards that calls for the establishment of a law of the organization. In imposing internal obligations to the group or network upon the holder of the power, the law may encourage the organization to monitor this, and therefore standardize it.

Ultimately, the development of a law of the organization recognizes a gradual change of perspective. It is no longer possible to restrict employment law to relations between an employer and an employee or a community of employees. Employment relationships can no longer be considered independently of inter-company relationships between legal entities, directors, partners, and so on. In addition, the law of the organization requires a break with the traditional separation between employment law and corporate law. Moving away from references to abuses of legal personality or excess of power, the law of the organization builds on the spread of power within the organization much more than it condemns it. Although it is the expression of a constitutionalization of private powers, this route carries with it the ambiguity inherent in any process of legal construction of a power, which reflects both its legitimacy and its limitations. It is, however, based on this condition that the law can draw the organization out from the shadows in which it has long been allowed to shelter.

Part II

The concept of constitutionalization

5 Reflections on the constitutionalization of the World Power System

Gunther Teubner

The Paris research project on transnational companies corporate citizenship raises one of the most difficult issues of our time, that of the new constitutional question. Can the power that private collective actors build up in the transnational space be effectively limited through constitutional constraints?

A series of public scandals has erupted in recent years: Multinational companies have violated human rights; the WTO has taken controversial decisions that threaten the environment and people's health in the name of global free trade; there has been doping in sport and corruption in science and medicine; private intermediaries have threatened freedom of expression on the Internet; private organizations have gathered information that has greatly infringed upon the private sphere; and, most recently, catastrophic risks have been unleashed on the global financial markets with clear disregard. As the writings of Jean-Philippe Robé clearly illustrate, all of these scandals not only pose problems for regulation, but also pose constitutional problems in the strict sense. It is the constitutionalization of social dynamics that is at stake and not merely the adoption of State regulation policies. Compared with the constitutional question of the eighteenth and nineteenth centuries, these are problems of another sort, but no less concerning, which arise today. If it was once about releasing the political energies of the power of the nation-state and, at the same time, effectively limiting them by the rule of law, it is now, in the case of the new constitutional question, about releasing completely different social energies – particularly significant in the economy, but also in the areas of science and technology, medicine and new media – and effectively limiting their destructive effects.[1] Nowadays, these energies – in productive and destructive ways – are unloaded in social spaces beyond the nation-state. The recent scandals cross the borders of the nation-state in a dual manner. Constitutionalism beyond the nation-state means two things: Constitutional problems arise simultaneously outside of the boundaries of the nation-state in transnational political processes, and outside the institutionalized political sectors in the "private" sectors of global society.

The remarkable outcome of the Paris project is, in my view, how it succeeded in linking three different approaches: a comprehensive theory of the power of multinational companies, an original vision of the constitutionalization of the so-called private collective actors and detailed reform proposals that indicate how such constitutionalization can be reached.

1 Philip Allott goes as far as to describe the new constitutional question as the "central challenge facing international philosophers of the twenty-first century" in "The Emerging Universal Legal System", *International Law Forum du Droit International*, 3, pp. 12–17 (2001), here: p. 16.

I fully agree with these three approaches. It seems to me that with the chapter in this volume by Jean-Philippe Robé, the Paris project has made a big step forward, not only in terms of considering the new constitutional question as a problem, but also in terms of showing wide-ranging, yet at the same time, very detailed possible solutions. There is one point about which I would formulate some qualifications. It is about the question of which of the following two options should be preferred: (a) whether constitutional rules for enterprise will be part of the constitutions of the State world or (b) whether they will form part of a societal constitutionalism.[2] There are, in my opinion, three difficult problems, which would suggest a preference for the second option. These three problems are posed by (1) the impossibility of a world constitution, (2) the difficulties of a perspective focusing on the State and (3) the reduction of constitutional problems to problems of social power. I would like to stress the importance of a constitutional pluralism in national and transnational, in public as well as in private contexts, and I'd like to discuss one of the many examples offered by transnational societal constitutionalism, namely the codes of conduct for multinational firms.

1. Three problems

A. The impossibility of a cosmo-political world constitution

With a sober sense of realism, Robé denies a world state as a substrate of a single constitution. Instead, he claims that there

> exists a global "system of power", the "public" and "private" components of which have a constitutional origin rooted in positive state constitutions, which has subsequently been extended by means of international treaties. This system has an effectiveness and, in this sense, a world constitution is already at least partially in place.[3]

If one takes serious the idea of a world constitution, the constitutionalization of international law would be considered, as far as possible, by analogy with the constitutional law of nation-states: a hierarchy of constitutional law against ordinary law. The entire world would be seen as a single domain of validity extending to all national, cultural and social fields.[4]

The project of a world constitution presents spectacular extensions with respect to the constitutional tradition – but it ultimately is not able to free itself from the fascination with the architecture of the nation-state and instead simply seeks to offset the obvious shortcomings by suggesting all kinds of compensations, supporting elements, reconstructions, foundations and decorative facades, which serve only to complicate the construction instead of building anew. The problem for such an approach lies in the fact that it centers on the State

2 Robé formulates his reservations against societal constitutionalism in such a way that his "analysis differs from certain current attempts to develop a constitutional theory free of any reference to the nation-state", J.-P. Robé, "Globalization and Constitutionalization of the World Power System", in this volume, note. 68.

3 Jean-Philippe Robé, "L'entreprise et la constitutionnalisation du système-monde de pouvoir", in *L'entreprise, formes de la propriété et responsabilités sociales*, Roger Baudoin (ed.), Paris: Lethielleux (2012), pp. 281–354, 313. A rigorous analysis of the different variants of a cosmo-political world constitution is offered by Ignacio de la Rasilla del Moral "At King Agramant's Camp: Old Debates, New Constitutional Times", *International Journal of Constitutional Law*, 8, pp. 580–610 (2011).

4 A well-conducted critique of such "constitutional illusions" of a world state constitution is in Andreas Fischer-Lescano, *Globalverfassung: Die Geltungsbegründung der Menschenrechte*, Velbrück: Weilerswist (2005), p. 247 et seq.

constitution. It must be recognized that this approach has the courage to rethink the constitution towards a political whole, in the light of inter-governmental process, via the inclusion of social actors, through the structural effect of fundamental rights in society, but it nevertheless remains committed to an understanding of the constitution whose role would be to liberate and to limit State action.

My main hypothesis is the following: We are witnessing the emergence of a multiplicity of civil constitutions. The constitution of a world society does not exclusively occur in the representative institutions of international politics. It can equally no longer take place in a world constitution encompassing all sectors of society. Rather, it develops gradually around the constitutionalization of a multiplicity of autonomous subsystems of world society. This is the central message of a transnational societal constitutionalism.

B. The fixation on the State

A sociological theory of societal constitutionalism, which has thus far remained unheard in the debate on the constitution, reduces the State-centricity of traditional constitutionalism. This constitutional theory relies on four distinct variants of sociological theory. It essentially uses general theories of functional differentiation according to which the internal constitution of the social subsystems – and not only of the State – is the central problem.[5] In addition, it relies on a particular field of sociology – a recently developed sociology of constitutions[6] – and on the theory of private government[7] and the concept of societal constitutionalism.[8] In addition, a sociological theory of the constitution promises to connect historical-empirical analyses that have been made from constitutional phenomena, standardized perspectives.[9]

What is it that makes the sociology of constitutions different? The fact that it not only raises the constitutional question within the context of the relationship to politics and the law, but that it also poses the question for all areas of society.

In this sense, the problem has been completely changed. It is not only that the question of constitutionalization arises with regard to the world state of international politics or international law, but that it does for other independent sectors of global society as well, for the global economy first of all, but also for science and technology, education, media and public health. Does a societal constitutionalism have the necessary potential to stem, in addition to expansionist trends in the political system, the expansionist trends (which are no less

5 General sociological theories of functional differentiation in the tradition of Emile Durkheim, Georg Simmel, Max Weber, Talcott Parsons, Pierre Bourdieu, and Niklas Luhmann give a different slant on the issue of whether the state constitution can serve as constitution for the whole society, or whether the social sectors develop autonomous constitutions.

6 From a programmatic viewpoint, see Chris Thornhill, *A Sociology of Constitutions: Constitutions and state Legitimacy in Historical-Sociological Perspective*, Cambridge: Cambridge University Press (2011); see also Gert Verschraegen (2013), "Differentiation and Inclusion: A Neglected Sociological Approach to Fundamental Rights", in *Making Human Rights Intelligible: Towards a Sociology of Human Rights*, Mikael Rask Madsen, Gert Verschraegen (eds.), Oxford: Hart, pp. 61–80.

7 The theory of private government has been developed by Philip Selznick in *Law, Society and Industrial Justice*, New York: Russell Sage Foundation (1969).

8 The concept of a *Societal Constitutionalism* (as opposed to a narrow *Political Constitutionalism*) was brought up for discussion by David Sciulli, *Theory of Societal Constitutionalism: Foundations of a Non-Marxist Critical Theory*, Cambridge: Cambridge University Press (1992).

9 Chris Thornhill, "Towards a Historical Sociology of Constitutional Legitimacy", *Theory and Society*, 37, pp. 161–197, 163 (2008) et seq.

problematic today) of many other social subsystems that threaten the integrity of individuals and institutions? Can constitutions effectively fight centrifugal dynamics in the subsystems of global society and thereby contribute to social integration – in a totally different manner from that of the classical understanding of integration by the constitution? Sociological theories can give a boost to these questions, which arise with new urgency in the face of globalization and privatization trends.[10] They call into question the fundamental assumptions of the current debate on transnational constitutions, replacing them with other hypotheses and thus identifying problems of a new kind and suggesting different practical consequences.[11]

C. Beyond social power

This approach considers, incorrectly, that the constitution of companies and, in particular, the horizontal effect of fundamental rights is exclusively a problem of social power. Their real objective is missing: to limit by law the expansion of social subsystems that do not always take place through the medium of power.

If the task is to limit by constitutional means the strong expansionist tendencies that have their origin in the specific logic of social subsystems, then a State conception of fundamental rights is no longer preserved. We cannot assign them to the individual players only,

10 For first steps toward a transnational societal constitutionalism – which states that in transnational space, numerous social subsystems develop specific constitutions beyond the state – see Gunther Teubner, "Global Private Regimes: Neo-spontaneous Law and Dual Constitution of Autonomous Sectors?", in *Globalization and Public Governance*, Karl-Heinz Ladeur (Hrsg.), Oxford: Oxford University Press (2003) pp. 71–87; ders., "Societal Constitutionalism: Alternatives to state-Centerd Constitutional Theory?", in *Transnational Governance and Constitutionalism*, Christian Joerges, Inger-Johanne Sand & Gunther Teubner (Hrsg.), Oxford: Hart (2004), pp. 3–28. Ibid., *Constitutional Fragments: Societal Constitutionalism and Globalization*, Oxford: Oxford University Press (2012).

11 Meanwhile, research (significantly different in detail) on transnational societal constitutionalism has proliferated: see Jean De Munck, "Law in the Global Age: Heading toward a Societal Constitutionalism", in this volume; Poul F. Kjaer *Constitutionalism in the Global Realm: A Sociological Approach*, London: Routledge (2014); Verschraegen, "Differentiation and Inclusion"; Hugh Collins, "The Constitutionalisation of Private Law as a Path to Social Justice", in *The Many Concepts of Social Justice in European Private Law*, Hans Micklitz (ed.), London: Edward Elgar (2011), pp. 133–166; Pablo Holmes, "The Rhetoric of Legal Fragmentation and its Discontents: Evolutionary Dilemmas in the Constitutional Semantics of Global Law", *Utrecht Law Review*, 7, pp. 113–140 (2011), here: p. 121 et seq.; Lars Viellechner, "The Constitution of Transnational Governance Arrangements: Karl Polanyi's Double Movement in the Transformation of Law", in *Karl Polanyi, Globalisation and the Potential of Law in Transnational Markets*, Christian Joerges & Josef Falke (eds.), Oxford: Hart (2011), pp. 436–464, here: p. 449 et seq.; Gralf-Peter Callies and Peer Zumbansen, *Rough Consensus and Running Code: A Theory of Transnational Private Law*, Oxford: Hart (2010), *passim*; Chris Thornhill, "Niklas Luhmann and the Sociology of Constitution", *Journal of Classical Sociology*, 10, pp. 1–23 (2010); Hans Lindahl, "A-Legality: Postnationalism and the Question of Legal Boundaries", *Modern Law Review*, 73, pp. 30–56 (2010), here: p. 33 et seq.; Riccardo Prandini, "The Morphogenesis of Constitutionalism", in *The Twilight of Constitutionalism?*, Petra Dobner & Martin Loughlin (eds.), Oxford: Oxford University Press (2010), pp. 23–46, here: p. 40 et seq.; Larry Catá Backer, Transnational Corporate Constitutionalism? (2009): http://lcbackerblog.blogspot.com/2009/06/gunther-teubner-on-complications-of.html; David Schneiderman, *Constitutionalizing Economic Globalization: Investment Rules and Democracy's Promise*, Cambridge: Cambridge University Press (2008); Marc Amstutz *et al.*, "Civil Society Constitutionalism: The Power of Contract Law", *Indiana Journal of Global Legal Studies*, 14, pp. 235–258 (2007); James Tully, "The Imperialism of Modern Constitutional Democracy", in The Paradox of Constitutionalism: Constituent Power and Constitutional Form, Neil Walker & Martin Loughlin (eds.), Oxford: Oxford University Press (2007), pp. 315–338, here: p. 328 et seq.; Reinhart Koselleck, "Begriffsgeschichtliche Probleme der Verfassungsgeschichtsschreibung", in Studien zur Semantik & Pragmatik der politischen & sozialen, Reinhart Koselleck & Begriffsgeschichten (eds.), Sprache: Frankfurt (2006), pp. 365–401, here: p. 369 et seq.

nor focus them exclusively on the social phenomena of power, nor provide them with the form of autonomous spaces guarded by subjective rights. Can we develop an approach here that declares that fundamental rights can work against the media of social communication themselves – power, but also profit, technology, knowledge, information media – instead of against the actors? Is it not then a case of protecting not only the fundamental rights of individuals, but also those of social institutions? Should the social effect of fundamental rights not be implemented through organization and procedure rather than through subjective rights?

2. Constitutional pluralism

The alternative route to statist societal constitutionalism is a constitutional pluralism on a national as well as transnational scale. In this, it's necessary to see the result of experiments that were carried out in the past with four different concepts of the constitution of society.[12]

A. The autonomy of societal constitutions

The tendency of liberal constitutionalism to ignore social sectors is discredited today. The totalitarian model that extended a massive regulation of the State to all sectors of society is rightly discredited. In contrast, we find the current concepts of the welfare state on the right, which emphasize that the State must prescribe the constitutions of the social sectors but at the same time respect their autonomy. However, the incessant injection of uniform political procedures of power and the consensus in the various social sectors has a counterproductive effect. Economic theories of law rely on the autonomy of the sectorial constitution of the economy, but they lose their credibility by relying exclusively on economic rationality, deeming all other rationales to be irrational and relying on integration of the whole society via market and competition.

It therefore comes down to sailing between the Scylla of the societal constitutions of the welfare state and the Charybdis of a purely economic constitutionalization. A compass is provided by the "law of conflict of rights" in the sense of Rudolf Wiethölter, according to whom sectorial societal constitutions are self-contained and have no need of political intervention in the event of a crisis:

> Taking autonomy seriously means relying on self-determination and at the same time on the inevitable externalization which should not be understood as outside determination but rather as potential support from outside in situations where self-help is not possible. It could be compared to therapeutic assistance or support structures outside the law.[13]

12 Véronique Champeil-Desplats, "Constitutionalization Outside of the State? A Constitutionalist's Point of View", in this volume, develops an informative typology for different versions of societal constitutionalism – (1) structural, (2) institutional, (3) contractualist and (4) axiological – that highlights relevant differences among them. My own version seems to be close to the institutional and the structural, but none of them really fits. I would suggest a fifth type, a socio-legal version. It would stress the co-originality of the social and the legal processes within a constitution, their clear-cut autonomy and separation, and their mutual interrelation in a "hybrid", "symbiotic" or "co-evolutionary" process.

13 Rudolf Wiethölter, "Zum Fortbildungsrecht der (richterlichen) Rechtsfortbildung: Fragen eines lesenden Recht-Fertigungslehrers", *Kritische Vierteljahreszeitschrift für Gesetzgebung & Rechtswissenschaft*, 3, pp. 1–28

Indeed, different variants of constitutional pluralism try, in effect, to maintain this difficult pathway.[14] The sociological theory of private government has conducted pioneering work here insofar as it has analyzed the companies and other private organizations such as political power associations and has encouraged, therefore, a transfer of political principles towards private organizations.[15] It is, therefore, in terms of legal policy, a criticism and a dismantling of the power and, in any case, of the legitimacy and limitation – and even the constitutionalization – of economic power. Just as with the constitution of politico-state power, private governments should establish their legitimacy in combining their organizational rules in an explicitly political way and by protecting their members' areas of freedom by equivalents to fundamental rights.

However, the theory of private government is too closely related to formal organizations or even only to financial companies. That the claim to constitutionalization be extended to the entire financial process and other societal processes at the same time is what theories on a larger scale supporting a societal and financial constitution of the welfare state are calling for. The starting point was the political idea of the "constitution of labor" (Sinzheimer), i.e. "of each order that calls for employees – in the areas determined by law or by contract – to exercise all rights of decision, reserved previously and exclusively to employers".[16] This idea became more widespread as a consequence. Democratic participation and the guarantee of fundamental rights should be extended to all socially relevant organizations.[17]

Western Europe is experimenting with a multiplicity of social constitutions granting the political constitution only the status of *primus inter pares*. Constitutions are everywhere in society: not just *ubi societas, ibi ius*, as Grotius once said, but *ubi societas, ibi constitutio*. Self-founding orders are developing at numerous places in society and are being stabilized by constitutional law. Law must accordingly develop a "multilateral constitutionalism" that does not bind social orders unilaterally either to the constitution of the State or to the economy, but rather models specific constitutions that do justice to the peculiarities of the various orders.

The far-reaching influence of interest groups on politics, extending from sheer lobbyism to genuinely public functions of private actors, the institutionalization of labor co-determination in corporations, the control of markets through the self-regulation of business associations, the strong role of professional organization in almost all social sectors – in the health service, sport, culture, science, education, the mass media – all these neo-corporatist arrangements institutionalize the representation of various social interests. In each case they are based on a special constitution that contains constitutive rules for self-regulation and at the same time permits the private associations to function as participants in the broader political process.

It is with a remarkable realism that neo-corporatist theories analyze the competition between State regulation and social self-regulation. In contrast to the rigidities of the

(1988), here: p. 27 et seq. Ibid. "Justifications of a Law of Society", in *Paradoxes and Inconsistencies in the Law*, Oren Perez & Gunther Teubner (eds.), Oxford: Hart (2005), pp. 65–77.

14 The main representative of constitutional pluralism is Neil Walker, "The Idea of Constitutional Pluralism", *Modern Law Review*, 65, pp. 317–359 (2002).

15 The key texts are Philip Selznick, *Law, Society and Industrial Justice*, New York: Russell Sage (1969); Robert A. Dahl, *After the Revolution? Authority in a Good Society*, New Haven: Yale University Press (1990), p. 80 et seq., 100 et seq.

16 Hugo Sinzheimer, "Das Wesen des Arbeitsrechts" (1927), in ibid., *Arbeitsrecht & Rechtssoziologie*, Frankfurt: Europäische Verlagsanstalt (1976), pp. 108–114.

17 Gavin W. Anderson, "Social Democracy and the Limits of Rights Constitutionalism", *Canadian Journal of Law & Jurisprudence*, 17, pp. 31–59 (2004).

authoritarian State corporatism of the 1930s, they submit, it is only freely formed social groups, without compulsory membership and without comprehensive State regulation, that are capable of making productive use of the interaction of spontaneous and organized elements within social subsystems. Although co-determination was institutionalized by State legislation, neo-corporatist theories make the point against the welfare state's fantasies of omnipotence, that co-determination cannot work successfully without the self-foundation and self-regulation of labor unions and corporations. Finally they turn against the frequent criticism of the associations' political influence and they emphasize auto-constitutional elements in the mediation of interests, which reflects the functional differentiation of society within politics.

At the same time neo-corporatist theories keep their distance from constitutional economics. While also stressing the self-foundation of social institutions, neo-corporatist concepts do not, however, engage in the artificial assumptions of rational choice. Moreover, they argue that the influence of social self-regulation depends to a very large degree on its protection by the State constitution. Finally, they account for the role of formal legal rules. The law places the spontaneous organization of employee interests on a permanent footing so that their influence on business decisions can be stabilized relatively independently of market and power fluctuations.

The "triangular constitutionalization" of social subsystems – a division of labor between their self-foundation in society, the constitutional interventions of the State and the stabilizing role of the formal law – may be considered as the important practical and theoretical contribution of neo-corporatism. Co-determination is the paradigm for the intricate interaction of societal constitutions and their external constitution through politics and law. State coordination through statutory laws are closely coordinated with social self-organization in corporations and trade unions, and with the courts constantly readjusting the balance.

B. Societal constitutionalism

David Sciulli developed the concept of "societal constitutionalism", which concentrates on another weak point of neo-corporatism.[18] Neo-corporatism is far too beholden to the dualism of politics and economics and to a large extent ignores other social sectors. As the repeatedly used term of "interest mediation" suggests, it focuses too narrowly on the relations between institutionalized politics and the economy. According to its self-understanding, neo-corporatist arrangements transform trade associations and labor unions into participants of the political system and turn their institutionalized interest mediation into political decisions. Neo-corporatism underestimates the autonomy of other social subsystems, which makes it relatively distant from institutionalized politics. At the same time, the concept is too close to the economy and takes only trade associations, corporations and trade unions into account. What is missing is to re-specify neo-corporatist institutions in other independent logics in society. Societal constitutionalism in fact corrects this deficit, because it is aimed from the outset at society in all of its subareas.

Starting with the dilemmata of rationalization in modernity, keenly analyzed by Max Weber, Sciulli attempts to identify counterforces that would work against the massive

18 David Sciulli, *Theory of Societal Constitutionalism, op.cit.;* ibid., "The Critical Potenzial of the Common Law Tradition: Theory of Societal Constitutionalism: Foundations of a Non-Marxist Critical Theory", *Columbia Law Review*, 94, pp. 1076–1123 (1994); ibid., *Corporate Power in Civil Society: An Application of Societal Constitutionalism*, New York: New York University Press (2001).

evolutionary drift towards an increasing authoritarianism. This drift is pushed by four impulses:

1 Fragmentation of action logics results in escalated differentiation, pluralization and reciprocal compartmentalization of separate spheres: Each area of action in society develops its own formal rationality that is in insoluble conflict with the rationalities of other areas.
2 Dominance of instrumental calculation is the only rationality acknowledged in all areas: Given the collision of rationalities in modernity, the logic of instrumental calculation alone is becoming generally accepted in economics and politics, but increasingly in other action sectors as well.
3 Comprehensive replacement of informal coordination by bureaucratic organization: Increasingly, in all areas of life, formal hierarchically structured organizations staffed by experts are proliferating as promoters of formal rationalities.
4 Increasing confinement in the "iron cage of modernity": Particularly outside politics, formal organizations are proliferating within different social areas, leading to a comprehensive rule-based orientation of the individual.[19]

This drift inevitably ends, society-wide, in intensive competition for positions of power and social influence, in highly formalized social control and in political and social authoritarianism. The only social dynamics that have effectively opposed this evolutionary drift in the past, and that will do so in future, are to be found according to Sciulli in the institutions of a "societal constitutionalism". It is crucial to institutionalize procedures of non-rational norms (non-rational in the sense of rational choice) that can be empirically identified in "collegial formations", i.e. in the professions and other norm-producing and deliberative institutions. They are

> typically found not only in public and private research institutes, artistic and intellectual networks and universities, but also within legislatures, courts and commissions, professional associations and, for that matter, the research divisions of private and public corporations . . . and even the directorates of public and private corporations.[20]

All these variants of constitutional pluralism fundamentally differ from their economic rivals and the welfare state by the role they attribute to State policy in the process of the constitutionalization of society. Unlike proposing a constitutional economy, the State is not limited to standardize minimum preconditions for an autonomous economic constitution or to only issue corrections in the case of self-destructive trends. In addition, constitutional pluralism cannot be identified with achieving political organizational goals throughout society, contrary to the intention of the concepts of the welfare state. It adds to the role of politics, the role of establishing constitutional guidelines for social sectors in a manner that close cooperation between the State and social players could put a brake on the centrifugal tendencies of the functional differentiation. What counts is that there is an interaction between the societal auto-constitutionalization and state-political impulses. It assigns to the political institutions of the nation-state the task of integrating the subsystems in conflict, not by taking

19 D. Sciulli, *Theory of Societal Constitutionalism*, op. cit., p. 80.
20 Ibid., p. 208.

concrete decisions that are collectively binding, but by coordinating the cooperation of social and political organizations.

C. A transnational constitutionalism?

Obviously, such an arrangement is made to measure for the special conditions of the nation-state. Constitutional pluralism has been having a lot of success but it depends on social and institutional conditions that occur only within the context of the nation-state.[21] This raises the question of whether, under the conditions of globalization, equivalents to such constitutional pluralism can be institutionalized. But the discussion of the different approaches should have clearly shown to which problem the constitutionalism of society reacts: to the idea of establishing an external pressure to contain both negative externalities as well as the centrifugal tendencies of the autonomous subsystems by their self-restraint.

With regard to the transnational space, there is a misconception that is widespread and that explains that the current debate underestimates the radicalism of societal constitutionalization. In principle, a need for a constitution is only due to particular forms of political "*governance*" that have been formed in global society and that differ from the "*government*", i.e. the traditional government practices of the nation-state. The "*governance*" is considered to be the result of socio-political administrative interventions, in which public and private players solve social problems.[22] The interconnection of different specialized bureaucracies of nation-states with players from around the world, transnational corporations, financial groupings, NGOs and hybrid schemes is seen as the new issue of global governance, which should now be overcome by constitutional institutions.[23]

Without a doubt this socialization of political domination encounters one of the central elements of global governance, but nevertheless, this analysis is short-sighted. It minimizes the problem when one only thinks of limited new private players, which include the power structures of global governance, by constitutional standards. Again, it should be pointed out that the narrow view of the politico-legal theories of the constitution, which also only focus on transnational reports and phenomena of the policy (in the narrow sense of institutionalized politics). From a sociological point of view, it becomes clear, however, that the real problem is the constitution of autonomous spheres of action in global society – precisely outside of international politics – and that the role of the standards of constitutional law in this process must be discussed. It is only when one goes beyond the transnational political processes in the narrow sense and it is understood that social players are involved not only in the process of global governance but that they establish themselves in autonomous global regimes outside of institutionalized policy – they can, however, become political players themselves and react to the policy – that the problems of constitutionalism in the strongest sense of the term become visible in global society.

21 Wolfgang Streeck, *Re-Forming Capitalism: Institutional Change in the German Political Economy*, Oxford: Oxford University Press (2009).

22 Jan Kooiman, "Societal Governance: Levels, Modes, and Orders of Social-Political Interaction", in *Debating Governance*, Jon Pierre (ed.), Oxford: Oxford University Press (2000), pp. 138–163, here: p. 139 et seq.

23 A well thought out concept of *governance* is found in Edgar Grande, Markus König, Patrick Pfister & Paul Sterzel, "Politische Transnationalisierung: Die Zukunft des Nationalstaats – Transnationale Politikregime im Vergleich", in *Globalisierung: Forschungsstand & Perspektiven*, Stefan Schirm (ed.), Nomos: Baden-Baden (2006), pp. 119–145.

Thus the differences between the sectorial constitutions and the political constitution come to the foreground. The constitutionalization of global governance has therefore always been understood as the constitution of transnational political processes in the narrowest sense. On the other hand, the sociological analysis of the global subsystems – the economy, science, culture and the mass media – is facing much more difficult questions: global subsystems now deploy a dynamic of uncontrolled growth, but must these be subject to constitutional restrictions? Are there, in these areas, similar things to expansive dynamic safeguards, in particular regarding the political separation of powers? More fundamentally, the question further asks to what point is it necessary to generalize the principles of political constitutions in order to escape the traps of methodological nationalism? And how should they be specified again to take into account the characteristics of a social institution of globality?[24]

Sectorial constitutions do not aspire to a stable equilibrium but follow the chaotic model of a 'dynamic imbalance' as a result of contrary developments – empowerment and limitation of the functional logic of the subsystems.[25] The new world constitutional orders have, until now in the west, only established *constitutive rules*, which normatively support the release of different systemic rationalities on a global scale. Today, however, it is clear that reorientation is needed. After long experiments in the history of the strong tendencies towards expansion of the global functional subsystems and after the shocks of the endogenous crises, countermovements take place which draw up – after violent social conflict – *limiting rules* that counteract self-destructive trends and limit the damage to social, human and natural environments. Of course, since the beginning of globalization, the 'vertical' problem of the constitution has been politically besieged: thus compared to nation-states, the borders must be imposed on the new global regimes. But the most serious constitutional problem, the 'horizontal' problem, is absolutely not taken into consideration "if the autonomy of functional systems cannot lead to mutual charges that will limit the structural adaptability of functional systems to their own differentiation".[26]

This blindness towards the negative externalities produced by systems that are clearly expanding with respect to their self-destructive potential was revealed by the financial markets crisis. The world constitution of financial markets, valid until that point, was simply the result of a blind evolutionary process where markets automatically turned global. Rather, this took place through the active participation of politics and law. In terms of dismantling national barriers and an explicit policy of de-regularization, a global constitution of financial markets, politically desired and legally stabilized, which freed uncontrolled dynamics, was established. But that which would replace national regulations and standardize restrictive rules at the same time was not planned by the political agenda, and was even opposed for years as being counterproductive. It is only today, following the experience of several

24 For generalization and re-specification, see Talcott Parsons & Charles Ackerman, "The Concept of 'Social System' as a Theoretical Device", in *Concepts, Theory and Explanation in the Behavioral Sciences*, Gordon J. DiRenzo (ed.), New York: Random House (1996), pp. 19–40. For more on the re-specification of basic political rights in financial organizations: Jens Schierbeck, "Operational Measures for Identifying and Implementing Human Rights Issues in Corporate Operations", in *Human Rights and the Oil Industry*, Asbjorn Eide, Ole Bergesen & Pia Goyer (eds.), Antwerpen: Intersentia (2000), pp. 161–177, here: p. 168.

25 Karl Polanyi analyzes the historic "double movement" of the expansion of markets and their limitation Karl Polanyi, *The Great Transformation: The Political and Economic Origins of Our Time*, New York: Farrar & Rinehart (1944), p. 106 et seq., p. 182 et seq. In a generalised form – not only for the economy but for the different social sectors as well Wiethölter, "Justifications" op. cit. here: p. 20.

26 Niklas Luhmann, *Die Gesellschaft der Gesellschaft*, Frankfurt: Suhrkamp (1997), p. 1087.

quasi-catastrophes that led to a collective learning process where we are seeking to limit finance by constitutional law on a global level in the future. In this regard, my thoughts are directly in line with those of Jean-Philippe Robé. It is very urgent to limit the social dynamics that are raging in their negative externalities by means of constitutional rules. And it is here especially that the finance constitution and the constitutions of transnational companies are at the center of constitutional attention.

D. A final example

It is possible to observe the first steps toward transnational societal constitutionalism in the social conflicts the result of which are corporate codes of conduct. Massive international and much-publicized public criticism plus the actions of protest movements and non-governmental organizations (NGOs) of civil society, compelled many transnational companies to "voluntarily" establish business codes of conduct. In these codes, they claim to commit to resolve certain types of problems with regard to the public interest and promise to implement them internally.[27] The question of how the effects of these business codes in the areas of labor, products, the environment and human rights must be assessed remains ambivalent. The commitments in the "private" codes are often simple public relations strategies that do not lead to effective changes in behavior.[28]

But our attention may be held by empirical studies which, in some cases, indicate that codes have brought about real changes. They have improved working conditions, increased protection levels for the environment and for human rights.[29] Ongoing monitoring by NGOs or the contracts that bind companies to certifying bodies in civil society seems to be the most important conditions for success.[30]

What matters are the pressures of learning, i.e. external constraints that are exerted on transnational companies with a view to gradual change. This means that communication is not simply by the medium of the law and legal sanctions are not the only ones to transfer expectations from the outside to the inside. Instead, through non-legal media – through the knowledge of experts, political and social power and economic incentives and monetary sanctions – learning processes are triggered.

Of what do the pressures consist? The sanctions of the law do not play a decisive role in this process. Mechanisms outside of the law act in their place. First of all, the process of inter-organizational power – unilateral pressure and political exchange – is forcing companies

27 For details, Kenneth Abbott & Duncan Snidal, "Strengthening International Regulation Through Transnational New Governance: Overcoming the Orchestration Deficit", *Vanderbilt Journal of Transnational Law*, 42, pp. 501–571 (2009).

28 For a critique of corporate codes, Tim Bartley, "Institutional Emergence in an Era of Globalization: The Rise of Transnational Private Regulation of Labor and Environmental Conditions", *American Journal of Sociology*, 113, pp. 300, 327 (2007) et seq.; Harry Arthurs, "Private Ordering and Workers' Rights in the Global Economy: Corporate Codes of Conduct as a Regime of Labor Market Regulation", in *Labor Law in an Era of Globalization: Transformative Practices and Possibilities*, Joanne Conaghan, Richard Michael Fischl & Karl Klare (eds.), Oxford: Oxford University Press (2002), pp. 471–488.

29 Martin Herberg, *Private Regulative in den Lücken der Staatenwelt: Umweltschutz im multinationalen Konzern zwischen staatlicher Steuerung & gesellschaftlicher Selbstregulierung*, Frankfurt am Main, NY: Campus; Olaf Dilling (2006), Martin Herberg & Gerd Winter (eds.), *Responsible Business: Self-Governance and Law in Transnational Economic Transactions*, Oxford: Hart (2008).

30 Annegret Flohr, Lothar Riethe, Sandra Schwindenhammer & Klaus Dieter Wolf, *The Role of Business in Global Governance. Corporations as Norm-Entrepreneurs*, Basingstoke: Palgrave (2009).

to develop their own codes. It cannot be emphasized enough that this external pressure is a prerequisite condition in order for corporate codes to really have an effect.[31] Here are found the pressures of the nation-state, as argued by Robé, as well as the pressures of social movements, such as I see them, to prove themselves as necessary mutual additions. In line with experiences so far, the States, as well as international organizations of the world states have, with their multinational company codes of conduct, generated resources of power that required external pressure. So far the pressures of offensive power from protest movements, NGOs, trade unions, nonprofit organizations and public opinion have proved to be just as strong. These are economic sanctions that often ultimately decide in the end: companies depend upon sensitive consumers and their buying habits and groups of investors who, with their investments, exert financial pressure on the companies.[32]

Behind the metaphor of "voluntary codes" hides something totally unlike volunteering. If transnational companies adopt the codes, it was not after having considered the request for the common good or due to corporate ethics. They resign "voluntarily" themselves to adopting, when massive learning pressures come from the outside. The learning process does not take place within the legal system, from code to code, through a transfer of validity, but it follows detours through other functional systems. In a complicated "translation process", the boundaries between systems are crossed; a perturbation cycle forms between the legal acts of international organizations, the pressures of political and social power, knowledge operations in epistemic communities, economic sanctions and legal acts of multinational companies. Initial content is radically changed when the code of conduct for international organizations is "translated" into the scholarly language of the experts, who design models and organize the monitoring, into the inter-organizational power of political attitudes among international organizations, NGOs and multinational enterprises, into the power of the regulatory mechanisms of public space and of incentives and financial sanctions and when lastly, everything is "retranslated" into the legal language of the internal codes of the company. This kind of complicated link between the two codes clearly shows that an auto-constitutionalization of the company does not stem from intrinsic reasons of volunteering, but is only due to external and diverted learning pressures.

31 Abbott & Snidal, "Strengthening International Regulation Through Transnational New Governance" op. cit, 506 resume: "These norms are 'voluntary' in the sense that they are not legally required; however, firms often adhere because of pressure from NGOs, customer requirements, industry association rules, and other forces that render them mandatory in practice".

32 For a detailed analysis of the relation between external pressures and internal enterprise structures see Jennifer Howard-Grenville, Jennifer Nash & Coglianese, "Constructing the License to Operate: Internal Players and Their Influence on Corporate Environmental Decisions", *Law and Policy*, 30, p. 73 (2008).

6 From orthodox to societal constitutionalism

Jean De Munck

The expansion of a global law plays a major role, without a shadow of doubt, in the transformation of contemporary societies. At a transnational level, the law has the purpose of serving three basic functions (Luhmann): the stabilization of normative expectations of behavior through the diffusion of a shared legal culture, the regulation of the conduct of private individuals and those involved in collectives (public or non-public) and the resolution of conflicts via the involvement of courts. In these three areas, one notes a transnationalization process. The spread of a global *legal culture* was initiated by major legal international bodies and is supported by several operatives in legal life, ranging from law schools to transnational law firms to NGOs and associations that advocate a culture of human rights. *Conduct regulation* goes through various transnational legislation and administrative bodies. On a global level, there are new authorities: functional organizations such as the World Trade Organization (WTO) and the International Labor Organization (ILO), which are formed in a very traditional manner by interstate agreements, but also authorities whose shape and function are more innovative, such as the International Olympic Committee or the International Standards Organization (ISO). Finally, the *resolution of conflicts* on a transnational level is supported by new courts. Some of them are of public origin, like the UN initiatives in international criminal courts or the various regional courts and commissions responsible for defending human rights. Other forms of transnational jurisdiction have emerged in the private domain, in which the arbitration courts for business, trade and sports matters are nowadays very important.

The national law must now deal with this transnational legal order. Here, I would like to comment on one of the problematic consequences of this situation: the mutation of the notion of constitution. There is no doubt that this notion provided a cornerstone of the rule of law the way it was theorized by the school of natural law and progressively implemented as a result of certain historical experiences in the eighteenth and nineteenth centuries. Whether it was written down or not, the constitution unified the two new sources of the legitimacy of the law: (a) the principles of rational law as conceived by philosophers, which provide the basis of a universal right to freedom (property, association, conscience, and so on.); and (b) the existence of particular nations, resulting from stories of territorialization. By linking these two (antagonistic and additional) principles in a single legal configuration, constitutions have allowed for the effective institutionalization of the idea of modern democracy. The question we are confronted with is one of knowing whether or not this notion will retain its organization power in the new world, both normatively (i.e. what should be law) and positively (what the law is).

There are many signs that reflect constitutionalization processes at work in the global world. More than ever, the idea of national constitution appears, at a domestic level, to be the royal path to democracy: This long tendency of modernity is not denied. But, more than anything else, forms of constitutionalization of international law can be observed (through the promotion of human rights as sources that are hierarchically superior to the law, through the globalization of "judges' dialogue" and the establishment of transnational judicial and legislative bodies). One can also observe a constitutionalization of non-state transnational regimes. To add to this, one can speak of "cosmopolitan constitutionalization from below" (Boaventura de Sousa Santos) in cases of new social movements that occupy the transnational political scene.

These indisputable indices of *constitutionalization* give rise to new forms of *constitutionalism*, i.e. political, sociological and legal doctrines that interpret these phenomena according to contrasting scales. First I will locate these various forms of *constitutionalism* in a range of large positions that indicate the central issue in the debate: knowing whether or not globalization calls only for an adaptation of our most basic intuitions concerning the law and democracy, or if, on the contrary, we are required to perform a thorough revision of these intuitions inherited from our history, or even, to a certain extent, abandon them (1).

Among the constitutionalisms most open to change, one highly promising route would seem to be that formed by Gunther Teubner. It is formulated within the framework of the systems theory. This theory, while powerful in its description and explanation aspects, received no normative concern from the one who conceived it (Niklas Luhmann); it was also indeed no subject of any constitutional claim. However, as Emilios Christodoulidis and Lyana Francot-Timmermans say (2011: 187), we should give Gunther Teubner the credit of a "normative turn" at the heart of the systems theory.

This "normative turn" manifested itself in the 1980s, in a timid form, in the theory of "reflexive law". This becomes quite obvious in the 1990s with the adoption of the exciting "societal constitutionalism" program. In a case such as this, one should note that a very high level of sensitivity regarding the current problems combines with a deep and subtle understanding of the complex transformations of positive law.

I would like to comment on this option, as a research and political-legal program. In order to set the scene I will first sketch the spectrum of positions of schools and authors on the issue of guiding principles of global democracy: The "societal constitutionalism" is clearly a "transformationalist" approach to classical constitutionalism (1). After that, I will make some comments on three of its basic components. I will first explain the key idea: Constitutionalism should not be focused on the State. This is to give a sociological and legal consistency to the idea of civil constitutions as an extension of the democratic ambition that stimulated the first constitutional phase of our societies (2). Second, I will comment on the interpretation that, in this context, can be stated as the first ambition of any constitution, namely the configuration of political sovereignty. We will see that the *demos* idea must be made more complex if it is to adjust to this new context (3). Finally, I will make a few remarks on the second key component of democratic constitutions: reference to fundamental rights. There is no constitution in effect if no hierarchy of norms is specified. Within the overall framework that applies to us, fundamental human rights play this central role. They cross over each other and require not only a specific kind of judicial monitoring (judicial review), but also a renewed political culture (4).

1. Constitutionalizations and constitutionalism

The concept of constitutionalization takes into account several social and institutional phenomena whose consistency is uncertain, to say the least. The aggregation under a single unique analytical category poses considerable interpretation problems. In constitutionalization practices, people will certainly come across ideas, theories and doctrines that are more or less articulate and coherent, expressed in individual texts and in several speeches, whether they are experts or laypeople. But there are also non-ideational components: power relationships, economic constraints, cultural practices, and so on.

With this, it is necessary to distinguish *constitutionalization* practices from *constitutionalisms*. These are *interpretations* that simultaneously provide a description of the reality of the constitutionalization phenomena; an explanation of how they emerged, their development or their blocking; and an assessment of their desirability and their normativity, which could generate policy options.

A. Orthodox constitutionalism

Let's start with simple and well-established ideas, before deconstructing and complexifying them. One particular form of constitutionalism occupies a central position in both the awareness of those it affects and among lawyers, sociologists and political scientists: liberal (or neo-liberal) inspiration constitutionalism. In such a case, the concept of constitution remains a very classic one. It is in line with liberal doctrines. This form of constitutionalism is defined by the following principles:

1. The constitution has the aim of establishing a State legal order via fundamental norms (not just political philosophy principles), which have higher status than ordinary laws.
2. It proclaims the rights and liberties of individuals (human and citizen rights). Civil and political liberties are at the center of it. They must be respected by all members of society, including the State, whose regulatory power is thus strictly limited.
3. It establishes a government based on popular will. This is expressed via the election of representatives during regular polls conducted by universal suffrage.
4. It establishes a national State that respects the separation of powers and the fundamental principles of the law.
5. The constitution takes precedence over all the other acts of the government. It establishes a judicial review of the constitutionality of the laws and regulations. It may only be changed via a special procedure.

Everybody will have recognized this doctrine, which originated in the constitutions of the eighteenth and nineteenth centuries. It is certainly not out of date in today's world. It has been an accompaniment to the implementation of the "Washington consensus" since the 1990s. Its various components are constantly repeated in the practices and the doctrines.

However, it is subject to strong protests. On one hand, these criticisms are internal and normative: it has been accused of failing to adhere to the promises of democracy and law that it claims to respect. The reasons for this failure are said to recognize implicit assumptions of political and legal philosophy. Meanwhile, these criticisms also have a sociological element (i.e. the claim that this constitutionalism would remain blind to multiple constitutionalization trends that have arisen, and continue to arise, in speeches and arrangements of positive law). In a way, one could say that real constitutional practices would be richer, and even "surplus", compared to the classic sketch whose content we have just recalled.

B. The four blind elements of orthodox constitutionalism

Without going back to discussing historical details – this would be tedious – we can roughly categorize the criticisms that this form of constitutionalism is subject to today under four headings. Following these criticisms, we can *at best* consider the latter to be a reductive constitutional version of democracy, which must be completed (but with what?). *At worst*, we can see in it a political danger and a form of ideology (in a Marxist sense).

1. First criticism: This type of constitutionalism is focused on the nation-state. It claims to legitimize the national State political power and to configure the institutions that work in a given territory. However, globalization leads to the pursuit of policies and the establishment of political institutions that transcend borders. It is not just a spatial overshoot for englobement in a wider area. It's about going beyond the territory *criterion* (as a pre-given context) that cannot be violated by any regulation. International commerce, online communication, the configuration of the mass media, finance flows, the mobility of migrants, and a thousand other processes that generate public problems, are no longer just "territorializable" in stable and recognized borders. Even though territorial constructions of a scale greater than nation-state (like the European Union) are desirable and useful, they are not sufficient for addressing these issues. However, constitutionalization processes that are already observable worldwide do concern these deterritorialized institutions e.g. the constitution of the WTO, that of the OIT and even the procedures of the UN Security Council.

2. Second criticism: This constitutionalism certainly effectively protects individual liberties against State power by limiting its scope, but it remains blind to the threats that they are exposed to from private powers that are formed outside the State but that have an extremely wide scope. These non-State powers may be of various kinds: church, media, health care system, and so on. More than anything else, one should think of businesses (financial or industrial) that have acquired an ability to dictate the standards in a way almost equivalent to that of States. It is important to understand that this normative capacity does not lie outside of the constitution. It is derived directly from a constitutional order that grants individuals property rights. In a strictly individual sense, the right of ownership certainly represents the condition of independent living. It provides the individual with their base in the material and objective world. But, with this individual basis, a new *sovereignty* developed (born of "organizational contracts", Lyon-Caen, 2014). By accepting the constitution of capital companies that become increasingly important, the law thus allows for the establishment of new powers that change the living standards of thousands, even millions of people. Civil society has thus become the playground of corporations – these entities formed of inter-individual contracts that acquire a real and autonomous existence through the mediation of law.[1] However, as has been emphasized by Robé (2013: 343), corporations, existing as systems of private governance, "carry with them the seed of a new feudalism". Globalization only intensifies this constitution process with private national powers that have become transnational; powers that may, as a result of international treaties, be of legal forms that are very restrictive on individual States.

However, one should note attempts to constitutionalize these private legal orders in order to promote new supervisory powers. These trends were already apparent, at national level, with the emergence of labor law and related collective negotiation institutions. Since the Weimar constitution, we know that the rights of union representatives can be legally enshrined. In 1946, Georges Gurvitch (2009) sought to constitutionalize the labor law. The German basic law of 1949 integrated the *Tarifautonomie,* which gave collective negotiation the status

1 See in this volume the shining explanations of Jean-Philippe Robé and Larry Catá Backer.

as a fundamental institution of the Republic. Permanent consultative structures have been established in many countries. Social dialogue as a method for the production of norms was enshrined in the constitutional texts of the European Union, even though one can judge that its position was marginal in the basic institutions.

3. Third criticism: Orthodox constitutionalism remains linked to a restricted version of democracy. The primary emphasis was on the legitimization of the representatives of general will via free and regular elections on the basis of universal suffrage. This is certainly a necessary condition for democracy. But is it a satisfactory condition, even at global level? The limits of representative democracy are well known: the principal (the people)/agent (the representative) relationship is a complicated one, and it becomes virtually impossible to monitor when the chain of agents grows disproportionately, just like with large institutions that have tangled levels, where orders are issued from an opaque expertocracy. Representatives may constitute a globalized elite who co-opt at a global level. They are no longer subject to popular verdict. With this, "the field of 'constitutional form and constitutional power' is really a game between the constitutive sovereign and the constituent people . . . a game that, according to realists, the sovereign dominates" (Tully, 2008: 472).

With representative democracy, it is necessary to add institutions of *deliberative* democracy and *participative* democracy (Nanz & Steffek, 2004). This is what non-governmental organizations in particular demand. Orthodox constitutionalism does not seem to allow for sufficient room for the same. Given the current situation, one cannot speak of a public global space and political engagement processes that are constitutionally protected.

However, we should take into account innovations that could initiate some constitutionalization processes. In transnational institutions for instance, we see the development of new instruments for recognizing "global civil society" groups. In this way, the "First Nations" obtained an embryonic level of international recognition. In certain global forums, NGOs are recognized as *ex officio* members. The European Union has constitutionalized a right of petition granted to its citizens.

4. Fourth criticism: Orthodox constitutionalism recognizes a limited concept of human rights. These include the first generation of rights (civil and political), at the expense of the second generation (social and cultural rights). However, the *real* freedom of individuals cannot be understood negatively (to borrow the distinction of Berlin, 1979); it must also incorporate a positive element. This was the prerogative of the welfare state: In their constitutions, Western welfare states have, to a large extent, internalized so-called second-generation rights regarding access to resources and socio-economic opportunities: the right to education, the right to work, the right to property, the right to guaranteed income, and so on. In modern society, we can mention the persistence of requests for the constitutionalization of *redistribution* policies. Some of them have already been consecrated by positive law: This is the case in particular with requests for the constitutionalization of the right to social security, or the right to work, in several national constitutions or international texts. We thus see the emergence of new requests such as that of the "right to food sovereignty" characteristic of transnational rural associations (Claeys, 2012).

Some of these four criticisms are not new. The second, third and fourth ones in particular have undergone formulations since the nineteenth century, which, in the twentieth century, had a profound impact on the constitutions of democratic nations.

In the history of constitutions, the contemporary situation seems to be ambivalent. On one hand, in Western countries, we share the feeling that orthodox constitutionalism in reality brings us back to an earlier phase of the constitutional evolution: that which precedes the advent of the "second constitutional revolution" (Robé) (i.e. the development of the welfare state). On the other hand, in developing countries, this constitutionalism may appear as a first step towards the rule of law and may, consequentially, adorn the feathers of democratic progress. This differentiation of historical temporalities must be overcome if one desires the establishment of a minimally acceptable North-South dialogue.

Anyway, among these four criticisms, the first one is the newest one. If the nation is no longer the obvious "container" of the ideas of the people, sovereignty and legitimate law, we are faced with the need not only to review constitutional order but also all the responses so far established in the pursuit of a solution to the other three problems. Until now we have assumed that the national State framework was not a fundamental problem but the key to solve all the problems of the orthodox constitutionalism.

C. A range of positions

The debate on constitutionalism in the global age is confronted with all these difficulties. Schools and propositions differ according to the position that they occupy, both internally and externally, with each of these criticisms. In an attempt to get a clear view of the positions in relation to each other, I propose the use of a distinction that originated from David Held. Regarding *Global Studies*, he noted that the approaches can be roughly divided into two broad categories: the "gradualists" and the "transformationalists" (Held et al., 1999: 7–9). With *gradualists*, on one hand "it is the form of democracy that is transformed, not its substance and guiding principles" (Bohman, 2005: 294). Politics and law must adapt to new dimensions of pluralism and governance, but they should not change their founding principles. The concept of democracy that was formed in the eighteenth century certainly deserves to be corrected, even reformed, but not reformulated or outright abandoned. We cannot close down old local legal services as a result of globalization. With *transformationalists*, on the other hand, it should be considered that globalization forces us not only to review the procedures of politics and law, but also its ideals and objectives and its theory and practice, where it is agreed that globalization would leave us in a radically new kind of world where old models would no longer be useful. We must conceive radically new institutions. We must change our theories of justice, and our vision of applicable law.

One of the domains where these "gradualist" (*gradualists*) or "transformationist" (*transformationalists*) concepts are confronted with ongoing changes is, quite simply, the concept of constitution. One could classify the prominent positions of the debate on a continuous arc from the first to the second.

On one side of the spectrum, one can find schools and authors who do not conceive any radical change to the idea of constitution. This would be the case with "orthodox" constitutionalism, which we have just talked about, for it can certainly envisage limited forms of global status constitutionalism favorably – for example forms of judicial review of human rights (first generation) proclaimed by an International Court of Justice. But it remains fundamentally subject to the rather severe restrictions that orthodox constitutionalism assigns to the very idea of constitution, which is a condition required for it to be effective. More open to change, neo-Kantian constitutionalists, such as Habermas and his school of thought, are open to a quite radical revision of the premises of liberal constitution, with the integration of the first and third criticisms in particular. They seek to promote, with much imagination and sophistication, a kind of post-national constitution (Cohen, 2012) that will give way to a concept requiring deliberative democracy (Bohman, 2007). However, they do not reflect a great deal of sensitivity with regard to the other two criticisms (2 and 4). This does not mean that they will be politically insensitive in any way; but they probably share a belief that management of these problems demands political struggle rather than a revised constitutional architecture.

The partisans of social constitutionalism, such as Gunther Teubner and Jean-Philippe Robé, being more "transformationist", tend to address the four criteria as a matter of priority pending the acceptance of a very radical revision of the idea of constitution. They seriously envision the formation of civil constitutions, which will supplement the already existing state constitution without abolishing it. However, a link is still maintained with the original idea of constitution: the basic features that characterize this formation can be likened to a distant star that, however, is progressively depleting on the horizon.

This transformationist orientation has been radicalized by authors like James Tully (1995) and Boaventura de Sousa Santos. The latter is the promoter of a "counterhegemonic constitutionalism", and the first one to uphold a "constitutionalism from below"; and both seek to inject dynamism into the institutional forms of global hegemony of which orthodox constitutionalism is an ideological component and a fundamental practice.

Finally, at the end of this curve, one can find authors for whom the very idea of constitution has lost its value not so much for normative reasons but for social ones. According to them, the concept of constitution is becoming less and less relevant in globalized, postmodern capitalism. The very functioning of the law has changed under the influence of dominating economic and political forces, up to the point where the old claims of the State to sovereignty and constitutional review are rendered incongruous. The position of Michel Freitag is a good example of this, as is that of Negri, who states that "the passage from government to governance fractures the control unit of the public law system" (2008: 105).

For them, postmodern law has become "management-based" and "operational". It is no longer ultimately based on the principles of rational law. Rather, it is oriented by efficiency and "problem-solving" processes localized in all-powerful organizations that have become impervious to the axiological rationality characteristic of historical constitutionalism. Given this, one may argue that constitutionalism has become obsolescent. Certainly, constitutional law retains a certain level of relevance as far as the organization of public powers is concerned. But one can no longer speak of constitutional *foundation*. On one hand, the constitution now includes, in its very formulation, contingent policy rules that are subject to strategic calculation (e.g. monetary regulations, economic and social aims). To put it in other terms, constitutional law absorbs more and more substantive ordinary rules (even though the former is still hierarchically superior). On the other hand, constitutional law becomes sectorial when it no longer organizes all legal order from a central position. It is overwhelmed by private legal constellations (such as *Lex mercatoria*, for example, or *Lex sportiva*). In short, this would mean that we have gone from "the political-legislative production of the law to its conventional and pragmatic production" (Freitag, 2002: 77). Normatively, Michel Freitag laments this development, but his relentless description leaves little room for doubt as far as the exhaustion of democratic possibilities is concerned.

The debate is therefore conducted from a range of positions: orthodox, gradualist, transformationist and post-constitutional. Here I would like to head down the trail opened up by the central intuitions of social constitutionalism. Sociologically, they appear to be better articulated than the others, while not losing sight of the normative requirements. Indeed, gradualist positions (Habermas) are often linked to a very normativist conception of constitution, and their selections are based on the aspects of social reality that fit their theories, with little consideration of the real processes that could jeopardize them. In particular, in my opinion they remain blind to the many privatization and autonomization processes of global legal systems emphasized by societal constitutionalism in a very realistic manner; they are also insensitive to the increasing difficulties that apply with the solutions that the welfare state provides in response to social claims.

The domination theories (Negri, Freitag) err on the opposite side. They underestimate the semantic and political potential that sustains constitutional discourses. Being fully occupied with showing the efficiency of the new powers unleashed on the world, they forget to question the resistance debates and the innovative practices that "take law seriously" (as Boaventura Sousa Santos and James Tully did). This means that they have to rely on anarchic "exceedances" when they don't simply end up in melancholy. Societal constitutionalism takes into account the "repoliticization" processes of the law and the perspectives that they open to new regulations.

2. Constitutions beyond the boundaries of the state

The concept of societal constitutionalism was developed by Gunther Teubner (Teubner, 2004). As he often recalled, he found the work of David Sciulli (1992), of Weberian inspiration, to be decisive. It underlined the reality and the necessity (evolutionary and normative) of extending the concept of constitution not only beyond the nation – as was demanded by all contemporary theorists (gradualists included) – but also (in particular) beyond the state and the political sphere. From this point of view, a constitution is defined as a coupling (very specific and dated) of an autonomous social system (the political system) with the legal system, which is also autonomous. This coupling allows for the provision of solutions to problems concerning the social system in question under conditions in which it is fundamentally threatened by dedifferentiation.

A. The political constitution

So what does a political constitution truly consist of, on a sociological level? It produces and stabilizes institutionally three major functional differences.

First differentiation: When regarded as an *organization*, the state must be distinguished from the public space. In sociology, an organization is defined as a set of connections between individuals that allow for the generation of *decisions* according to a set of objectives that are defined in advance. These decisions pertain to the use of resources or the content of communications. The organization obeys a division of work in which the roles are distributed during the decision process. Parliament, administration, judiciary, political parties and interest groups each occupy their role in the state. But this organization must be distinguished from the public opinion that is generated from spontaneous and informal meetings of citizens engaged in discussion in a public place. Regardless of how this public space is conceived (Habermas version or not), it is clear that it must be established as an area that is protected by the law. The constitution establishes this founding difference of political-administrative organization and public area via civil, political and religious liberties. Its erasure would forever be acknowledged as problematic from the perspective of the efficiency of decisions (whereby the elite would become deaf to external information) and their legitimacy (when there is no public debate).

Second differentiation: The political system, understood as a sphere of *specific normativity*, must be distinguished from several other kinds of sphere. By proclaiming the neutrality of the State, for example, the modern constitution establishes (negatively) the borders of a normativity field that is specifically political. Its border with religion is regarded as a necessary one that can never be legally superseded, whatever the discussions of its exact course may be. More positively: the constitutional discourse assigns legitimate values to political rationality (the target of general interest, the pursuit of the common good, the defense of territorial integrity), which do not include the values that are pursued in the other spheres. In such a case, constitution is an institutional condition for the autonomy of the churches (via religious rights), of the market (via property and contract laws), of science (via freedom of conscience, research, expression), and so on. The spheres of normativity outside of the political sphere are thus protected against State intervention, and reciprocally.

Third differentiation: As a *collective actor*, the State has its own personality. It is distinguished from the other actors (individual or collective) that populate civil society. It focuses an existing collective power, and acquires for itself the means to intervene in society via taxation, the armed forces, administration, and so on. As such it is about the stable establishment of normative expectations of behavior ensuring respect for the different agents rather than allowing for their aggregation in the large "political body" of Léviathan. This is why a constitution explicitly defines the scope of the power of the State (the "competencies") and sets the general operating conditions in a restrictive manner.

According to the sociological interpretation of human rights proposed by Luhmann (Verschraegen, 2002), these three differentiations allow for the protection of all persons (individuals or corporations) as well as all the autonomous normativity spheres. The State has been constitutionalized since the end of the eighteenth century due to the enormous accumulation of power reflected by the establishment of absolutist early modern monarchies. Whereas traditional society exploded as a result of the pressure imposed by various functional differentiations (scientific, economic, artistic . . .), political power emerged as a particularly strong aggressive threat to an earlier stage of social differentiation (a threat that would be confirmed by the totalitarian regimes of the twentieth century).

The constitution is the *legal institution* of this differentiation/articulation of the state in these three perspectives. This institutional dimension must be strictly distinguished from the organization (Boltanski, 2008). The organization coordinates functions and assigns roles, while the institution exercises a categorical feature: The institution has "the task of confirming what the current situation is; to say what is indicative of what and what is important" (Boltanski, 2008: 26). Certainly, the law itself, as far as its implementation is concerned, recognizes specific organizations that are partially mixed with those of the State. But we can in no way reduce the constitution to an affair of coordination means.

What is the object of this institution? It is not just the State, as is sometimes understood, but the *society* itself. After all, a constitution empowers not only the State but also private individuals and corporations. It allows multiple normative spheres to coexist. It determines things with the application of categories that are forever brought up in political discussions, as well as differences and fundamental references that distinguish it from the contingent categories of ordinary legislation.

B. Civil constitutions

Societal constitutionalism seeks to provide a structural response to the two first criticisms of orthodox constitutionalism. Gunther Teubner (2010: 328) writes that "today's constitutionalism moves beyond the nation-state. It does so in a double sense: constitutionalism moves into the transnational context and into the private sector". One notes the constitution of specialized transnational legal regimes at global level: sports law, *lex mercatoria*, cybernetic law, and so on. These regimes go over the authority of national legislators and judges.

In these multiple fragmented legal orders, it is already possible to observe trends toward constitutionalization, which does not necessarily respond to traditional formal criteria. Constitutions can certainly be in written form, in France or in the United States, but certain unwritten customs may also be considered as a constitution (like in Britain or Israel), in which case they are set forth and continuously repeated in the legal system. It is not necessary to proclaim the constitution in a solemn moment that is born of a revolution: for constitutionalization is not a separate event, but a process that repeats itself and affirms itself mid-term and long-term. However, if a form of judicial control (*judicial review*) is necessary for the discussion of constitution, we will not necessarily be required to wait until a specialized court is authorized to occupy itself with this task:

> judicial review of standard business contracts, of private standards of due diligence, of standardization by private associations, of arbitration court decisions in both national and international spheres, are examples of a de facto constitutional review of non-legislative law.
>
> (Teubner, 2004: 20)

Besides this, one can also put forward normative arguments for civil constitutionalism. The different social systems are *all* a threat to the integrity of individuals. With the development of systemic society, one should note a new danger in social relationships: It no longer stems only from individuals, but also from anonymous processes affected by science, money, the media, and so on. The bioethics committees deal with situations of extreme vulnerability in medical procedures all the time. Monetization corrupts the world as it is actually experienced; it transforms identities into goods. The media stalk private life, invade privacy spaces and overturn reputations. Far from being confined to the State, as is believed by liberals, the threat factor proliferates everywhere in our decentralized world. Threat also affects association and sociality patterns. The autonomous normativities of the systems encounter major obstacles in their environments, for other, more powerful social systems fragment them and annex them in their own operations.

The objective of civil constitutions is the selection and reinforcement, in non-State spheres, of the specific normative elements that are compatible with a perspective of democratization. For example: In the scientific and academic community, the principle of *academic liberty* is a long-recognized one. Its pedigree dates back to the Middle Ages. It allowed for the establishment of protected discussion areas meant specifically for communities of researchers. In the Middle Ages, it was considered a privilege to be able to argue against the various powers of the Prince or the Church. In the modern era, it's a matter of the expression of free opinion and searching for the truth, while allowing the researchers to escape the subordination links mandated by a private labor contract, or the reserve duty that a civil servant is supposed to recognize. Thanks to this type of autonomy, a certain type of teaching (typically the university kind), has been able to emerge and mature. The *principle of collegiality* also enjoys a position of acclaim in university life – it assumes that decisions that affect the community stem from discussions and decisions between and among peers. In some contexts, this collegiality extends not only to academic colleagues but also to students. Today we know that this principle is extremely important when it comes to immunizing scientific life against the pressures that can arise from the political or economic domain. In the legal culture of all spheres of society (press, businesses, health, cyberspace, and so on.), one can bet that they will be able to find similar principles that could justify their constitutional protection.

C. Beyond the State . . . but not without it

However, civil constitutionalization conditions continue to depend on the attitude of the State. One can certainly extend constitutionalization outside the State, as Gunther Teubner proposed, but one cannot head there without the State. There are two reasons for which the State is a necessary partner on the road toward civil constitutions.

The first reason concerns the accumulation of resources at its disposal, and in particular the monopoly on lawful violence. Even in the civil sphere, one cannot imagine the law being efficient without State enforcement. Not that any form of legal efficiency depends on this. There are indeed types of legal efficiency that are a matter of incentives and semantic framing rather than sanctions. But the resources for constraint measures remain a necessary recourse option in the event of non-execution. However, an alternative already exists: the redistribution of resources for lawful violence amongst the different spheres of society. This redistribution is already the trend in several regions across the globe. But the constitutionalization of civil spheres cannot (normatively) be confused with the lawful privatization of violence. Teubner's approach appears poorly equipped to face this risk. In this regard, a kind of sociology of Weberian inspiration would seem better equipped for acknowledging the problem of violence in circumstances of domination. Even with a societal constitutionalism, it remains impossible to avoid the asymmetrical function of the State in the legal processes.

The second reason with the essential character of the State lies with the fact that, to this day, it represents the only social world that has *already* been constitutionalized in a relatively satisfactory manner. As such, it should not serve only as a paradigm or *analogon* (public) for future (civil) constitutions; it is also a *political instrument* that lets one intervene in the various civil sectors, directly, via the route of legislation. It is true that this recourse to the State (with the aim of empowering legal domains that must, as a matter of principle, remain outside of it) recognizes certain risks, for the State itself constitutes a threat of dedifferentiation. Political action can certainly achieve convincing results without going through the State apparatus, which is not always necessary or adequate. However, given the magnitude of the task, and the possible resistances and the difficulties to be overcome, it is hard to imagine that the different spheres could be constitutionalized with no decisive contest (however limited) on the part of the State apparatus.

The decentering of the State therefore should not be radicalized, such as Günther Teubner tends to do (see also, in this sense, Lindhal, 2011). Societal constitutionalism calls more for a transformation of state intervention methods (in particular with regard to the link between administration and civil society) than the peripheralization that some formulations of Gunther Teubner seem to resemble.

3. What is the *demos* of a civil constitution?

For a democracy to function, it is necessary to recognize the sovereignty of the people. But the question is one of knowing who belongs (or does not belong) to the sovereign people. As Goodin (2007: 43) says, "constituting the demos is the first step in constructing democracy". The legal constitution would usually respond to this problem via the principle of nationality.

However, in a perspective of societal constitutionalism, this response is no longer valid. On one hand, when territorial limits are crossed by global policies or institutions, it is no longer possible to equate those who lay down the law and those who suffer the consequences thereof according to a strict principle of territory; on the other hand, the perspective of a civil constitution lays down the question of civil sovereignties, *alongside* political sovereignties. I would like to explore this question briefly, citing progressive substitution, on the principle of nationality and the "all affected principle" that is promoted by certain globalization theorists.

A. The constitution as an institution of the sovereign people

Before I address the question as such, it is worth clearing up a misunderstanding concerning the actual effectiveness of the constitution in the process of the establishment and maintenance of political sovereignty. The constitution limits the power of the State via a set of fundamental laws, and the system for the division of powers, thereby imposing a priori a framework for the exercise of sovereignty. With this, one could understand the constitution as a means for the containment of popular power- – and it is true that the paradigm of *restricted democracy* accompanies orthodox constitutionalism like a shadow. This weak version, often designated as "American", invokes another version in response; one that is willingly designated as "French" (although it is just an historical reduction). In such a case, constitutions and legal norms are not constraints or restrictions in the democratic process but expressions of the general will of the sovereign people (formed by means of political coalition and cooperation actions).

The two poles of this conflict share a single concept of legality as an external reality that does not mix with the processes of will formation and decision. But the truth is that the constitution does not just play a role of sheer *limitation*; it allows a people to exist and function *as a* self-determined people. To explain this point, we should remember the famous distinction of John Searle between two types of regulation functioning. The first purpose of the rules is one of limitation. For example, the Highway Code regulates traffic flows, imposes levies, and mandates drivers and pedestrians to observe certain behaviors in specific contexts. But traffic would exist without the intervention of these rules. It's not the regulations that create pedestrians, drivers or the flow of traffic as such. However, there are other rules that function as constitutive rules of the activities to which they apply. For example, one cannot play a game of chess if there are no rules for the game; after all, the simple moving of pieces on a board cannot in itself be classified as a game. Similarly, going back to the example of the highway code, one could say that, while this code does not create pedestrians, it does create the red light as a red light; for the significance of this light, which is well-known among drivers, owes its presence only to a convention established by the code, and it makes sense in relation to other rules.

A rule can therefore be applied in the creation of a new social reality (which is shared), thanks to the symbolic operation that lets one treat something *as though it were* something else. By virtue of a rule, a river can count as a border, a hammer and sickle can become symbols of Communism, and a raised arm may, in certain defined circumstances, count as a vote. And a heterogeneous multitude can turn into a sovereign people.

I hope you will pardon me for this formula that appears to be nothing more than tautological: a constitution is truly *constitutive*. Contrary to the myth of the "presence" of the people (as Derrida would put it), and contrary to the myth of the general will born of the simple combination of individual wills or a combination of forces that existed prior to its introduction, it is important to keep alive the awareness of this symbolic mediation of democratic power. As Ulrich Preuss (2010: 36) wrote:

> "Constitutionalist" is a notion of self-rule according to which the will of the united body (of the people) is embodied in a system of rules, institutions and procedures which determine the principles of how a free society wants to be ordered. Here the multitude is transformed into "the people"; but "the people" does not rule by joining the individual wills into to one collective will but by the application of these rules to the relevant cases through the competent institutions.

When looked at from this angle, a constitution is certainly constitutive, but it is not at all transcendent. It does not create the people (as a whole), but rather redescribes the people and, at the same time, transforms it. The fetishizing of the constitution turns into a means for depoliticizing social relationships, and therefore for sanctifying domination relationships. The constitution must therefore be dislodged from the "imperial throne", as Tully (1995: 183–184) explains when discussing the confines of orthodox constitutionalism.

> Constitutions are not fixed and unchangeable agreements reached at some foundational moment, but chains of continual intercultural negotiations and agreements in accord with, and violations of the conventions of mutual recognition, continuity and consent.

Constitutions are implemented during several discourse and practice type actions that result in a recreation of its scheduling. In other words, the constitution is a process rather than a structure. One of the advantages of societal constitutionalism is that the formalist account of the constitution is played down, allowing it to be distributed in the multiple social auto-institution processes.

B. Beyond the territory: All affected principle

So what are the boundaries of a people governed by a post-national regime? Today, the convention of territory is undermined. We are obliged to reconnect the constitution with the social action of the participants (more on this subject: Whitt, 2014). In order to go beyond the territoriality principle, some political thinkers put forward the idea that a norm becomes legitimate if it is developed by all persons concerned. Jürgen Habermas, David Held and James Goodin in particular, advocated this substitution. It has three clear advantages. First, it is in line with the founding principle of democracy: the law should be developed by those who are governed by it. However, it subtly extends this concept, with corrections to it: the law must be developed by those to whom it applies or *who are affected by its conditions*. Second, this formulation does not preclude the pertinence of a territoriality principle: in this vision of democracy, the nations retain a place while ceasing to occupy the entire field. Third, this formula respects the principle of equality that "all affected interests principle is fundamentally equalitarian, counting all interests equally; and equality of power is arguably the cornerstone of democracy"(Goodin, 2007: 50).

The renewed constitutional norm should establish the legal guidelines of such a principle. Even if the principle is a convincing one, its implementation will prove difficult, especially in a global context. One immediately acknowledges that it is open to two conflicting interpretations.

On one hand, the problem is one of determining the level of the legitimate extension of this public. It seems that we could extend these limits very far. In a company, the *stakeholders* have as much right to influence decisions as the *shareholders* do; in the media, the journalists and the public would be every bit as involved as the owners of the equipment; in schools, parents would have a real kind of power, just like professors, and so on. But this principle also implies that the public in question also goes beyond roles and functions that are *already* established. A group of subcontracted workers has a direct interest in the internal decisions of a contracting company even if they are independent from it legally. Certain segments of the public may have an interest in the broadcasts of information by media groups, and so on.

A principle of openness and uncertainty would therefore be recognized as an accompaniment to the application of this principle. The size and nature of the public in question must be surveyed, but these surveys may only be conducted by the public in question itself – the public has the final word regarding its own composition.

On the other hand, the constitution must also guarantee that the decisions will be made according to established roles and within an acceptable time frame. Keohane (2003: 141) discusses this concern:

> Merely being affected cannot be sufficient to create a valid claim. If it were, virtually nothing could ever be done, since there would be so many requirements for consultation and even veto point.

It's not just about establishing a "weak" public location (to borrow the terms of Frazer), but also a strong public committed to the formation of collective will. Under these conditions, infinite openness to the voices of minorities and permanent questioning of the decisions made would also be contrary to the requirements of a democracy. The endless deliberations of an inclusive public could lead to a democratic fatigue, which would undermine confidence in the process. With this, it is necessary to apply a principle of closure and therefore exclusion of the *demos*, as well as a principle of openness and participation.

C. The dual structure of the constitutional Demos

I see only one response to this issue: the separation and articulation between the decision forums on one hand, and the deliberation forums on the other. These forums would be sectorial in that they relate to a particular activity sector without any of them – not even the State – being able to assume total governance of the society.

The principles, means and functions of these forums differ, and as such they should be institutionalized just as they are. This is why Gunther Teubner (2004: 23) was correct when he remarked a distinctive trait in the very notion of democratic constitution in the distinction between what he called a "formalized" sector and what he called a "spontaneous" sector. However, the concept of "spontaneous public" is somewhat confusing. The "spontaneous" element is also shaped and formalized a certain way, for transferring information and for bargaining or deliberation procedures (on the distinction between negotiation and deliberation, cf. De Munck & Ferreras, 2012). Basic rights form the legal infrastructure of this informal sphere.

Table 6.1 Duality of the constitutional *demos*

Formalized forum	*Informal public*
Decision	Opinion formation
Representative democracy	Participative democracy
Negotiation	Open discussion

If one can thereby outline a structural similarity between political *demos* and civil *demos*, it should not be forgotten that there are major differences between these two types of public. One should not expect to find *similarities* between these two types of sovereignty exercising on a structural level, for the civil circles display unique features absent in other spheres. We should thus get the theory of democracy to move into non-political spheres in order to identify specific traits from it. With this – as an example – a company is a very unique environment that combines complex normativities that are well-outlined by work sociology and management sciences. A new reading of civil society should identify potential constitutional structures in the already existing normative fabric. One such attempt has been made by Isabelle Ferreras (2013), who sought to identify the traces of a potential bicameralism in a company using the model of the formation of the parliamentary states. This exercise shows both similarities and significant differences.

The paradigm of an already existing civil constitution at national level can doubtless be found in the mechanisms for collective negotiation and social dialogue that have allowed for a constitutionalization (if a partial one) of the industrial sector and the economic-type public policy. Contrary to the claims of Michel Freitag,[2] who sees the social state as a phase of the dissolution of modern law (a step towards management postmodernity), societal constitutionalism restores its value of democratic demands extension. In particular, in the systems including dual representation of workers – the union route and the electoral route – one can see a draft of this dual *demos*, which is demanded by democracy. Examination of this phase of our socio-economic history would also reveal pathological elements: neocorporatism, very present in national post-war structures, evidences an overvaluing of negotiation procedures over deliberation procedures. This tendency has resulted in the generation of a technocratic oligarchy that acts like a highly exclusive club that, ultimately, has led to democratic deficits. In our social history, certain self-management experiments demonstrate the intractable problems that forms of direct democracy yield when it comes to making coherent decisions Right now, we should be pondering the conditions of the institutionalization of a genuine social dialogue at the level of multinational business firms. The same reasoning could apply, *mutatis mutandis*, for other normative spheres.

4. Fundamental rights in civil spheres

The institution of a sovereign *demos* is only one side of a constitution. One can also ask what civil constitutionalization could signify, not within the context of the first differentiation (state apparatus/public space), but in the sense of the other two (systems/individuals and normativity/normativity)? This means that what is at stake is the diffusion of human rights throughout the civil society.

A. Respecification of fundamental rights

Two problems can be distinguished: the protection of the difference between *individuals* and systems, and the protection of the difference of the normative *spheres* in their relationships with each other.

2 Michel Freitag remains a prisoner of a foundationalist version of the constitution and a statocentered understanding of democratic law. This understanding of our story has led him, inevitably, to be all reactive and nostalgic in connection with "postmodernism" developments. Sadly, this position is inconsistent with the aims of a critical sociology which currently seeks to awaken those possibilities that have not yet been realized.

Regarding the first problem, the fundamental rights indeed provide an institutional response to the threat of the invasion of a person's integrity by the systems. One recognizes here the problem of "negative" liberty promoted by liberalism, which now pervades all spheres of civil society. But the fundamental rights are not limited to this immunological version of liberty. The "positive" side of the same suggests that they also guarantee *access* to the various subsystems while avoiding barriers to entry that could be indicative of absence of resources or lack of participation. Thus, for example, the right to education enables an individual to access the labor market and the cultural system. In this way, the connectivity of the individual with the differentiated systems is institutionally maintained by the society's legal infrastructure. One can apply the same reasoning for all economic, cultural and social rights. Societal constitutionalism seeks to meet the fourth criticism of orthodox constitutionalism listed earlier.

Regarding the second problem, the fundamental rights have a function of establishing limits between the extension zones of the different normative spheres. For example, the right to religious freedom grants churches self-organization options (a right to a form of sovereignty). Just like organizations, churches are protected against intrusions from other organizations (the State, scientific powers, economic powers, and so on.). Simultaneously, a religious person's specific rationality can flourish while non-religious elements are purified and rejected outside the scope of it. Contrary to the claims of Latour, Teubner thereby suggests that we are fully modern. The same reasoning can be applied for all the spheres. Of course, each sovereignty must be recognized by the others as having its limits. Thus, one can see Kantian reasoning of mutual limitation of freedoms applying with whole ensembles of social connections (as far as Kant was concerned, it applied only to individuals).

As explained, the implementation of fundamental rights is in no way an exclusive function of the State; it extends to all systems and it should be supported by them with no fantasizing of a global political power. This was already the case with national societies; and it's even more so in a global context, as there is no State jurisdiction. The extension of the fundamental rights to the spheres of civil society therefore requires an adjustment; or rather, more exactly, to borrow the concept of Teubner: a *respecification*. This is a very difficult task, since it must satisfy two demands at once.

On one hand: rather than being a marginal adaptation, it's a "translation" (a term taken from Teubner that we are going to criticize) that must respect the specificity of the civil sphere, its semantics, its particular actors, its irreducible objectives, and its "medium". For example, the economy functions according to the market rules, and there can be no question of treating these rules as State rules where the legislator would occupy a central position. This is why private law is not public law. They are not confused in societal constitutionalism. We must place trust in the creativity of the actors to fabricate a system of fundamental rights that itself also generates specific legal subsystems. On the other hand, constitutionalization calls for a form of hierarchization of norms in civil environments – for without them, one could no longer speak of constitutionalization, only juridicization. The expanded constitutional project calls for a coupling of standards and values of different spheres on one hand, and fundamental rights on the other hand.

Legal pluralism demonstrates the need for the law to be linked to societal differentiation. It is for this reason that we should not transform fundamental laws into a new unitary super-constitution imposed by a global State, covering all social interactions. According to Teubner, this "neo-Kantian" version should be avoided. The respecification-related difficulty, however, is obvious: it stands in a difficult balance between too much hierarchy (which would introduce an unfortunate heteronomy) and not enough hierarchy. The first trend would, at best, generate a new moralism in connection with human rights, and a postmodern version of the Hegelian beautiful soul; the second trend would generate a so-called human-rights crusader cynicism, which would, under its moralizing image, mask the unshifting approach of indifferent systems in the face of any form of corrective judicial intervention. We can already observe these two excesses in contemporary society.

B. A pragmatic version of respecification

However, it is not for certain that the systemic sociology espoused by Gunther Teubner is sufficient for highlighting the practical dilemmas and the normative possibilities that apply with this problem of *tuning* with respecification.[3] It is happy to indicate the direction and to warn against excesses and deficiencies, but it cannot tell us the position of the "good fence" between the spheres. In confidence, it leaves functional self-regulation to resolve this critical issue.

Here it seems possible and necessary for us to return to the actors, their practices and their discourse, in order to shine light on this question. After all, it is not necessary to assume that what Gunther Teubner has described in the language of the theory of systems, cannot be described and explained using the vocabulary of the theory of action. Viewed from the point of view of the actors, the systemic closures observed by the neo-functionalist theorist are experienced as problems of categories in conditions of uncertainty. True, it is the case that the actors certainly can and will make the difference between what is the law and what isn't (or what is politics and what isn't, or what is the economy and what isn't, and so on.). But this difference originates from discourse of justification where borderline arbitration is not *already* resolved by an overhanging systemic logic. This transition from a functionalist perspective to a pragmatist perspective can demonstrate the potential cross-fertilization of sociologies that are different in their axioms but that converge with regard to some of their objectives.

From a pragmatist point of view, the differentiation problem is not a translation problem of semantic contents crossing the borders of ready-made languages. The "legalization" of semantic contents (for instance, the transformation of academic freedom into a constitutionalized freedom) is a question of discursive imagination, not of application of codes. The ordinary language is an open language with many semantic potentialities. "Vagueness" and under-specification of concepts (like the concepts of "rights") are overcome by inferences and indexicalization in specific contexts. The difference between a legal and a moral use of the concept of "right" is always vague and can only be clarified in a specific speech situation. What Teubner describes as "systemic closures" can only take place in *a posteriori* context of sociological description. From a pragmatist point of view, there is no translation problem; instead we are facing an ongoing creolization of words, concepts, categories and arguments.

From the pragmatist point of view, the differentiation process is not an evolutionary law but only a semantic possibility that must be decided in situation. In the context of art differentiation (De Munck, 2015), we have attempted to identify three ideal-typical attitudes that reflect the actors' reflexivity with regard to differentiation. They could also designate the legal field. The first is the desire of strict autonomy of the legal domain, as reflected by legal *formalism* in its different variants. This attitude has been highly cultivated by law faculties, the majority of that are still oriented towards a kind of positivism of legal reasoning. Meanwhile, the second attitude seeks to *materialize* the law, as part of a desire to juridicize all spheres of society. The perspective of the "social engineer" lawyer is therefore a privileged

3 A good example of this is included in the work by Sheldon Leader on multinational business, in this volume.

one. In a case like this, the law has a claim to sovereignty over other social spheres: Its premise is to intervene in their normative production approach in a heteronomous manner, from an overlooking viewpoint. The third attitude consists of seeking a middle ground between the two approaches listed earlier through a process of *coupling* between multiple fields, which includes the legal section among others. In such a case, the various legal actors learn of the other actors and vice versa. There is no doubt that these three versions of the law should be supplemented by a fourth version that anchors the law in morality and axiological values. It can be easily understood that different versions of the relationship between human rights and social normativity derive from these four reflexive attitudes.

Gunther Teubner certainly defends a *normative* preference with the third attitude. But the other options – formalism, regulative statism and natural law – are not just description errors of *sociologists* who would not understand the reality of the functional dynamics of differentiation (and coupling). These are attitudes that are espoused by the actors themselves, who execute these guidelines in everyday legal life and allow these alternative legal worlds to actually exist. That which Teubner describes as conflicts between schools of sociological thought that it is necessary to choose from, in reality consists in conflicts related to social practices that are resolved (or not) in creative controversies and compromises. These practical attitudes should be described by a kind of sociology more attentive to different practical situations than that of Luhmann-type systemism. Unlike the latter, this pragmatist sociology does not ontologize any kind of social approach of which the social structure[4] is supposed to provide an a priori definition. Rather, one should recognize that the differentiation and recombination processes are heading in the direction of contingent fates that are not rendered necessary by any immanent logic.

As far as sociology is concerned, the societal constitutionalism program leads to a new research request regarding the semantic compromises through which fundamental rights penetrate the differentiated spheres of global society. How can one, in the sphere of global health, register fundamental rights in medical, hospital and sanitary categories? How does "care", for example, today constitute (or not) a creative metaphor for such a conciliation? Another example: Is the concept of "stakeholder" a good metaphor in order to introduce the "all-affected principle" in the management discourse? The emerging discipline of Corporate Social Responsibility contributes to the systematization of the arguments, at the same time providing a major theoretical contribution toward a potential constitutionalization of the domain of business.

C. Constitutionalization and soft law

This semantic problem allows us to approach one final aspect of the current constitutionalization processes: their connection with processes of soft and diffuse juridicization. To provide a clarification of the difference between *hard* and *soft law* here, one can distinguish between three types of criteria (Abbott et al, 2000):

1 The obligation criterion: a legal provision can be more or less obligatory. The *ius cogens* provisions are strictly obligatory. But certain legal rules only offer "menus" (i.e. ranges of options that leave the recipients free to choose).

4 Despite his desire to desontologize sociology with the use of a vocabulary for procedures and events, Luhmann maintains a residual kind of "necessitarism". For all his "constructivist" denials, the trend of systemism to ontologise societal differentiation often leaves him pursuing an unjustified kind of evolutionism.

2 The precision criterion: by formulating a regulation in vague and abstract terms (standards, for example, such as the interests of children or abuse of the law), or by specifying the conditions of its application, the field of interpretation of the regulation is liable to vary considerably. There is no one-to-one relationship with the first criterion: vague principles may be particularly obligatory (or not), while specific regulations may be left as recommendations or options (or impose strict limitations).
3 The delegation criterion: the execution and monitoring of the application of a regulation may be formally assigned to specific bodies or authorities. However, in other cases, the responsibility for the legal enforcement is left more or less open.

It is easy to understand that each of these criteria can be distributed over a continuous line from maximum to minimum intensity.

> Consequently, the concept of legalization encompasses a multidimensional continuum, ranging from the 'ideal type' of legalization, where all three properties are maximized; to 'hard' legalization, where all three (or at least obligation and delegation) are high; through multiple forms of partial or 'soft' legalization involving different combinations of attributes; and finally to the complete absence of legalization, another ideal type.
> (Abbott et al., 2000: 402)

Such levels are recognized with constitutionalization. International criminal courts, or transnational courts responsible for the protection of human rights, are testimony to the development of *hard law* devices. However, the processes of *soft law* increasingly innervate plural and fragmented law, for two reasons. The first reason is that these processes are better suited to a situation where the authority is not identifiable because there are too many candidates exercising it (States, transnational agencies, and so on.). The characteristic of *soft law* is that it is oriented toward the establishment of *agreements* via the non-binding diffusion of norms that focus on the shared need for coordination. Its second advantage is its flexibility: Because it is not formalized, in the event of any uncertainty the normative system may evolve and therefore accompany the learning processes. It is perfectly adequate for semantic innovation and discovery procedures. This is why one can find several references to *soft law* in literature dedicated to constitutionalization. With this there are multinational codes of conduct (for example, those promoted by the OECD) (Backer, 2005–2006); or even ISO procedures in the domain of certification matters, which now include procedures relating to corporate social responsibility and climate change; or even guidelines proposed by the UN.

Societal constitutionalism hinges a great deal on such procedures. It depends not only on these procedures by default. It is important for one to fully dismiss the idea that legal efficiency depends only on the existence of a formal sanction. Societal constitutionalism invokes a new legal culture that is not just about behavioral control and limitation. It is especially necessary to coordinate the (semantic and pragmatic) *inferences* that will allow for the regulations to be interpreted in diverse and evolving situations. To borrow a clarification proposed by the economics of conventions (Batifoulier, 2001): If the rules coordinate behavior (conduct, actions) and are going to be applied to particular situations, they require an interpretation process. This has been stressed throughout the hermeneutic tradition, from Dilthey to Ricœur; and it is being rediscovered within the theory of incomplete contracts. At this level of reflexivity, we need a "conventional evaluation model" that allows for the coordination of *representations* (not only *behaviors*). This may not happen without an agreement on the interpretation framework. There are several possible interpretation frameworks, for there are several models of justice and morality. As far as this plurality goes, there are certain *conventions* allowing for selection and prioritization.

The law is just one of the channels via which an interpretation convention may be stabilized. This relieves us from the Kelsenian reading of law as a system of rules, bringing us closer to a Dworkin kind of interpretativism. Societal constitutionalism must touch on that level of depth if it is going to successfully create a new legal culture allowing for a productive confluence between human rights and legal cultures in the different civil spheres.

There is some evidence to suggest that this transformation is already under way. If we observe the evolution of social movements across the world, we can only be struck by their progressive permeability to human rights discourse and their increased level of attention to changes in the law. A "constitutionalization from below" (Boaventura de Sousa Santos) is blossoming. To a certain extent, this new culture is at odds with an older culture, derived from the workers' movement and its many offshoots, which valued the class struggle and the rejection of the law. To put it in simpler terms: One can distinguish the *labor movements* from the new *human rights movements*. The former sought to expand their mobilization capacity, and their actions were, as a matter of priority, oriented towards strikes and political negotiations. In the latter, the emphasis is more placed on the acquisition of knowledge, the establishment of relevant discourse and competent participation in consultation bodies. David Kennedy wrote:

> human rights movements tend to understand problems as political and solutions as legal. By contrast, labor rights movements have generally regarded problems as primarily economic and social, and solutions as primarily political.
>
> (quoted by Kolben, 2009–2010)

Initially, it was possible to believe that this difference in legal cultures was closely related to the sociological composition of the social movements in question: On one hand, the *human rights movements* were led by highly educated people from the middle or upper classes; on the other hand, the *labor movements* were formed of workers or peasants who had suffered greatly as a result of legally formalized domination and who sought to resist it via fundamental political movements. But this first reading is becoming less and less pertinent – and this is because, in many movements, it disappears in favor of a new culture of struggle that both reconciles popular movements with legal discourse and reformulates or even subverts it (Claeys, 2012). A good observer, such as Boaventura de Sousa Santos (1998: 354–355) may note that, even if the human rights policy can be identified within orthodox constitutionalism, which covers a hegemonic policy,

> this is not the only aspect of the issue. Throughout the world, there are millions of people and thousands of NGOs fighting for human rights, frequently taking major risks as they do so, in defence of the oppressed classes and social groups who have often been victims of authoritarian capitalist States. The political agendas of these struggles are frequently (either explicitly or implicitly), anti-capitalist ones. Anti-hegemonic discourse and practices in support of human rights have emerged; they have offered non-Western conceptions of human rights, with the development of related cross-cultural dialogues.

5. Conclusion

Societal constitutionalism meets the conditions for building an alternative to the orthodox constitutionalism that arose from the Washington consensus. It is part of the posterity of the social state, and renews its approach to the relationship between law and society. It is adjusted to contemporary globalization requirements. It renews our concept of democracy and human rights, at a profound level. Part of it is a very powerful normative onus, all for the purpose of a radicalization of the demands for democracy extended to the various spheres of civil society and their accumulative responsibility regarding the promotion of human rights.

There are two major questions that remain open. On one hand, the relationship with the State should be reclassified: a simple differentiation between the legal system and the political system does not allow for consideration of a special relationship that remains between the two systems; this is a privilege not shared by other spheres of society. On the other hand, outside of the automatic closing of these systems, one should call pragmatic behaviors, which are themselves plural and differentiated, into question, as well as the actors who make the differentiations in the authorized practices and discourses.

Anyway, the democratic perspective has not been exhausted as a result of the fragmentation of legal spheres and the specializations gathered from the spheres of social activities. Consequentially, when it comes to shifts in concepts demanded of us in the future, we are compelled to make them a reality, with audacity and imagination.

Bibliography

Abbott, K.W., R. O. Keohane, A. Moravcsik, A.-M. Slaughter & D. Snidal (2000). The Concept of Legalization, *International Organization*, 54, pp. 401–419.

Backer, L. C. (2005–2006). Multinational Corporations, Transnational Law: The United Nations' Norms on the Responsibilities of Transnational Corporations as a Harbinger of Corporate Social Responsibility in International Law, *Columbia Human Rights Law Review*, 37(2), pp. 287–390.

Batifoulier, P. (ed.) (2001). *Théorie des conventions*, Paris: Economica.

Berlin, I. (1979). *Four Essays on Liberty*, Oxford: Oxford University Press.

Bohman, J. (2005). From *Demos* to *Demoi*: Democracy Across Borders, *Ratio Juris*, 18(3), pp. 293–314.

Bohman, J. (2007). Institutional Reform and Democratic Legitimacy: Deliberative Democracy and Transnational Constitutionalism, *Revue européennes des sciences sociales*, XLV(136), pp. 95–110.

Boltanski, L. (2008). Institutions et critique sociale. Une approche pragmatique de la domination, *Tracés: Revue de sciences humaines*, 8, pp. 17–43.

Christodoulidis, E. & L. Francot-Timmermans (2011). The Normative Turn in Teubner's Systems Theory of Law, *Rechtsfilosofie & Rechtstheorie*, 40(3), pp. 187–190.

Claeys, P. (2012). The Creation of New Rights By the Food Sovereignty Movement: The Challenge of Institutionalizing Subversion, *Sociology*, 46(5), pp. 844–860.

Cohen, J. (2012). *Globalization and Sovereignty. Rethinking Legality, Legitimacy, and Constitutionalism*, Cambridge: Cambridge University Press.

Cotterrell, R. (2009). Spectres of Transnationalism: Changing Terrains of Sociology of Law, *Journal of Law and Society*, 36(4), pp. 481–500.

De Munck, J. (2015). Qu'est-ce que la critique artiste? in *Le tournant de la théorie critique*, B. Frère, (ed.), Paris: Desclée De Brouwer.

De Munck, J. & I. Ferreras (2012). The Democratic Exchange, as the Combination Between Deliberation, Bargaining and Experience, in *Renewing Democratic Deliberation in Europe. The Challenge of Social and Civil Dialogue*, J. De Munck, I. Ferreras, C. Didry & A. Jobert (eds.), Brussels: P.I.E. Peter Lang, pp. 149–171.

de Sousa Santos, B. (1998). *De la mano de Alicia*, Colombia: Siglo del Hombre Editores.

de Sousa Santos, B. & C. A. Rodriguez-Garavito (2005). *Law and Globalization from Below. Towards a Cosmopolitan Legality*, Cambridge: Cambridge University Press.
Ferreras, I. (2012). *Gouverner le capitalisme?*, Paris: Presses Universitaires de France.
Freitag, M. (2002). *L'oubli de la société. Pour une théorie critique de la postmodernité*, Rennes: Les Presses de l'université Laval, Presses Universitaires de Rennes.
Goodin, R. E. (2007). Enfranchising All Affected Interests, and Its Alternatives, *Philosophy and Public Affairs*, 35(1), pp. 40–68.
Gurvitch, G. (2009). *La déclaration des droits sociaux*, Paris: Dalloz.
Held, D., McGrew, A., Goldblatt & D., Perraton, J. (1999). *Global Transformations*, Cambridge: Cambridge University Press.
Keohane, R. O. (2003). Global Governance and Democratic Accountability, in *Taming Globalization. Frontiers of Governance*, D. Held & M. Koenig-Archibugi (eds.), Cambridge: Polity Press, pp. 130–159.
Kolben, K. (2009–2010). Labor Rights as Human Rights?, *Virginia Journal of International Law*, 50, pp. 449–484.
Lindhal, H. (2011). Societal Constitutionalism as Political Constitutionalism: Reconsidering the Relation between Politics and Global Legal Orders, *Social & Legal Studies*, 20(2), pp. 230–237.
Lyon-Caen, A. (2014). Le droit sans l'entreprise. *L'entreprise*, in *Point aveugle du savoir. Colloque de Cerisy*, B. Segrestin, B. Roger & S. Vernac (eds.), Auxerre: Editions Sciences Humaines, pp. 23–31.
Nanz, P. & J. Steffek (2004). Global Governance, Participation and the Public Sphere, *Government and Opposition*, 39(2), pp. 314–335.
Negri, A. (2008). La souveraineté aujourd'hui: entre vieilles fragmentations et nouvelles excédences, *Tracés: Revue de sciences humaines*, 8, pp. 101–119.
Preuss, U. K. (2010). Disconnecting Constitutions from Statehood: Is Global Constitutionalism a Viable Concept?, in *The Twilight of Constitutionalism?*, P. Dobner & M. Loughlin (eds.), Oxford University Press, pp. 23–46.
Robé, J.-P. (2013). Les entreprises multinationales, vecteurs d'un nouveau constitutionnalisme?, *Archives de philosophie du droit*, 56, pp. 337–361.
Sciulli, D. (1992). *Theory of Societal Constitutionalism: Foundations of a Non-Marxist Critical Theory*, Cambridge: Cambridge University Press.
Teubner, G. (2004). Societal Constitutionalism: Alternatives to State-Centered Constitutional Theory?, in *Constitutionalism and Transnational Governance*, C. Joerges, I.-J. Sand & G. Teubner (eds.), Oxford: Oxford University Press, pp. 3–28.
Teubner, G. (2006). The Anonymous Matrix: Human Rights Violations by 'Private' Transnational Actors, *Modern Law Review*, 69(3), pp. 327–346.
Teubner, G. (2010). Fragmented Foundations: The Constitutionalism Beyond the Nation-State, in *The Twilight of Constitutionalism?*, P. Dobner & M. Loughlin (eds.), Oxford: Oxford University Press, pp. 327–341.
Tully, J. (1995). *Strange Multiplicity. Constitutionalism in an Age of Diversity*, Cambridge: Cambridge University Press.
Tully, J. (2008). Modern Constitutional Democracy and Imperialism, *Osgoode Hall Law Journal*, 46, pp. 461–493.
Verschraegen, G. (2002). "Human Rights and Modern Society: A Sociological Analysis from the Perspective of Systems Theory, *Journal of Law and Philosophy*, 29(2), pp. 258–281.
Whitt, M. (2014). Democracy's Sovereign Enclosures: Territory and the All-Affected Principle, *Constellations*, 21(4), pp. 560–574.

7 Constitutionalization outside of the State?

A constitutionalist's point of view

Véronique Champeil-Desplats

One of the characteristics of contemporary constitutional theories is the linking of the concepts of State and constitution to the extent that they become inseparable. On one hand, the State would not exist without the constitution and in the absence of a specific document, one quickly resorts to the notion of an unwritten constitution. On the other hand, the constitution is an inherent part of the State. This could be applied to other modes or organization of power only conceptually by extension and thus the opportunity to think about the existence of a constitution or a process of constitutionalization outside the framework of the State is quite reduced. It requires a certain change in the dominant conceptual frameworks on which current constitutional and State theories are built. To understand this, it is necessary to first outline a summary of definitions used before providing a short historical perspective on the subject.

Definitions. After briefly recalling the ways in which the concept of "constitution" is formally defined in terms of constitutional law, the possible meanings of the more recent concept of constitutionalization shall be examined in greater depth.

Constitutions. In terms of constitutional law, two meanings of the word "constitution" are commonly distinguished: constitution in the formal sense and constitution in the material sense.

In the formal sense, the constitution "is a set of rules, regardless of their purpose, as outlined in the constitutional form. They are generally contained in a special document, but above all, they have a value greater than that of all other positive standards and they may only be amended in accordance with a special procedure that is more difficult to implement than one that allows another standard to be modified, such as an ordinary law".[1] Three elements do need to be pointed out: (a) in the formal sense, the constitution may focus on various themes and establish any type of political regime; (b) insofar as it has a greater value than other standards, the constitution is closely linked to the concept of the sovereignty of the order that it establishes; (c) it "generally" takes the form – and therefore, not necessarily – of a special document. In other words, the formal meaning of the term constitution does not presuppose the existence of an *instrumentum* called "constitution". England and Israel are two typical examples.

In the material sense, the constitution refers to the content of the formal constitution. It relates to "the organization and the functioning of the public authorities and the division of competences among them".[2] This definition gives rise to two points.

1 F. Hamon & M. Troper, *Droit constitutionnel*, Paris, LGDJ (2013), 34ème édition, p. 44.
2 Ibid., p. 49.

First, in historical and geographical terms, the content of constitutions varies and evolves substantially. Constitutions can divide competences in a very diverse manner. They can vary in terms of length and detail. They may or may not proclaim lists of rights and freedoms, and when they are present, they give variable importance to different "generations" of rights. Finally, they may include the drafting of chapters laying down the basic principles of particular branches of the law – civil law (family law and property law), criminal law and criminal procedure (prohibition of the death penalty, torture, forced disappearance, and so on.) – these initiatives are often the result of a specific reaction to the acts of authoritarian regimes overthrown by the new constitutional order.

Second, there are two epistemological approaches to the concept of material constitution: a descriptive and a prescriptive approach. In the first case, the constitutionalist is content not to take sides and to describe the general structures and content of constitutions both past and present. In the second case, the constitutionalist evaluates these constitutions against an ideal constitutional model and even recommends content that should provide a set of standards to support the quality of constitution: a guarantee of rights and a separation of powers, as envisaged for example by the French revolutionaries in article 16 of the Rights of Man and of the Citizen, 1789.

Constitutionalization. The concept of constitutionalization refers to a process.[3] It may be considered from the bottom up or the top down.

In terms of the bottom up, constitutionalization leads to conferring a hitherto-lacking legal order upon a constitution – either in a formal or material sense. Historically speaking, it's the first manifestation of constitutionalization. If it is to be assumed that this ultimate expression should take the form of a written *instrumentum,* then with the exception of Israel and England, this process has now been completed on a State level. However, as evidenced by the dissemination of the concept of the "constitution of England",[4] the absence of writing is not an invalidating element. Outside of the State framework, however, this process of constitutionalization is barely outlined. At the very least, this is the case with some sections of Europeanist or internationalist doctrine.[5] What therefore opens up here is a wide scope of reflections on its forms and its conditions of execution.

From a top-down point of view, constitutionalization, within the meaning of constitutional standards, tends to disseminate its content to the whole of the legal order. It is also possible to distinguish a *stricto sensu* top-down movement and a *lato sensu* top-down movement.

Stricto sensu, constitutionalization refers to a historical process transforming into legal relationships, more particularly into relationships framed by constitutional law, the relationships among the public authorities exercising political powers. Once again, the existence of a written constitution is not necessary: In Israel for example, the Supreme Court holds a central function in the legal framework of relations among public authorities.[6] Within the framework of the State, this process is engaged to a greater or lesser extent. Its degree of completion

3 See R. Guastini, Leçons de théorie constitutionnelle, Paris: Dalloz (2010), collection Rivages du droit, pp. 80 et seq.; M. Loughlin, "What is constitutionalization?", *Jus Politicum*, 3: http://juspoliticum.com/article/What-is-constitutionalization-157.html

4 See D. Baranger, *Ecrire la Constitution non écrite. Une introduction au droit politique britannique*, Paris: Presses Universitaires de France, Coll. Léviathan (2008).

5 See S. Hennette-Vauchez & J.-M. Sorel, *Les droits de l'homme ont-ils constitutionnalisé le monde?,* Bruxelles: Bruylant (2011).

6 See Guastini, Leçons de théorie constitutionnelle, op cit., p. 81 et seq.

depends on the binding force that the established authorities attach to the constitution in order to regulate their competences and their relationships, as well as the extent of the powers conferred in this area to the constitutional courts. Outside of the framework of the State, no general conclusion can currently be drawn. Everything depends on what each particular non-State organization considers being its "constitution" and the way in which their decision making bodies refer to it.

Lato sensu, the top-down process of constitutionalization, refers to the transformation process of a legal order at the end of which it gradually becomes "irradiated", "'impregnated', 'saturated' or 'immersed'" by constitutional standards and, more specifically, by the rights and freedoms that they proclaim.[7] Constitutional standards tend to be packaged predominantly as "legislation, case law, doctrine and the behaviour of political operators" rather than private operators.[8] The constitutional text is therefore an "over-interpretation" in the sense where, on one hand, it tends to determine the interpretation of any legal statement and to guide political and social debate but also, on the other hand, where it supports the production of other constitutional standards (of new principles, rights or freedoms) that it does not explicitly state, but which are deemed implicit by those who interpret it.[9]

This form of constitutionalization is based on two essential elements: a constitutional review mechanism that ensures the binding nature of constitutional standards and a quantitative element that transforms into a qualitative element – recurrence, references to the text of the constitution in legal, political or social debates. It is this tendency towards the "constitutional omnipresence",[10] this ultimate level of the process of constitutionalization promoted by the combined action of constitutional courts and a proactive doctrine, which theorists of Italian law have successfully called neo-constitutionalism.[11] Within the State framework, this process has been initiated and expands at times and in varying degrees according to the States. In brief, this occurred from the beginning of the twentieth century in the United States, in the 1960s in Italy and Germany, in the 1980s in Spain, Portugal or France (in terms of the latter, for different reasons and under different forms than its two Iberian neighbors) and during the 1990s in Latin America, Eastern Europe, India and South Africa. In extra-State frameworks, this manifestation of constitutionalization is at its most evanescent and contrasting to the extent that it assumes the existence of a body of judicial control that ensures the dissemination of standards that, whether by extension or analogy, are deemed to be "constitutional". According to some authors, this would be initiated on the continents of Europe and South America through the development of the jurisprudence of the European Court of Human Rights or the Inter-American Court of Human Rights.[12]

At the end of this initial perspective, links between the "State form" and the concepts of constitution and constitutionalization are very close. If the space for considering the State without a constitution appears reduced, it appears to be more open to considering the

7 See Guastini, op. cit.; M. Barberis, "El neoconstitucionalismo, Third Theory of Law", in *Neoconstitucionalismo, Derecho y derechos*, S. Pozzolo (ed.), Lima: Palestra editores (2011), p. 251.

8 P. Comanducci, "Constitucionalización y neoconstitucionalismo", in *Positivismo jurídico y neoconstitutionalismo*, P. Comanducci, M. Angeles Ahumada & D. Gonzales Lagier (eds.), Madrid: Fundación coloquio jurídico europeo (2009), p. 86; S. Pozzolo, "Notas al margen para una historia del neoconstitucionalismo", in *Neoconstitucionalismo, Derecho y derechos*, S. Pozzolo (ed.), op. cit., p. 48.

9 Guastini, op. cit., pp. 163 et seq.; see also Comanducci, op. cit., pp. 86–87.

10 Pozzolo, op. cit., p. 22.

11 See Pozzolo, *Neocostituzionalismo e positivismo giuridico*, Torino: Giappichelli editore (2001).

12 See Hennette-Vauchez & Sorel, op. cit.

constitutional notion outside the competence of the State. It is this which also suggests a return to the history of the concept of a constitution.

Historical perspective. Historically speaking, the links between the term "constitution" and the form of power structure that is the State are formed gradually. The term "constitution" was indeed first used outside the political and conceptual frameworks that relate to the State. As O. Beaud points out: "Originally, the term constitution, from the Latin *constitutio*, is as much a product of medicine (where he describes the idea of State, order or a whole organisation), as it is law where it refers to both a set of papal or monastic texts and a procedural act or the drawing up of an official deed (for example in private law, in French, a '*constitution de rentes*' [annuity purchases] or '*constitution d'hypothèques*' [granting of mortgages])"[13] Similarly, it refers as much to the body of an individual ("the human constitution") as a social or abstract body, thereby designating very early on "the manner in which something is made, the composition of something". The author explains: "With regard to the particular case of France, it is proven that the same word, 'constitution', used without qualification, for a long time had no real political meaning in the Ancien Régime".[14] When this meaning came into existence in the middle of the eighteenth century, it did not exclude those pre-existing concepts. The word was still particularly used at the turn of the eighteenth and nineteenth centuries in civil law where it referred to the organization of the Church, and references "to ecclesiastical constitutions" were commonplace at the time.[15]

The emergence of the political meaning of the word "constitution" does not immediately lead to its association with the concept of State. It is rather more the concepts of nation or government to which it is related. The expressions "national constitution", "constitution of the Republic", "monarchical constitution", "the people's constitution" and, above all, "governmental constitution" (understood in the broad sense and the substantive action of governing) are the most frequent. On one hand, when the State is discussed, the concepts of nation and government are never far away.[16] On the other hand, the use of the word "constitution" in the political field is still marked by one of its first meanings that related it to the human body. Locke, Bolingbroke, Montesquieu and Sieyès – key authors on the conceptualization of the political meaning of the word "constitution" – as well as American and French constituents by the end of the eighteenth century, had indeed developed a so-called mechanical design for the constitution,[17] which was built principally from an analogy structured between the constitution of the human body and the constitution of the social or political body: "in the same way that one distinguishes in humans between the head and arms, or distinguishes will and action, legislature power is similarly distinguished in the State between the will and the executive power, which is the action".[18]

13 O. Beaud, "L'histoire du concept de constitution en France. De la constitution politique à la constitution comme statut juridique de l'Etat", *Jus Politicum*, 3, p. 8 (2009), http://juspoliticum.com/L-histoire-du-concept-de.html, pdf.

14 Ibid.; see also J.-M. Denquin, "L'objet du droit constitutionnel: Etat, Constitution, Démocratie", in *Traité international de droit constitutionnel*, D. Chagnollaud & M. Troper (eds.), Paris: Dalloz (2012), t.1, pp. 51–53.

15 Beaud, op. cit., p. 9.

16 See, for example, the *Dictionnaire universel et raisonné des connaissances humaines* (F.-B. de Felice, Yverdon 11, pp. 189–191 (1772), cited in Beaud, op. cit., p. 9; see Montesquieu, *L'Esprit des Lois*, particularly Book XI.

17 See A. Papatolias, *Conception mécaniste et conception normative de la constitution*, op. cit. (2000); M. Troper & L. Jaume, *1789 et l'invention de la constitution*, Paris: LGDJ (1994); M. Troper, "La machine et la norme. Deux modèles de constitution", *Le droit, la théorie du droit, l'Etat*, Paris: Presses Universitaires de France (2001).

18 F. Hamon & M. Troper, *Droit constitutionnel*, Paris: LGDJ (2013), 33ème éd., p. 99.

The junction between the political concept of constitution and State, which crystallizes the creation of the terms "State constitution" or "constitution of the State", is not therefore an obvious one, either from a historical point of view or from a conceptual point of view. It is the result of a gradual transformation of the meaning of the word "constitution" and its construction as a new politico-legal concept designed to frame the form of power structure that is the State.

It remains that once the concept of constitution has emerged to refer to a form of framework of State power, new theoretical proposals have ended up in systematizing the association. Hans Kelsen is undoubtedly one such person who has gone the furthest in arguing the indivisibility of the concepts of State and constitution. This indivisibility can be understood as a consequence of the manner by which the author distinguishes his identification of State from law. For Kelsen, the State is indeed a set of legal standards and it does not predate these standards. In fact, it is specifically "made" by them. Furthermore, at risk of repeating oneself, the constitution is the "constitutive act" of the State: "through the multiple transformations it has incurred", explains Kelsen, "the concept of constitution has retained a permanent nucleus: the supreme principle idea determining the entire order of the State and the essence of the community established by this order. In whatever way the constitution is defined, it is still the foundation of the State . . ., it is the standard that regulates the development of laws, the general standards in performance from which the activity of the State bodies is exercised".[19] From Kelsen's point of view, every State therefore necessarily has a constitution. Conversely, as long as it is a supreme standard of legal orders, and consequently the monistic perspective supported by Kelsen, the constitution necessarily relates to the State or else the word is used by analogy or metaphorical extension.

Such an approach has strongly influenced the constitutional thinking of the twentieth century.[20] Rethinking it today from a constitutional perspective, the dissociation between State and constitution therefore implies a certain number of shifts occurring in the conceptual frameworks that were established more than a century ago. How should this happen (1) and at what epistemological cost (2)?

1. Changes and conceptual reconstructions

Thinking of constitutionalization outside of the State expects a distancing from the way in which the concept of constitution was built within the State framework. The main change is undoubtedly that of identifying the concept of constitution, which proceeds with a particularly formal definition to all the highest standards of a sovereign State. This change does not, however, mean that any formal characteristic or any reference to the idea of supremacy be dismissed. It implies rather to accept, on one hand, in a pluralistic perspective that everything organized together can be endowed with supreme standards that are thought to have established a "constitution" and, on the other hand, that the concept of normative supremacy be dissociated from that of State sovereignty.

What remains, therefore, is to determine what types of understanding of the constitution make this change possible. Until now, four principal ways have been explored and respectively, they provide a structural approach (A), institutional approach (B), contractualist approach (C) and finally, an axiological approach (D) to the concept of constitution.

19 H. Kelsen, "La garantie juridictionnelle de la Constitution", *Revue de droit public* (1928), §2, vol. 35, p. 197.

20 See for example, G. Burdeau, "Une survivance: la notion de Constitution", in *Etudes offertes à Achille Mestre*, Paris: Sirey (1956), p. 57.

A. Structural approach

An initial way of thinking about the constitutional idea outside of the State is to conceive it as a way of power structuring, irrespective of its form. As Olivier Beaud points out, this avenue has been considered by the German historian Reinhart Koselleck.[21] This author presupposes opposition between "the constitution in terms of its structure (i.e. a repetitive political form)" and "the event, the flow of political developments".[22] Seen in a structural dimension, the constitution would necessarily be long-lasting. As a sustainable phenomenon, it would distinguish itself in particular from the contingency of political decisions taken in the short term.

This distinction directly leads Koselleck to criticize the reduction "of constitutional history to the history of the 'constitution of the State' (*Staatsverfassung*)".[23] In other words, for the author, in terms of a structural phenomenon, the constitution is likely to refer to any form of group or organized power. The author then invites "legal historians to extend the scope of their study and to simultaneously study State constitutions and the law that relates to companies (private law, economic law or employment law) and the relationships between State and civil society, in order to build a bridge 'between the history of pre-modern law and modern constitutional history'. Its watchword is to integrate both 'pre-State as well as post-State' history into such a study".[24]

Koselleck also notes that the reduction in scope of constitutional thinking about the State was accompanied by a switch between using the term "constitution" in the plural, to "constitution" in the singular, in addition to which, a capital *C* is sometimes used.[25] Considering the constitutional idea outside the framework of the State would therefore require a reconnection with the original plural of the term, insofar as the non-State powers that frame it express themselves under multiple forms of organization.

B. Institutional approach

From Santi Romano[26] in Italy or Maurice Hauriou[27] in France, lawyers have proposed numerous variations on institutional theories. The point in common to consider is that social organizations pre-exist their legal format, and that the law itself is produced by social issues. Moreover, institutions as specific forms of social organization characteristically combine a temporal element, a duration or permanence, a structural element, orderliness or a normative power, and a teleological element, a common goal pursued by its members, the construction of an "undertaking", as Hauriou explains.

From an institutional perspective, it is not preexisting supreme legal standards that fix the supreme values of the social order or the institution, but the opposite in fact: It is "the order with fundamental values that generates hierarchically superior standards".[28] In other words, the concept of constitution is not conceived as the product of an act of native will that would

21 See R. Koselleck, *Begriffsgeschichten. Studien zur Semantik & Pragmatik der politischen & sozialen Sprache*, Frankfurt aM, Suhrkamp Verlag (2007), pp. 365–401, cited in Beaud, ibid., p. 2.

22 Beaud, op. cit.

23 Ibid.

24 Ibid., p. 3.

25 Ibid., pp. 4–5.

26 Santi Romano, *L'ordre juridique*, Paris: Dalloz (1975).

27 M. Hauriou, "La théorie de l'institution et de la fondation. Essai de vitalisme social", *Cahiers de la Nouvelle Journée*, 23 (1925), pp. 90–128; see E. Millard, "Hauriou et la théorie de l'Institution", *Droit et Société*, 30/31, pp. 381–412 (1995).

28 See S. Pozzolo, *Neocostituzionalismo e positivismo giuridico*, op. cit., p. 18.

lay down certain values becoming constituent of the legal order. On the contrary, "the constitution exists only as a summary of principles already embodied in the institution, and therefore exists thanks to an intellectual operation that extracts the method of being from the institution itself".[29] Therefore any institution (the family, the church, associations, trade unions, enterprises, international organizations, and so on.), the State being only one of them, has a capacity to produce and generate its own constitution based on its supreme values. The constitution is then defined as the set of standards that express the supreme values of an institution.

C. *The contractualist approach*

The contractualist approach has enjoyed remarkable success over the previous years in German constitutional doctrine under the influence of Jürgen Habermas.[30] Under this framework, the constitution is designed as a contract that covers the political method of organization under which individuals want to live. This mode of organization is not necessarily a State and therefore it is no longer necessary, nor are the usual forms of State powers: legislative, executive or judicial powers.

The contractualist approach of the concept of constitution was specifically revived at the time of the debates on the European constitution. The prospect was to promote a "constitution created by Europe", the product of a "European social contract".[31] This contract would be concluded by the European States who agree to give a portion of their power to a supra-State political organization.

This proposal concerns the interest in creating a new avenue, with a theoretical and ancient philosophical background and a new way of thinking about the decoupling of the concepts of constitution and State. It cannot escape, however, the conventional difficulties that are encountered in social contract theories, including that of solid identification, history and the key moment. In terms of the European framework in particular, it has to cope with the added difficulty of determining the parties to the contract: Are these European States? People from the European States? The people of Europe? In the latter case, how can they be identified?

These questions have not been ignored by the proponents of this model. The response then was to assume the original, unprecedented nature of the constituent moment under consideration, i.e. to conceive the European social contract as an analogous act, only and not identical to the contractual-constituent phenomenon that characterized the States. The constitution of the European Union would thus be the work of an original "multilateral constituent power",[32] which is not a sudden revolutionary fact, but a process that is long-lasting.[33]

D. *The axiological approach*

The recent neo-constitutionalist movement offers a final way of considering the idea of constitutionalization outside the framework of the State. This movement promotes a specific

29 Ibid.

30 J. Habermas, *Sur l'Europe*, Paris: Seuil (2009); La Constitution de l'Europe, Paris: Gallimard, NRF Essais (2012).

31 See I. Pernice, *Fondements du droit constitutionnel européen* (2000): www.whi-berlin.eu/documents/fondements.pdf

32 J. Gerktath, *L'émergence d'un droit constitutionnel pour l'Europe. Modes de formation et sources d'inspiration de la constitution des Communautés et de l'Union européenne*, Les éditions de l'Université de Bruxelles (1997).

33 J. Habermas, *Sur l'Europe*, op. cit., p. 59.

material dimension of the concept of constitution, which essentially structures it around moral values expressed in the form of rights and fundamental freedoms. The constitution therefore becomes both a set of standards and a set of values. No longer content with establishing "*who* has the competences and *how* to create valid legal standards of the system", the constitution also wants to determine "*what* content" must have these standards.[34] The constitution is no longer a case of a " 'simple technique' of scheduling" and the "legal limitation of power" but "conversion into a citizenship pact" as guarantor of shared values considered to be fundamental at any given time.[35] The constitution is considered to be the collection of the highest standards of a legal system provided that it conveys a certain moral content. It is "a moral document legally in force", which should set out principles, rights or fundamental freedoms supposed to be shared by all and deemed to be enforced by all: dignity, freedom, nondiscrimination, security, and so on.[36]

Neo-constitutionalists most often conceive constitutional values in a pluralistic manner. In other words, the fundamental rights and freedoms of the legal order are likely to express conflicting claims.[37] They offer a matrix of common values that function as a framework and support to multiple and sometimes antagonistic claims. The question is then to know who and how these various claims were articulated, for example, those that were expressed in the form of economic freedoms (freedom of movement of capital, freedom of enterprise, and so on.) and those who defended the right to health or employment. This critical issue has been particularly invested in by the neo-constitutionalist movement.[38] Several techniques and often very thin theories of conciliation, weighting or proportionality have been available from, or destined for the decisions of constitutional courts, as well as regional courts (European Court of Human Rights, the Inter-American Court of Human Rights or the Court of Justice of the European Union).

This is because in the neo-constitutionalist model it is the judge who becomes the main actor of an axiological reading of the constitution and, therefore, the axiologization of the whole of the legal order. After the Second World War, a number of constitutional courts have thus benefited from, or have seized considerable powers, exercising at the same time judicial competence, legislative competence and, on occasion, constitutional competence. Even though the origin of the power of judges, in particular their mode of appointment is often subject to discussion, their activism has eventually found legitimacy in the objective pursued: a guarantee of rights and fundamental freedoms.

In designing the constitution primarily as a place of expression and the protection of fundamental rights and freedoms, current neo-constitutionalist thinking has also opened up the possibility of thinking about the process of constitutionalization in other spaces of power than that of the State. This avenue has been explored. The idea of constitutionalization won supranational legal orders within which courts (European Court of Human Rights, the

34 M. C. Redondo, "Sobre principios y estado de derecho", in *Estado de Derecho y decisiones judiciales*, M. C. Redondo, J. M. Sauca & P.A. Ibañez (eds.), Madrid: Fundación coloquio jurídico europeo (2009), p. 23.

35 Pozzolo, "Notas al margen para una historia del neoconstitucionalismo", op. cit., pp. 24–25.

36 See M. Atienza, F. Laporta, "Imperio de la ley y constitucionalismo. Un dialogo entre Manuel Atienza y Francisco Laporta", *Isonomia* 31 (2009), p. 209 et seq.

37 G. Zagrebelsky, "Storia e costituzzione", in *Il futuro della costituzione*, G. Zagrebelsky, P. P. Portinaro & J. Luther (eds.), Torino: Einaudi (1996), p. 76 et seq.

38 R. Dworkin, *Taking Rights Seriously*, Cambridge, MA and London: Harvard University Press (1977), p. 3 et seq; R. Alexy, *Teoria de los derechos fundamentales*, Madrid: Centro de estudios constitucionales (1993), trad., E. Garzon Valdès., p. 160 et seq.

Inter-American Court of Human Rights or the Court of Justice of the European Union) multiply case law constructions on the basis of rights and freedoms, to the point where some have questioned whether human rights had not in fact "constitutionalised the world".[39] Nevertheless it should be noted that at the supranational level, moments of axiologisation and constitutionalization become reversed with regard to their manifestation within the State. While in this framework the constitutionalization of the legal order produces its axiologization, at the supranational level, it is the latter that would lead to constitutionalization and, in the last instance, to State control of the legal order. The development of the decisions of the European Court of Human Rights within the Council of Europe, the binding force of the European Charter of Fundamental Rights, accession to the European Convention on Human Rights and the changes in the Court of Justice in favor of fundamental rights within the European Union would thus be the vehicles of the constitutionalization of each of these organizations or, with regard to the European Union, of its State control.

Thought has also been expressed at an international level. Some are ready, the heirs of Georges Scelle, to not only accept the concept but also to assert the existence of an "international constitution".[40] This existence is based on three assumptions: (1) "the Constitution is an inherent part of the concept of law" and, conversely, there would be no "Law without a Constitution". It channels power and allows "an agreement to be reached between coercion and freedom". (2) "In addition to the protection of freedoms", this channeling of power is embodied by "the implementation of international constitutional functions" (legislative, executive and judicial functions"). (3) The constitution is not necessarily in a written format.[41]

This representation of the international constitution remains strongly anchored in the conceptual apparatus of the State. Not only are "international constitutional functions" similar to State functions (legislative, executive, judicial) but, in addition, the constitutional idea is essentially promoted here to establish a framework for inter-State relations. The next step would then be to attain a worldwide, global, or even transnational dimension. The idea is to think of "a world constitution"[42] or "global constitutionalism"[43] covering any type of power relations, just as much the conventional relations between the State and individuals or between the States themselves, as those between States and international organizations, States and multinational enterprises, multinational enterprises and individuals, and so on. It is finally at this level that neo-constitutionalism would find its fulfillment if one accepts, like Suzana Pozzolo, that despite its name, it "is not only a constitutionalist doctrine", but "presents itself primarily as a general theory of law".[44] Rather than "limiting power", this theory would then seek to "found a new one" [45] on moral values expressed in the legal form of rights and fundamental freedoms. The re-founding of the constitutional idea would be no longer

39 Hennette-Vauchez & Sorel, op. cit.

40 See O. De Frouville, "Le paradigme de la constitutionnalisation vu du droit international", in S. Hennette-Vauchez & J.-M. Sorel (eds.), op. cit., p. 198.

41 See De Frouville, op. cit., p. 200.

42 A. Cassese, *I diritti umani nel mondo contemporaneo*, Roma-Bari: Latera (1994); see also M. Loughin & N. Walker (eds.), *The Paradox of Constitutionalism: Constituent Power and Constitutional Form*, Oxford: Oxford University Press (2007).

43 See Barberis, op. cit., p. 8. See also J. De Munck, "From Orthodox to Societal Constitutionalism," in this volume.

44 Pozzolo, "Notas al margen para una historia del neoconstitucionalismo", op. cit., p. 29.

45 Ibid., p. 30.

intended to confront the "old political powers" so much as provide a framework for the decisions and behaviors of the "new actors" that emerged with the "growing globalisation of the market, such as central banks, and various supra-national organizations".[46] In some respects, this general theory of law is continuing along foundations renewed by moral contemporary philosophies based on former jusnaturalist ideals, with the difference that these ideals were forged against the States, while neo-constitutionalism also applied to forms of power extracted from it or exceeding them.

2. To what extent can there be constitutionalization outside of the State?

The various proposals that support the prospect of constitutionalization outside of the State framework, provided that we take them seriously, present a number of overlooked elements. Four sources of questions will now be specifically discussed: (A) the form that this constitutionalization can take (global constitution or constitutional pluralism?); (B) the actors involved in constitutionalization (who is behind it?); (C) the risks of privately reappropriating the constitutional idea; (D) the need and even relevance of an analogical recourse to concepts that were established over two centuries under the State framework, in order to think of non-State forms of exercising power.

A. Global constitution or constitutional pluralism?

There are two ideal-typical ways of spatially conceiving constitutionalization outside the State. It is possible to envisage a unified and centralized constitutionalization, "a unique global State-political constitution" or even "a global constitution", or it is possible to adopt the perspective of "constitutional pluralism" or a "multilateral constitutionalism". In this instance, constitutionalization is seen to be a progressive, heterogeneous, complex polycentric process that takes shape through "a multiplicity of autonomous subsystems of the global society".[47] Each of the subsystems, be they social, economic, financial or political, will develop its own specific form of constitutionalization. In other words, "Does every person have their own constitutionalization?"[48] The fact remains that each of these levels of the constitutionalization process is a gray area.

The route of "global constitutionalization" quickly questions its specific methods of implementation: a global constitution by whom, for whom, and how? To what extent would it be able to grasp and to limit the multiple forms of power that are outside the States? Would these lend themselves to a uniform supervisory framework or regulation?

The reverse perspective of favoring the route of constitutional pluralism seems, in this regard, more suitable. However, insofar as each of the potential constitutions of the subsystems is likely to adopt the most varied forms and content, do they not risk resulting in a "dislocation" of the constitutional idea?[49] This dislocation can be considered at two levels.

46 Ibid., p. 36.

47 See G. Teubner, "Réflexions sur la constitutionnalisation du système-monde de pouvoirs", Work session of the research group "Constitutionnalisation du système monde de pouvoir", Collèges des Bernardins (June 28, 2013). See also L. Catá Backer, "The Concept of Constitutionalization and the Multi-Corporate Entreprise in the 21st Century", in this volume.

48 J.-M. Sorel, "Le côté obscur de la force", in S. Hennette-Vauchez & J.-M. Sorel (eds.), op. cit., p. 226.

49 M. Barberis, *Stato Costituzionale. Sul nuovo costituzionalismo*, Mucchi editore (2012), Modena, p. 21 et seq.

On a pragmatic level, first of all, how is it possible to specifically coordinate the multiple subsystems and constitutional levels? Subsequently on a conceptual level, to what extent can the dissemination of the concept of constitution to qualify very heterogeneous forms of the framework of power not result in making it devoid of meaning? Here is not the place to defend the existence of a supposed true meaning of the word "constitution", but instead to question the limits of recourse of a concept whose usefulness for knowledge is based, like any other, on a minimum of uniformity or, if preferred, on diversity controlled by its uses. Is it not forbidden to call constitution or constitutionalization everything and anything but what does one really gain? The thoughts put forward by Georges Burdeau conducted in a completely different context, have a particular resonance here: "Pluralism led to the relativity of constitutional standards that are no longer as popular as recipes appreciated or discredited depending on the circumstances. The concept of constitution then takes on a character of fluidity where it dissolves. There is only a constitution in terms of a firm policy option".[50]

B. Constitutionalization: Who makes it happen?

Who are the actors of the constitutional process that would emerge outside the States? The answer varies once again in terms of concepts adopted.

If it is viewed through the perspective of constitutional pluralism, each subsystem produced its own constitution. It was then a safe bet that everyone would follow specific processes of constitutionalization involving different actors that are difficult to identify a priori. If one prefers the opposite perspective of a "global constitutionalization" or "holistic constitutionalization", the main difficulty, which was raised *mutatis mutandis* during the debate on the European Constitution (*supra*), is identifying the constituent "people" or the ultimate legitimating entity on behalf of which constitutionalization is undertaken.

Without doubt, it is neo-constitutionalist theories that more precisely determine the actors in the constitutionalization process: the actors of constitutionalization are the judges. This recovery, or overvaluing, of the role of judges does however highlight the weakness of basing the whole process on a parameter of trust. The success of constitutionalization depends, "to a large extent on the deliberative virtues of the legal grounds"[51] and its ability to commit to certain values. It is certainly possible to provide good reasons to trust in the judges: their retreat when faced with immediate and passionate public opinion, their detachment in respect of the short-term calculations of traditional political powers which, in some States, are also discredited by corruption,[52] their habit of handling abstract principles and relating them at the end of a "reflective equilibrium"[53] to specific cases, their "previous ethics",[54] or even their code of conduct.[55]

50 G. Burdeau, "Une survivance: la notion de Constitution", in *Etudes offertes à Achille Mestre*, Paris: Sirey (1956), p. 60.

51 L. G. Sager, *Juez y democracia*, Madrid: Marcial Pons, trad. (2007), V. Ferreres Comella, p. 212.

52 J. C. Henao, "De nouveaux acteurs pour la démocratie? Le cas de la Cour constitutionnelle colombienne", in *La démocratie, du crépuscule à l'aube*, V. Champeil-Desplats & J.-M. Denquin (dir.), Paris: Mare et Martin (2016, forthcoming).

53 Sager, op. cit., p. 203; see also P. Rosanvallon, *La légitimité démocratique*, Paris: Editions du Seuil, Points (2008), p. 217 et seq.

54 See V. Ferreres Comella, "Estudio introductorio", in L. G. Sager (ed.), op. cit, p. 19; see also L. G. Sager, op. cit., pp. 92–93 and pp. 202–203; P. A. Ibanez, "Justificación de las decisiones judiciales: una aproximación teorico-practica", in M. C. Redondo, J. M. Sauca & P. A. Ibañez (eds.), op. cit., p. 101 et seq.

55 See L. Ferrajoli, *Dei diritti e delle garanzie*, Bologna: Il Mulino (2013), p. 41 et seq.

So far, nothing ensures the systematic or institutional sustainability of these virtuous factors.[56] Several moments in the jurisprudential history of the US Supreme Court, the Constitutional Council in France or the Court of Justice of the European Union, for example, allow doubts to be raised that priority has always been given to the guarantee of rights and freedoms with regard to other requirements (security, public order, economic freedoms, and so on.). Neo-constitutionalist theories are thus faced with the age-old question: *Quis custodiet ipsos custodes?* Breaking this deadlock would require that which is still missing,[57] thinking of this new role conferred on judges in more sophisticated theories of separation and the redistribution of powers. The constitutionalization process could not therefore be based exclusively on one single actor, but – and here, one aspect of constitutional pluralism is reached – shared between various actors (associations for the defense of rights and freedoms or even consumers, non-governmental organizations, trade unions, social actors, and so on.) according to the locations of proposed powers: international organizations, boards of directors of public or private bodies and so on. This consideration of the diversity of possible actors in constitutionalization would then progress to the question of "Who takes care of the caretaker?" – that of the coordination of the plurality of competing perceptions of constitutional property.

C. The publicizing of private relationships or the privatization of the constitutional idea?

Under the State framework, meaning and a binding force is conventionally conferred upon the constitution both to those who are responsible for imposing it and those to whom it applies. On one hand, the separation of the constituent power and constituted powers is supposed to prohibit any reappropriation of the former by the latter. On the other hand, the bodies responsible for ensuring compliance – its "caretakers" – are either progressive or conservative, and are public authorities reputed to act in the benefit of an interest that is not personally theirs. At least, they can act in the interest of the institution they embody. In all cases, the use of the constitution is deemed to be separated from private interests, otherwise it would be interpreted as an abuse of authority or an act of corruption.

Outside of the State, the actors involved in constitutionalization are essentially private entities that are stakeholders in the determination of its rules and its implementation. The detachment between constituent power, on one hand, and the constituted powers or recipients of constitutional standards on the other, tends to diminish and, potentially, to bring a contractual element to the constitutionalization process. Rather than a form of publicizing the private reports,[58] should this new regulatory horizon not also engage or rather move towards a "privatization of the constitutional idea"? We can at least hypothesize that in terms of the "public/private" issue, constitutionalization outside the State promises to be an ambivalent process, a space of tension and dialectical relationships between movements of deprivation and publication, at best complementary and virtuous, and at worst contradictory and subject to manipulation.

56 See E. Millard, "Quelques bonnes raisons de douter du néo-constitutionnalisme", in V. Champeil-Desplats & J.-.M. Denquin (dir.), op. cit.

57 See in this respect Pozzolo, "Notas al margen para una historia del neoconstitucionalismo", op. cit., p. 36.

58 J. De Munck, "From Orthodox to Societal Constitutionalism", in this volume.

D. *Is there a necessity for and a relevance of the analogy with the State framework?*

The evocation of a constitutionalization outside of the State finally questions the purposes of this initiative as well as the adequacy of the means envisaged to meet those purposes. At this stage, reasoning will mainly be by virtue of raising questions.

What is exactly being looked for when there is talk about the prospect of a constitutionalization that would extend to relations breaking away from the State framework? "Is it really constitutionalization that we are looking for, or is it a simple arrangement of standards in order to achieve a legal order"[59]? Is this really constitutionalization or a way of effectively regulating new actors who defy any restrictive order to which they have not directly consented? Or further still, to what extent is it necessary to go through the "constitutional case", [60] which was established as a founding moment in the construction of modern States in order to think about the framework for the behavior of actors who, to a large extent, escape to the latter?

By thinking of constitutionalization on the other hand "by analogy with the constitutional law of nation States"[61] does this not force an adherence to conventional representations of new forms of power that have become inadequate? While attempting to grasp this through concepts forged in a State-centric framework over the centuries, is there a risk of missing an historic opportunity for a comprehensive renewal – not to say paradigmatic renewal – of theoretical frameworks and modes of conceptualization of legal thought? The inventiveness that is at work in establishing new forms of power is a challenge not only for the old powers, but also for those who undertake to grasp and understand it. It should be noted that nearly two centuries have passed between the emergence of the "modern State" and the thoughts on its limitation by contemporary constitutionalists. Therefore let us show enthusiasm for the work ahead awaiting legal thought, although one may not share the same enthusiasm for the phenomena that defy it.

59 J. M. Sorel, "Le côté obscur de la force", in S. Hennette-Vauchez & J.-M. Sorel (eds.), op. cit., p. 221.
60 Ibid.
61 Teubner, op. cit.

8 The concept of constitutionalization and the multi-corporate enterprise

From body corporate to sovereign enterprise

Larry Catá Backer[1]

1. Introduction

Constitutions and constitutionalism have become critical elements of global institutional discourse. The purposes of constitutions are well known. From modest beginnings in the West during Greek and Roman times,[2] referencing the organic rules for the construction of the political society of the State,[3] they had become the means by which a political community evidences the organization of its political order and the institutional structures that are charged with its operationalization.[4] Constitutions are static, at least in the sense that that they provide the framework for government and the instructions for the deployment of group power to be exercised by that government. Constitutions manifest a community – the aggregation of individuals (or other entities) – that have formed a body corporate. It is the product of a formation (*corporare*) to form a body out of the union of otherwise distinct parts. This incorporation was once understood as virtually completely self-referencing. Its context was essentially internal and once effected was as stable as the nature of the *genius* (understood in its ancient sense of the spirit attendant at birth, as something innate in itself) of the society that produced it. It's most important characteristic, then, was to evidence the creation of something tangible and autonomous (e.g. a State or an enterprise) from the union of parts (territory, inhabitants, shareholders, productive capacity).

Increasingly, the process of formation acquired a more dynamic and ideological element. The dynamics of that process are bound up in the ideologies of constitutionalism. The purposes of constitutionalism are rather newer. It frames an ideological universe, increasingly influential after 1945 and developed in parallel to the international institutions that arose after the Second World War, that provides a normative structure for validating constitutional instruments as legitimate. Constitutionalism, made manifest through constitutional instruments, might also be understood as theological[5] – at least in the sense that it is meant to

1 W. Richard & Mary Eshelman, "Faculty Scholar & Professor of Law", *Professor of International Affairs* (2013–14), Pennsylvania State University. The author may be contacted at lcb911@gmail.com

2 Aristotle, *The Athenian Constitution* (Sir Frederic G. Kenyon, trans.) MIT Classics online (original c. 350 B.C.) http://classics.mit.edu/Aristotle/athenian_const.1.1.html; Ancient History Sourcebook: Aristotle: *On the Lacedaemonian Constitution*, c. 340 BCE, www.fordham.edu/halsall/ancient/aristotle-sparta.asp

3 Generally Polybius, *The Histories* (Evelyn Shirley Shuckburgh, trans.), London: MacMillan / Co. (1889): www.gutenberg.org/files/44125/44125-h/44125-h.htm and www.gutenberg.org/ebooks/44126; Aristotle, *Politics: A Treatise on Government* (William Ellis, trans.), London &.Toronto: J. M. Dent & Sons Ltd. and in New York by E. P. Dutton &. Co. (1912): www.gutenberg.org/files/6762/6762-h/6762-h.htm

4 Cf. *Constitution of the United States of America as an Early Template*: www.gutenberg.org/ebooks/44126

5 Cf. Carl Schmitt, *Political Theology: Four Chapters on the Concept of Sovereignty* (George Schwab, trans.), Chicago: University of Chicago Press (2006) (originally *Politische Theologie: Vier Kapitel zur Lehre von der*

define a systematic and rational study of truths that exist beyond the will or control of any constitutionally constituted body – be it State, enterprise or religious community.

That "beyondness" of constitutionalism is critical because of its arguably theological feature – constitutionalism's sustained focus on the incarnation of abstraction outside of the natural persons whose coming together produces the body corporate. This also parallels strong currents in Western theology, and the philosophical movements that have sought to construct theological structures without reference to historical divinities. All have recognized the reality of the incarnation of abstraction – animating clay,[6] the Logos,[7] population[8] – and now the multinational enterprise, the subject of this chapter. More important, perhaps, is not the focus on the animation of the abstract, but its ensoulment[9] – its infusion with those characteristics and normative values, that fidelity to rules and principles, that themselves also manifest a greater abstraction – Truth, Justice, Fairness and the like. While constitutions can be understood as the means of making communities tangible, constitutionalism gives these concrete abstractions a soul, that spark of greater truth that marks the character of the incarnation and by their acts distinguishes between legitimate and illegitimate operation ("And the Lord God said, "The man has now become like one of us, knowing good and evil)".[10] Constitutionalism, then, provides the normative foundation applied, in context, through constitutions, by States (certainly) and other non-State actors (more recently) that seek to not merely make themselves tangible, but self-governing in ways that are deemed so both by internal stakeholders and external constituents (from the community of nations to transnational consumers and investors).

There are a number of significant schools or approaches to constitutionalization.[11] One strand can be identified as "global constitutionalism".[12] It has as its object the ordering of the community of political persons, States, within one organized world order. It would attain this objective by aggregating the political authority of States through international superstructures

Souveränität (2nd edition), Munich (1934) (e.g., asserting that concepts of modern political thought may be understood as theology and theological premises that have been secularized), nicely discussed in David Bates, "Political Theology and the Nazi State: Carl Schmitt's Concept of the Institution", *Modern Intellectual History*, 3(3), pp. 415–442 (2006).

6 Genesis 1:27.

7 John 1:1–18.

8 Foucault, Michel. *Security, Territory, Population, Lectures at the Collège de France 1977–1978* (Graham Burchell, trans.), New York: Picador Palgrave Macmillan (2007).

9 The concept of hominization is difficult today to separate from the obsession in the West about abortion – a site chosen for the ongoing war for dominance in moral governance between the institutions of the State and those of religion. See e.g. John Finnis, *Aquinas: Moral. Political and Legal Theory*, Oxford: Oxford University Press (1998). Yet the notion of hominization continues to resonate in its more classical meanings, the core of which was to distinguish inanimate organics (the biblical "clay") from the sentient, autonomous and self-conscious and self-referencing "person" around whom society grows and governance is built. It is that ensoulment that incarnates God in human and thus provides the claim to superiority and dominance, as well as the basis for distinguishing the good (legitimate). Cf., Center for Bioethics and Culture, Ensoulment and the Sacredness of Human Life (2006): www.cbc-network.org/2006/11/ensoulment-and-the-sacredness-of-human-life/. As such, ensoulment can be understood as much as a *political* subject in religion as it is a *theological* subject in politics.

10 Genesis 3:21.

11 It is worth taking seriously Roger Cottrell's argument, made in the context of the direction of socio/legal theory, that law is a composite of competing and unstable authority claims. Roger Cottrell, "Spectres of Transnationalism: Changing Terrains of Sociology of Law", *Journal of Law and Society*, 36(4), pp. 481–500 (2009).

12 See Anne Peters, "The Merits of Global Constitutionalism", *Indiana Journal of Global Legal Studies*, 16(2), pp. 397–411 (2009).

as new global government. It has sometimes an administrative character.[13]The recent global embrace of judicialization of State and inter-State activities suggests one aspect of this construction. It is built from interlocking State and international judicial and quasi-judicial bodies (ICC, WTO, human rights courts, and so on.) whose pronouncement of outcomes in disputes that come before them build a large well of customary practice that might form a singular legal edifice. Similar efforts have been attempted through global administrative bodies (WTO and standard setting agencies), and less successfully with executive bodies. It is premised on the ideal of a unitary system of constitutionalism which produces all sorts of entities each derived from a "legal" person of higher station.

Another important strand may be identified as "transnational constitutionalism". It seeks to manage the tendency toward nihilism in the anarchy of the Westphalian system[14] by positing constraints on the constitutional choices that might be made by any polity. It recognizes a customary and communal ordering of States, whose community is held together through mutual enforcement of a common core of customary principles. This common core of constitutional principle is made flexible through elaboration of complex notions of margins of appreciation exercised by States. The common constitutional traditions of States serve as a focal point of transnational substantive constraints on individual State power.[15] It is the most traditional of the modern constitutional ideologies. It is grounded in the idea that constitutions and States form a closed circuit into which non-State actors play no role. It reinforces the primacy of law as a field and as a mechanism for legitimate expressions of political authority closely tied to the State.[16] It is premised on rule of law as a political concept that may only be asserted by a sovereign polity defined by the territory its apparatus can control. But it substantially constrains the flexibility of a sovereign polity by the application of supra constitutional principle.

A third strand is sometimes identified as "polycentric constitutionalism".[17] It is anarchic (in the sense that there is no normative or institutional power center) and it applies

13 See e.g., Daniel C. Esty, "Good Governance at the Supranational Scale: Globalizing Administrative Law", *Yale Law Journal*, 115, p. 1490 (2006); Richard B. Stewart & Michelle Ratton, "Sanchez Badin, The World Trade Organization: Multiple Dimensions of Global Administrative Law", *I CON*, 9(3), pp. 556–586 (2011).

14 Recall the basis of the Westphalian system, which posits States at the apex of political hierarchy, which engage internally as they see fit but with each other on the basis of principles of non-interference in internal affairs of other States, and the legal equality of States. See, generally, Kurt Burch, "Changing the Rules: Reconceiving Change in the Westphalian System", *International Studies Review*, 2(2), pp. 181–210 (Summer 2000) and citations therein.

15 Larry Catá Backer, "God(s) Over Constitutions: International and Religious Transnational Constitutionalism in the 21st Century", *Mississippi College Law Review*, 27, pp. 11–65 (2008). Cf. Ernest A. Young, "The Trouble with Global Constitutionalism", *Texas Journal of International Law*, 38, p. 527 (2003).

16 That connection is nicely summarized in Roger Cottrell, "Spectres of Transnationalism: Changing Terrains of Sociology of Law", *Journal of Law and Society*, 36(4), pp. 481–500 (2009).

First, it makes the State and its agencies central. Second, it sees law as monistic, not pluralistic, in form (with international law as an extension of the reach of nation-state legal authority through treaties and the recognition of shared customs). Third, it assumes law's autonomy. Fourth, it almost always assumes settled internal/external distinctions that define the legal field. And fifth, it assumes that State law makes a practical difference; it has general effects in society of such significance that this law cannot safely be ignored in social practice. Ibid., 483.

17 Larry Catá Backer, "A Conversation About Polycentricity in Governance Systems Beyond the state", *Law at the End of the Day* (November 11, 2013): http://lcbackerblog.blogspot.com/2013/11/a-conversation-about-polycentricity-in.html; Larry Catá Backer, "Transnational Corporations' Outward Expression of Inward Self-Constitution: The Enforcement of Human Rights by Apple, Inc"., *Indiana Journal of Global Legal Studies*, 20(2), pp. 805–879 (2013).

contextually to all institutional aggregation of groups of constitutive entities (States, corporations, religions, non-State organizations) each organized according to the logic of the organization – functional differentiation serves as marker. Although polycentric constitutionalism posits common structures and principles of constituting legitimate communities[18] the details of such constituting organization, their character and scope are understood as functions of the consent of the individuals or institutions that have come together to form (constitute) the entity. For political organs, political constitutionalism is the rule. For the rest, non-State actors mostly, principles of *societal* constitutionalism predominate[19] – these suggest the forms of political and legal constitutionalism applied extra-legally. This gives rise to all sorts of formalist fussing about the legitimacy of non–law-based governance, fussing that is grounded on the fundamental ordering premise of political constitutionalism that, under rule-of-law principles, holds legislatively authorized law at the highest level of authority. For some, each governance order exists autonomously and both are horizontally arranged. For others, societal constitutionalism is a polite way of suggesting forms of constitutional delegation to creatures that must be understood as derived from and subordinate to States.

A fourth strand posits a "World Power System" (WPS) as a constitutional system.[20] It is one that suggests a malleable notion of constitutionalism, one that stretches its traditional notions, but one that remains loyal to its core values. That controlled malleability suggests the application of traditional though reshaped constitutional notions beyond the nation-state, to enterprises that occupy a de-territorialized space (and are thus in a sense societally constituted, though they do not embrace the notion of societal constitutionalism per se). Yet the possibility of the constitutionalization of (that is, the process of constitutionalizing) the extra-territorial governance space that enterprises increasingly occupy can be enhanced through an instrumental approach grounded in legislation that might contribute to the normative project of fashioning a "good" consolidation of the auto-constitutionalization of the WPS through a variety of micro-devices. This constitutionalizing strand effectively detaches constitutionalism from States and then, so detached, applies them with equal force to all governance institutions – all understood as incarnations of power.

Constitutionalization, in contrast to constitutions and constitutionalism, "stands as an expression of a set of processes that are now having an impact on decision making at all levels of government – local, national, regional, international. It concerns the attempt to subject all governmental action within a designated field to the structures, processes, principles and

18 Cf. Poul Kjear, "The Constitutionalism of Intra- and Trans-Normative Orders", *Indiana Journal of Global Legal Studies*, 20, pp. 777–804 (2013); Jayne Ellis, "Constitutionalization of Non-Governmental Certification Programs", *Indiana Journal Global Legal Studies*, 20, pp. 1035–1059 (2013).

19 Discussed in Gunther Teubner, *Constitutional Fragments: Societal Constitutionalism in the Globalization*, Oxford: Oxford University Press (2012).

20 See Jean-Philippe Robé (in collaboration with Antoine Lyon-Caen and Stéphane Vernac), "Enterprises and the Constitutionalization of the World Power System" (2013 paper on file with author); also see Jean-Philippe Robé, *L'Enterprise et le Droit*, Paris: Presses Universitaires de France (1999); Jean-Philippe Robé, "Enterprises and the Constitution of the World Economy", *International Corporate Law*, 2, pp. 45–64 (2003); Jean-Philippe Robé, "Conflicting Sovereignties in the World Wide Web of Contracts – Property Rights and the Globalization of the Power System", in *Soziologische Jurisprudenz, Festschrift für Gunther Teubner*, Gralf-Peter Calliess, Andreas Fischer Lescano, Dan Wielsch & Peer Zumbansen (eds.), Berlin: De Gruyter Recht (2009), pp. 691–703; Antoine Lyon-Caen, "Le Pouvoir entre droit du travail et droit des sociétés", *Revue de Droit du Travail*, 9, pp. 494-498 (2010).

values of a "constitution"[21] – but it is more than that. Globalization has untethered politics from the State. But it has not unmoored the standards and indicia of legitimacy and institution creation from its State-based origins. By the beginning of the twenty-first century, constitutions and the ideological basis for its legitimate operation, had become the standard for judging the legitimacy of governance organs. As non-State actors increasingly sought to assert governance authority – from those activities once understood as inherently political and administrative, executive or judicial in character – they turned to the forms of legitimacy used by States and embraced constitutions, and with it the normative framework of constitutionalism. Constitutionalization, then, refers to those processes that subject all efforts to incarnate intangible aggregations of governance power in the structures constitutions and the ideology of constitutionalization.

The concept of constitutionalization, then, focuses on the *drive* to apply the insights of constitutionalism to incarnated abstractions, to engage in ministry. Where once it applied almost exclusively to religious and political orders, the early twenty-first century has seen the expansion of the notion to practically every form of institutional aggregation. That movement has changed the world. To grasp the meaning of constitutionalism, to be able to see through constitutions to the abstractions made flesh which in turn themselves build communities among other animated abstractions within national, international and transnational spaces, then, requires a close study of the basic principles of constitutionalism. But such enterprises requires a magisterium, a Sanhedrin, an imam – those who teach the faithful about what is expected of them, who arbitrate the meaning of the normative principles that frame judgment about the legitimacy of action. There are many of those, each vying for recognition as the authoritative voice both to describe the universe within which these abstractions live and operate, and to elaborate the principles through which they may be judged and validated, and may thus exercise their power without opposition.

Constitutionalization makes constitutionalism unavoidable – and constitutionalism is now marked by constitution-making in accordance with the normative rule systems of constitutional construction. But beyond these generalities, there are deep theoretical schisms. These schisms are made more interesting as constituting agents increasingly "make theory" from their own actions – and theory is then put in the embarrassing position of having to catch up to facts on the ground. That certainly has been the story of the march of constitutionalization for non-State actors, especially multinational enterprises.

This chapter considers this concept of constitutionalization in the context of the multinational enterprise. The baseline for that consideration is the WPS approach – the notion that the global project of constitutionalization is as yet incomplete – and requires for its completion the absorption of non-State actors, and principally the large transnational economic enterprises that have become sometimes more powerful political actors than many States. The framework for that consideration is the framework of constitutionalism itself – the drive to find structures for the incarnation of abstractions whose force can be readily felt but which can be felt only in the effects it produces. But just as constitutionalism is not solely about *form* – the self-referencing self-constituted entity – so the analysis also looks to the *function* of this structuring, the ensoulment of the enterprise. That ensoulment is represented by the normative premises (or deep structures) of constitutionalism, those rules that constrain the intangible person in its constitution and operation. Yet it is the malleability of that soul, and

21 Martin Loughlin, "What is Constitutionalization?", *Jus Politicum*, 3: www.juspoliticum.com/What-is-constitutionalization.html

the identity of those who may speak for it, that provides as difficult a set of issues for non-State bodies corporate as they do for States.

Constitutionalization, and its theoretical structures, if only considered as an amalgam of the *desire* or *intent* (understood as a cultural instruction or preference) to invoke the frameworks of constitutionalism for the formation and interactions of bodies corporate merely provides only a static view of the revolution in the rearrangement and control of governance authority. But constitutionalization serves, or ought to serve, a deeper purpose, and one that serves as the *underlying thesis of this chapter*: Constitutionalism provides a framework applicable to any organized group, from States to non-State actors, that seeks to govern itself through an entity autonomous of other entities and of its constituent parts. In globalization, all self-governing groups necessarily interact, as equals or otherwise. There is a need, therefore for a common platform for interaction among bodies corporate, that is for the intermeshing of governance personalities that "bump up" against each other as equals or otherwise.

Constitutionalization is the way that we organize the study of the search for (and theory of) a common platform among self-governing groups which are related by their interactions but which need a system for identifying each other and organizing those interactions. It serves as the meta-structure for the space within which the community of believers may interact within a shared ideological space, one that is both compelling and mandatory. It posits meta-principles for constitutionalism that ought to make it possible for States to engage with commercial enterprises and universal religious bodies. But it also suggests an obligation to constitutionalize along its terms – there is an aspect of *ministry* in constitutionalism that is manifested through its works – what it offers constitutional actors and their constituent members that is deemed "good" as a guide to behavior. The chapter thus ends with a brief view toward application – what does all this theory mean for the way States and enterprises ought to act, that is ought to perform their constitutional roles in the world in which they occupy substantial positions of power over individuals, who now appear dwarfed by these institutional giants. It is the constitutionalist system that in its operation is most compatible with the expectations and customs of stakeholders that will succeed, in the end, as setting the parameters of constitutionalism going forward.

2. Incarnation – constitutions: The enterprise made flesh

Let us consider the way that each of the distinct strands of constitutional systems tend to approach the issue of the incarnation of aggregations of power and governance. The differences in basic premises contribute to differences in approaches and conceptualizations of the possibilities of constituting governance units beyond the State – or, to the extent that such conceptualization is possible, of the relationship between these governance units and the State. I start with WPS's constitutionalism and then contrast its premises to those of global, transnational and polycentric constitutionalism.

WPS approaches seek to construct frameworks for identifying those governance organisms that exist within globalization spaces but outside the governance territories of traditional political governance centers (States). They first seek to localize globalization within the WPS and identify its most significant actor, a precisely defined concept labeled – "the enterprise". To that end they reject the grounding premises of global and transnational constitutionalism, which defines constitutional spaces as for all practical effects, proceeding from or through States. That immediately presents a normative conundrum: Our social sciences are ideologically constructed to be in sync with our basic political premises. Because those basic premises posit the State as the basic organizing incarnation of autonomous abstract power, with other juridical persons inferior to and creatures of this basic and wholly autonomous aggregation of communal governance authority.

If that is the case, WPS analysis confronts a fundamental challenge similar to that of polycentric constitutionalism: how to understand the structures of global society as it moves from a law-state model to something else, when the classical approaches of the social sciences are no longer relevant to the problem as it is actually evolving. The social sciences are encased within the analytical structuring parameters of the law-state system. These have two substantial deficiencies. First, they presume one idealized "master template" State. Second, they presume one idealized "master template" social order within the framing embrace of the State. These serve the State order system and are less useful as that becomes less central to the realities of power allocation in the global order.

In both cases, the language of constitutions by its terms excludes the possibility of incorporation of entities that are not States. To the extent that such incorporation is possible it is wholly derivative – non-State entities may be incorporated only through an act of "creator" enterprises, much like "woman" was made of "man".[22] But it is that very premise that sits at the center of the critique of the constitutional enterprise of conventional constitution systems. WPS analysis proposes an analysis the purpose of which is to embrace the actual functioning of global power systems, that is, where there are no longer external factors to a power (functional) analysis. Polycentric constitutionalism shares this objective with WPS analysis to a point, but would reject any analysis that posits any singular referent or ordering center to global power systems. Polycentricity posits global anarchy in the sense of multiple autonomous systems in need of coordination or cooperation or accommodation;[23] WPS analysis intimates the possibility of aggregation and coherence if not unity. That difference will significantly affect the way in which either views the constitution of non-State actors, and the range of enterprises within which such analysis applies. While WPS analysis focuses on economic enterprises, polycentric analysis would embrace all communal incarnations within cross-cutting systems of power that may intermesh but which may not converge.

Focusing on the enterprise has the effect of narrowing the scope of WPS constitutional analytics within the confines of globalization – that is within the governance spaces opened when States made their borders porous and governance power fractured.[24] This distinguishes it from other approaches. Thus, while the central problem of polycentricity is the construction of self-consciously autonomous organization distinct from its constituting elements, and where the central problem of global and transnational constitutionalism is the (re)construction of systems grounded in politics and expressed through law enacted by representatives of natural persons organized as territorial States that recaptures the cohesion of the ideal of the Westphalian system and its international organs, that of WPS centers on the problem of the enterprise in globalization.

That problem of the enterprise in globalization is interrogated by considering the enterprise in two broad respects. First, true to its mission of "seeking truth from facts",[25] WPS

22 Gen. 2:21–23.

23 Cf. Surya Deva, *Regulating Corporate Human Rights Violations: Humanizing Business*, London: Routledge (2012), pp. 200–231.

24 See Gralf-Peter Calliess & Peer Zumbansen, *Rough Consensus and Running Code: A Theory of Transnational Private Law*, Oxford: Hart (2010); Larry Catá Backer, "The Structural Characteristics of Global Law for the 21st Century: Fracture, Fluidity, Permeability, and Polycentricity", *Tilburg Law Review*, 17(2), pp. 177–199 (2012).

25 Deng Xioaping, "Emancipate The Mind, Seek Truth from Facts and Unite as One in Looking to the Future", *Selected Works of Deng Xiaoping* II (1975–1982) (December 13, 1978): http://english.peopledaily.com.cn/dengxp/vol2/text/b1260.html

analysis engages in a diagnosis of the position of the enterprise invoking the techniques of deconstruction and reconstruction. The deconstruction analysis seeks to uncover the "enterprise" from out of its hiding places within the open spaces created by globalization. WPS analysis understands open spaces as those areas of governance into which the domestic legal orders of States cannot reach. That exercise, in turn, requires a distinction between the formal structures of enterprise formation and regulation – the corporation – and the functional repositories of corporate power in an "enterprise" that is the aggregation of multiple formal corporate structures the totality of which may evade the law of any one place.

This process unveils the realities of the spaces now open within which enterprises exist as ghosts – they are functionally tangible but formally nonexistent creatures that occupy a space between formal law-state governance zones in ways that would ultimately tear the conventional law-state system apart. It is in this sense that under a WPS analysis enterprises are recognized as "extra-legal." This state of extra legality results from the effects of property regimes that, once conceived for the management of things by natural persons, have been able to be used to animate aggregations of things in corporate form. Its principal perversions follow from the invisible visibility of enterprises within the current WPS – no equal treatment of persons and entities under law. These "un-natural" persons, thus incarnated, exceed the powers and authority of their creators. This imbalance is exacerbated by the logic of globalization that has made borders quite porous to capital and enterprise (as complexes of juridical persons) but which remain highly regulated for the free movement of natural persons.

This imbalance frames the reconstruction analysis. It is based on the premise of equality between natural and legal persons, between natural and bodies corporate. That requires a rebalancing of relations between natural and legal persons to reduce the advantages of the latter. And that rebalancing requires a reconstitution of the incarnate enterprise by limiting the existing split between control (functional and in the hands of the enterprise) and ownership (formal and in the hands of the entity). This rebalancing is made necessary because of the failure of traditional shareholder wealth maximization and fiduciary duty premises, which have proven to be illusory. What is needed, then, is to incarnate the "enterprise" within systems of law, constrained by constitutional principle. And that, in turn, requires a rethinking of the structures of the constitutionalism of the law-state system itself. The problem of the enterprise, then, is a problem of incarnation – not self-incarnation, but one that is captured within law and politics systems that these "enterprise ghosts" have managed to evade. Having revealed these horrors, that is, the perversions of a WPS of full and empty governance spaces, WPS analysis then offers a solution to these "perversions" through a process that extends the constitutional project of States to economic enterprises, a process of ensoulment discussed later.

While WPS analysis seeks to uncover the unitary nature of enterprise self-constitution from out of its component parts, and to incarnate it within a WPS, other approaches might attach a wholly different set of characteristics to the phenomenon of the enterprise, which is at the center of WPS condemnation. Global constitutionalism and transnational constitutionalism might well share the WPS's suspicion of uncontrolled self-constitution.[26] While WPS analysis recognizes the incarnation of enterprises as substantial actors "in fact" (and would seek to bring them into a comprehensive constitutional system with specific objectives) both

26 See, generally, Vlad Perju, "Cosmopolitanism and Constitutional Self/Government", *I CON*, 8(3), pp. 326–353 (2010).

global and transnational constitutionalism do not recognize the enterprise at all for precisely the same reason. Transnational constitutionalism is bounded by the limitations of the traditional law-state. It recognizes those legal or juridical persons it creates, or those it recognizes as created by other States, but beyond that, these enterprises are thought to exist in "social" space. They are beyond the reach of the domestic legal orders of States precisely because they have refused to recognize the power of the State to manage them. They are thus ghosts in the sense that they remain invisible to law, except through the actions of their recognized components (those corporate entities that operate within the territories of these States). Global constitutionalism would add a layer of regulation of corporate activity between States, and might harmonize the approaches of States to those aggregate incarnations they recognize, but they would not reach an enterprise that will not exist within its legal structures. Both are satisfied with this arrangement because of the basic "deal" inherent in corporate law, that in return for conformity to law in their formation and operation, lawfully incarnated enterprises are recognized as autonomous by the State, and are free to take full advantage of the law system of the State in which they operate and within which they remain subordinate beings.[27]

Polycentric constitutionalism understands this differently. It attaches a substantially different character to the incarnation, the self-formation, of the enterprise so carefully described in WPS analysis. What WPS analysis describes as a ghost, polycentric constitutionalism would characterize as the solidity of formation under constitutional rules autonomous of those that bind natural persons. Indeed, polycentric constitutionalism might recast the WPS analysis as a double incarnation – the possibility that corporations, as incarnate abstractions within the domestic legal orders of States might combine to create enterprises that exist outside of the law-state system, and operates solely in so-called social space. That produces the power and imbalance noted by WPS – not because of the possibilities for abuse within law systems, but despite them. That enterprises can exist, can be formed in this governance space, is a function not of the power of law bound to States, or to the international order, but to the consent of these bodies and the willingness of others to interact with them or their constituent parts. It is in this sense that these enterprises are not ghosts so much as strangers to the governance systems of States with which they must interact (and certainly so through their constituent corporations). More importantly, perhaps, polycentric constitutionalism understands the power of self-constitution as neither inherent solely in the economic enterprise nor unique to it. Rather it posits the possibility of multiple governance systems within which people may form any manner of structures of governance that can exist independent of their creators and that can operate within their own logic to develop operational rules based only on the rules of a constitution. These "feral incarnations" exist within their own governance spaces and may interact with but are not necessarily subsumed within those of other systems. The question for polycentric constitutionalism, then, is not about the legitimacy of formation, but of the problem of ensoulment – the rules and principles within which these feral creatures ought to operate.

Taken together, it emerges quite clearly that each variation of approach specifies a different relationship between corporate incarnation and law. Global constitutionalism embraces law as the basic form of legitimate governance, understood in its narrow and classical sense of command produced through democratic processes specified by law. However, that concept of law would be extended to the global State. Transnational constitutionalism embraces

27 See, e.g., David A. (Bert) Westbrook, *Between Citizen and State: An Introduction to the Corporation*, Boulder, CO: Paradigm Press (2007).

the traditional approach, based on national law, disciplined only by the constraints of the common constitutional traditions of the community of nations. Polycentric constitutionalism reduces law from its traditional status as the only source of governance, to one that expresses *only* the governance authority of States. It offers *societal* governance as an alternative – a governance system established outside of law and the structures of the State – one that treats State-based law-constituted governance systems as equivalent in dignity within the societally constituted communities that may serve as the basis for the establishment and enforcement of rules within societally self-constituted units. WPS recognizes the product of societally constituted incarnations, like enterprises, but would have them brought back into the framework of law, now extended to all self-constituted governance communities. These distinctions have significant consequences for the ideological basis of constituted legitimacy that is constitutionalism, a subject to which the chapter turns next.

3. Ensoulment – constitutionalism: Entities as moral/ideological constitutional creatures

If the multinational enterprise perverts the actual system of world power by strategically using its private status to avoid public obligation, then the constitutionalization of the enterprise sector, now a lawless zone, is the necessary next step. This turns on WPS's very specific conception of constitutionalization, one that charts a path that is unique, though not without its troubling aspects. It is with this project that one moves from the issue of the possibility of constituting an organism other than a State, to the issue of the principles under which it may be recognized by others as legitimate. That is, having incarnated the non-State actors (solely the enterprise for WPS analysis), we move to the possibility of giving it a soul and a moral system within which it might operate unmolested (though constrained).[28]

For WPS that system embraces the highest aspirations of liberal western rights based rule of law democratic power constraining model – "*indivisible, laïque, démocratique et sociale*".[29] WPS argues, in its most provocative insight, that this constitutional extension is necessary because it represents the unfinished trajectory of Western constitutionalism. It is made necessary by the extra-constitutional growth of private power under the shadow of the State. Thus understood, the extension of universalist constitutional principles is necessary to domesticate private power and to rebalance global power systems by recentering the public interest within both States and economic enterprises not otherwise subject to management by the State (or through constitutional constraint directly applied as principle or as command). The contours of WPS constitutionalism are thus tied to public law internationalism, with no margins of appreciation against constitutional consensus among States. WPS thus resonates with global constitutionalism, but is irreconcilable with transnational constitutionalist objectives. WPS is, in this sense, aligned with global constitutionalism, and may be coherent with the thrust of transnational constitutionalism. The grounding of all three is on the product of State-based public law, grounded in the core principles of individual human dignity and rule of law as applied through the operation of democratic principles. It embraces much of

28 Cf. Christopher Thornhill, "A Sociology of Constituent Power: The Political Code of Transnational Societal Constitutions", *Indiana Journal of Global Legal Studies*, 20(2), pp. 551–603 (2013).

29 *Constitution de la République française*, Art. 1: www.assemblee-nationale.fr/connaissance/constitution.asp

the principles of the International Bill of Human Rights. That aligns it as well with soft law projects like the UN Guiding Principles for Business and Human Rights.[30]

Indeed, for transnational constitutionalism, the possibility of extension of constitutionalist principles to the formation of political communities other than States is heretical – the broaching of a possibility of reducing the uniqueness of States and of reducing the structures of rule of law governance from something inherently tied to the sovereignty asserting principles of mass democracy falls beyond the essential logic of transnational constitutionalism and would be rejected.[31] That, indeed, underlies the rejection of the Norms for Transnational Business in the first years of the twenty-first century, which I have elsewhere discussed.[32] If this is so – synthesis may produce a movement toward deep or substantive constitutionalism that is distinct from the traditional State-based constitutionalism. How to subject all forms of power to the principles of constitutional government to (a) ensure respect of the rights of individuals and (b) promote the development of the exercise of all forms of powers in the common interest of the organization exercising power. This project is more compatible with global constitutionalism than with the more traditionalist transnational constitutionalism that remains a powerful force.

Yet its potential coherence with the logic of global constitutionalism is also limited. WPS analytics are also, and perhaps uneasily, tied to the long development and ideological foundations of the liberal politics of the West, now rendered both universal in the political realm and among a larger class of governance institutions by seeking to bring enterprises (now recognized incarnate form) into its ambit. This is thus meant to recognize both the true form of the enterprise as a government[33] and also as bound by a duty, like those of States, to comply with the principles of constitutional organization heretofore applied to and developed for States. But these Western liberal constitutional notions may have little resonance with the constitutional structures of Marxist Leninist States, like China.[34]

Here lies one of the great practical consequences of this approach: If enterprises are both incarnated as public persons autonomous of their creators and ensouled by extending the constitutional constraints of States to these enterprises, then the force of the agency and fiduciary principles at the heart of corporate law must give way to the superior constitutional obligations of the exercise of public power. Now bound by notions of public duty, the *demos* of the enterprise necessarily expands from the shareholder to the stakeholder. And thus the

30 Cf. John G. Ruggie, *Just Business: Multinational Corporations and Human Rights*, New York: W.W. Norton (2013).

31 See José A. Alvarez, "Are Corporations 'Subjects' of International Law?", *Santa Clara Journal of International Law*, 9(1), pp. 1–35 (2011).

32 Larry Catá Backer, "Multinational Corporations, Transnational Law: The United Nation's Norms on the Responsibilities of Transnational Corporations as a Harbinger of Corporate Social Responsibility as International Law", *Columbia Human Rights Law Review*, 37, pp. 287–389 (2006).

33 This is an old insight, see David Vogel, "The Corporation as Government: Challenges and Dilemmas", *Polity*, 8(1), pp. 5–37 (1975); Arthur S. Miller, "The Corporation as a Private Government in the World Community", *Virginia Law Review*, 46(8), pp. 1539–1572 (1960). It has now acquired a societal element as well as a the traditional public law element either within domestic or international law structures. See, e.g., David Sciulli, *Theory of Societal Constitutionalism: Foundations of a Non-Marxist Critical Theory*, Cambridge: Cambridge University Press (1992).

34 Cf. Karin Buhmann, *Implementing Human Rights Through Administrative Law Reforms: The Potential in China and Vietnam,* Copenhagen: Djøf (2001); Larry Catá Backer, "China's Corporate Social Responsibility with National Characteristics: Coherence and Dissonance with the Global Business and Human Rights Project", in *Human Rights and Business: Moving Forward, Looking Back*, Jena Martin & Karen E. Bravo (eds.), Cambridge: Cambridge University Press (2015), pp. 530-558.

shareholder wealth maximization model of corporate governance must necessarily give way to a public law model that (applying principles of mass democracy and empowerment) produces a stakeholder model that would align corporate objectives with public policy norms, one that is limited by constraints of individual rights, process rights and the need to avoid detrimental externalities.

However, its structural framework is quite distinct. Unlike transnational constitutionalism, WPS would extend public law based deep constitutionalism (principles of conduct) directly onto enterprises (though not to other non-State actors). It would not merely internationalize a coherent constitutionalism (the object of global constitutionalism) or harmonize common constitutional traditions the traditions of which are memorialized as universal constraints on government action (the objective of transnational constitutionalism) but would extend them to on-public actors. That notion is incompatible with either global or transnational constitutionalism, both of which might embrace the notion of enterprise management, but not as subjects of law, whether domestic or international. It is also incompatible to conventional approaches to the governance of non-State actors.

WPS also rejects the fundamental approach of polycentric constitutionalism. It its form as an anarchic system, it provides none of the certainties of global, transnational or WPS constitutionalism, each of which points to a singular set of guiding principles within which constitutions are structured. Instead, anarchic polycentrism holds only the promise of shared custom, and the certainty of group values, but ones defined solely by the incarnating group. It is reduced to nothing more than (1) a system of classification (2) the core object of which is to define the characteristics of constitutions (3) to be used to determine the legitimacy of the constitutional system as conceived and as implemented (4) based on rule of law as a fundamental postulate of government (5) and grounded on a metric of substantive values derived from some source beyond the control of any individual.[35] In its form as societal constitutionalism, it again draws on general custom, something that echoes the processes of transnational constitutionalism's values generating process, but retains an elasticity that goes beyond fidelity to a single set of specific core values grounded in a particular ideology. Yet societal constitutionalism is tied to the great movements in global customs among the distinct groupings that might seek to come together to effectuate self-consciously autonomous entities. In the area of business practice, those customs increasingly develop in tandem with human rights norms produced through international public and private organs, themselves autonomous self-constituted extra national organs. But these also may not come completely within the constitutional traditions meant to be captured by WPS. Indeed, WPS might be understood to seek to recapture the enterprise for or within the State constitutionalist system by recognizing the State power of enterprises. It would follow that societal constitutionalism and anarchist governance systems would tend to be viewed as part of the problem, rather than as contributing to a solution, precisely because it acts as an impediment to the core goals of extending the heretofore State-based constitutionalism project to economic enterprises.

It is possible to stand back from this discussion and seen increasingly dense set of flora populating a forest of governance without government and government without a State.[36]

35 From Larry Catá Backer, "From Constitution to Constitutionalism: A Global Framework for Legitimate Public Power Systems", *Pennsylvania State Law Review*, 113(3), pp. 671–732 (2009).

36 Discussed in Larry Catá Backer, "Governance Without Government: An Overview", in *Beyond Territoriality: Transnational Legal Authority in an Age of Globalization*, Günther Handl, Joachim Zekoll & Peer Zumbansen (eds.), Leiden, Netherlands and Boston, MA: Martinus Nijhoff (2012), pp. 87–123.

This forest, though, might be better understood as a market – where competing visions of "the good" are displayed for the consumption of those who might profit thereby. But constitutionalist systems are not tangible commodities; they are more fundamentally choices about notions of the reality within which this self-interacts with others. On one hand, that may suggest anarchy within constitutionalism – as a number of distinct realms of constitutionalism congeal around their own normative ideals and processes. On the other, it may suggest not so much a stable but a competitive anarchy in which all constitutionalism view themselves as universalist and each then vies against the others not merely to dominate but to obliterate their rivals in a dynamic contest to shape the world. They thus acquire the characteristics of movements – political or religious – in the sense that each others a closed view of the world that excludes others and on which is based social, political, economic and moral interaction. The object of these movements is not merely to explain the reality around us, but to provide a choice for a way of ordering that reality in accordance with its terms. Thus constitutionalism in its many forms may suggest a *respublica constitutionalis.*[37] That impulse, if true, requires a move *from constitutionalism* (as a descriptor and value marker) *to constitutionalization* (as a cause and a set of cultural assumptions, with its markers and taboos that manages understanding). It is to a brief consideration of this phenomenon of constitutionalization that I turn to next.

4. Ministry – constitutionalization: Common platforms, structures, language; multiple objectives

The differences to the content of constitutions, and to the means for expressing both rules for managing formation of these entities and their value content, suggest a *relationship between constitutionalism and constitutionalization.* Constitutionalism not only posits the structure of the values within which entities may be incarnated (its soul), but it also binds the content of ensoulment with a necessity of its transmission. Constitutionalism drives constitutionalization precisely because by its very terms constitutionalism defines "the good" and thus makes alternatives impossible. It makes mandatory the formation of entities under its value terms. If constitutionalism touches on ensoulment, constitutionalization touches on ministry, and thus provides a common platform for interaction and further development. Here the earlier reference to Martin McLoughlin's definition of constitutionalization becomes more pointed.[38] Yet this "discipline of constitutional procedures and norms", as I have suggested earlier, is made more complicated by its indeterminacy, on one hand, and its fracture among distinct sects of constitutionalism on the other.

Thus, for example, WPS constitutionalism has a direct impact on its approach to constitutionalization: It would require all enterprises (States and economic entities) to conform to

37 I draw an obvious analogical reference to the more ancient and partisan notion of a *respublica christiana*. See F. Urquhart, "Christendom", in *The Catholic Encyclopedia,* New York: Robert Appleton Company (1908); contra John Locke, "A Letter Concerning Toleration," in *A Letter Concerning Toleration and Other Writings* (1689) Mark Goldie (ed.), Indianapolis: Liberty Fund, 2010. Again, the structures of the political organization around theology provide a rhetorical and conceptual structuring framework for constitutionalization, and especially that of non-State organizations.

38 "We are today witnessing the emergence of a new phenomenon in the public sphere: the phenomenon of constitutionalization. . . . It concerns the attempt to subject all governmental action within a designated field to the structures, processes, principles and values of a 'constitution" Martin Loughlin, "What Is Constitutionalization?", *Jus Publicum* No. 3, *supra* 21.

its precepts and to embrace its values if they are to be recognized as enterprises. In addition, it would permit the suppression of non-conforming enterprises. The same is the essence of transnational constitutionalism, but only with respect to the governments of States. That serves as the basis for intervention by States in the affairs of others and to justify revolution. Polycentric constitutionalism would also ensoul, in the sense that it would demand a normative system that must be derived and exercised beyond the will of any of the constituent parts of a governance organism incarnated through constitutional means and seeking the benefits of legitimacy on that basis. But the actual scope of those norms might differ, and perhaps considerably, among governance communities. Still, all of these ideologies are held together by the basic objective of providing a common way of organizing reality – in this case, governance spaces – so that governance organizations can be identified, disciplined, categorized and engaged with. It is the need to create this field of play, this community of believers, within which the rules of the game are all embraced in equal measure by all players.

Constitutionalization, then, implies a drive toward universalism in the constitutionalist, which is necessary for the triumph of the normative reality at the heart of each version of constitutionalism: constitutionalization thus describes both the attempt to fit all governance within constitutionalist ideals, but also to fit all constitutionalist ideals together into a coherent framework. It is not enough to embrace constitutionalism – all constitutionalist enterprises ought to embrace *the same* constitutionalism. That is the notion at the foundation of WPS, global and transnational constitutionalism in the sense that even the diversity of expression permitted within each is derivative of and disciplined by the structures of each system's basic premises. It is in this sense that each would establish a version of a *respublica christiana* within the governance space it claims for its constitutionalist project. Even polycentric constitutionalism adheres to a form of this notion, with its emphasis on the process structures for investing a self-referencing self-governing community with constitutionalist characteristics. This follows from the *core premise of constitutionalization* – that self-constitution is a communal act *both* (1) in the sense that it brings constituting actors together to create a new being from out of that aggregation, and (2) in the sense that such constituted actors (States and enterprises for example) must exist within a community of actors similarly constituted. Such self-constituting governance actors are neither constituted in isolation and out of whole cloth, no do they exist in isolation untouched by persons and actors around them.

There is a corollary to this notion of constitutionalization as a positive and communal movement. That corollary is that there is also a sense of fundamental *ministry*[39] in each of these systems, ministries that are central to the concept of the constitutionalism expressed by each. A community requires actors and each constitutionalist system must acquire a large enough share to make their joint discipline and welfare increasing existence possible. But that ministry cannot be made up solely of pretty words and complex theories of the "the good" and "the right" at the heart of constitutionalism. Instead, in its aspect of ministry, constitutionalization brings us ultimately to operationalization. This is so because the abstractions of constitutionalization, can only be solidified by acts – and acts of constitutionalization are necessarily felt through the specific operationalization of constitutional systems – not

39 See, e.g., Elaine L. Graham, *Transforming Practice: Pastoral Theology in an Age of Uncertainty*, Eugene, OR: Wipf & Stock (2002). The connection between law, governance and theology bound up in this concept are old. See, e.g., A Ministry of Justice, *Harvard Law Review*, 35(2), pp. 113–126 (1921). In its modern incarnation cf. Emmanuel Y. Lartey, *Postcolonializing God: New Perspectives in Pastoral and Practical Theology*, London: SCM Press (2012).

their structuring so much as what they produce and how they relate to each other and to their stakeholders, and not just that relation but the nature of the discipline possible for those enterprises (States or other actors) that would deviate from constitutionalist norms.

The concept of constitutionalization, then, has as its foundation, a *performative* element – it exists only through its manifestation in context of relations among actors and their constituents.[40] This also performs ancient patterns deep within the politico-cultural bones of the West – "You see that a person is considered righteous by what they do and not by faith alone".[41] Thus, it is one thing to constitutionalize the enterprise space; it is quite another to operationalize that constitutionalization. It is to the hard task of operationalization that this section turns. For WPS, operationalization at the heart of constitutionalization consists of a number of micro-devices. The first distinguishes between firm and corporate governance as a means of decentering shareholders and equity from governance decisions. The object is to move toward stakeholder governance at the firm level while retaining shareholder power of some sort at the corporate level. It requires reshaping fiduciary duty. The second is to modify the management structures of the enterprise itself, grounded in the provisions of incentives as micro-devices founded on "true value" concept. That requires changing accounting rules to change the way the value of the enterprise is understood. For this task there is the possibility of considerable intermeshing with non-constitutional actors. The object would be to reframe the conception of accounting from its current narrow financial focus. To one in which social, cultural, and environmental values are also incorporated. The third is to limit shareholder rights and power in corporate governance. Board election would be retained, with greater protection for board (an enterprise model) and with a broadening of business judgment rule coupled with a limitation of shareholder limited liability (liable for a broader abuse of position and value destruction. The fourth would expand role of the judiciary (bring the State back in through the back door). Judicialization model would be shifted form constitutional to corporate sphere along with a transposition of the rule of law model to corporate sphere. The object would be to transform private to public normative framework through a bottom up approach (use courts as common law vehicle) but instrumentally driven by public principles underlying decision making. Here the State makes a grand reentrance in ways that might make the system coherent with aspects of transnational constitutionalism.[42] Most interesting in this respect would be the openness to extraterritorial power in the service of public law principles (ostensibly universally embraced).[43] The fifth would open the possibility of additional interventions. These include a modestly larger role for non-governmental organizations, acceptance of universal jurisdiction, expansion of criminal prosecution, class action reform in line with reduced role of shareholding (but States have been taking this role away from individuals for decades now), clarifying and simplifying unfair competition

40 Generally John L. Austin, *Sense and Sensibilia* (G. J. Warnock, ed.), Oxford: Clarendon Press (1962). In its application to the performance of economic reality, see Donald MacKenzie, Fabnian Muniesa & Lucia Siu, "Introduction", in *Do Economists Markets? On the Performativity of Economics*, Donald MacKenzie, Fabnian Muniesa & Lucia Siu (eds.), Princeton: Princeton University Press (2007), pp. 1–19.

41 James 2:24.

42 Cf. Jiunn-Rong Yeh & Wen-Chen Chang, "The Emergence of Transnational Constitutionalism: Its Features, Challenges and Solutions", *Pennsylvania State International Law Review*, 27, p. 89 (2008–2009).

43 Cf. Daniel Augenstein & David Kinley, "When Human Rights Responsibilities Become Duties: The Extra-Territorial Obligations of States that Bind Corporations", in *Human Rights Obligations of Business: Beyond The Corporate Responsibility to Respect?*, Surya Deva & David Bilchitz (eds.), Cambridge: Cambridge University Press (2013), pp. 271–294.

actions, the reform of domestic legal orders to permit actions to recover the cost of negative externalities (problems of certainty and proof of course) and an extension of consumer protection rules (technology as bio power!).

In contrast, polycentric constitutionalization offers the mediating power of investors and consumers. Many of the micro-devices of WPS may be compatible with polycentric constitutionalism's project. For polycentric constitutionalism, though, operationalization focuses more on the structural control of markets and sites for intermediation than on the substance of commands beyond those evolved and embraced through the consent of the governance community – and notions such as extraterritorial jurisdiction and mandatory judicialization would likely be incompatible with polycentric ideals. I have, for example, considered the power of disclosure as a tool to socialize business entities and others into compliance with emerging social norms (that is to behavior rules that are not transposed into the laws of nation-states necessarily but which have binding effect within social, economic and other communities).[44] To that end, it is well-known that both State and non-State regulatory systems play an essential role.[45] Among the most important players in the context of structuring markets and business behavior expectations are the securities exchanges vital to the operation of global investment. The community of exchanges structures its operations and disciplines its members through an organization of exchanges, the World Federation of Exchanges.[46] That organization has itself sought to revamp corporate sustainability reporting with the object of institutionalizing, routinizing and harmonizing sustainability reporting. The goal is to produce systems that might be used, like current financial reporting systems, to evaluate companies for purposes of making investment and other pricing-related decisions. The centrality of routinization, institutionalization and reporting coherence[47] is the stuff of polycentric constitutionalist discipline.

What are the consequences of this constitutional analysis? What follows from the unearthing of the theological bones of the concept if constitutionalization? There are a number of consequences worth considering. The first proceeds from the state of the developmental stage of most constitutionalist systems. These are all relative new ideologies. Few have existed outside of the writings of their adherents. None has reached a mature stage of development. But all have reached the stage of application and each has seen some movement toward operationalization. Each borrows from the others to construct a new synthesis on which a universal or more comprehensive community could be built, within which the faithful can

44 See, e.g., Larry Catá Backer, "From Moral Obligation to International Law: Disclosure Systems, Markets and the Regulation of Multinational Corporations", *Georgetown Journal of International Law*, 39, pp. 591–653 (2008).

45 See, e.g., Larry Catá Backer, "On the Problem of the State in the State Duty to Protect Human Rights—Fostering National Action Plans as a Means of Refocusing the State Duty on the Business of the State Itself", *Law at the End of the Day*, May 10, 2014: http://lcbackerblog.blogspot.fr/2014/05/on-problem-of-state-in-state-duty-to.html

46 See Larry Catá Backer, "Disclosure Systems and Securities Exchanges—On the World Federation of Exchanges Creation of a Sustainability Working Group and the Proposal to Require Extra Financial Disclosure", *Law at the End of the Day* (May 31, 2014): http://lcbackerblog.blogspot.com/2014/05/disclosure-systems-and-securities.html

47 See, Larry Catá Backer, "On Moving From Theory to Practice of Corporate Responsibility to Respect Human Rights—Thoughts on the Human Rights Reporting and Assurance Frameworks Initiative (RAFI) Project", *Law at the End of the Day* (May 18, 2014): http://lcbackerblog.blogspot.fr/2014/05/on-moving-from-theory-to-practice-of.html

more efficiently build relations and increase their collective welfare brining order or at least cohesion to the world in a manner agreeable to the community.[48]

The second consequence proceeds from the first. Operationalization suggests that each if the constitutionalist systems considered have acquired a substantial enough following to make some form of implementation action possible. That is certainly the case with transnational constitutionalism, but it is also the case with polycentric constitutionalism. Beyond the obvious power of enterprises in fact as self-constituted centers of governance[49] the hybrid efforts to fashion multipolar systems of law and governance with constitutional implications at the transnational level remain potent.[50] Most important among these are the UN Guiding Principles framework and with it the buy-in of substantial elements of States, public international organizations and large enterprises. Each of these systems is plausible and internally coherent; each presents a distinct vision of the world, inconsistent with the others. Together they produce autonomy and intermeshing among their respective adherents, along with a drive toward conflict and unification.

The third consequence proceeds from the advanced state of contestation among constitutionalist systems. That contestation has produced both risk and opportunity for constituents and partisans but also for those who would seek to impede constitutionalization.[51] Global constitutionalism offers this through the centralization of the State within the administrative apparatus of a global administrative technocracy. Transnational constitutionalism offers the best and most advanced version of the Westphalian State System, one in which the anarchy of classical State System organization is replaced by a common core of principles, a *jus gentium*, for constitutional restraint. Polycentric constitutionalism offers the anarchy (in the sense of a lack of a center) of the classical Westphalian system but now opened to all plausible governance organizations in a world in which the differences between States and non-governmental actors disappears, but in which multiple distinct governance systems emerge and interact with each other, sometimes coherently and sometimes in conflict. It permits every governance entity to develop within its own logic, constrained only by the cultures of governance to which its communities subscribe.[52] It offers internal logic but at the price of systemic coherence. Lastly, WPS offers the discipline of public constitutionalism to non-public governance organs, principally economic enterprises. Its singular insight is to detach constitutionalism from the State, but retain its essence, and then apply it uniformly to all organisms that function in the manner of States. It is simple, transposable and, if developed appropriately, might well provide a simple set of implementing mechanisms that would not require any great conceptual leap. But WPS's systemic coherence sacrifices the autonomy of enterprise governance within a State System that remains fractured. It might require a pairing with transnational constitutionalism to make it work.

48 Cf. Walter T. Wilson, *Pauline Parallels: A Comprehensive Guide*, Westminster: John Knox Press (2009) (intertextualism in the service of a new synthesis).

49 Cf. Fabrizio Carfaggi, "Newfoundations of Transnational Private Regulation", *EUI Working Papers*, Robert Schumann Center for Advanced Studies (RSCAS 2010/53) (2010).y.

50 See A. Abbegg, "Regulation of Hybrid Networks at the Intersection Between Governmental Administration and Economic Self-Organization", in *Networks: Legal Issues of Multilateral Co-Operation*, Marc Amstutz & Gunther Teubner (eds.), Oxford: Hart Publishing (2009), pp. 255–289.

51 See Peer Zumbansen, "Comparative, Global, and Transnational Constitutionalism", *Global Constitutionalism*, 1(1), pp. 16–52 (2012).

52 Cf. Andreas Fischer Lescano and Gunther Teubner, "Regime Collisions: The Vain Search for Legal Unity in the Fragmentation of Global Law", *Michigan Law Journal of International Law*, 25, pp. 999–1045 (2004).

The fourth consequence proceeds from the differences among these principal constitutionalist systems. Each of these systems offers quite distinct possibilities for the organization and management of corporate (enterprise) constitutional systems – yet each of them may also be captured by the stakeholders to which they are most bound. On one hand, it has been suggested that States have sought to hijack the UN Guiding Principles project by refocusing attention on a State-centered basis for regulating business and human rights and that enterprises have sought to hide behind mere legal compliance within domestic legal orders as a means if shriveling the corporate responsibility to respect human rights, at the heart of that polycentric enterprise.[53] On the other hand, individual enterprises have begun to supplant the State as sources of human rights–based regulation.[54]

The fifth consequence proceeds from a general consideration of the issue of constitutionalization. The process of constitutionalization is in an advanced stage. It is unlikely to be reversed. The greatest of the affected institutions – States and enterprises – can no longer hope that this phenomenon is a passing fad. Indeed, each sees advantages in one or another of the constitutionalist systems in gestation. No governance institution can remain aloof and all will have to choose guiding ideologies going forward – or one will be selected for them by default.

While States might be inclined toward transnational constitutionalism, enterprises may find polycenteric constitutionalism more valuable. WPS will require the exercise of political will at the national and international level that may be well beyond the capacities of elected officials, but it is not beyond the capabilities of well organized communities of consumers and investors who with civil society might invoke the mechanics of mass democracy to force adoption of WPS implementation strategies. Global constitutionalism remains a mainstay of academics though some of its undertones might be usefully deployed by other systems. Societal constitutionalism remains a powerful instrumental outlier. It is that because the phenomenon remains difficult to manage instrument ally, yet it is quite powerfully directed by evolving cultures of forming and operating groups in ways that mirror the desires of its constituents. That it continues to develop is a warning to those constitutionalist systems that believe that constitutionalism proceeds from theory. That was the value of the UN Guiding Principles and the hole that it sought to fill that was missing in transnational and global constitutionalism. But of course both transnational and global constitutionalism preserved that "hole" intentionally. The core foundation of both of these ideologies of constitutionalism rests, after all, on a rejection of the subjectivity of non-State actors within any sort of constitutional system. Indeed, both are grounded on the principle that the legitimacy of their legal orders is dependent on the subordination of non-State Systems to both the law systems of domestic legal orders and the emerging international State-based international order. WPS offers an intriguing alternative – one that recognizes the legitimacy of the governance power of enterprises but which seeks to embrace the fruits if the long process of Western rights – based constitutional development and recast it as cultural *jus cogens*, perhaps better understood as natural law universally applied.

What emerges from this very small glimpse into operationalization is the last and perhaps most important insight for the concept of constitutionalization and the multinational

53 See Backer, "On the Problem of the State in the State Duty to Protect Human Rights", *supra* 45.

54 Jan Wouters, Axel Marx, Nicolas Hachez & Private Standards, "Global Governance and Transatlantic Cooperation: The Case of Global Food Safety Governance", *Leuven Center for Global Governance Studies* (2008): www.transatlantic.be/publications/wouters-marx-hachez_final.pdf

enterprise in the twenty-first century: In the absence of practical application, no amount of constitutionalism will succeed in capturing the imagination and the project of constitutionalization will stall. Constitutionalism, like other great political and religious movements before it, must be able to offer not just a clear sense of right and wrong, but a system that, in congress with other like-minded persons or entities, constitutes a community within which all actors share a common platform that (self-reflectively perhaps) can be reproduced not as theory but as the very acts that make the constitution and operation of bodies corporate worthwhile.

In early 2014, the Center Pompidou hosted a Manifesto-Exhibition entitled *Modernités Plurielles; Plural Modernities from 1905–1970.*[55] The organizational principle of this Manifesto-Exhibition was to recast the way we think about what for many of us was once understood as a singular and Western modern art movement directed from Paris through the 1930s, and thereafter New York. The movement that became modern art must be understood in the plural, and less either in the singular and as a directed movement. Instead modern art movements were both distinctive but deeply intertwined with each other across five continents over nearly a century and also significantly affected by connection with the academic, publishing and art market worlds. Viewed from the distance of time, what emerges is a leaderless movement within which "the complex and dynamic relationships between universality and vernacular culture, purity and hybridity" produced the appearance of aggregation around what became in hindsight the modernist sensibility.[56]

The same can be said for the various strands of global or transnational constitutionalism that are now taking definitive shape among its "artists" in academia, business, States and international organizations. Constitutionalization is proceeding along parallel but sometimes quite distinct tracks. Each seeks to weave in distinctive ways synergies of procedural principles, rule of law values, customary notions of good governance (as legally or societally constituted), and human rights or personal autonomy values.[57] Most everyone involves agrees the same perception of the functional shift of power, and of the State within it – but there are substantial differences between this constitutionalist movement that makes a single characterization difficult.

5. Conclusion

In this age, the world structures of reality and comprehension have produced a peculiar orientation, one in which individuals are abstracted and abstractions are incarnated in their place. Enterprises no longer have stockholders; they have mutual, pension and sovereign wealth funds that serve as autonomous embodiments of a now-abstracted individual shareholder. States no longer have individual voters expressing collective will in republics; they have democratic organization in which aggregations of individuals (civil society, businesses and other organized elements) engage with administrative aggregations for the ultimate benefit of a now abstracted individual natural person citizen. Aggregations of economic activity

55 Direction de la Communication et des Partenariats Press Kit, Multiple Modernities 1905–1970, from October 23, 2013, Museum, Level 5, Multiple Modernities: www.centerpompidou.fr/Fen/Fcontent/download/14570/129106/version/14/file/PRESS+KIT+MULTIPLE+MODERNITIES.pdf

56 Catherine Grenier, "A History of Global Art", in *Modernités Plurielles 1905–1970*, Paris: Center Pompidou (2013): http://slash-paris.com/en/evenements/modernites-plurielles-1905-1970.

57 Cf. Carol Harlow, Global Administrative Law: The Quest for Principles and Values, *European Journal of International Law*, 17(1), pp. 187–214 (2006).

are no longer legally constituted businesses subject to the management of States; they are societally constituted enterprises. All of these realities are in search of a legitimating ideology and an expressive form through which they might perform their realities. They are maneuvering among a set of competing ideologies under which these realities may be disciplined. These ideologies themselves operate theologically to incarnate, ensoul and provide a structure for their performance (ministry) that realize the reality of abstract individuals and incarnate entities.

This chapter has considered the conception of constitutionalization as a structure for theorizing a space within which constitutionalized entities may interact in accordance with the ideological principles of legitimizing constitutionalism. It has grounded this conception in the theological frameworks of Western conceptions of organizing society in values enhancing structures. That theology produces both a way of structuring the way constitutions are conceived, invested with value and then incorporated into a mandatory ministry to create a community of believers that eventually would embrace the world.

Constitutions have been the means through which States have expressed their organization and ruling ideologies. Constitutionalism provides the normative ideology for expressing the core rules and values that determine the legitimacy of variations in constitutional embodiment. Once associated with the construction of political "persons", the normative structures in constitutionalism have opened the possibility of using its frameworks for the embodiment of any organized group that wants to govern itself. Constitutionalism provides the structure for incarnating an institutional entity that is ensouled in the sense that it is separate and autonomous from its creators, though operated through them. In globalization all self-governing groups interact beyond the territorial borders of States. That interaction requires a common platform for intermeshing among quite different classes of constitutional entities. Constitutionalization is the way one understands the science of that search for a common communicative platform among self-governing groups related by their interactions but that need a system for identifying each other and organizing those interactions. It posits meta-principles for constitutionalism that ought to make it possible for States to engage with commercial enterprises and universal religious bodies.

The chapter suggested the ways in which the WPS approach to constitutionalism seeks to vest these meta-principles to the process of constitutionalization, and suggested some of its strengths and difficulties. It also suggested that within emerging discourses of entity organization and interaction that (1) it is the form of constitutions that now serve as the basis for institutional formation; (2) it is the normative structures of constitutionalism that provides the "soul" of those institutional forms, that serve as the basis of their autonomy from their creators and operators and that guide them between right and wrong; and (3) it is constitutionalization that serves as the foundation for a common language of interaction among an increasingly diverse set of constitutional creatures, through an application of the notion of community and ministry inherent in the concept of constitutionalism. But critically, for this enterprise of constitutionalization – as each of these variations on possible cosmologies of constitutionalism vie for control of the discourse of constitutionalism and for prominence in the process of constitutionalization – it is to those constitutionalism that are most compatible with the customs and expectations of key stakeholders, those that make it easiest for enterprises and States to discipline themselves advantageously in the world, that are likely to set the tone for constitutionalism and constitutionalization in the decades to come.

Part III

The concept of constitutionalization applied to the firm

9 Human rights and the constitutionalized corporation

Sheldon Leader

1. The question

In the course of building and operating the petroleum pipeline for the export of oil from Chad through Cameroon, ExxonMobil issued the following statement: "[We are] steadfast in promoting respect for human rights throughout the world. We believe corporations play an important role in supporting human rights and that our presence in developing countries positively influences issues relating to the treatment of people".[1] If these words are not simply intended to warm the air but are to be taken seriously, how are we to understand them? What, in particular, would it mean were we to manage to incorporate such a commitment to human rights into the company's constitution – either voluntarily or by requirement? How does this incorporation relate to the overall project of constitutionalization of economic power in civil society?

2. Demands to make of any constitutionalizing strategy

Such a constitutionalizing strategy has to respond to the following requirements: It must specify the *interactions* between internal standards contained in the company's constitution and external guarantees contained in human rights instruments, national constitutions, etc.; it must specify *modes of exercising* fundamental rights as they constrain other corporate objectives and interests; it must indicate who has *standing* to pursue a remedy; and it must specify modes of stakeholder *participation* in corporate decisions.

A. External/internal norms and their interaction

There are two ways in which norms guaranteeing fundamental rights can take effect for an enterprise: externally and internally. Externally, their source can be a national constitution, legislation with constitutional status or a treaty binding the State. These norms can give rise to constraints on companies as entities: sometimes via the State's obligation to "protect" individuals/groups from abuse by third parties and sometimes directly. Internally, there are the company's own articles of association or their equivalent in other jurisdictions, which can contain commitments to fundamental rights.

Should the internal constitution "mirror" the rights guaranteed in the wider national constitution or legislation together rules of an international organization exercising jurisdiction over both? For example, should fundamental labor rights contained in ILO conventions

1 ExxonMobil, Corporate Citizenship Report Summary (2003): www.exxonmobil.com/corporate/files/corporate/CCR_2003.pdf

binding the State, and informing national labor law legislation, also be imported inside the corporate constitution with the same scope and weight as they do in labor law? In that case, an obligation to respect, say, trade union rights also becomes an obligation that directors owe to their employees *via* their obligations to act in the best interests of the company. The obligation falls within the directors' fiduciary obligation to the company, such that if he or she fails to respect this labor right, they have – by definition – damaged the interests of the company in preventing it from following through on its own constitutional commitments.

If there is no such incorporation into the corporate constitution, then the *company* continues to owe the obligation to its employees to respect their basic labor rights, but simply externally – as an entity bound by labor law. In this latter case the announcement of a corporate commitment to respect human rights may be well meant but is ultimately banal: It simply recalls the fact that the company is bound to obey those laws that themselves may reflect the State's obligation to protect its subjects from human rights abuse, as provided by various core human rights instruments.

As a further example of the potential reach of an internal constitution that has been enriched by incorporating external standards, consider investment contracts between companies and host States – as distinct from investment treaties among States. These contracts sometimes contain clauses that can require the State to do things which would, apart from that undertaking, violate the human rights of its citizens. This can particularly happen with the so-called stabilization clause, which are undertakings by the State not to apply new law to the project from the date the contract is signed. This could result in the State not living up to its obligation to apply fresh rights to those working on the project, where the rights arise from treaties it has ratified but after the investment contract has been signed. There can be two consequences for a company in this situation: It might be considered complicit with the State in violating the rights in question; or its attempt to make such a contract with the State might be void due to its lack of capacity to make such an agreement. The latter would be a possibility if the constitution of the host State were imported into the company's own norms governing the responsibilities of its officials.[2]

B. The need to specify the appropriate mode of exercising a basic right

A corporate constitutional commitment must indicate the way in which basic rights are to be given scope and weight as they compete with other interests and rights that the company is meant to respect. This balance is sometimes not adequately specified. This is a problem, for example, with Afghanistan's effort to inject wider social concerns into mining corporations' operations. On one hand, its draft Minerals Law requires a company to carry out mining operations in a way that interferes as little as possible with the rights of any lawful occupant of the surface land, such as a farmer.[3] The company is entitled to pursue its commercial objectives, but must adjust them so as to do least damage to the interests of the population at large. However, elsewhere in the same draft statute the reverse happens: At the exploration phase of mining, the company's commercial interests take automatic priority over the interests of the local population when the two compete. The law thus stipulates that farmers

2 See "Labor Rights in the World Economy", in *Evaluate Labor Law*, A. Lyon-Caen & A. Perulli (eds.), Milan: CEDAM (2010), pp. 113–122.

3 Cf. Draft Minerals Law of 2012, Article 42 (2) (a) and Article 42 (1) (a): http://mom.gov.af/Content/files/Mineral_Law_Consultation_English.pdf

have a right of access to suitable water – a key human right – but only on condition that they do not interfere with the company's right to carry out exploration activity.[4] A constitutional commitment that incorporates such a fundamental right into internal corporate standards has to take a coherent view about the way it is to be exercised: in this case about the weight assigned to the farmers' or residents' rights to property.[5]

C. The need to specify standing to pursue a remedy

ExxonMobil's commitment to human rights is a commitment to individuals and to groups. If it is to be respected as a *constitutional* commitment, a position has to be taken about a potential gap between those damaged by corporate activity and those entitled to pursue a remedy for that damage. It is a gap between the group of victims and the potentially smaller group of legitimate plaintiffs. There can be liability for damage caused by faulty behavior by a company official. It may be due, for example, to his or her negligence. To what group of potential plaintiffs should a duty of care extend in this situation and what would corporate constitutional principles indicate?

A further issue about constitutional standing arises when, for example, a mining company makes an undertaking in an investment contract with the host State that contains a clause committing the company to respect access to water for surrounding farmers. This is provided, for example, in a contract between the government of Afghanistan and a Chinese mining company, which stipulates that the company "shall not utilize agricultural water or deprive any lands, villages, houses, or watering places for animals of a reasonable supply of water insofar as such water has, through custom, been utilized for such lands, villages, houses or animals".[6] What should a corporate constitution, suitably enriched by incorporation of external constitutional guarantees, say about such an undertaking? Should it require the company to insist that the farmers damaged also be entitled to sue under the contract between itself and the host government? Is it, as an alternative, acceptable that the farmers be content to hope that the State, as party to the agreement, will sue on their behalves? Will it be acceptable that the company provide internal grievance mechanisms as an alternative?

Closer to home, the UK Companies Act 2006, section 172 requires directors – in discharging their fiduciary obligation to promote the success of the company – to "have regard" for the interests of employees and for the impact of the company's operations on the community and the environment. Do constitutional principles concerned with standing tell us anything here? If directors in a particular situation have totally failed to turn their minds to such impacts, and hence have prima facie violated the terms of the legislation, would it be appropriate for a corporate constitution to stipulate that these employees, or members of the

4 Article 42 (2) (a) requires "exercise [of] the rights of the license reasonably and in such a way as to affect as little as possible the interests of any owner or lawful occupant of the land on which such rights are exercised". This is the direct opposite of the direction of adjustment called for in the same article, which provides that the owner/occupant "retains the right to graze livestock upon or to cultivate the surface of such land including the use of water, in so far as such grazing or cultivation does not interfere with the use of such area for reconnaissance, exploration". The former is an appropriate human rights standard.

5 If there are no effective external regulators of corporate activity in Afghanistan, then the enterprise itself – however clear its commitment to social responsibility – will favor the spirit behind the second part of the law over the first.

6 *Contract Between the Government of Afghanistan and MCC – Jiangxi Copper Consortium (Mcc) for Development of the Aynak Copper Deposit.* (On deposit with the author.)

damaged community, may bring actions against the directors for damage done to the company here, or should that be left to shareholders?

D. Participation in corporate decisions

A constitutional commitment must indicate the mode of participation in corporate decisions to which stakeholders' fundamental rights entitle them: This ranges from a potential right to vote for representatives on the board of directors through to rights of stakeholder groups within the local population to participate in decisions about the location or design of a mine, oil extraction installation or highway. Which of the stakeholders should be entitled to vote for the leadership of the company? Which should be entitled to participate in decisions for particular projects?

3. Different ways of trying to meet these demands – three approaches to corporate accountability

An obstacle to meeting these demands lies in disagreement – not about the relevance of human rights to corporate activity (we are familiar with that debate) – but over the way in which such rights are to be *deployed* in regulating corporate behavior.[7] Standing behind any given human right, be it freedom from gender discrimination, the right to trade union activity or the right to respect for property, are alternative ways of connecting the enterprise to the interests that the rights are meant to protect. Human rights norms can announce the entitlements but still leave us in the dark about the way in which any particular interest is to be given its place as a constraint on corporate power. That place is the product of a conception of corporate accountability. Those conceptions may well differ among themselves. In turn, that difference will affect what one considers to be success or failure in meeting the demands made of a constitutionalizing strategy.

Consider three ways in which the interests of those affected by corporate activity can appear on the agenda of a corporate constitution:

1 There are those interests for the protection of which corporate management is *strategically* accountable. In failing to attend to these interests a miscalculation might be made about the best way to further the company's – usually commercial – purposes. This is the most prevalent way policy makers aim to link the corporation to a human rights of people it affects. Respect for the right can be an effective way of advancing the business. It also follows that if a right claimed serves no such corporate purpose, or even harms it, then the case for the right disappears.
2 There are those interests for which management is *equitably* accountable. On this approach, the interests of, say, local farmers or employees are to be protected by the company not with the justification that doing so helps to further the enterprise's purposes, but for independent reasons of social justice. This gives any particular fundamental right more weight and steady presence than does the strategic approach. At the same time, such an approach faces resistance from those who see this equitable link as

7 For the distinctions that follow, see Leader, "Corporate Accountability", in *The Oxford Handbook on Public Accountability*, M. Bovens, R.E. Goodin & T. Schillemans (eds.), Oxford: Oxford University Press (2014), Chapter 22; and Leader, *The Reach of Rights* (forthcoming).

cutting across corporate purposes too strongly. One can see an example in the larger place for human rights created by this approach in the protocol for deciding when a company – complicit with the State – would contribute to an illegitimate eviction of e.g. farmers from their land in order to make way for a project. If the farmers' interests are given equitable and not just strategic status, then they might be able to hold on to their land more effectively than the company's strategic interests would allow, since under international human rights law, "evictions may only be carried out *as a last resort, once all other feasible alternatives to eviction have been explored* and appropriate procedural protections are in place".[8]

3 There is finally a set of interests for the satisfaction of which the company is *ultimately* accountable. This type of interest operates in a fundamentally different way than do the other two. It indicates a "sovereign" entitlement to have the last word in answering the question, what is this particular enterprise here for? Who is the company committed to benefit as part of its reason for existing in the first place? Sometimes it is the State itself that will answer that question, in the name of its sovereign duty to advance the public interest. At other times, individuals or groups lying outside of the State can possess that power of ultimate authority: Shareholders do so via their right to vote to accept or reject a fundamental change of corporate objectives as contained in the corporate constitution. There is no reason in principle to limit this special sort of interest to shareholders. Employees might also be placed in this position, with their own representatives on the board of directors. In principle, other groups as well – such as members of the local community – can have this special role if it is clear that the company's purpose – i.e. its reason for existence – includes working for their benefit, and not simply avoiding damage to them.

4. How the three strategies shape the constitutional demands

We can now draw together the concerns of Sections 2 and 3, seeing how the distinct approaches to corporate accountability can affect the ability of a constitutionalizing strategy to meet the several demands properly made of it.

A. Strategic accountability

1. Interactions between internal and external norms

It makes sense, from a strategic perspective, to separate external standards binding the company per se from internal standards binding management to the enterprise from within. A boundary thereby appears, separating actions that serve the interests of the company from the damage that those same actions can do to those notionally 'outside' of the company, and whose rights are embedded in domains such as labor or human rights law. It is quite possible, on this approach, for management to act under what company law says is *required* for the good of the company, while at the same time being condemned by e.g. human rights law for doing the exact same thing. This has emerged in striking form in a recent dispute concerning a UK company's attempt to develop a massive open-pit coal mine in Bangladesh that

8 Based on CESCR, General Comment 7, particularly paragraphs 3 and 11–16.

will displace 40 000 people, only 10 000 of whom will have meaningful compensation. The company argues that, given the size of its investment as a proportion of its overall activity, withdrawing from the project on grounds of human rights impact would inflict such a large loss on its long-term investors that the directors would be in breach of their fiduciary duty to work for the overall long term benefit of the company, defined as the benefit for shareholders "as a whole" as required by section 172 of the Companies Act 2006. From a strategic point of view, this argument can look plausible. It does not ignore the interests of the local population: Instead, it shapes the point of contact between itself and those impacts. Its predominant obligation is to serve the purpose for which the company exists: to mine coal at a profit. The directors can be legitimately concerned about the harm the company might do, but *internally* the only way that such harm can outweigh the potential gains to the company from opening the mine will be if the latter has to pay costs for the damage done and these costs are likely to be greater than the revenue it will earn.

This strategic reasoning can afford to admit, in a particular situation, that the company – as an *external* matter – is in breach of an important human right. It can hold to the prospect of going ahead with a project such as the coal mine, earning the revenue, and then standing ready to pay any damages to successful plaintiffs, hoping that the latter will not swallow too much of the earnings. Similar reasoning pervades the world of mergers and acquisitions. In carrying out its due diligence, a purchaser may confront part of the labor force that would have strong prima facie claims for unfair dismissal, for example. If the size of the compensation for the illegal act is a relatively small part of the overall value of the transaction, the advice often given by lawyers structuring the deal is to proceed with the dismissals and stand ready to compensate. In short, strategic accountability calls for purchasing an ability to violate basic rights by having the room to pursue the company's objective despite the social damage done, dipping into the company's treasury to pay the bill.

2. *Strategic approaches to the exercise of a basic right*

If the scope of a corporate obligation to respect certain rights flows from its strategic priorities, then the right demands attention when – and only when – it aligns with those priorities. The right must, however, cede to corporate purposes whenever the two clash. This affects what can be called the direction of adjustment between rights and corporate interests. On the strategic approach, a basic right is recognized as requiring respect, but the *degree* of such respect owed is dictated by the need to choose the means of protecting the right that does least damage to corporate objectives. This is what we have seen in the example of part of Afghanistan's draft Minerals Law, protecting as it does the rights of occupiers of local land, but adjusting their exercise of those rights so as to interfere least with the company's activity of exploration.[9]

The strategic approach also provides one response to a persistent concern when project planners carry out human rights risk assessments. There is ambivalence in these exercises: Is the concern to identify the risk to the *company* in the event that it violates human rights, or is it the risk to the *potential victim* in the event that his or her right is violated? The question persists, and is acute when the equitable species of accountability is in focus. From the strategic perspective, the hope is that the results of the two enquiries will come together. This approach will acknowledge the need to *avoid* violating a right – rather than let the violation

9 *Supra* note 3 and accompanying text.

happen and compensate for it – only when the right is a relevant concern in planning: when, and only when, recognizing the right advances a corporate commercial purpose.

3. The strategic approach to standing to pursue a remedy

The strategic perspective tailors remedy for victims to the successful promotion of corporate objectives, and to the promotion of the outlying objectives of national and international policy designed to assist with that effort. For example, government policy might aim to restrict access to a remedy for damage done by enterprises – including damage to their fundamental rights – to a relatively narrow portion of those injured in order to encourage inward investment. This restrictive approach to standing for breaches of, for example, labor or land law can have enormous impacts on injured workers, displaced farmers and others. Since the ground for protecting a fundamental right is, from this perspective, strategic, then standing can in this way be adjusted to corporate strategy.[10]

4. Strategic approaches to participation in corporate decisions

A corporate constitution must deliver and distribute entitlements to influence or control corporate power. How does a strategic approach to corporate accountability try to accomplish this? As indicated earlier, we can divide participation rights into two categories: First there are those rights to elect and remove the leadership of the enterprise and second there are rights to participate in decisions about corporate policy.

4.1. RIGHTS TO VOTE FOR CORPORATE LEADERSHIP

Here, a strategic orientation takes as its point of departure an assumption that a set of fundamental purposes or objectives for a given company are already in place and seeks the best way to further these. From this it follows that the power to elect or remove directors should be in the hands of those who are best placed to vote for the people who will stay within the boundaries of, and most effectively further, these corporate aims. These anointed as electors are often shareholders. However, the reason for so allocating the right to vote is strategic: It does not emerge from a more fundamental conviction about what is equitable, or fair. Thus, a reason that is often proffered on strategic grounds for limiting the vote to shareholders is that doing so avoids a confusion and dilution of the mandate given by the company to directors. If the leadership is accountable to an electorate widened to include, e.g. employees, then corporate objectives will in turn become an unclear mix dictated by these diverse interests. Life is already difficult enough with occasional splits among shareholders, says this view, so there is no need to increase the difficulty by adding the interests of other stakeholders to this unstable mix.

A competing strategic vision can take the same point of departure but reach a very different conclusion. It can, that is, assume a set of fundamental corporate purposes in place, and look for the spread of rights to vote for the leadership that will best further those purposes. However, it is possible to argue for a wider franchise, that this right to vote should be extended to employees, relevant members of the local community in which the enterprise

10 It is possibly for these strategic motives that the UK legislature considered but rejected the possibility of giving employees derivative actions for breach of section 172 of the Companies Act 2006.

is located, etc. This would not be because the company must take account of their interests *despite* the solutions called for by corporate objectives, but rather *because* those objectives are better served by widening this part of the franchise. This argument arises from a fundamental feature of corporate law: However firmly one might declare that the commercial company exists in order to further the interests of its shareholders (a view to be considered further on), this is a requirement over the lifetime of the company. It concerns the body of shareholders "as a whole", to use the language of the UK Companies Act 2006, section 172. This cannot be distilled into an obligation to further the immediate or short-term future interests of a particular body of those shareholders. Many jurisdictions have celebrated cases in which shareholders have sought to overturn or prevent directors' decisions on particular matters, and which the latter have been able to resist on the ground that they are acting bona fide in the interests of the company.

4.2. RIGHTS TO PARTICIPATE IN CORPORATE DECISIONS

These modes of participation can vary, from consultation requirements for works councils or trade unions, consultation requirements with local populations whose land or environment risk damage, through to shareholders and other stakeholders having a direct right to vote on the internal policies of the company. The strategic approach to these modes of participation tailors them to best fit with pre-existing corporate objectives. Participation, on this approach, cannot involve attempts to alter corporate objectives – which are in place – but can bring to bear distinct views about how best to further those objectives. This has the concrete result that the predominant mode of interaction between company and stakeholder is one of consultation, not consent. The latter, if withheld, can yield a right to veto corporate policies, while the former obliges the company to listen but reserves to it the power to take the final decision alone.

B. Equitable accountability

This approach to accountability stands in sharp contrast to the strategic mode. This can be seen by going back to each of the elements of constitutionalization of the company, and seeing the difference that an equitable outlook makes.

1. Interactions between internal and external norms

Equitable accountability seeks a stronger link between the internal corporate constitution and external sources for human rights norms, be they in wider national constitutions or international instruments. If we go back to the commitment to human rights made by ExxonMobil in the introduction, in the equitable mode this can be understood as a demand made for independent reasons of social justice, not tied to the requirement of showing that these reasons merge into a further way of meeting the enterprises' core objectives. This is an approach that wants symmetry between corporate and national constitutions. This means that the scope and weight of the human rights that the corporation embraces are given not by the corporation itself, but by external bodies whose mandate is to provide authoritative interpretations of those rights which guide the use of power across all domains, be this the State or civil society. Notice that in this equitable mode, this search for symmetry goes still further. It is not only aiming at correspondence between corporate and national constitutions, but also between all of the distinct domains of law that impinge on the company and its activity. It is a demand that one and the same basic right has the same features inside labor, investment, corporate, and human rights law. The lead is given by the last set – human rights norms – since these are seen, in the equitable mode, as providing the core principles to be followed by any body that considers itself to follow human rights requirements. The scope and special weight of that right given to it by, for example, the European Court of Human Rights or other regional human rights courts, would be incorporated into these other bodies of law without transformation.

Finally, equitable accountability does something that strategic accountability cannot countenance. It distinguishes between risk to the company and risk of damage to victims, refusing to allow the latter to be subsumed by the former. This creates a difficult but crucially important task for the decision makers in the company if they are to be plausible supporters of its constitutional legitimacy. It is often thought, from within their role, that the only way the company can legitimately allocate its resources so as to prevent human rights abuses is that those abuses must appear as risks to the enterprise per se. This would, of course, be the filter imposed by a strategic mode of accountability. In the equitable mode, the risk of damage to human rights is a freestanding concern and is *at the same time* meant to figure as a concern for directors of the company. It may indeed require that they increase risk of loss to the company in commercial terms in order to avoid risk to the rights at stake. This is a central challenge: it is, for example, one of the central dilemmas faced by the recent UN Guiding Principles on Business and Human Rights.[11]

2. *The equitable approach to the exercise of a basic right*

The demands of equitable accountability reverse the strategic way in which basic rights and core corporate commercial purposes are balanced against one another. What is altered is what was earlier called the "direction of adjustment". Whereas the strategic mode looks to shape the scope and weight of a human right so as to allow it space but at the same time to minimize its quality as an obstacle to corporate objectives, here the opposite occurs: Corporate purpose must be tailored so as to do least damage to the rights in play. This aligns corporate human rights policy to that which the State itself is meant to follow. The many objectives of the State that are important, such as the pursuit of foreign policy objectives or the encouragement of investment in a strategic sector of the economy, are meant to be pursued in a way that does least damage to human rights, not the reverse. Equitable demands on the corporation require the same direction of compromise.

3. *The equitable approach to standing to pursue a remedy*

Here again the contrast with the strategic approach is striking. The latter is willing to draw the boundary line between legitimate plaintiffs and the wider group of those who suffer damage from e.g. corporate negligence with an eye on what will be best for advancing inward investment and minimizing the obstacles to risk taking by enterprises. The equitable approach is wary of drawing the boundary line this way. If the damage done by corporate negligence arises from a given event, such as negligently causing an oil spillage, then justice

11 For an argument that tries to resolve the dilemma in favor of the equitable species of accountability, see Leader, "Collateralism", in *Global Governance and the Search for Justice*, R. Brownsword (ed.), Oxford: Hart Publishing (2005), pp. 53–67.

requires compensation for clear but remote victims as much as it calls for compensation for clear victims who are in proximity.

The equitable approach would also increase the scope of those entitled to sue the company on the basis of undertakings it gives to the State about the welfare of local populations within an investment contract. In the example of the contract between the government of Afghanistan and a Chinese mining company, an equitable approach would demand that the local populations that are meant to benefit from the undertaking not to use their agricultural water should be entitled to sue on that contract.

Finally, in the example of a legislative demand that a company have regard for interests other than those of shareholders, as we see in the earlier example of the United Kingdom's company law, an equitable approach to standing would demand that those intended to benefit from this obligation on corporate directors be entitled to activate the legislation by suing. This would be a suit for a breach of company law – a domain normally preserved for the other directors who can be trusted to be impartial, or if none is to be found, for shareholders. The equitable approach could go further, widening the group of those to whom the company becomes directly accountable.

4. The equitable approach to participation in corporate decisions

The equitable approach that divides risk to rights from risk to the commercial objectives of the company calls for holding in balance these disparate demands, not allowing one to be subsumed by the other. That balance calls for leadership that is sensitive to the disparate constituencies that stand behind these disparate demands. It follows from this that an equitable approach to participation must empower a variety of representatives. This yields a wider group of stakeholders entitled to participate at both levels identified earlier: that of selection and removal of leadership and participation in corporate decisions. The former has its well-known example in the German system that gives these selection powers to a supervisory committee that is in turn elected partly by employees. The latter is equally demanding on constitutional principles. Like the strategic approach, an important place is given to consultation rather than demanding veto powers for the affected population. However, the equitable approach demands that consultation take place well before key decisions about projects, and indeed about policies, are taken by the company. This mode of early and thorough consultation is precisely designed to impinge on a terrain that the strategic approach often leaves untouched: the terrain of basic decisions to pursue or to abandon, or to seriously modify the whole design and rationale of a project.

C. Ultimate accountability and constitutional principles

This ground of accountability asks a question that the other two are not equipped to answer: *For whom* does the company exist? This aims to identify the interests which it is the very rationale of the company to serve. It probes into the heart of the company's reasons for existence rather than ask who, along the way, the company should not injure because of e.g. its negligence or unwillingness to pay a decent wage. If one imagined both of these problems as well as all similar ones solved, this question would remain to be answered. There are positive as well as negative responses to be given here. Negatively, a mistake is often made in arguing that because certain stakeholders are strongly affected by a corporate decision, as are employees, they should therefore be seen as entitled to share in the exercise functions as sovereign stakeholders. But to reach that conclusion a further step needs to be taken. It must be shown that the company isn't just bound to be fair to the employee in its decisions about his or her conditions of work, but also that the company exists at least in part *in order* to advance the welfare of these employees. If the latter can be demonstrated, this changes the picture. It is no longer simply a question of being *fair* to the employee, as the earlier account of equitable accountability would require. It is also a question of moving the employee into the center of the stage – possibly along with other stakeholders who might also be there – but at the center. As is often said of shareholders in classic arguments for giving them priority, so here, in a way that is extendable to certain other stakeholders: If these individuals' interests are not advanced by the company, then it might as well shut its doors. It has no reason for being here.

This yields a central question for the strategy of bringing the private commercial company under the control of wider constitutional principles. It may be necessary, in the name of the basic rights that the constitution serves, to make a shift in the very foundations of a corporate mandate. It may be necessary to widen the group of those the company exists to serve so as to conclude that, for example, a pharmaceutical company exists partially in order to further the health interests of the least-well-off in the population. The least-well-off would then move from being a group to which the company gives sincere but collateral attention, as a poor relation to its core objectives, to being a part of those core objectives. They become those to whom the company is ultimately accountable. Constitutionally, they would be entitled to participate in decisions about the character of or any shift in core company objectives. Such a shift in the rationale for a corporation's activity may also require an external demand – one that comes from a State – to see how they can best deliver the basic goods that human rights demand in a world in which the initiatives are ever more in the hands of private actors.

5. Conclusion

To bring the private economic actor such as the company within the reach of constitutional logic marks a decisive step. It is a way of crossing a line we have known for a long time that needs to be crossed: between public and private centers of power. The distinct dimensions of constitutional demands described here force us to be clear about the distinct types of accountability that is being sought. Hard choices have to be made – choices to which constitutional principles are no strangers, and that private economic power needs to encounter.

10 The responsibility of multinational enterprises

A constitutionalization process in action

Antoine Lyon-Caen and Tatiana Sachs

The Rana Plazza disaster evidences the failures of a system allowing the spreading of power without responsibility. Economic organizations grow by making use of the limited liability entailed by the legal corporations they are made of, corporate law and the compartmentalization of national legal systems. The people and entities running these organizations thus avoid any responsibility towards the people and entities over which they nonetheless have significant influence.

In the face of this lack of responsibility, created in part by law, there is a rising movement that is requiring States to "take the necessary steps to prevent abuses committed abroad by business enterprises within their jurisdiction".[1] This movement can be witnessed in most international organizations. Alongside the United Nations, the OECD has expanded its guiding principles for multinationals with recommendations covering corporate conduct, inter alia, in the areas of human rights and the environment. The European Commission, for its part, calls on Member States to incorporate the United Nations' principles into their national laws.

There is thus a favorable international environment for the emergence and recognition of the duty of care, sometimes called the "principle of national diligence", applied to the leading companies with regard to the entities that are within their sphere of influence.

In any case, this context has been used by certain French deputies on the left in drafting and submitting to Parliament a proposed law that establishes a duty of care to be applied to parent companies and hiring companies with regard to the entities they influence. This proposal has gone through various versions. It was adopted by the National Assembly at first reading[2] on March 30, 2015.

This legislative initiative has already provoked reactions, those that criticize it all saying the same thing: The intention of the proposal is commendable, but it is not feasible.

The first line of criticism questions whether a State legislative initiative is even appropriate. As attractive as its aim may be, it would damage the competitiveness of the companies under the proposed provisions, and also that of any country that enacts them.

The second line of criticism concerns how the types of organizations to be subjected to normative requirements are to be determined. This criticism is based on a well-known argument: It would be difficult, if not impossible, to define what is meant by a group, a network or a sphere of influence.

1 Guiding Principles on Business and Human Rights adopted in June 2011 by the UN Council on Human Rights.

2 In a bicameral system such as the French parliamentary system, a proposed law (introduced by Parliament) or a bill (introduced by the government) does not become law until its terms have been adopted by both houses. In case of disagreement, the National Assembly (elected by universal suffrage), has the final say.

The third line of criticism concerns the type of responsibility that the proposal seeks to attribute to parent companies and hiring companies: personal responsibility or responsibility for others' actions? Liability for misconduct or responsibility for the risks created? All known distinctions of tort law, which are not easily comparable from one country to the other, are being reviewed to discuss the choices made by the authors of the proposal.

The issues discussed are sensitive because they affect the very purpose of the initiative, which is to discipline private power with regard to human and social needs. Indeed, this proposal seeks to compel economic organizations, via a duty of care, to integrate into the value chain a concern for the fate of the workers and communities affected by their economic activities and for the protection, both of natural resources and the lifestyle of the indigenous populations. Through the enactment of a duty of care, the strength and spread of basic human rights are reaffirmed in the face of privately held power rather than governments.[3]

This legislative initiative is an example of a measure emphasizing the constitutionalization of private power. By analyzing it, we can better see the overall architecture of the constitutionalization of private power (1), but we can also witness a moment when this is taking place (2).

1. The architecture of constitutionalization

The proposed law, passed at first reading on March 30, 2015, establishes the obligation for companies of a certain size to set up a vigilance plan and provides for possible governmental penalties against companies that do not establish such a plan, ensure its execution or fulfill the commitments made within the context of their own plan.

Formally, the plan is a document to be included in the non-financial reporting that all major companies headquartered in a country of Union must establish from now on under the European Directive of October 22, 2014.[4]

This union of a vigilance plan devised by companies and included within a network of rules, some of which provide for State penalties, constitutes the technological originality of the measure.

A. The vigilance plan

At first glance, the use of a plan as a mechanism may appear surprising. In a borderless world driven by market capitalism, in which companies are elusive, where the strategic decision centers are evasive, this mechanism may seem to hark back to the era of central planning.[5] However, a "plan", far from being obsolete, can prove to be a very useful tool for the tinker trying to cobble together a global law that the contemporary writer invites us to be.[6] It should first be stressed that since referring to a plan helps to draw a parallel between State power and the power of multinational companies over the entities within their "sphere of influence",[7] it probably offers a suitable mechanism for constitutionalizing companies.

3 See *L'entreprise, formes de la propriété et responsabilité sociales* (Baudoin Roger, ed.) Paris: Collège des Bernardins (2012).

4 Directive No. 2012/34/EU of the European Parliament and of the Council, October 22, 2014, Article 19a.

5 L. Sfez, *L'Administration prospective*, Paris: Armand Colin, 1970.

6 This metaphor is taken from B. Frydman (*Petit manuel pratique de droit global*, Académie royale de Belgique, coll. "L'académie en poche", p. 103 et seq.), who was inspired by C. Levi-Strauss.

7 On the virtues of this expression, see C. Hannoun, "Propositions pour un devoir de vigilance des sociétés-mères", *Mélanges en l'honneur de Michel Germain*, Paris: LGDJ, Lextenso (2015), p. 342 et seq.

Reference to a plan, a tool used by centralized governments, constitutes and implies the intention of controlling the power of multinational corporations. Thus, even as large companies defy the limitations of the law – conceptual limitations, geographical limitations – in order to free their power of decision from all coercion and responsibility, the introduction of an obligation to implement a plan – here a vigilance plan – constitutes a means to seize power where it is used.[8] In this sense, a plan is a realistic legal mechanism. Moreover, such a realistic goal is reflected in the definition of the range or scope of the duty of care, which extends to the activities of the company and those of the companies it controls,[9] directly or indirectly, as well as the activities of their subcontractors and suppliers, with which the company has an established business relationship.

Subject to bitter controversies, the wording adopted in the end has two advantages. First, the notion of control is not merely control through the holding of capital. Control can be understood as a "dominant influence over a company by means of a contract or through bylaws".[10] Moreover, the purpose of listing all the legal forms under which relationships between companies are formed (parent-subsidiary relationships, hiring firms, subcontractors and suppliers) is to close loopholes for avoiding the law.

So what type of power may devise, develop and implement a "vigilance plan"? The old vocabulary of the "plan", widely used in administrative science,[11] establishes a model for efficient, preventive State intervention. As noted by the authors who studied the legal tools at the disposal of the administration, the plan is classified under "forward-thinking legal instruments".[12] It is designed to deal with the uncertainties, contingencies and risks the future holds. Achieving this goal presupposes that the means of action are combined and organized. Moreover, in referring to State planning, A. Hauriou stressed that the distinctive feature of a plan is its "behavioral obligations".[13] Born within the scope of governmental action, the idea of a plan then moved to private activities in which the State took an interest, not in order to prohibit or punish them, but rather to guide them.[14]

A plan is constructed. Emphasis is placed on discussion and negotiation.

A plan is carried out, and is of necessity respected by those responsible for complying with its objectives and analyzing any obstacles encountered. Thus, as materialized in a so-called vigilance plan, the duty of care is not simply an act of good will. It calls for deeds and actions to achieve a purpose: "the prevention [of] serious damage in the areas of health and the environment, and of human rights abuses"[15] in the area covered by the duty of care.

Based on a program, the plan requires activities to be rationalized, that is to say, the mobilization of resources organized around a purpose.[16] The means thus used must allow for the

8 In this respect, a parallel can be drawn with the notion of decision which has emerged to better understand the use of economic management power, creating a shift with respect to types of decisions. In this sense, see F. F. Guiomard, La justification des mesures de gestion du personnel. Essai sur le contrôle du pouvoir de l'employeur, Thèse Université Paris Ouest Nanterre La Défense (1999); P. Lokiec, Contrat et pourvoir, Paris: LGDJ, coll. "Bibliothèque des thèses", 408 (2004); E. Lafuma, Des procédures internes. Contribution à l'étude de la décision de l'employeur en droit du travail, Paris: LGDJ, coll. "Bibliothèque de droit social", 46 (2008).

9 Control, as referred to here, is as it is understood under company law.

10 Article L. 233–16 of the French Commercial Code.

11 Just think of the employment safeguard plan, formerly referred to as downsizing measures.

12 L. Sfez, *L'Administration prospective*, Paris: Armand Colin (1970).

13 A. Hauriou, *Mélanges offerts à M. le Doyen Trotabas*, Paris: LGDJ (1970).

14 See A. "Lyon-Caen, Le plan, l'entreprise et l'emploi, la loi du 25 janvier 1985", *Critiques de l'économie politique*, 32, p. 13 (September 1985).

15 The newly created Article L. 225–102–4 of the French Commercial Code.

16 The preamble to the proposed law is in this respect symbolic.

spread of decent practices and behavior from a centrally devised strategy. In this regard, two lines of reasoning can be considered. The first is based on setting specific targets and allowing the organization's entities to use whatever means they deem appropriate. It would still be necessary to be able to set precise objectives. In the alternative, a second line of reasoning assumes that the means should be precisely defined and the objectives to be pursued left somewhat indeterminate.[17] This line of reasoning should prevail for the implementation of the duty of care, for two reasons. On one hand, the law does not impose specific objectives in the areas covered by the duty of care on companies that have an influence on other entities. What is required, rather, is the rationalization of the latter's deeds.[18] This orientation is clear from the words chosen by Parliament, which merely delivered a statement that the plan must contain "reasonable diligence measures". On the other hand, the "dominant" company cannot simply impose objectives on the entities it influences without giving them the financial, temporal and organizational means to achieve them. Otherwise, the duty of care would be meaningless.

Finally, referring to a plan leads us to reflect on the way it is developed. What place is there for consultation or other forms of participation for stakeholders? Such questions are bound to arise, particularly when it comes to the involvement of employees and their representatives. This is an illustration of the hybrid nature of the plan, a micro-measure for managing power that is both political and legal.

B. Accomplishing the duty of care

"Effective": This word appears twice in the legislation adopted by the National Assembly, reflecting the legislature's concern that the duty of care should not remain a dead letter.[19] In this regard, the measure contains two very different modes of realization for the vigilance plan: one is based on the independence of the actors, while the second is more concerned with moving the company's actors towards the public authorities. Far from being mutually exclusive, these modes of realization may be linked.

The first mode of realization requires a company with the power to influence the management of other companies to publish the vigilance plan as part of its non-financial reporting. This obligation extends the transparency requirement for non-financials, which France has been promoting for several years, and which Europe encourages through a directive adopted in 2014.[20] The first recipients of this transparency are the "influential" shareholders, but more broadly the investor market. Thus, the use of non-financial reporting is inseparable from the emergence of social – or societal – rating agencies responsible for evaluating and ranking companies on their social, environmental and human rights record. These tools use and even imitate the instruments of regulatory competition, turning them away from purely economic and financial purposes.[21] Corporate governance rests on indicators. In this type of model, the legal rule prescribes no other behavior than to report on actions in areas that are subject to this reporting.[22] This means comparing the performance of the various

17 On these two lines of reasoning for State planning, see L. Sfez, *L'Administration Prospective*, op. cit., p. 190.

18 This is also the line of reasoning followed by the courts in monitoring employment safeguard plans.

19 In this sense, the remarks of N. Cuzacq, *Le devoir de vigilance des sociétés mères et des entreprises donneuses d'ordre*, coll. Paris: Dalloz (2015), p. 1049.

20 Directive No. 2012/34/EU of the European Parliament and the Council of October 22, 2014, Article 19a.

21 In this sense, see B. Frydman, *Petit manuel pratique de droit global*, op. cit., p. 102.

22 This is clearly reflected in the penalties for noncompliance with reporting obligations.

players in a market, leading to the pressure that such a comparison may produce, which then drives the action. The legal rule of transparency – by this we mean the transparency of non-financials – then provides the conditions for market discipline to function properly. In this type of legal measure, the role of law is to make the means of independent regulation available to the actors. In this sense, the obligations of non-financial reporting, which includes transparency concerning vigilance measures, is part of a policy of empowering multinational corporations.

These tools are favored by companies and their managers, who appreciate the merits of a soft law that produces results without actually forcing them. However, given the legal weaknesses of certain instruments dealing with Corporate Social Responsibility), the legislature chose to place the implementation of the duty of care under the eye of the public authorities – and this is the second mode of realization. Thus, noncompliance with the duty of care exposes the company to civil liability, in accordance with the very traditional principles of liability for misconduct or negligence. The choice of this basis can be discussed.[23] As it stands, the establishment of fault, in the case of injury, will be based on an assessment of the reasonable diligence measures undertaken. It is important to note the word "reasonable" here. It suggests a twofold evaluation of the means used: that of their rationality (i.e. the instrumental consistency of the means with the ends) and that of their suitability (i.e. an assessment of their proportionality in view of the company's means).

The establishment of a vigilance plan and the measures associated with it powerfully show the function of micro-measures supporting a company's constitutionalization: a sophisticated normative co-mingling, where the independence of actors meets heteronomy.

2. A moment of constitutionalization

Why does this French legislative initiative, the fate of which cannot easily be determined, moreover, have a particular value, especially from the point of view of heuristics? It allows us to see, at a given time and in a specific context, how the constitutionalization of the private power belonging to large economic constellations works. It involves an exchange or interaction between the independence of these constellations and State standards. Others may say, between private law and public law.

But what needs to be better described and analyzed from the example of the French initiative, whose fate is still uncertain, is how such an exchange takes place.

A. Description

Multinational power, which uses corporate techniques to limit responsibility and exploits the barriers between the various national legal systems, has dipped deeply into the resources provided by national rights. Just consider the use that these companies make of entrepreneurial freedom and the freedom of economic initiative, and of national and international rules that protect competition, thus limiting the ability of the States to intervene. To this State law on markets and competition should be added company law, with the limitations on responsibility that it makes possible, and tort law, which largely respects the legal segmentation of economic organizations.

23 See, in particular, C. Hannoun, "Propositions pour un devoir de vigilance des sociétés mères", in *Mélanges offertes à M. Germain*, Paris: Dalloz (2014), p. 381.

The French legislative initiative seeks to introduce the need to take account of damage to the environment, health and basic human rights into the management of such economic organizations, in order to identify the risks and to design and implement preventive measures. Thus, it is a question of enhancing the regulation of these organizations' activities, this enhancement resulting from the legal obligation to establish and implement, even within these organizations themselves, a set of measures designed to identify and specify particularly serious violations due to the nature of the damage likely to be caused.

Constitutionalization thus results, in the sense that a number of the norms and standards that make up the legal order of large multinational corporations are revealed with this legislative initiative. As a counterpart to this, *constitution* also results, with the integration into this order of standards and benchmarks that were originally created in order to subdue and restrain governmental power, and which will thus enter into the experience of private power. In this respect, at least, it is not appropriate to speak of a juridification process, because the purpose is not to introduce ordinary State standards into the internal organization of multinational corporations, but rather standards that are similar to so-called constitutional standards.

B. Analyze

A careful examination of what the French law is attempting to do will allow us to better understand what is produced – or what can be produced – by an interaction between a State initiative to integrate the prevention of damage to the environment, health and basic human rights with the management and standards of large corporations.

The background to this integration that the French law is attempting to achieve is particularly rich. The duty of care that this law seeks to institute has already been examined, designed and formalized in many of the international organizations where multinational corporations exert influence. In other words, upstream of the French legislative initiative, the companies themselves have helped to determine the configuration and conditions of acceptance for the vigilance expected – and soon probably required – of them. The bed in which the duty of care is to be planted has, in large measure, been prepared.

Therefore, the integration of concerns for the environment, health and human rights will not be a mere copy of State constitutionalization. The term used has its originality; to some extent, the chosen wording uses the standard terms and references of organizational management; the envisaged procedures and modes of action are a far cry from those used in the field of public policy. The process includes a selection of references, along with a translation from one language – that of corporate management – into another – that of the law. This selection, with its accompanying translation, is undoubtedly one of the factors fueling skepticism about the scope that the legal institution of the duty of care can have. But it also represents the concessions that a national legislature has to make if it is to ensure that the procedures it designs are operative.

Another feature of this original co-mingling of insightful heteronomy (Parliament) with independent power (organizations) results from this selection and its accompanying translation. The constitutional principles – as experienced by the States – that are to be introduced into the sphere of private power are not "directly applicable horizontally". In other words, they cannot be invoked, without mediation, by a local authority whose rights have been harmed through the activity of a subsidiary company, or by employees of a subcontractor treated in violation of their dignity. The exercise of private power is not directly subject to the constitutional principles designed to be set against governmental power. It is first governed by the multinational corporations' own standards for ensuring the respect of the environment, health and human rights.

If any State penalties are to be imposed, it would be due to the multinational corporation's failure to comply with its own vigilance procedures, which it defined and declared it had implemented.

As we can see, this moment of constitutionalization sheds light on the process deserving of the name.

11 Constitutionalization and the status of the director

The test of "Say on pay"

Charley Hannoun

"Say on pay" is a topical issue that can be viewed as a demonstration of the process of "constitutionalization" of the status of the director. "Say on pay" is a requirement for shareholders to approve the pay of the director. This debate originated from certain excesses criticized by the media. However, the need for control over the shareholder now seems to lead to a global convergence of legislation, which could reinforce the idea that a "constitutionalization" process would be in at work. Analysis of "Say on pay" will then allow this hypothesis to be put to the test in assessing the scope of practices that sustain it and the power relations that bind several categories of interests: shareholders, directors and those who are called stakeholders. However, in this complex relationship, the director is placed in two positions that could lead to the revelation of certain paradoxes and an interpretation of the work structuring processes in very different ways.

The director is at the heart of economic power. Spotting the signs of a global construction of his or her status could probably give credence to the idea of an active process of structuring the company. Should we find confirmation of the hypothesis of the "constitutionalization" of private economic powers? The answer is not easy to formulate. Not only does the concept, derived from an analogy using the organization of public authorities, assume several meanings, but the figure of the director is still, despite appearances, very unclear.

Assuming that the concept of "constitutionalization" is fixed, at least provisionally in a broad sense, such as the organization of private powers in a spontaneous manner, or in accordance with rules of a procedural nature used to set limits and prevent abuses, there also remains the need to specify the category of director. However, the law offers a variety of statutes that give rise to confusion between the director and other categories of interest that should distinguish them, that of the employee or of the partner. But in practice, the director can fall under several categories at once. He or she can be an employee of the company. He or she can be a shareholder or even the majority shareholder. He or she can be a legal entity or an individual. He or she can exercise legal power, but also de facto power. He or she can be in charge of the general management or only have an administrative post. If one expands the category of director into a purely sociological field, things become further complicated, because the director may be an employee, or a member of a technostructure, to use Galbraith's terminology.[1] To add a little more confusion, in groups of businesses and in large companies, businesses are composed only of representatives of interest categories. Individuals are kept at a distance from the company. Some have spoken of tiered capitalism.[2]

1 J. K. Galbraith, *Le nouvel état industriel* (3rd edition), Paris: Gallimard (1967, 1989), p. 100 et seq.

2 P. Bissara, "Les mutations de l'actionnariat et le fonctionnement des sociétés cotées", in *Mélanges D. Schmidt*, Paris: LGDJ (2005), p. 61 et seq.

The shareholders are primarily the companies represented in the assemblies by the directors. Even investment funds are represented by managers, hence directors. In short, the word hides a multitude of possible situations and statutes through which the director can potentially raise several categories of interest.

To clarify the status of the director, it is therefore necessary to take sides in specific situations while knowing that, in a way, the risk is that he or she is sometimes a prisoner of the agenda of a formal message and that the reality can be quite different.

Faced with a very general hypothesis, such as the concept of "constitutionalization", it can be useful to employ the testing method. In this way, the idea is to put the hypothesis to the test with regard to a particular issue, that of "Say on pay". The point is particularly controversial because it affects the remuneration of the director and his or her control. The pay level is discussed on a recurring basis. Highly publicized in recent years, "Say on pay" has the advantage of entering an international debate around the governance of large companies. In addition to the issue of the definition of the purposes of the management of the companies, it introduces the question of control over the director's remuneration.[3]

Study of "Say on pay" also allows better identification of the figure of the director. It is best to come to terms with it through the status of the corporate officer named by the board of directors with an executive function. The target category is more precise still, that of leaders of large listed companies. In addition, this particular subject may, in a number of ways, be a good litmus test regarding the "constitutionalization" hypothesis. This is because "Say on pay" seems to be just the beginning of a global convergence process in legislation in the sense of the same control of remuneration. It might then be a particularly significant sign of a general movement of the structuring of practices aimed at framing financial power by formalizing an important element of the status of the director. Many countries in the world have already adopted a tool for shareholders to have a vote on remuneration: Shareholders vote on the remuneration policy (*ex ante*) or the amount of remuneration (*ex post*). These decisions may be of a binding nature, or merely come under a consultative remit.[4]

The analysis of "Say on pay" will thus allow the hypothesis of "constitutionalization" to be put to the test in assessing the scope of practices that sustain it and the power relations that bind several categories of interest: shareholders, directors, but also those that are termed "stakeholders", with the employees being the first to be considered. However, in this complex relationship, it will be shown that a director can be placed in two positions that could lead to very different interpretations of the work processes. On one hand, the director can be considered, in substance, as an "owner" of the company who should be accountable to the shareholder, the true "owner" of the company and exclusive financial beneficiary of their management. On the other hand, the director could be seen, one might almost say, as "constituted", as a "trustee" or a "steward" in charge of a multitude of interests, including those of the stakeholders, who would then be able to state their opinions on the legitimacy of his or her remuneration.

3 P.-H. Conac, "Le contrôle de la rémunération (*Say on Pay*)", Paris, *Revue des Sociétés* (2013), p. 400; J. O'Donnell & J. Merriman, "EU's Barnier urge binding shareholder vote on pay" (May 16, 2012): www.uk.reuteurs.com; A. Tonnelier, "Le long chemin des actionnaires français pour voter la rémunération des patrons", *Le Monde* (March 1, 2013); A. Viandier, "L'avis consultatif de l'assemblée des actionnaires sur la rémunération des dirigeants sociaux", Paris, *Semaine Juridique Entreprise et Affaires,* 29, p. 1416 (2013).

4 *Rapport Autorité des Marchés Financiers 2012 sur le gouvernement d'entreprise et la rémunération des dirigeants*, p. 30; P.-H. Conac, "Le contrôle de la rémunération (*Say on Pay*)", cited earlier.

With regard to these positions, which will be subsequently analyzed, "Say on pay" leads to very different conclusions about the scope of the process of structuring at work.

1. "Say on pay" of the shareholders, the true owners of the company, against the director controlling the company

At first glance, "Say on pay", as all of the debate elsewhere on the governance code, is clearly an expression of a strengthening of the institutional nature of large corporations. The temptation is great to find the catalyst of the "constitutionalization" process of corporate governance. Yet "Say on pay" could also lead to an analysis that is exactly the opposite, in that it would reveal the truth, a paradoxical return to the agency theory and the emergence of new forms of control that are dependent on this theory.

A. The paradoxical return of agency theory

Affirming a return to the agency theory and a decline in institutional theory at a time when the company and its board of directors seem to be bureaucratic in significant, even disturbing proportions is without doubt an unexpected observation. Several elements usually argue in the opposite direction. The need for boards of directors to develop internal guidelines would lead to strengthening of the quality of the body empowered with its rules of operation intended to improve its functioning in the interests of the company.[5] This approach would find several endorsements in substantive law. One would cite the Motte judgement, which dealt with the anonymous company as a set of hierarchical bodies equipped with statutory powers that cannot be altered by the effect of agreements or practices that would remove the substance.[6] The exclusive competence of the board of directors to set the remuneration of corporate directors, like the noncontractual nature of that compensation, would be elements that confirm the institutional nature of public limited liability companies. But this functional perspective is perhaps misleading, as the study of "Say on pay" shows, for behind the strengthening of the regulations on independence of the board of directors, a reverse process could be hiding that is a weakening of this form of internal control and a return to the contractual design of the management of the companies.

1. The weakening of internal control of the board of directors

The questioning of the exclusive authority of the board of directors to set the remuneration of directors has consequences for its institutional basis as a body of the company[7] and must be registered in the general debate that aims to thoroughly reconsider the governance of large companies. As a first approach, all the debate on corporate governance has contributed to the strengthening of internal control of companies and hence their institutional form. In this way there is a desire to strengthen the independence of the board to give shape to the concept of interest of the legal person, the separate interest of shareholders and the leaders themselves.

5 D. Miellet, "Le règlement intérieur: un moyen simple d'améliorer le fonctionnement du conseil d'administration", Paris, *Juris-Classeur périodique (JCP) Entreprise*, 2243 (2006); A. Viandier, "Le règlement intérieur du conseil d'administration des sociétés cotées", Paris, *Revue de Jurisprudence de Droit des Affaires*, p. 1003 (December 2003).

6 Civ. June 4, 1946, Motte judgement, J.C.P. (*Juris-Classeur périodique*) 1947, II, 3518, note D. Bastian.

7 J.-P. Berdah, *Fonctions et responsabilité des dirigeants de sociétés par actions*, Paris: Sirey (1974), p. 85 et seq

The technique of independent administrators appears on one hand to reinforce the idea that the board is an independent body – but it also accredits a contrary idea, to know that the natural tendency of the board had been until now, fading for the benefit of the director of the company.[8]

In the same way, it can be seen that the breakup of the board of directors in specialized committees seems to strengthen the capacity of the body and the institutional nature of the company, but on the other hand this process began a transformation of internal control that could ultimately perhaps eliminate this body in favor of other forms of control. Some do not hesitate to announce that these specialist bodies will one day be elected directly by the assembly.[9]

Another example, the recent development of the technique of the referent administrator, seems to introduce a new way of articulating the interests of the dominant shareholder with the directorate on corporations.[10]But isn't this referent administrator a way to develop a new form of shareholder control[11] in the margins of the board – which does tend to become a room for rubber-stamping decisions taken elsewhere in committees and negotiated between the corporation's management and the leading shareholder via the referent administrator?

These different clues to a deep transformation of the board of directors appear ultimately as ways to correct a tendency moving towards the closing down of this body. On one hand, they can be seen as ways to save it from a decline by the institutionalization or even increasing bureaucratization, but on the other hand, they may be perceived as makeshift solutions that are only the preliminary step before a profound transformation of the governance of large companies.

So, after abandoning the purely functional perspective exclusively focused on the means of improvement of the governance of companies, the way can be opened to wonder about the underlying forces that compete and the stakes of the debate for the control and distribution of the value created by the company. In this regard, the link cannot fail to be made between the process of "financialization" of companies, the transformation of the shareholder and the questioning of modes of governance that themselves are structured in a different context, that of heritage and industrial capitalism.[12]

8 See A. Tunc, "Supprimer ou renforcer le conseil d'administration des sociétés anonymes?", Paris, *Revue droit des affaires internationales*, p. 669 (1991).

9 See C. Bébéar, *Ils vont tuer le capitalisme*, Paris: Plon (2003), esp. p. 95.

10 F. Basdevant, "L'administrateur référent: un nouvel acteur dans le gouvernement d'entreprise", Paris, *Revue trimestrielle de droit financier* (*RTDF*) 1, chr. p. 85 (2010) et seq.; P. Le Cannu, "L'administrateur référent: un nouveau personnage au théâtre du conseil", Paris, *Revue trimestrielle de droit commercial*, p. 625 (2013); M. Germain, V. Magnier & M.-A. Noury, "La gouvernance des sociétés cotées", Étude et rapport, Paris, *Juris-Classeur périodique*, *JCP*, Entreprise esp. No. 10, p. 1638 (November 21, 2013), et seq.

11 Thus, according to P. Le Cannu: "Relations with shareholders are no doubt delicate to put in place within the French context. The British do not have this reserve: relationships with the major shareholders fall within the job description of the senior independent director. Equality between shareholders and the fear of letting slip inside information must also be present to incite prudent practice. The shareholders clubs already give ideas on what can or cannot be done in this area. In addition, it is no longer the case that the corporate directorate refuses to meet institutional shareholders or funds when they hold a significant share of capital and ask questions or request a meeting. It is therefore desirable that the personalities established communication in terms of leadership to be able to cope with these demands. The CEO can respond continuously to the solicitations, and it is understand that the vice president can be in charge of it. When this is the case, they are often also given the title "Vice President of the Board of Directors". This task is defined only in the rules of procedure of the council, or in statutes, which brings the vice president into play in legal technique terms (Cf. "L'administrateur référent: un nouveau personnage au théâtre du conseil" see note 10).

12 See J. Peyrelevade, *Le gouvernement d'entreprise ou les fondements incertains d'un nouveau pouvoir*, Paris: Economica (1999).

The institutional idea of the company and the quality of the company body are born in legal terms in this particular context. Some saw a functional perspective in it and the determinism of a natural given: the functioning of the company would dictate its rules to the law by arguing its economic and operating principles. But it also perhaps allows a rhetorical method of justification of the power taken by the directors to overcome the power of the shareholders to be seen in the perspective of a strategic analysis of organizations. It is no coincidence if employers who have been (oddly enough) the best defenders of the concept of the interest of the company, at the time of the debate on corporate governance, to emphasize that this interest would be distinct from that of the shareholders;[13] in the 1970s, this notion was the object of a virulent debate when employees invoked it to limit the decisions taken by the majority shareholders.[14] At this time also, the interests of the shareholders and directors were confused. Directors clearly did not appear as a distinct interest category.

This implicit return to the agency theory can then be measured not only in the decline of the internal control exercised by the board, but also in the transformation of the relationship of the management with the company.

2. *The weakening of the notion of a governing body*

Indeed, the institutional approach determines the quality of the management body of the company. The director is historically representative of the shareholders and the company as a legal entity. This contractual relationship of mandate persists even in the terminology used, as they are most often referred to with the label of "corporate officers". But, as for the board of directors, the industrial period also known as managerial capitalism has helped the director overcome the shareholder; the institutional approach can be perceived, not really as one might be tempted to think like a natural given related to the functioning of companies, but in part also as a rhetorical justification to strengthen a strategic position. As this strategic position is put to poor use by the transformation of the shareholder into a time of "financialization" of the economy, it is not surprising to witness a return of the rule of the contract and the idea that the director is less a body than a service provider, linked together with the company by a contract.

In this perspective, the predictable submission of the completeness of the remuneration of directors in the system of regulated agreements leads to a questioning of the quality of body to replace them in a contractual relationship with the company.

B. Agency theory and the development of external control

Putting forward the hypothesis of a return to the agency theory within a context that is seemingly favorable to the theory of institution suggests new observations. Companies traded on the stock exchange have reached such a degree of organizational and legal complexity that they might easily think that they no longer belong to the shareholder, who ends up dissolved and scattered on the financial markets. Economic players with a strong social impact would

13 Cf. Viennot reports, AFEP and CNPF reports on the board of directors of listed companies, July 1995; AFEP and MEDEF report on corporate governance, July 1999.

14 Cf. Paris May 22, 1965, Paris, Recueil Dalloz 1968, p. 147, note R. Contin; Paris, *Juris-Classeur périodique, JCP* 1965.II.14274 bis, concl. M. l'Av. Gén. Nepveu; Paris, *Revue trimestrielle droit commercial*, 1965, p.619, obs. R. Rodiere; Paris: Recueil Dalloz (1968), chr. p. 45 of R. Contin, "*L'arrêt Fruehauf et l'évolution du droit des sociétés*".

then carry corporate responsibility, like the declining welfare states that they should take over. Yet the pressure exerted by financial investors on directors through the debate on corporate governance gives a powerful reason to think that what the first observers significantly named "the return of the shareholder"[15] actually aims only to replace the director in an officer position and to reinvigorate the agency theory. Power that is returned to the shareholder to influence remuneration has a symbolic element in that it replaces the director in his or her position of service provider in the service of the interests of its corporate officer.

The pressure of the financial shareholder goes beyond a simple exchange of ideas. It builds on new tools created by the practice. The return of the position of corporate officer borrows new ways that precisely reveal "Say on pay". Shareholder control is exercised remotely and externally to the company or through institutions that seek to re-create a direct link to the market with the directors without necessarily going through the corporate bodies that have been created for this purpose. The increase in the influence of consultancies in voting agencies is a primary illustration. The role of the proxy advisors has become a concern to the financial authorities both in France and on a European level.[16] In response to a specific need of the financial shareholder, they offer a special and unprecedented service akin to a real internal control normally dedicated to corporate bodies but carried out externally. Studies have pointed out that the recommendations of the major agencies are followed by institutional investors, which leads companies to revise their remuneration policy before even the corporate bodies are solicited on this point.[17] Consultancy agencies for voting are thus at the origin of a form of standardization that emphasizes the creation and sharing of the value.[18] A standard dialogue established between the institutional shareholder and directors explains the low rate of negative opinions of the general assemblies and the reduced impact of "Say on pay" on levels of pay.[19] Through this standard dialogue, an informal agreement can be reached outside the social organs. As a matter of fact, for the financial shareholder it is less the amount of money paid to the director than the rate of return on their investment that is important. However, this rate depends much more on performance and management orientation in favor of the shareholder than the director's level of remuneration. A ratio was even developed to facilitate the decision making of the financial shareholder based on that criterion.[20]

These forms of external control are based on new institutions such as proxy advisers, but also institutions such as the referent administrator that can be used to link informally between the leading shareholder and the directors. Actually, these forms of external control meet the needs of the financial shareholder, which, by way of its remoteness, is not in a position to personally exercise monitoring as a heritage or industrial shareholder would. The forms of control are intimately related to the structural needs of the shareholders. The

15 For example, see J.-J Caussain, Le gouvernement d'entreprise. *Le pouvoir rendu aux actionnaires*, Paris, Litec, 2005.

16 AMF Recommendation 2012–4; see also, "Report on agencies consulting on the vote or 'proxy advisors'" published (February 19, 2013) by the ESMA.

17 E. Ginglinger, "Say on Pay: quelles conséquences pour les entreprises?", Paris, *Option Finance* (September 9, 2013).

18 F. Palomino, "Rémunération des dirigeants d'entreprise: que peut-on attendre du 'Say on pay'?", *EDHEC Business School* (November 2012).

19 See Ernst & Young study in partnership with Labrador, *Panorama des pratiques de gouvernance des sociétés cotées françaises* (2013), p. 27.

20 For a Canadian study, see J. Mc Farland, "Say-on-Pay Votes Increasingly Tied to Performance", *The Globe and Mail* (September 7, 2014).

governing body was born of the need to delegate the management function in the large industrial company. From this necessity to delegate the management function derives the idea expressed in a famous American doctrine initiated by Berle and Means[21] highlighting that the need to delegate gives rise to an asymmetry of information giving the officer in charge of the daily management a strategic position that is characteristic of managerial capitalism. The statutory auditor is a correction instrument for this asymmetry and was established precisely at the origin to allow the shareholder to control through its accounting operations that which they are no longer able to monitor by themselves.[22]

But today, for the delocalized financial shareholder anxious to invest in the financial markets, the needs of control pass through the creation of new tools. The techniques of agencies (ratings agencies, voting consultants and perhaps one day management consulting agencies), that of the vice president, and the standardization of the governance of large companies and bodies in charge of internal audits, should allow the financial shareholder to take informed remote decisions and have a direct influence on the management without bypassing the handover of the legal bodies provided for this purpose, the board of directors and general assembly, which appear to be no more than chambers for rubber-stamping decisions prepared and decided upstream in an informal and direct relationship organized by new bodies as a result of practice.

In this perspective, if the debate on corporate governance were to be apprehended under the assumption of "constitutionalization", it must be observed – as is revealed in particular by the question of "Say on pay" – that economic structuring introduced by spontaneous institutional practices of external controls are for the moment only aimed at replacing the director in his initial position of corporate officer.

Could the 'constitutionalization' process, however, find other resources in a rising force, that of the stakeholders who tend to challenge the power of the shareholder and demand the quality of economic beneficiary in the action of the leaders? From this point of view, indeed, the question of remuneration and its legitimacy may arise in very different terms.

2. The "Say on pay" of stakeholders and economic beneficiaries against the trustee director

Under the perspective of stakeholders, the issue of "Say on pay" has, for the moment, never really been raised, as company law predominantly organizes the power of the shareholder. The challenge most often deals with compensation levels and the media denunciation of excess, which resulted in France in a measured intervention by the legislature and forms of self-regulation through employer institutions. But the movement in favor of corporate citizenship could well lead to new calls for an expansion of "Say on pay" to stakeholders and in particular to the company employees. If big business is considered to be a public good run in the general interest, it would be possible to find in this enlargement of the aims of the management the catalysts for a "constitutionalization" process aimed at framing the powers of leaders and their remuneration. Thus the director should be regarded as a "trustee" and the "stakeholders" would have a vocation to be endowed with "Say on pay".

21 Berle & Means, *The Modern Corporation & Private Property*, New York: Macmillan (1932).

22 Cf. J. Hilaire, "La formation du commissariat aux comptes. De la surveillance par les actionnaires à la certification", in *Le commissariat aux comptes, renforcement ou dérive?*, A. Sayag (Dir.), CREDA, Paris: Litec (1989), vol. 1, p. 13 et seq.

A. *The trustee director*

The return of the agency theory found through the "Say on pay" debate conducted on a global level could nevertheless lead, under pressure from stakeholders, to putting the director in a new position that can restore legitimacy to managerial capitalism. The debate on corporate governance has in effect prompted directors to overcome the shareholder and to claim the position of "trustee" in charge of a multitude of interests. But from this perspective, the agency report then binds the director with all stakeholders and not just with the shareholder, as is the case in standard theory. The return of the agency theory would therefore not be a simple regression to an original situation.

This evolution is probably controlled by the societal impact of big business and the decline of legal individualism that accompanies it. This movement is no more irrelevant to the dispersion of share ownership and organization of groups that cause a stripping of the duties of the legal entity. In effect, you can distinguish between three functions of legal entity: the function of de-materialization of assets (transformation of real rights into personal rights), which from an economic point of view is also a function of financing; a function of the transformation into assets; and a function of representation and asset management. From these three functions, personification allows, in principle, the definition of the scope of the association of the categories of interest and corporate law, which does not take into account the reality of this stripping back and considers only the partnership agreement that was founded thanks to the partners' contributions, in essence, is a kind of "condominium" made into an asset by the legal agent and managed by corporate officers responsible for the common interest of the only "co-owners", who are the associates. However, in groups and in the context of "financialization", these three functions are no longer met within the same company. They are completely relocated, or even globally scattered. In a large company, the holding company is generally listed, thus ensuring the transmission function on the market of the value of the underlying assets of its subsidiaries. The management itself is carried out by a steering committee, which brings together leading company executives and the productive assets are the property of the subsidiaries that are controlled to a greater or lesser extent. In this setup, the legal entity is no longer allowed to precisely define the scope of the association and property rights. It even allows a dissociation of the power and legal title. The forms of control and management tend to develop externally. All categories of interests affected by the activity of issuers and the trustees seem to be in a position to claim ownership of the leaders' actions and, as such, become the beneficiary of a right of control. It is no surprise then to find, in such a context, that the director of the principal company is placed in the position of a trustee or a steward in charge of the interest of a multitude of categories of interest. Therefore, he or she imperceptibly transforms the management role, which tends to become a function of governance. The decline in power of the shareholder does not only take place alongside the dispersion of capital in a large company,[23] but also in organizational terms and forms of legal structuring that promote the identification of the company through its only governance and crystallizes claims in a direct relationship with all stakeholders while placing the director in a position of trustee.

This position is not without consequences for the basic concepts such as those of corporate interest, or for the purposes of management.[24] Corporate citizenship is another way to

23 Cf. R. Aron, *Dix-huit leçons sur la société industrielle*, Paris: Gallimard (1962), p. 276.

24 Cf. Focus group chaired by J. Attali, *Pour une économie Positive*, Fayard/La Doc. française (2013), which includes several proposals to that effect made in different forms, the creation of a status of director, creation of a form of company with the purpose of expanding, and reform of article 1833 of the civil code in order to broaden the definition of the aims of the management in order to integrate the creation of environmental and social value, building in particular on the works of B. Segrestin & A. Hatchuel, *Refonder l'entreprise*, Paris: Le

understand the duties and obligations of the trustee director. This responsibility is no longer the only one that leads to the imputation of harmful consequences of an act of leadership, and it tends to become that of support for the interests of stakeholders and a guarantee of risks created by the company. It is a responsibility of the same type as that which is expected from the welfare state – although it would perhaps allow the emergence of a new model, that of "corporate welfare" that would allow thoughts of "constitutionalization".

B. "Say on pay" for the benefit of the stakeholders?

The logical extension of such a movement would be recognition for the benefit of the stakeholders of a scrutiny right on the legitimacy of the remuneration of the director. The result would probably be felt on the evolution of the level of remuneration, as if for the shareholder it is the rate of return that controls the evaluation, stakeholders may have more diverse views. To focus on employees, the criterion of legitimacy would be rather inferred from the remuneration gap within the company. Sociologists have been able to show that levels of inequality that are too high are experienced as a form of injustice and are a demotivating factor in terms of work.[25]

"Say on pay" thus appears to be placed at the crossroads of several paradoxical justifications. On one hand, if public opinion is set to stir up through the media the amount of remuneration the directors receive, it also appears that the shareholders' control that would result in new forms, would be the source of this progression, right there where he or she is asked to take to the floor to limit pay. It is often observed that the directors' remuneration may have never risen as much as when opinion and legislators became involved. It is questionable to wonder if the obligation that would be made to the shareholder to speak in assemblies would not be a means intended solely to silence the public and stakeholders, giving the shareholder an opportunity to be reaffirmed in the power that gives him or her ownership of the capital – especially when we have seen that "Say on pay" appears to already exist in the informal relationships between the leading shareholder and the director.

Establishing a "Say on pay" for the benefit of stakeholders – submitting for example the remuneration directors receive to the vote of the works council – would no doubt give a different scope to this procedure, as the goal would be to limit excessive inequalities in terms of remuneration. But such a prerogative would probably mean a profound change in the approach there is towards corporate law, especially in France.

Ultimately, "Say on pay" could, from the point of view of stakeholders and employees in particular, be the manifestation of a "constitutionalization" process, the source of procedural rules to give shape to the status of the director as part of a social contract in training.[26] For the time being, however, the clearest finding remains that the "financialization" of the economy tends to re-create, on the margins of the legal bodies and institutional theory that underlies them, the model of the agency theory whose return in an external and unpublished form may well for some time remain the unsurpassable horizon of the market economy.

Seuil (2012); of Y. Queinnec & W. Bourdon, *Réguler les entreprises transnationales*, Forum for a New Global Governance (2010); and of G. Giraud & C. Renouard, *Vingt propositions pour réformer le capitalisme*, Paris: Flammarion (2012).

25 P. Fenot, "Eléments de sociologie de la rémunération des dirigeants: de la légitimité de la rémunération au besoin social d'encadrement", *Revue Lamy Droit Affaires* p. 85 (2013).

26 See V. Champeil-Desplats, "Constitutionalization Outside of the State? A Constitutionalist's Point of View", in this volume.

12 Can States regain fiscal sovereignty over globalized business?

Christian Chavagneux

The different estimates available lead one to believe that the largest States lose the equivalent of at least 2 to 4% of their GDP each year in tax revenue, with tax havens being one of the reasons behind these losses. These are colossal amounts. Two-thirds of the losses are supposed to be due to aggressive tax planning strategies on the part of businesses; the rest are from high earners.

Tax havens also exert strong pressure in favor of decreasing tax rates. Total tax revenues for the OECD countries, measured as a percentage of GDP, continued to grow from the mid-1960s until the mid-1990s, before stabilizing since the beginning of the twenty-first century at slightly below 35%. Within the European Union (28 States), the tax rate of businesses lost 12 percentage points between 1995 and 2014, dropping from 35% to 22.9%. The States have integrated the existence of tax havens and internalized the need not to ask too much from businesses, despite huge social and financial needs required by a successful and equitable integration into globalization. The problem is even more glaring for developing countries that are deprived of budgetary revenue necessary to their development because of multinational corporations evading tax and the embezzlement of funds by corrupt public elites.

The aggressive tax planning strategies of enterprises aim at building an alternative tax system based on a purely fictitious geography of activities designed by private actors. It infringes on the State power to tax and is as such one of the source of power of firms. The good news is that, to paraphrase Jean-Philippe Robé (p. 35) the G20 is now attempting to clarify what is the appropriate use of tax sovereignty in a global economy and to police improper uses. What is at stake is no less than an attempt to constitutionalize the tax power of multinationals by rewriting tax laws in an age of globalization. Firms do not observe passively what the G20 is doing. They intent to keep as much tax power as they can. But the fight is on – and it is the first time since the 1920s that States have tried to establish tax rules in a globalized world.

1. A private financial geography of globalization

As Ronen Palan writes in his contribution to this volume, "one of the mainstay of corporate power originates in the discrepancy between the 'legal personality' corporate forms that are located within territorial boundaries of sovereign states, and economic personality of the firm, which consists of a string of companies located in various jurisdictions". Among those jurisdictions, tax havens are fictitious legal spaces that allow disassociating the place where a financial transaction occurs (wages, financial income, profits, and so on.) from the place where it is recorded and therefore taxed. These artificial capital flows lead to statistical inconsistencies that are indicators of a globalization whose level is in fact largely unknown, as the available data does not reflect the reality of the functioning of the global economy.

Take the example of the United States. At the end of 2013, the largest national holder of foreign investment stock from American multinationals was the Netherlands (15.5% of the total) and if we include Ireland, Bermuda, the British Caribbean, Luxembourg, Switzerland and Singapore, we are nearing half of the total stock. Canada, Germany, France, China, and so on., natural candidates to have a strong presence from large US companies, are actually at the lower end of the official classification.

In Europe, the LuxLeaks scandal highlighted the place occupied by secret tax agreements negotiated by the tax authorities of the country with companies from around the world in order to offer them low taxation. In its 2014 World Investment Report, UNCTAD looked closely at the influence of Special Purpose Vehicles – clearly shell companies – in Luxembourg. The result was that only 8% of Luxembourg's investment abroad and 5% of investments received corresponded to real financial activity. The rest related to artificial streams allowing companies to escape the tax authorities of their country of origin.

In summer 2014, in accordance with a European Union Directive, French banks published the total amount of their turnover and the number of employees for each country where they operate. When calculating the turnover per employee, it is apparent that with the exception of Société Générale, Ireland plays an important role for the French banking system. The country is located in the leading trio of territories where the turnover per employee is the highest. For BPCE, it is even eleven times greater than for the average of the bank's subsidiaries, and for its financial subsidiary Natixis, eight times higher! A bank with a smaller surface such as Crédit Mutuel is also subject to strange subsidiaries: Behind the United States and the United Kingdom, Luxembourg, the Dutch Antilles and the Bahamas top the list of the most "productive" subsidiaries. An analysis carried out by the NGO Weed on Deutsche Bank data points out the important role played by the Luxembourg subsidiary where productivity is nearly four times higher than the average of its other subsidiaries.

Another case is the Cayman Islands, which for decades have regularly ranked among the first financial centers in the world. While the City of London handles only about three times more capital (4,900 billion of assets as opposed to 1,500 billion), it employs a hundred times more people in its financial sector (approximately 360,000 people rather than 3,600)! Maybe the residents of the Caymans are exceptionally productive, or maybe its "financial sector" has few actual activities and serves to record fictitious transactions for tax purposes, or to take opaque financial risks.

There are many examples, all of which are heading in the same direction: Public data measuring investment and international capital flow do not reflect the reality of globalization of firms and finance. The magnitude of this is overvalued, inflated by artificial flows and distorted geography. Companies and financial investors impose a representation of globalization that does not match that of the real economy and it is this fictitious globalization that is taxed.

2. The G20 counterattack

The year 2013 was marked by the late-summer political launch of an OECD action plan to combat the questionable tax practices of multinationals. Nicknamed BEPS (Base Erosion and Profit Shifting) this plan targeted, as its name suggests, practices that enable global companies to reduce their taxable base by moving the profit that they make to territories where they will be taxed less. The G20 countries reached an agreement to list fifteen specific points that merit political action on their part if they wish to regain fiscal sovereignty against multinationals. They delivered their action plan in October 2015. (The G20 countries have also approved the development of a global standard for the automatic exchange of tax information to combat the aggressive optimization practices of individuals, see Chavagneux, 2015.)

The fifteen points raised, which are quite technical, are all relevant targets with the intention of trying to correct current flaws that result in the low taxation of large groups. The fifteen points of the BEPS plan are the subject of preliminary analyses and reflections undertaken by the OECD. The documents are then open for public comments. The institution synthesizes the proposals and attempts to find compromise positions. Debates on each of the points of the action plan are therefore very technical. Without going into the details of the expert debate, the important points that are currently being negotiated may be highlighted.

Action 1: The digital economy

Taxing digital businesses does not pose a different problem than that of the taxation of other companies, according to the OECD. The problems of the erosion of tax bases and transfers of profits are, however, exacerbated because companies in this sector are more aggressive. The measures proposed by the OECD are primarily aimed at preventing companies in this sector from being able to localize intellectual property items in tax havens before forcing other subsidiaries to pay for the use of this property and thus siphoning off profits. The OECD wants to propose detailed arrangements for value added taxation on this type of activity, reflecting on what could be the legal expression of a "permanent digital establishment" (taxation occurs where the permanent establishment has been established).

Action 2: Neutralize the effects of hybrid arrangements

Hybrids are financial products that change depending on the place where they appear. For example, they take the form of shares in countries that do not tax dividends, and become bonds in those that do not tax interests. Two subsidiaries placed in appropriate countries that exchange such products therefore escape any taxation. The OECD brings to the table the legal instruments that should allow neutralizing the effects of hybrid products, which should lead to their disappearance.

Action 3: Strengthening rules on transfers from subsidiaries

Each country implements specific tax regimes governing the arrangements for taxation of income originating from subsidiaries located abroad. The OECD wants these different regimes to be reconciled and therefore limit the incentive to preserve profits in tax havens. Within the European Union, since the Cadbury judgement of May 2006, European countries can intervene in transfers made between subsidiaries in tax matters insofar as subsidiaries are considered to be "purely artificial".

EU countries had until 31 December 2015 to convert the amendment of January 2015 of the mother-daughter directive, which now incorporates an anti-abuse clause enabling national authorities to not grant the benefit of double taxation to schemes that are "not genuine", in other words, schemes put in place to obtain taxation benefit that are not based on any economic reality.

Action 4: Limit base erosion via interest deductions

One of the tools used by companies to reduce their tax base is that of a subsidiary located in a tax haven that provides a loan to another localized in a country with higher taxation. As the repayment of interest on borrowings is deductible from profits, business has found a way of siphoning profits to tax havens. The OECD is considering several methods to limit recourse to this type of practice.

The institution does not wish to set standards for the financing of multinationals, in particular regarding their choice to resort further to borrowing or equities. However, even if the use of this aggressive tax optimization tool seems less widespread than the manipulation of transfer prices, the subsequent orientation often involves limiting misuse of the recourse to debt.

Action 5: Counter harmful tax practices

The OECD considers competition is good in itself, including in the field of taxation. But it becomes "harmful" when States go too far in offering products aimed at deliberately deducting tax revenues from their neighbors. The OECD has begun to build a consensus on two points.

On one hand, on the reconsideration of the "patent box" – laws that offer tax breaks for multinationals' patent research and localization activities. Belgium, Spain, France, Hungary, Luxembourg, the Netherlands, Portugal, the United Kingdom and Switzerland all offer this type of legislation and Ireland has announced they want to join them. In late 2014, the European Commission requested that Belgium, Cyprus, Spain, France, Hungary, Luxembourg, Malta, the Netherlands, Portugal and the United Kingdom provide them with information about their "patent boxes".

On the other hand, a consensus is also under way on the monitoring the famous tax rulings – a prior agreement outside of common law between the tax authorities of a country and companies regarding the procedures relating to taxation of their profits. The OECD condemns the practice of "rulings".

On the basis of documents covering the period 2002–10, the international consortium of investigative journalists showed in November 2014 that through the audit firm PwC, Luxembourg has signed 548 agreements of this type with more than 340 multinational companies as well as companies of average size. No doubt the other major audit firms are no exception.

In practical terms, this means that the Luxembourg tax authorities are to validate profit minimization practices in order to achieve a low tax rate, on the order of 0.5 to 3%. It brings low revenues but, multiplied by the large number of firms concerned (plus some fees) it ultimately allows Luxembourg to build its wealth and tax receipts on the basis of a diversion of revenues from other countries.

The OECD calls for an obligation for tax authorities to carry out a "spontaneous exchange" of information between them on such practices, while the European Commissioner Pierre Moscovici spoke of "automatic exchange" – on a perimeter that could be broader than that of BEPS. However, the principle is the same: Luxembourg, for example, will be supposed to inform the tax authorities in other European countries that it has agreed to aggressive optimization rulings with companies originating in their countries. In all fairness, it is possible to doubt the will to implement this on the part of Luxembourg and other countries that follow such practices. The OECD responds that Action 12 of the BEPS plan requires companies to declare their aggressive tax arrangements to authorities and that thanks to Action 13, tax administrations will benefit from country-by-country accounting reporting that should enable them to see to what extent the tax base is artificially moved (see following).

The European Commission seems to be more on the ball. It has launched several investigations into such practices in 2014, including agreements concluded by Luxembourg with Amazon and Fiat, by Ireland with Apple, and by the Netherlands with Starbucks. In the case of the agreement implemented since 2003 between Amazon and Luxembourg, noting that "most European profits of Amazon are recorded in Luxembourg but are not taxed in Luxembourg", the Commission considers that the country is "grant[ing] a financial advantage to Amazon by allowing the group to pay less tax than other companies whose profits are allocated in line with market terms", which equals for the Commission to a type of disguised State assistance.

An important development because it would allow these procedures to be considered illegal under European law. Agreements in 1991 and in 2007 between the Irish tax authorities and Apple are also being targeted. First, the Commission launched investigations into cases related to Belgium, Cyprus, Ireland, Luxembourg, Malta, the Netherlands and the United Kingdom before getting in touch at the end of 2014 with all EU member States to provide them with all rulings given between 2010 and 2013.

Action 6: Ending treaty shopping

Companies are entitled to use tax cuts offered by such countries for foreign investors to reduce their taxation in order to attract them. In this way, many multinationals are for example artificially headquartered in Mauritius to take advantage of this country's agreement with India. BEPS provides that there will now be minimum standards for the use of these treaties that will make treaty shopping impossible. All countries have agreed to move forward on this point, for which the OECD listed no fewer than twenty issues to settle in late 2014! The work is currently done.

Action 7: Prevent the artificial avoidance of permanent establishment status

The entire action of BEPS aims to ensure that activities can be taxed on the territories where the added value is created and not where it is artificially transferred. This legally requires a reflection on permanent establishment status, which affects several points of BEPS. That which is contained in this action aims specifically to address the problem of companies acting on behalf of other companies, specific proposals to the insurance sector, and so on.

Action 8–9–10: Action on transfer mispricing

At the heart of the BEPS action is the need to combat the technique most used by multinational corporations to avoid tax, the manipulation of transfer pricing. Notably, this includes the point of manipulation of transfer pricing on intangible assets (brands, software, and so on.) for which there is no international market. Telling Google that the transfer price it imposes on its subsidiaries for the right to use its brand is abusive is one thing; measuring the extent of this abuse is another: There is no comparable international market in this area.

The OECD wants to set new rules for transfer pricing correcting the defects of those currently in force and based on the principle that the subsidiaries of the same multinational represent separate entities and are supposed to exchange goods and services at prices "comparable" to those prevailing on the international markets between businesses that are not connected in any way. The OECD maintains the same principle of reasoning but seeks to minimize as much as possible how multinationals manipulate these transfer prices, manipulations that in recent years have led to increasing clashes between multinationals and tax authorities.

Technical details of the regulations under negotiation make it the privilege of a number of experts who will be able to continue to live by their capacity for interpretation of tax laws, on behalf of governments or private companies, and often both during their professional career. As has been recognized by the OECD experts, the definition of transfer pricing is not a science: Their aim is to reach a compromise on interpretations allowing the best limitation of the double non-taxation of companies. Let's be clear: What the Commission is doing here is a public intervention to question the internal rules of exchange within enterprises.

Action 11: Building Data *on* BEPS

The OECD has launched an appeal to all experts who would like to contribute to reducing aggressive tax optimization by multinationals, by providing the tools to properly measure it, both on a macro-economic basis and micro-economic basis. This data would represent an interesting tool to track the progress – or not – made in the questioning of dubious tax practices of companies.

Action 12: Declaring aggressive optimization schemes

The plan asks for mandatory disclosure to the tax authorities of aggressive tax planning schemes used by companies. While it is an information of interest, the existence of such constraints in the United Kingdom has not transformed the country into a virtuous territory.

Action 13: Improve documentation on transfer pricing

This action owes everything to the British NGO Tax Justice Network, where one of the experts, Richard Murphy, proposed the following idea several years ago, namely the request made to multinational enterprises to provide country-by-country reporting. The OECD will therefore establish a framework for data concerning turnover, the number of employees, the amount of physical assets, profits made, taxes paid as well as tax debts. Only companies with a turnover higher than 750€ million are affected. The latter point will, according to the OECD information, leave 85% of companies outside the process while focusing on the most powerful. They will provide their data to the tax authorities in each country of residence in 2016 and they can exchange information on the subject from 2017.

Only the tax authorities will have this information. It will not be made public, which is a pity because it would be important information for employees, shareholders, journalists and civil society organizations. The OECD intends to review in 2020 the operating conditions for country by country reporting, which will perhaps lower the threshold of the businesses concerned and consider that information could be made public, a development that does not gather a political consensus among the States for now but will need to be tabled at the time.

Action 14: Make dispute resolution more effective

With tax authorities becoming more aggressive in their audits, cases of conflict between authorities and between them and tax-paying businesses regarding interpretation are on the rise. Given the magnitude of the changes to be implemented within the framework of BEPS, the trend should not falter. Making conflict resolution and arbitration instruments more effective is therefore necessary. All countries are not in agreement over making arbitration procedures mandatory. This is why much weight is still afforded to the small community of experts able to navigate these rules in all their growing complexity.

Action 15: Develop a multilateral instrument

Finally, many developments put on the table by the OECD can be active only when they are included in all existing international tax treaties. This is because, when establishing the rules concerning the problem of double taxation of multinationals – once in the country of the subsidiary, once in the country of the parent company – in the 1920s, the League of Nations chose to focus on bilateral tax treaties rather than a large multilateral convention.

Today, dealing with the non-taxation of companies brings about significant changes. To speed up the process, the countries have found it feasible and desirable that the OECD proposes an international convention allowing the one-off approval of new rules for the taxation of multinational companies.

The fifteen actions described are surely moving in the right direction for the reconsideration of aggressive fiscal optimization practices employed by companies. Never since the 1920s has the international community of States gone so far in its attempt to define a tax framework for multinationals. This includes making the effort to involve, by way of various measures, developing countries that are suffering the loss of tax revenues in significant proportions. The OECD highlights that for some countries the taxation of multinational companies corresponds to 90% of their revenues.

But if the principles are laid down, their realization remains to be seen. It is now necessary to wait until the end of 2015 for the OECD to deliver the precise content of its fifteen actions.

3. The conditions for a return to fiscal sovereignty

Once the OECD's technical work has been completed, the next step will be its implementation towards 2017–8. The concrete work of regaining the fiscal sovereignty of States will begin at that time. It is already possible to list the measures that seem necessary for its success.

Strengthening tax administrations

The fight against tax havens does not stop at information obtained from these territories through country-by-country reporting. On the contrary, this is where it starts. Tax authorities need a high capacity for investigation and processing of information in order that the current international diplomatic efforts translate into effectively recovered tax revenues. The technical capacity of public tax inspectors should be increased both by ongoing training tailored to the complexity and the increasing internationalization of fraud and possibly by recruiting professionals from the private sector in banking, accounting, financial and legal expertise. Their statutory and recruitment conditions may be subject to specific procedures.

However, developments in the last years have been going in the wrong direction. With a few rare exceptions, tax authorities' personnel are in decline and, for some countries, a very sharp decline. An effective policy to combat tax havens must reverse this trend.

Fix a target for the reduction of tax losses

In order to ensure the effectiveness of the arrangements being implemented, the European Parliament and the national parliaments should be informed annually of the results of the policies. This would notably allow new European and national legal frameworks to develop quickly and when needed.

The fight against tax havens is a long-term one. Public policies that are currently working in this direction will take several years to be implemented and will be subject to renegotiations. Thus, to maintain the dynamic policy of recent years, it is necessary to measure progress on a regular basis and maintain the pressure on governments and private actors to continue their efforts.

For example, at the level of each country of the European Union, at the level of their parliament and the European Parliament, tax administrations and the Commissioner in charge of taxation could be required to produce an annual document that would set out the effective tax rates of the more affluent people and multinationals (as a group), the number of tax recoveries carried out, the number of reports received via automatic exchange of information, from which countries, the amounts of tax recovered, and so on. The list is still to be negotiated. A parliamentary discussion could follow the publication of the report, for example at the time of the budget debates. The proceedings of the "European semester" could include this dimension in the opinions delivered by the Commission regarding dynamics of the public finances of EU countries.

Protect whistleblowers

The bursting of the financial bubble and the economic and social crisis that ensued were the opportunity for the mobilization of employees denouncing the activities of their companies, public or private, for doubtful moral – or even legal – purposes. If Edward Snowden is the most publicized case in the field of civil liberties, the denunciation of tax practices that are deemed scandalous has experienced strong growth. The revelation by Antoine Deltour – and another French individual whose identity is not known – of the behavior of the firm PwC in Luxembourg that gave rise to the LuxLeaks case, is only the latest episode in a series that saw the mobilization of employees of UBS Banks, in France and the United States, and of HSBC, Julius Baer, and so on. All have been prosecuted by their former employers.

Until now, these whistleblowers have not been able to receive adequate legal protection at a European level and within the various countries of the European Union. It is therefore necessary to make progress in this area. What are the possible routes?

In April 2014, the Committee of Ministers of the Council of Europe proposed a recommendation to lay down the groundwork for protection that would benefit whistleblowers, a law that could serve as a basis for reflection on the subject for many countries. On the most general level, the Council "recommends that member states have in place a standardized, institutional and judicial framework to protect individuals who, in the context of their work-based relationship, report or disclose information on threats or harm to the public interest" (Council of Europe, 2014).

The definition of what encompasses the activities of whistleblowers in the perspective of the protection of the general interest of the European States and the EU should then include protection against violations of the tax laws of the countries affected and the risk for their public revenue, and even for their financial stability. This is in the broadest possible sense because, as Australian legal scholar A. J. Brown says, "the complete character of protective legislation for whistleblowers, regardless of the sector in question, depends on three criteria:

the range of facts likely to be reported; the scope and diversity of the sectors of activity covered by the legislation; and, finally, the scope of persons eligible for the process and the protection set down in law" (quoted by Billard et al., 2014).

One point must be emphasized. The recommendation of the Council of Europe states that the protection granted should not undermine "the well-established and recognized rules for the protection of legal and other professional privilege" (see earlier statement). It is necessary to remain alert to the fact that the conditions for the protection of professional secrecy remain compatible with whistleblowers.

Act against the practices of legal professionals and financial professionals

An effective policy to combat tax havens must directly address practices undertaken by intermediaries in law and finance who promote their use – audit offices, tax experts, and so on.

Legal obligations could be put in place for consultants and tax advisers to declare tax optimization products they create to the administration, and also to identify their clients and consulting firms, thereby reducing aggressive optimization marketing. Tax administration must provide itself with the means of exercising a watch on aggressive optimization techniques.

It is possible to consider a method of rating tax consultants based on a model of notes received by the States, businesses, and so on. (AAA, AA, A, and so on.). Intermediaries to dubious practices would see their rating reduced whenever they are caught red-handed. Below a certain rating, these professionals would be forbidden to deal with local and national authorities and, under certain conditions, they may be prohibited from dealing with listed companies.

Generally speaking, with or without grades, professionals caught dealing in illegal schemes should be hit by heavy fines and these should be widely made known. Tackling those professionals that encourage tax fraud to make money themselves is an essential step in carrying out a real political fight against tax havens.

Remove the banks from tax havens

The presence of banks in tax havens poses a risk of financial instability. Financial institutions use these territories not only to reduce their taxation but also to take risks in an opaque manner.

The current US legal offensive against such practice involves heavy financial penalties with a request to bring down the leaders of the institutions (Miller, 2014). In the United Kingdom, the governor of the Bank of England is following the same pathway: The bankers at the head of the institutions of the country are seeing increased personal legal responsibility, while new rules allow for bonuses to be returned in the case of evidence of market manipulation.

Another possible route to consider is that since some banks pose an additional risk to the financial stability because of their presence in tax havens, they should incur a surcharge on capital in the image of what is imposed on banks considered to be systemic. An amount of capital to total assets should be added by 3 to 5 percentage points in a progressive manner, depending on the presence of establishments in tax havens.

4. Moving towards the principle of unitary taxation

As explained very clearly by the civil society experts gathered in the BEPS Monitoring Group, the underlying cause of the erosion of tax bases is the separate entity principle applied to the various subsidiaries of a multinational. "The underlying cause of BEPS is the separate-entity/arm's-length principle which the OECD itself has increasingly entrenched over the last two decades; it insists on treating the national operations of multinational enterprises as if they were independent of each other, whereas in reality they operate as an integrated whole under central direction. This principle creates a perverse incentive for multinationals to organize themselves as complex corporate groups with often hundreds of affiliates including many formed in convenient jurisdictions to facilitate base erosion and profit shifting"(Cobham and Loretz, 2014).

In a working paper published in November 2014, Alex Cobham and Simon Loretz present an alternative unitary taxation proposal put forward by professor and tax expert Sol Picciotto, which consists of "treating each multinational group of companies as a unit, regardless of the geographical and juridical rental of the individual subsidiaries; calculating profit and loss on a group-wide basis; and then allocating the taxing rights on this consolidated profit between the jurisdictions with which the group has a nexus, according to the extent of actual financial activity". The authors remind us that this kind of unitary taxation system with an allocation formula, only currently exists at a national level in the United States, Canada, Switzerland and – for local taxes – in Germany.

Cobham and Loretz used a database including 211,360 individual subsidiaries belonging to 26,795 companies to try to assess the consequences of the adoption of a unitary tax system. Their work leads to five important conclusions for supporters of this alternative: (1) there is no obvious formula, whether based on assets, turnover or the number of employees, which objectively takes account of the location of activity; (2) the exact design of the allocation mechanism is crucial for the redistribution of tax bases of companies between countries; but (3) the corporate tax base really moves from countries such as Luxembourg, the Netherlands and Ireland to countries with higher taxation; (4) the introduction of the consolidation of accounts leads to a significant reduction in the overall tax base of companies, by more than 10%; (5) the clearest result of this study, the authors conclude, is that there is insufficient data to perform a comprehensive analysis of the impact on the redistribution of revenue in the event of a switch to unitary taxation.

Unitary taxation is, intellectually speaking, the most satisfactory response to the erosion of tax bases due to multinationals. They are managed as a single unit and must be treated in tax terms as such. However, the proposal requires more technical work to establish an appropriate allocation formula, and for political work to take into account the importance of the induced redistribution. For the American Law expert Reuven Avi-Yonah, if the adoption of country-by-country reporting can be a basis for the implementation of unitary taxation, "the transition to UT is likely to be a long process".

5. The three strategies of companies

Companies do not passively observe the G20 trying to rebuild international tax rules in order to be able to regain sovereignty. October 2015 saw the complete definition of the BEPS plan – but until its implementation in 2017–8, months will pass that will provide them an opportunity for fighting this evolution. Firms seem to have adopted three strategies in this regard.

Influence the content of BEPS

The consultation process surrounding the BEPS plan allows all those who wish to contribute to the debate on the precise definition of the measures to be taken. In May 2014, during a

Table 12.1 Who wants to influence BEPS?

In % of total	*Transfer pricing*	*Transfer pricing on intangibles*	*Digital economy*	*Hybrid products*	*Abuse of the treaties*	*Total*
Lobby of companies	14.5	3.5	6.7	7.4	8.9	40.9
Multinationals	4.5	1.3	1.5	0.6	1.3	9.3
Legal and financial professionals	14.3	8.4	4.5	6.5	5.8	39.6
NGOs	3.9	0.2	0.2	0.4	0.4	5.2
Academics	1.9	1.1	0.4	0.2	0.6	4.3
Non-member States	0.2	0.0	0.0	0.0	0.0	0.2
TOTAL	39.4	14.5	13.4	15.2	17.1	100.0

(Source: OECD – Author's calculations)

webcast, the OECD provided interesting information on who seeks to influence the content of the program the most on five key issues: the politics of transfer pricing on goods and services and on intangible products, on the digital economy, on hybrid financial products and on the abuse of tax treaties. It can be summarized in the following table.

Totaling the intervention of business lobbies, companies themselves, and legal and financial professionals gives a figure of 90% of contributions. Certainly, the amount is not reflective of the quality or originality of the contributions, which are often redundant. NGOs and representatives of civil society are doing their best to be present, but the disparity of means results in accounting for only 5% of contributions, just ahead of academics who hardly seem passionate about the topic, for this kind of democratic exercise counts for nothing in their careers.

If we now look at priority issues, it can be seen that the primary topic by far, with nearly 40% of all interventions, relates to transfer prices. NGOs have been right to mobilize for years on the subject for this where companies are fighting the hardest to preserve their interests. They are also present on the issue of the abuse of tax treaties and transfer pricing of intangible assets, where the legal and financial professionals are by far most active

It is clear that one of the current strategies of multinational companies is to mobilize their expertise to influence as much as possible the implementation of the BEPS program.

Carry the political fight

Given that the final content of the BEPS plan may not suit them, multinationals are also looking for political allies, especially in the United States.

Mid-January 2015, *The Guardian* journalist Simon Bowers showed how several professional pressure groups in the high-technology service industries, whose members include Apple, Microsoft, Google, Amazon, Intel, Yahoo!, Facebook, Uber, Netflix, Hewlett-Packard, eBay, IBM, and Twitter, took forceful action to attack the content of the BEPS in the US and attempt to question it in political terms.

Indeed, part of the American Republicans, who control the Congress, is taking action to derail BEPS. But that is one part only, as others are sensitive to the fact that the budget will balance more easily thanks to recovered revenues. The Obama administration does not appear to retreat in this area, and the new standards were validated October 2015. A new Republican administration would potentially not come to power until 2017 at the earliest.

It is clear that current efforts in the fight against tax havens could not be initiated without the support of the United States. The precedent of 2000, when the election of George W.

Bush scuppered the ongoing initiatives, underlines how the role of American hegemony is always present in this issue: The findings of the political debates that take place there have an influence on the situation in the rest of the world.

Rebuild opacity

Finally, if influence and political mobilization efforts prove ineffective, firms may always try to rebuild opacity in other ways. It's possible to get an idea of this when trying to measure the presence of a few large companies in tax havens.

In December 2014, *The Economist* asked two specialists to study the annual reports of US companies between 2004 and 2012 to measure their presence in tax havens, the objective being to see to what extent it is recognized by the firms. Their results are astonishing: in 2012, nearly 300 companies declared a significant decrease – a decrease in the number of more than 50% – in their presence in tax havens.

Optimists will see this as a move towards healthier climates; others, as a desire to obscure the information available on this topic. *The Economist* falls into the second category, noting that where Google had declared the presence of more than 100 subsidiaries in tax havens in 2009, the number declared today is . . . two. This is something that is fairly widespread in this sector, with Apple declaring three subsidiaries in these territories and Microsoft five according to the latest figures from the NGO American Citizens for Tax Justice.

6. State tug-of-war

For their part, the States are encouraged to use a mix of cooperation and competition.

A need for cooperation

In terms of cooperation, the States should agree on the concrete definition of the content of BEPS. When the Saint Petersburg G20 summit politically validated the fifteen points of the project in September 2013, it established the possibility of an agreement between the States on what could be done by each of them to recover their tax base, without resorting to methods considered to be aggressive by others or a unilateral challenge to the interests of their multinationals. The OECD works within this framework.

Once solutions from the BEPS plan will be put on the table, all the countries that feel aggrieved by harmful tax practices will be able to use them. If Luxembourg wants to continue to offer opaque products, all the States that so wish may dip into the toolbox of possible actions put forward by the OECD and neutralize the effects. If only one country does it, he will meet difficulties. But all countries now need to recover tax revenues currently beyond their control.

The temptation of competition

Conversely, two elements push towards an increase in competition between the States.

If it becomes more and more difficult for some of them to provide fiscal and financial products that are opaque, there is a risk of increased tax competition. What comes to mind is Ireland announcing at the same time the closure of one of its flagship products – the famous double Irish – and the opening of a tax shelter – a patent box – to attract companies filing patents.

Moreover, an important policy question arises: If the announced measures are effective in recovering the tax base, which countries will benefit? If Google cannot siphon off profits to Bermuda, who will be able to tax its activity? “We” say the French, Germans, and so on., since the activity is with us. “No, we” say the Americans as the company works through an algorithm that come from American engineers brains, value added is in our home. Important battles are looming on the matter as to the redistributive effects of the new rules.

7. Conclusion: An historic moment

This is the first time in a century that the international community of States is undertaking coordinated action to set the rules for the taxation of multinationals in a globalized economy. History does not repeat itself. For all the governments, parliaments, NGOs, experts, academics, and so on, who think that just and universal taxation is part of the definition of the social contract, this period is historical: 2015–8 are the key years for mobilization.

In the 1920s, the League of Nations followed a set of standards aimed at preventing wealthy individuals and entrepreneurs involved in international activities from being taxed twice for the same activity, once in the countries where they were active and once in their country of origin. Today, the problem is radically reversed: It is about establishing principles of fair taxation of individuals and businesses that play upon their international presence to escape taxation with the active complicity of tax havens.

Let there be no mistake: Behind the technical discussions stirring up experts on the content of the new standards being defined, it is an essentially political battle that is unfolding. It leads to a questioning of powerful private interests and parasitic economies living in tax secrecy; it will result in a global redistribution of tax bases and therefore revenues that secure the capacity for action for European States in terms of public services, the welfare state, the fight against inequality and financial instability. In Jean-Philippe Robé’s words, it is an attempt to constitutionalize the power of enterprises through the definition of a macro-device in the realm of taxation.

The OECD defines new standards and norms that will be gradually implemented to give rise to a new fiscal world in 2017–8, in two years – an eternity, which still leaves the door open for a shifting balance of power in the face of uncertain issues. The battle for the end of secrecy for tax purposes has only just begun, and it will go well beyond 2018. Assuming that the new fiscal framework put in place will be at this height, it is already certain that it will be not perfect. It will reveal principles that are difficult to put into practice, holes in the net and omissions. We can’t wait another century to put them right. To achieve this, two key developments are needed: first, maintaining the possibility of political action on the subject through the permanent mobilization of national parliaments and the European Parliament, needed to define the institutional framework; second, the possibility of evolving technical standards through regular reviews of their operation, open to all interested stakeholders.

Finally, the ongoing tax revolution will be credible only if the deviants, those who will always seek to escape their tax contributions against all odds, suffer the consequences. The OECD will still be able to draw up lists of recalcitrant countries, but the potential penalty will remain at the mercy of the necessary compromises between States. All will be well when it comes to stigmatizing a small, weak country – but nothing will happen when it becomes necessary to tackle major financial centers. The solution involves the legal indictment of private actors. American justice has already paved the way in this area while there is a lack of doctrine in Europe. It must, as a last resort, provide serious means to act against recalcitrant.

Regardless of the outcome of the various strategies followed by one or the other, the actual results will be followed closely. As is rightly pointed out in *The Economist* (2014), the global debate on tax havens is now continuing under the gaze of mobilized media, especially investigative journalists who track the flaws in the system, of non-governmental organizations whose technical expertise has progressed significantly in recent years, and employees who are increasingly unhappy with the idea of dubious fiscal behavior and are more and more inclined to denounce them.

One final point: If BEPS measures are implemented on a large scale and we add to them the implementation of an automatic exchange of tax information, many artificial international transactions related to aggressive tax practices of individuals and private individuals will disappear or will be considerably reduced. These flows, currently registered in the international capital flows, would be brought out of the current measures, lessening the intensity of the globalization. Mechanically and statistically, the fight against tax havens would lead to a form of financial de-globalization.

Bibliography

Billard, A., M. Duranton, J.-P. Foegle & T. Martin-Teodorczyk (2014). The 'midstream' of the Protection of Whistleblowers, *The Journal of Human Rights* (online), May 20. http://revdh.revues.org/752

Bowers, S. (2015). US Tech Giants Launch Fierce Fightback Against Global Tax Avoidance Crackdown, *The Guardian*, January 21. www.theguardian.com/business/2015/jan/21/us-tech-tax-avoidance-google-amazon-apple

Chavagneux, C. (2015). *Fighting Tax Havens: What Has Been Done. What Should Be Done*, Report for Eva Joly, Greens/European Free Alliance Group in the European Parliament, February. http://cld.bz/fRy9uRo

Cobham, A. & S. Loretz (2014). International Distribution of the Corporate Tax Base: Implications of Different Apportionment Factors Under Unitary Taxation, *ICTD Working Paper* No. 27, November. www.ictd.ac/sites/default/files/ICTD%20WP27.pdf

Council of Europe (2014). Recommendation CM/Rec 7 of the Committee of Ministers to Member States on the Protection of Whistleblowers, April 30: https://wcd.coe.int/ViewDoc.jsp?Ref=CM/Rec(2014)7&Language=lanEnglish&Ver=original&Site=CM&BackColorInternet=C3C3C3&BackColorIntranet=EDB021&BackColorLogged=F5D383

The Economist (2014). The Openness Revolution, December 13: www.economist.com/news/business/21636070-multinationals-are-forced-reveal-more-about-themselves-where-should-limits

Miller, M. M. (2014). Remarks by Principal Deputy Assistant Attorney General for the Criminal Division Marshall L. Miller at the Global Investigation Review Program, New York, Wednesday, September 17: www.justice.gov/criminal/pr/speeches/2014/crm-speech-1409171.html

Afterword

The research leading to this book was conducted – at the initiative of the Collège des Bernardins (Paris, France) – by the "Économie, Homme, Société" research department. In 2009–11 and 2012–4, two research programs centered on the concepts of the firm and the corporation brought together a team of around thirty researchers from several disciplines (law, economics, management, sociology, political philosophy, anthropology and theology), as well as practitioners.

The research started from a negative observation, of which J.-P. Robé was the first to fully grasp the significance:[1] Ownership of a company's shares does not make the shareholders the company's owners. This observation, valid both under Romano-Germanic law and Anglo-American common law, caused us to revise a number of common representations of the company: It cannot be appropriated, its purpose cannot be reduced to the maximization of shareholder value and its leaders are not the shareholders' "agents". Hence the need to rethink the company, which is today in a conceptual "blind spot".[2] The work undertaken from 2009 to 2011 considered the company from four points of view:[3]

1 A device for personal achievement that should be institutionalized,
2 A cross-valuation device that should be democratized,
3 A device for collective creation that should be contractualized,
4 A device of private (non-governmental) power that should be constitutionalized.

Further work in 2012–4 deepened these reflections. The work on "constitutionalization" brought together international experts on these issues. By combining their contributions, this book builds on the approach and broadens the reflection to the international level. Other teams also analyzed the company as an organization designed for collective creation: by elucidating the need to think of the company as being based on the work of those who participate therein, by specifying the institutional and organizational conditions for their involvement in a cooperative system, upon which the company's performance largely depends, and by analyzing the influence of the financial sphere on the company and the changes needed to provide the long-term financial resources required for it to grow.[4]

1 See J.-P. Robé, *L'entreprise et le droit*, Paris: Presses Universitaires de France, *Que sais-je?* collection (1999), p. 128.
2 B. Segrestin, B. Roger & S. Vernac (publisher), *L'entreprise, point aveugle du savoir*, Paris: Éditions Sciences Humaines (2014), p. 343.
3 See O. Favereau, *Entreprises: la grande déformation*, Paris: Parole et Silence (2014), p. 155 – B. Roger (publisher). *L'entreprise, formes de la propriété et responsabilités sociales*, Paris: Lethielleux (2012), p. 569.
4 See O. Favereau & B. Roger, *Penser l'entreprise, nouvel horizon du politique*, Paris: Parole et Silence (2015), p. 120; O. Favereau (publisher), *Penser le travail pour penser l'entreprise* (forthcoming); B. Segrestin,

The Collège des Bernardins is an institution dedicated to the ambitions and hopes and questions of modern society and their intersection with Christian wisdom.

Building on the long-standing tradition of which it is the custodian within the University of Paris since it was built in the thirteenth century, the Collège des Bernardins has created a research center that is open to discussion on all issues relevant to our society.

This research center brings together researchers and practitioners in a place that combines freedom of thought and respect for academic standards, multidisciplinarity and international openness in order to contribute their knowledge and experience to the issues affecting the future of humankind.

It comprises of six departments, jointly managed by an academic and a theologian:

1 Biomedical ethics;
2 Human societies and educational responsibility;
3 Economics, Mankind and Society ("*Économie, Homme, Société*");
4 Society, Freedom, Peace;
5 Judaism and Christianity;
6 The Language of Art.

Olivier Favereau, Baudoin Roger
Co-directors of the "Économie, Homme, Société" research department
Collège des Bernardins

K. Levillain., S. Vernac & A. Hatchuel, *La "Société à Objet Social Étendu", Un nouveau statut pour l'entreprise*, Paris: Presses des Mines, Sciences de la Conception collection (2014), p. 122 T. Auvray, T. Dallery & S. Rigot, "L'entreprise liquidée, la finance contre l'investissement," Paris, Michalon (2016).

Index